Positive Psychology

Theory, Research and Applications

SECOND EDITION

Positive Psychology

Theory, Research and Applications

SECOND EDITION

Ilona Boniwell, PhD and Aneta D. Tunariu, PhD

 Open University Press

Open University Press
McGraw-Hill Education
8th Floor, 338 Euston Road
London
England
NW1 3BH

and Two Penn Plaza, New York, NY 10121-2289, USA

First published 2011
First published in this second edition 2019

Senior Commissioning Editor: Hannah Kenner
Editorial Assistant: Karen Harris
Content Product Manager: Ali Davis

A catalogue record of this book is available from the British Library

ISBN-13: 9780335262182
ISBN-10: 033526218X
eISBN: 9780335262199

Library of Congress Cataloging-in-Publication Data
CIP data applied for

Typeset by Transforma Pvt. Ltd., Chennai, India

 # Dedication

We would like to thank our families for their patience and generous support, and our students for their participation and feedback.

Contents

About the authors

Professor Ilona Boniwell is one of the world leaders in positive psychology, having founded and headed the first Master's degree in Applied Positive Psychology (MAPP) in Europe at the University of East London. Nowadays, she is the strategic head of the International Master's in Applied Positive Psychology (iMAPP) at Anglia Ruskin University (UK), teaches at Ecole CentraleSupelec and HEC (France) and consults around the world as the director of Positran. Passionate about practical applications of positive psychology to business, education and coaching, Ilona has developed the Toolkit for Well-being and Positivity at Work for the UAE and worked for the Government of Bhutan to construct a framework for happiness-based public policy at the request of the UN. She has trained thousands of positive psychology professionals around the world (in Australia, Japan, China, Singapore, Dubai, South Africa, Portugal, Iceland, France and the UK) and worked with multinational companies such as L'Oreal, Microsoft, Sanofi, Bullo, Mars, Alpro Soya, Engie and Orange. In the past, Ilona founded and was the first Chair of the European Network of Positive Psychology (ENPP), organized the fist European Congress of Positive Psychology in 2002, and was the Vice-Chair of the International Positive Psychology Association (IPPA). She is the author of ten books, five positive education programmes (including SPARK Resilience) and seven positive psychology tools.

Dr Aneta D. Tunariu is a Chartered Psychologist with the British Psychological Society and the Head of School of Psychology at the University of East London, where the first Masters programme in Applied Positive Psychology in Europe was established in 2007. The School that Aneta heads is a distinct blend of academic and professional training programmes which embody the aspirations of its founders and people everywhere who regard university education as personally transformative. Aneta's academic expertise, research, consultancy and applied practice in national and international settings are hinged on the Psychology of Relating and closely informed by concepts from social psychology, existential positive psychology, coaching psychology, psychoanalytic theory and counselling psychology. Her recent positive psychology coaching interventions (delivered in England, Morocco and France) incorporate the social justice and restorative practice agenda and focus on working with young people to acquire skills for flourishing and emotional agility, within a variety of professional, cultural and community-specific contexts.

Preface

Purpose of the book

Since the first edition of this book (2011) – and even more so since Ilona Boniwell founded the first Master's programme in Applied Positive Psychology (MAPP) in Europe (2007) at the University of East London, England – the field of positive psychology has been rapidly expanding. This expansion manifests in terms of advancements in theory development, topics of study, contexts for positive psychology interventions (personal development, education, health, workplace, social care, restorative justice) as well as in terms of the reach and popularity positive psychology has come to enjoy. Thanks to demonstrable scholarly and empirical rigour and notable benefits of its applications to enhancing well-being and improving performance, recognition of positive psychology as a significant field of study in today's higher education landscape continues to grow.

The purpose of this book is to contribute to the expanding academic citizenship of positive psychology with an up-to-date synthesis of the literature accompanied by dialogues of innovation and critical thought. It aims to offer a collective body of knowledge for students, whether in psychology or other fields, to refer to. It is designed as a textbook and offers lecturers, especially if relatively new to the area, a comprehensive and clear structure for teaching positive psychology.

Tone of the book

Major differences between this book and other textbooks within positive psychology include:

1 A message of balance

The second edition of this book emerges at a time of notable transition, which is not least made manifest by what has come to be known as 'the second wave of positive psychology'. The book captures the spirit of this new wave, which we see as an opportunity to reimagine and continue to expand the conceptual reach of 'positivity' while preserving the original scope of generating knowledge, research and practices that most optimally demarcate positive psychology as a science and area of applied psychology. For instance, Chapter 2 (Understanding Emotions) has received notable review and includes a substantial section on rethinking negative emotions. Chapter 8 (Positive Psychological Interventions [PPIs] offers a comprehensive mapping of major trends in PPIs and discusses novel ways to categorise the growing number of PPIs.

2 An integrative positive psychology

Both authors are seasoned lecturers, researchers and psychology practitioners. Both have longstanding track records of applied work designing, implementing and evaluating bespoke interventions informed by principles and research from positive psychology. Both seek an approach to practice that integrates knowledge from other areas of psychology such as social, developmental, counselling, coaching and business psychology as well as insights from aligned professions such as neuroscience and philosophy. In different ways, the chapters reflect this interest and regard of positive psychology as one of the multiple areas of contemporary psychology rather than an isolated field of study.

3 Critical perspective

Europeans have traditionally been trailblazers in the psychological sciences, with their critical and unfettered perspectives. By including exercises and critical perspectives throughout the book, we endeavour to maintain this important reputation. Criticality has been further expanded by considering the role of discourse in shaping truth-claims as well as subjective experience and action.

4 Fun and engaging voice while still adhering to academic evidence

We found that it is through our students' engagement and participation that the study of positive psychology translates into a genuinely transformative endeavour. To this end, we intend the book to be fun, informative and educational for the reader, and we have taken a great deal of time to ensure this is possible. The second edition features a new, guest chapter on physical activity from the lens of positive psychology (Chapter 9) – adding to this spirit of holistic engagement. The Guided Tour section of the book outlines the various pedagogical modalities used across the book chapters.

Set up of the book

The textbook is divided into 11 chapters, potentially but not restrictively representing 11 lectures across a 12-week semester (inclusive of reading break). The chapters also concentrate on one of the topics in more detail. Each chapter provides information about theories in positive psychology and offers numerous exercises to help meld together research and applications. The chapters finish with exercises for students to use and implement in daily life. Furthermore, each chapter provides lists of suggested reading and web resources to continue learning about that specific topic.

Beginning of chapter

We have set the book up so that the reader starts learning from the start. We initiate the chapter with clear *learning objectives* that help orientate the reader as to what the chapter will entail. We also offer three mock essay questions that we believe are appropriate for the chapter contents. We invite the reader to keep an eye out for what content would be useful when answering these questions.

Throughout the chapter

Throughout the chapter we have cleverly and creatively included several learning/interest boxes that will help the learning journey. The first box to look out for is:

Think about it...

These boxes are peppered throughout the book to get you thinking about the concepts and theories we have just relayed. This is a great way to collate what you've learned and to critically reflect on the subject matter.

The second type of box to look out for is:

EXPERIMENTS

We have also included sections within the textbook detailing appropriate groundbreaking research studies that link to the theories discussed. We have chosen sharp, quirky one-liner titles to describe the studies that the reader will hopefully find funny and easy to remember.

Finally, when we need to re-cap or refresh our knowledge on general psychology issues, look out for:

time out

These boxes take the reader on a time out to re-learn topics such as epistemology, validity, reliability, the brain, and so on. This is general information the reader should know or may need a refresher on.

End of chapter

From teaching on an applied positive psychology course, we know that the reader needs more than just being talked at, or given a book to read. The end of the chapter includes several ways for them to become active in their learning process, so at the end of each chapter there are the following sections:

1 *Chapter summary:* As we did in the beginning, setting out the learning objectives, we will summate all that the reader needs to know after reading the chapter. This way, they will be able to have a concise breakdown of the information.

2 *Suggested resources:* We have provided links and books with explanations of the usefulness of each. Have a look at them and see which ones will be most helpful to you in your learning process.

3 *Measurement tools section:* No psychological science is complete without an assortment of psychometric tools, so we have, with the permission of the original authors, included several well-used positive psychology tools at the end of each chapter for the reader to try out and reflect upon.

Positive psychology's ethos and philosophical ideas that underpin its approach to understanding the human capacity to flourish can be found and expanded through a variety of story-telling mediums. With this in mind, the book provides links to media materials within as well as beyond the typical academic literature.

List of Figures, Tables and Questionnaires

Figures

Tables

Questionnaires

The Gratitude Questionnaire-Six Item Form (GQ-6) (McCullough, Emmons and Tsang, 2002)

Positive and Negative Activation Schedule (PANAS) (Watson, Clark and Tellegen, 1988)

Scale of Positive and Negative Experience (SPANE) (Diener et al., 2009c)

Satisfaction With Life Scale (SWLS) (Diener et al., 1985b)

Subjective Happiness Scale (SHS) (Lyubomirsky and Lepper, 1999)

The Maximizing Scale (Schwartz et al., 2002)

Meaning in Life Questionnaire (MLQ) (Steger, Frazier, Oishi and Kaler, 2006)

Flourishing Scale (Diener et al., 2009)

Flow Experience Questionnaire (Csikszentmihalyi and Csikszentmihalyi, 1988)

Life Orientation-Revised (LOT-R) (Scheier, Carver and Bridges, 1994)

Generalized self-efficacy scale (GSE) (Schwarzer and Jerusalem, 1995)

Changes in Outlook Questionnaire (CiOQ) (Joseph, Williams and Yule, 1993)

Self-Determination Scale (SDS) (Sheldon and Deci, 1995)

Person-Activity Fit Diagnostic (Lyubomirsky, 2008)

International Physical Activity Questionnaire (IPAQ)

Physical Activity Enjoyment Scale (PACES) (Kendzierski and DeCarlo, 1991)

CHAPTER 1

Introduction to Positive Psychology

❖ LEARNING OBJECTIVES

Positive psychology is the study of topics as diverse as happiness, optimism, subjective well-being and personal growth. The opening chapter has two goals: (1) to describe and critically examine the emergence and development of this new field in recent years and (2) to orientate students to some of the topics studied by positive psychologists. At the end of the chapter, the reader will have the opportunity to complete questionnaires on some of the main topics in positive psychology.

Topics include:

- The scope and aim of positive psychology.
- The history of positive psychology.
- How we measure happiness.
- The good life and authenticity.
- Humanistic psychology.
- Topics within the textbook.
- Where positive psychology stands today.

MOCK ESSAY QUESTIONS

1 Critically discuss the differences between 'positive' psychology and psychology as usual.
2 Is positive psychology as different from humanistic psychology as it claims to be?
3 Why might we need positive psychology?

What is positive psychology?

In today's world, society is facing extremely tough challenges in the form of global warming, natural disasters, economic recession, unprecedented homelessness, terrorism and the draining continuation of war. With all this sadness and horror, where in the world does a science based on testing happiness, well-being, personal growth and 'the good life' fit in to a modern day agenda?

This textbook will take the reader through the new science of *positive psychology*, which aims to 'understand, test, discover and promote the factors that allow individuals and communities to thrive' (Sheldon et al., 1999). Positive psychology focuses on well-being, happiness, flow, personal strengths, wisdom, creativity, imagination and characteristics of positive groups and institutions. Furthermore, the focus is not only on how to increase individual happiness, which on its own would run the risk of merely preserving a self-centred, self-absorbed approach, but on happiness and flourishing at group and community levels as well. We will look at how individuals and groups thrive, and how increasing the well-being of one will have a positive knock-on effect on the other, equalling a win-win situation.

What we hope to demonstrate, throughout this textbook, is that positive psychology is not simply the focus on positive thinking and positive emotions. It is much more than that. Indeed, the area of positive psychology is focused on what makes individuals and communities flourish, rather than languish. *Flourishing* is defined as 'a state of positive mental health; to thrive, to prosper and to fare well in endeavours free of mental illness, filled with emotional vitality and function positively in private and social realms' (Michalec et al., 2009: 391). As such, a science that focuses on the development and facilitation of flourishing environments and individuals is an important addition to the psychological sciences.

Think about it...

Why have you decided to take this module? What was it about the syllabus that attracted you? Past experiences? A certain topic? Take a moment to reflect on this.

Positive psychology concentrates on positive experiences at three time points:
a) the past, centring on well-being, contentment and satisfaction; b) the present,
which focuses on concepts such as happiness and flow experiences and c) the
future, with concepts including optimism and hope. Not only does positive
psychology distinguish between well-being across time points but it also
separates the subject area into three nodes:

1 The subjective node encompasses things like positive experiences and states
   across past, present and future (e.g. happiness, optimism, well-being).
2 The individual node focuses on characteristics of the 'good person',
   (e.g. talent, wisdom, love, courage, creativity).
3 The group node studies positive institutions, citizenship and communities
   (e.g. altruism, tolerance, work ethic) (Positive Psychology Center, 1998).

Contrary to criticism, positive psychology is not a selfish psychology. At its best,
positive psychology has been able to give the scientific community, society and
individuals a new perspective on existing ideas as well as providing empirical
evidence to support the phenomenon of human flourishing. Above all though,
positive psychology has challenged and rebalanced the deficit approach to living
while connecting its findings to many different disciplines at the same time.
Throughout this textbook it will be apparent how inducing positive emotions,
committing acts of kindness and enhancing social connections enable individual
and societal flourishing, demonstrating the usefulness of the discipline for
individual, group and community well-being.

Authentic happiness and the good life

What is the good life? Socrates, Aristotle and Plato believed that when
people pursued a virtuous life, they would become authentically
happy. Epicurus and later utilitarians preached that happiness was indeed
the abundance of positive feelings and pleasures. Positive psychology has
traditionally conceptualized authentic happiness as a mix of *hedonic* and
eudaimonic well-being (Seligman and Csikszentmihalyi, 2000). Hedonic happiness
encompasses high levels of positive affect with low levels of negative affect, in
addition to high subjective life satisfaction. The notion of 'authentic happiness'
has been further broken down by Seligman to entail a life that is a combination
of a *pleasurable life,* an *engaged life* and a *meaningful life*. The pleasurable life
encompasses feelings of positive emotions (e.g. joy, gratitude, serenity, interest,
hope, pride, amusement, inspiration, awe and love), which are integral
components to our success and well-being. Positive emotions widen our thought
processes, which can be built up over time, and banked, to create a 'protective
reservoir' upon which a person can draw from during unpleasant or distressing
times (more about this in Chapter 2). Eudaimonic well-being focuses more on the
creation of meaning and purpose in life, although the distinction between these

two concepts is still subject to further unpacking and debate (Huta and Waterman, 2014).

The engaged life focuses on flow, engagement, absorption and well-being whereas the meaningful life encompasses the service to something higher than the self. Thus, individuals can find happiness with the pursuit of all three 'lives'. At present, the concept of authentic happiness is more a theory rather than a causal recipe for happiness (Rashid, 2009a). As positive psychology continues to grow and develop more longitudinal data-banks, we will know more about how these three 'lives' work in harmony to enhance well-being.

Think about it...

Sheldon (2009) defines authenticity as 'emotional genuineness, self-attunement and psychological depth'. Humanists originally believed that you couldn't study such abstract concepts, whereas other theorists, such as Freud believed that one could never be authentic.

1 Do you agree or disagree with these arguments?
2 Can you think of a time when you have been truly authentic or inauthentic to yourself?
3 How do you know when you are being truly authentic?

The origins of modern day positive psychology

The person attributed for the creation of the positive psychology movement is Martin E. P. Seligman, Professor at the University of Pennsylvania. After decades of experimental research and success from his learned helplessness theory, Seligman was appointed President of the American Psychological Association (APA) in 1998. It was during his inauguration at the 107th annual convention of the APA in Boston, Massachusetts, 21 August 1999, that Seligman decided to introduce his agenda to re-correct the trajectory of modern day 'pathologically focused' psychology. Since Seligman's presidential position, he has become a figurehead for the positive psychology movement and continues to gain support from research funds and governments across the world to include positive psychology theories and practices into daily life.

ROSES

Although not an experiment, the story of Seligman and his rose garden has become a folk legend in the discipline of positive psychology. As his

▶

▶

account goes, positive psychology started from an epiphany he experienced whilst attending to his rose garden. His daughter, who was five at the time, had been asking trying to get her father's attention, and, after her persistence, Seligman turned to her and snapped. Unhappy with this response, his daughter asked him whether or not he remembered how she used to whine when she was three and four. She further stated that when she turned five, she decided to stop. Thus if she was able to stop whining, then he was able to stop being a grouch! This revelation of developing what was right, rather than fixating on what was wrong, sparked what Seligman would go on to promote during his career as APA president: that we should be teaching our children and ourselves to look at our strengths rather than weaknesses.

See Seligman and Csikszentmihalyi (2000) for the original account.

Psychology as usual (pre-1998)

Unbeknown to the general psychology population, there were *three tasks* of psychology prior to World War Two (WWII). These were to: a) cure mental illness; b) enhance the lives of the normal population; and c) study geniuses. Due to the aftermath of two world wars and the return of many psychologically impaired soldiers, research funding focused on its first agenda, with the other two nearly forgotten[1] (Linley, 2009).

We must acknowledge that this funding for mental disorders has been immensely successful as at least 14 disorders can now be cured or considerably relieved (Seligman and Csikszentmihalyi, 2000). Unfortunately, these fixations on pathology led to psychology becoming a 'victimology'. Instead of viewing humans as proactive, creative, self-determined beings, psychologists viewed humans as passive individuals subjected to external forces (Seligman and Csikszentmihalyi, 2000).[2] Hence, the main difference between post-WWII psychology and today's positive psychology is in the question asked: 'Why do these individuals fail?' vs. 'What makes some individuals succeed?' See also the interview with Mihaly Csikszentmihalyi, co-founder of positive psychology (Csikszentmihalyi and Lebuda, 2017).

66 The message of the Positive Psychology movement is to remind our field that it has been deformed. Psychology is not just the study of disease, weakness, and damage; it also is the study of strength and virtue. Treatment is not just fixing what is wrong; it also is building what is right. Psychology is not just about illness or health; it is about work, education, insight, love, growth, and play. And in this quest for what is best, Positive Psychology does not rely on wishful thinking, self-deception or hand-waving; instead it tries to adapt

what is best in the scientific method to the unique problems that
human behavior presents in all its complexity.

– (Seligman, 2002b: 4). 🙶

The call for psychology to invest attention beyond deficits mapped against
'standards of normality' continues to evolve and encamps empirical endeavours
through the lens of positive psychology as a medium for social changes,
advocacy and responsibility not least relating to 'what is (could be) a good life'
(see e.g. the edited book by Biswas-Diener, 2011).

Originally, the idea of positive psychology was to move away from the
disease (medical) model (Figure 1.1) that fixated on moving people from a
−8 to a −3 or severely depressed to mildly depressed. Positive psychology, on
the other hand, situated its focus on people who fell at +3 (languishing) and
helping to raise them to a +8 (flourishing). We find this model an easy, simple
visual when teaching our students to differentiate between the 'main aims' of
positive psychology.

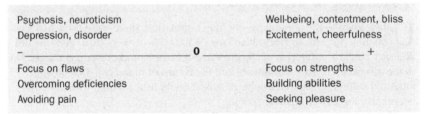

FIGURE 1.1 Disease/health model

Of course, the analogy is nice and simple and did the trick at a time when
clarification between the psychologies was needed. However, this theoretical
model assumes that people can be at zero; but what is zero? And what does it
really mean to be +3? In addition, the model assumes that positive psychology
cannot help those on the negative end of the scale. There is evidence that
positive psychology interventions can benefit people who are diagnosed as
clinically depressed in addition to the normal population (Sin and Lyubomirsky,
2009; Schotanus-Dijkstra et al., 2017). The growing number of supporters for the
development of positive clinical psychology found that 'positive characteristics
(such as gratitude, flexibility, and positive emotions) can uniquely predict
disorder beyond the predictive power of the presence of negative characteristics,
and buffer the impact of negative life events, potentially preventing the
development of disorder' (Wood and Tarrier, 2010: 819).

Since 1948, the World Health Organization has defined health as 'a state of
complete physical, mental and social well-being and not merely the absence
of disease or infirmity' (WHO, 1948: 200). Corey Keyes, an illustrative example of

a positive sociologist, has spent years looking at the relationship between mental health and mental illness. His work brought him to conclude that the two are not on the same continuum, and that they are two separate continuums. Thus, the absence of mental illness does not equate to the presence of mental health. Keyes proposed two strategies for tackling mental disorder: 1) The promotion and maintenance of mental health, and 2) The prevention and treatment of mental illness (Keyes and Michalec, 2009).

History of positive psychology (Ancient day)

One of the criticisms of positive psychology is that the ideas are not new. Even the term 'positive psychology' was used by Abraham Maslow, many decades before Seligman (Maslow, 1954: 201). However, Seligman and Csikszentmihalyi have succeeded in bringing forth the thoughts and ideas of past researchers, philosophers and scientists to our consciousness as individuals and as psychologists. We have identified four groupings that were examining and theorizing about 'the good life' before positive psychology came into existence.

1. The Ancient Greeks

Aristotle's (384–322 BCE) greatest contribution to philosophy is arguably his work on morality, virtue and what it means to live a good life. As he questioned these topics, he concluded that the highest good for all humanity was indeed eudaimonia (or happiness). Indeed, his work argued that although pleasure may arise from engaging with activities that are virtuous, it is not the sole aim of humanity (Mason and Tiberius, 2009).

2. Utilitarianism

Utilitarianism, created by Jeremy Bentham and carried on via John Stuart Mill, is a philosophy that argued that the right act or policy from government was that which would cause 'the greatest good for the greatest number of people', also known as the 'greatest happiness principal', or the principle of utility. Utilitarianism was the first sector that attempted to measure happiness, creating a tool composed of seven categories, assessing the quantity of experienced happiness (Pawelski and Gupta, 2009). Whereas philosophers before had assumed that happiness was immeasurable, utilitarianism argued and attempted to demonstrate that it was indeed possible. Pawelski and Gupta (2009) propose that utilitarianism influences some areas of positive psychology today, such as subjective well-being, the pleasurable life, etc. Ultimately, positive psychology accepts that while pleasure is a component of overall well-being, it is not enough, and the inclusion of eudaimonic pursuits is necessary as a compliment to utilitarian philosophy.

3. William James

A brilliant scholar, William James is best known for his contribution to psychology through his widely read text *The Principles of Psychology* (1890). James originally trained as a medical doctor at Harvard University, Boston, USA, before becoming interested in religion, mysticism and epistemology (Pawelski, 2009). His chapter, 'The Emotions', is most relevant for positive psychology to acknowledge. Within this, he suggests that emotions come after we have physically acted out. For example:

> 66… common-sense says, we lose our fortune, are sorry and weep; we
> meet a bear, are frightened and run; we are insulted by a rival, are
> angry and strike. The hypothesis here to be defended says that this
> order of sequence is incorrect […]that we feel sorry because we cry,
> angry because we strike, afraid because we tremble.
>
> – *(James 1890: 1065–6)*. 99

Thus, this is an early example of writing to connect emotions and expressions together. His years of intertwining physiology, psychology and philosophy still have an impact in philosophical issues surrounding the mind, the body and the brain today.

4. Humanistic psychology

Humanistic psychology emerged in the late 1950s early 1960s as a backlash to the predominant psychological theories of psychoanalysis, behaviourism and conditioning. In addition, the humanistic movement introduced and solidified qualitative inquiry as an imperative paradigm to research human thought, behaviour and experience, adding a holistic dimension to psychology. In a nutshell, humanistic psychology is the psychological perspective that emphasises the study of the whole person. Humanistic psychologists believe that a) an individual's behaviour is primarily determined by their perception of the world around them and their personal meanings; b) individuals are not solely the product of their environment or their genes; and c) individuals are internally directed and motivated to fulfil their human potential.

The main drive of humanistic psychology was to focus on mental health, specifically positive attributes such as happiness, contentment, ecstasy, kindness, caring, sharing, generosity, etc. Humanists felt that, unlike their behaviourist cousins, humans had choice and responsibility in their own destiny. This perspective ultimately views life as a process, with all humans beholding an innate drive for growth and fulfilment of potentials. The humanists even went as far as to include spiritual proprieties of the self, the world and well-being; an area that is controversial even in today's scientific societies.

So, even back then, psychologists were aware of the deficit in research on the positive side of life. Some positive psychologists have argued that the reason why the humanistic discipline never really took off stems from the fact that they never developed a respectable empirical basis. This lack of theoretical basis led to encouraging a narcissistic preoccupation with the self and self-improvement, at the expense of societal welfare (Seligman and Csikszentmihalyi, 2000).

time out

Abraham Maslow

Abraham Maslow was one of several eminent psychologists who embody the humanistic movement and what it stood for. Maslow was a very famous psychologist across all disciplines, and actually coined the term 'positive psychology' (Maslow, 1954: 201). Mostly known for his model on 'hierarchy of needs' Maslow eemphasized the need for psychology to focus on human potentialities rather than just human deficiencies (Bridges and Wertz, 2009). Thus, he desired a more positive approach toward psychology. His major contributions to psychology as a whole were his theories on motivation, needs, self-actualization and peak experience.

The science of psychology has been far more successful on the negative than on the positive side; it has revealed to us much about man's shortcomings, his illnesses, his sins, but little about his potentialities, his virtues, his achievable aspirations, or his psychological height.

(Maslow, 1954: 201)

Overall, it seems, positive psychology has not started on the right foot with regards to its humanistic cousins. In the beginning, there was a clear drive to separate positive psychology from the humanistic discipline, claiming a major difference in methodological inquiry: positive psychology is the scientific study of well-being, and therefore uses the scientific method to test hypotheses. We believe that there is much that positive psychology can learn from and continue to learn about the humanistic movement and this need to separate from the humanistic appears divisive and unnecessary.

Humanistic psychology criticizes positive psychology for its short-sighted drive to separate itself from the humanistic discipline, as by adopting this approach, it has left out vital areas of research, and methods of inquiry (qualitative) that limit the generalization of its main findings. Furthermore, humanistic psychologists feel that to prove that positive psychology is indeed 'scientific', it has over compensated and stuck to quantitative inquiry. This is a very important historical fact that students must be aware of when undertaking their studies in positive psychology. We truly believe that in order to understand where we are in positive psychology, we have to know where we have come from.

Can we measure happiness?

This is one of the most fundamental questions for positive psychology. Indeed, many reasons as to why the topics and concepts within positive psychology were not previously studied were because they were believed to be ephemeral and too difficult, if not impossible, to study and measure. By creating and testing using scientific measurement tools as well as experimental methods, scientists/ psychologists have taken philosophical concepts or virtue and happiness, and put them to rigorous, scientific testing.

Therefore, over and over again, the literature will state that positive psychology is a science, not a self-help technique that uses the scientific method to understand human thoughts, feelings and behaviours. When psychology was first making its way into history, it wanted to adapt the same scientific rigour as the natural sciences, such as biology and chemistry. These sciences are based on objective testing and the positivist epistemological paradigm. This epistemology ascribes to experimentation, logical deduction and rational thought to examine the world whereby knowledge is obtained by direct, objective observation. Facts and knowledge lead to laws and predictions for human nature and can determine causal relationships (cause and effect).

time out

Epistemology

Epistemology is a branch of philosophy concerned with the acquisition of knowledge through addressing related questions such as: what can we 'know' (ontology)?; what represents 'knowledge'?; how can we go about acquiring this defined knowledge? (methodology); what are the limitations of our 'knowledge'?; who/what shapes the process of 'knowledge – production'? Several philosophically grounded research paradigms emerge as a function of arriving at different answers to these questions. Researchers must therefore choose which epistemological position they believe best suits their research question. The main paradigms include post-positivism, constructivism (social constructionism), advocacy/participatory and pragmatism.

At its beginnings, in an attempt to be considered a 'proper science' positive psychology tended to distance itself from the use of qualitative methods. Over the recent years, however, qualitative research is increasingly regarded as imperative, and it is used to explain and explore topics and results within the discipline.

> ### Think about it...
>
> What is truth?
> What is knowledge?
> What is scientific knowledge?
> How can you best negotiate objectivity, subjectivity and relativity when delineating the parameters of research methods?
> Should positive psychology also use qualitative research methods?
> Write down your answers and think of examples to argue your points.

Considerations related to epistemology, methodology, tools, findings, and criteria for evaluation of these findings are crucial in establishing what constitutes good evidence in psychology. For any scholarly discipline, 'good evidence' is fundamentally necessary to substantiate 'truth claims'; that is, scientifically derived knowledge about a phenomenon established as part of a recognized system of methods and procedures for generating, analysing and making sense of direct observation or measurement of experience. Evidence refers to a study's results (processed data) and the interpretations these results afford in relation to a theory hypothesized (top-down, as in quantitative studies) or emergent from the data (bottom-up as in qualitative studies). Good evidence takes into account other established evidence (by noting how it refutes, expands or corroborates this). Evidence is evaluated through the set of criteria agreed vis-à-vis what constitutes good quantitative research – including validity; reliability; (ideally) absence of bias; and power to generalize results – or good quantitative research – including inductive rigour; credibility; transparency; reflexivity (accountability for subjectivity and co-authorship); and transferability (see e.g. Willig, 2013)

Where is positive psychology today?

Following Seligman's speech on 21 August 1999, researchers gathered in Akumal Mexico (regularly, from 1999–2002) to discuss the development of the new area of positive psychology (Linley, 2009). Since then the field of positive psychology has gained massive momentum. Positive psychology lecturers, researchers and practitioners have established formal platforms where students can study the syllabus of positive psychology (e.g. Method for Impact Assessment of Programmes and Projects (MAPP) programmes of study have been established across the world, beyond the USA and Europe) and forums to share scholarly publications and advance trends in the positive psychology field, such as the following:

- The European Network for Positive Psychology (see Boniwell, 2009) aims to share knowledge and research on positive psychology with all who have an interest in the subject. It will hold its ninth European Conference in Positive Psychology in 2018.

- The first World Congress of Positive Psychology was held 2009 in Philadelphia, USA. In 2017, the International Positive Psychology Association (IPPA) organized the fifth World Congress in Montreal, Canada with more than 1300 delegates from over 60 countries from around the globe in attendance.

- A further sign of the strength of today's status of positive psychology as a field of psychology are its peer-reviewed journals – *Journal of Positive Psychology*; *European Journal of Applied Positive Psychology*; and *International Journal of Applied Positive Psychology*.

Since the publication of the first edition of this book, the terms 'Positive Psychology 2.0' (Wong, 2011) and 'Second Wave Positive Psychology' (Ivtzan et al., 2016) have been coined and new trends mapped out – such as vis-à-vis our understandings of negative emotions. Important questions are also asked about best ways to professionalize the application of positive psychology to offering relevant and ethical interventions to real-life settings (Lomas and Ivtzan, 2016a). Such initiatives aptly demonstrate our current re-imaging of the field as we grapple with the nuanced philosophical, conceptual and applied complexities of the idea of the 'positive psychology in and of itself' (Lomas and Ivtzan, 2016b).

The second wave of positive psychology is also an opportunity to reimagine and expand its conceptual reach critically while preserving its distinct scope and interest in optimal human functioning and actualization. For instance, at a broader level, accepting a view of language as productive vs. descriptive meaning-making medium, pushes forth and makes obvious our capacity as social agents to destabilize dominant discourse and the realities and goals that it promotes, as well as those that it leaves out (Colahan et al., 2012). At a personal level, shifting perspective requires acknowledgement of the taken-for-granted world views that we have internalized and accepted as true. It involves noting the imposition and restrictions our habits of thought engender because of their familiarity, anxiety-reduction function and various other subtle yet pervasive mechanisms of self-surveillance. As discussed in Chapter 2, relative to the particularities of a circumstance, hierarchy goals and the ethics an individual subscribes to, negative emotions can be easily rendered as problematic. However, openness to rethinking their nature, deliberateness and optimally tolerating (learning from and through) their discomfort are emerging as central to developing agile mindsets, stamina and skills required for success and fulfilment.

Positive psychology's place in psychology as usual

There are a vast number of areas within the entirety of the psychological discipline. The American Psychological Association denotes over 50 branches within its department, while the British Psychological Association recognizes more than five chartered areas of psychology including: clinical, counselling, forensic, health, neuro-psychology, occupational, and sport and exercise. However, where exactly does positive psychology fit within the accepted psychology disciplines?

Arguments tend to surround whether positive psychology is a separate discipline in itself or if it encompasses the entire field of psychology. For example, Figure 1.2 shows how positive psychology can be situated within mainstream psychological disciplines. Others links can be drawn to humanistic psychology, psychiatry, sociology, biology and many more. However, whether or not positive psychology will become a separate discipline area remains to be seen.

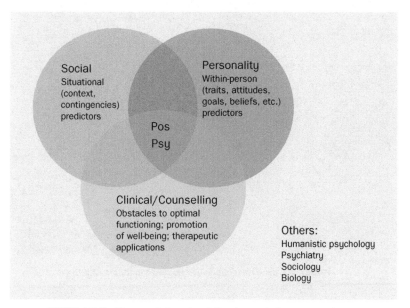

FIGURE 1.2 Positive psychology in relation to psychology as usual

Positive psychology spans a multitude of areas and disciplines – as illustrated by the mind map (Figure 1.3) below.

Think about it...

What might be missing from this mind map? As you go through this textbook to create your own visual mind map, helping you to understand the many links within positive psychology.

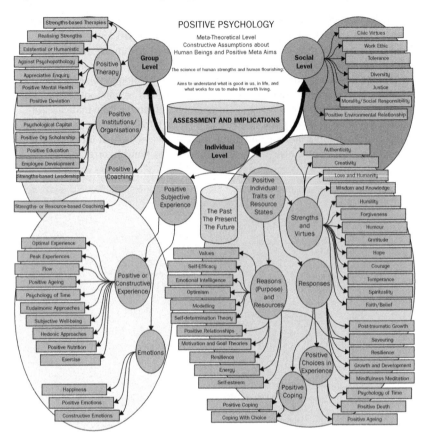

FIGURE 1.3 Mind map of positive psychology (Smith, 2008)

However, positive psychology would argue that psychology should also expand its focus to improving child education by making greater use of intrinsic motivation, positive affect and creativity; improving psychotherapy by developing approaches that emphasize hope, meaning and self-healing; and improving family life by better understanding the dynamics of love, parenthood and commitment. They argue it should improve work satisfaction across the lifespan by helping people to find authentic involvement, experience states of flow, and make genuine contributions in their work; that it should improve organizations and societies by discovering conditions that enhance trust, communication and altruism; and that it should improve the moral character of society by better understanding and promoting the spiritual impulse.

One thing to note is that many researchers within these areas of expertise were working in these before the area of positive psychology was even born. Thus, what suddenly makes some of these areas now positive psychology rather than say clinical or sport? For example, for the past 30 years, research has been accumulating on how coaches and athletes can achieve peak performance. From the vast amount of data collected, theories on motivation, planned behaviour, mastery and success have been cross-fertilized with other areas of psychology. In particular, the aims of sport psychology/performance psychology appear to seek that same outcome. Sport tends to look at the best performers and adapt their strategies to those who can improve further, as does positive psychology, which looks at those who are flourishing and shares this information with the normal population. The authors believe that the collaboration with these two areas is a strong point for future psychologists to note.

Topics we will cover in this textbook

The areas with sufficient amounts of research and interest to the well-being of the self and society include subjective well-being, positive affect, hope, optimism, resilience, post-traumatic growth, goals, meaning and strengths. Chapter 2 focuses on the concepts of *positive emotions, emotional intelligence* and *flow*. Chapter 3 discusses *hedonic happiness* and the concept of *subjective well-being* (SWB). Following from this, Chapter 4 will question the concept of SWB with theories of *eudaimonic* theories, including *psychological well-being* and *self-determination theory*. Chapter 5 discusses theories of *optimism, positive illusion* and *hope*. Chapter 6 is a follow-through of Chapter 5 focusing on *resilience, post-traumatic growth, wisdom* and *ageing*. Chapter 7 explores *meaning* and *goal theories* and their association with well-being. The last few chapters focus more on the applied nature of positive psychology, looking at *strengths* and *interventions* and how we can apply them within corporate organizations, schools, health centres and therapeutic surroundings. Finally, the last chapter looks at the discipline from a more critical viewpoint, with scholarly predictions of where this new and exciting discipline will end up.

From the review of positive psychology yesterday, today and tomorrow, we hope we have shown that although perhaps not labelled as such, the topics have history and decades of research behind them. What positive psychology has definitely achieved is to identify groups of fragmented researchers focusing on the positive side of human behaviour, thought and feelings and given them a common thread.

Chapter Summary

Reflecting on the learning objectives the reader should now understand the main aims of positive psychology and its components. In summary:

- Positive psychology is the science of well-being and optimal functioning.
- There are three levels to positive psychology: the subjective node, the individual node and the group node.
- Positive psychology has a rich history within ancient Greek philosophy, humanism and several areas of mental health.
- Humanistic psychology is a close cousin of positive psychology, with the main difference being positive psychology's focus on the use of the scientific method.
- There are a wide variety of topics that we will cover, ranging from positive emotions to trauma and growth.
- Positive psychology is not simply a 'happiology'; it is intended as a supplement to 'psychology as usual'.

Suggested Resources

www.youtube.com/watch?v=1qJvS8v0TTI
What is Positive Psychology? Published on 10 October, 2012. A 'white board animation' sponsored by Test Prep Gurus (www.TestPrepGurus.com).

www.ted.com/talks/martin_seligman_on_the_state_of_psychology
TED Talk Lecture. Published on 21 July, 2008. *Martin Seligman talks about psychology,* as it moves beyond a focus on disease, what can modern psychology help us to become?

www.brainpickings.org/?s=Popper
In Search of a Better World: Karl Popper on Truth vs. Certainty and the Dangers of Relativism. 'Knowledge consists in the search for truth … It is not the search for certainty.' Blog by Maria Popova.

www.positivepsychology.org.uk
This is our positive psychology UK website that focuses on leading positive psychology researchers and their findings.

www.authentichappiness.org
The original 'go to' website, authentic happiness is a place where you can access all of the leading positive psychology tools, as well as participate in research and learn up-to-date research from Seligman himself.

www.ippanetwork.org

This is a website dedicated to researchers in positive psychology, with access to full membership reserved for psychologists and MSc graduates of positive psychology. The details of conferences are available to the public.

www.enpp.eu

This is the European network of positive psychology, with highlighted representatives for countries within Europe, as well as their conference details and abstract submission deadlines.

Further questions for the reader

1 What do you feel is novel about positive psychology?

2 If this is positive psychology, does that mean all other psychology is negative? Discuss.

3 Why do you think positive psychology is needed in today's society?

4 Which topics do you relate to and why?

5 What do you think the potential dangers of positive psychology are?

Personal Development Interventions

Before we start the course, we would like to you to think about your current state of happiness. How happy are you? Try out the following exercises to help raise awareness around your current happiness levels and how you can potentially improve them.

1 First is an interesting exercise involved in the rapidly growing therapeutic intervention, Quality of Life Therapy (Frisch, 2006) and is known as 'The happiness pie'. In order to do this, you need to get a sheet of blank paper, and make a large pie chart that represents your life and how you separate/allocate your energy. Some examples include: family, health, exercise, goals, spiritual practices, work, and play. Now, as you reflect on it, visually make 'slices' into this pie, to identify which pieces of the pie are most important to you and important to your well-being.

▶

▶

Once you've identified these, make a note of whether or not the size of the slice represents the importance of the slice. For example, if family is very important to you and yet it represents only a small fraction of the pie, then maybe it's time to start thinking of how to scale back other areas and increase the particular one. Finally, list five ways you can make time for these slices and thereby increase your well-being.

2 The second exercise we would like you to do is something that you may already do instinctively, and thus, this is simply putting a name and some structure to your daily routine. If you do not already do this, then you're in for a powerful surprise (Seligman et al., 2005)!

This exercise is called 'Three good things' and was developed to enhance your sense of gratitude. For the next week, before you go to bed, write down three good things that happened to you that day. The 'things' do not have to be monumental such as winning the lottery or graduating, and it is surprising how hard it can be at the start. Eventually, you will start to see and appreciate the smaller things in life that add up over time.

We would suggest that, after you complete the three good things for one week, you continue for the remainder for the course. Use the gratitude scale below to document your pre- and post-gratitude scores.

Measurement Tools

Before we start asking you to fill out all of the included questionnaires, we would like you to review the 'time out' section below to refresh your memory on what constitutes a 'good' questionnaire. Remember, the data collected is only as good as the questionnaire it was taken with. Enjoy!

time out

Assessing quality within questionnaires

The following section will review the main components involved in creating a good quality questionnaire (Howitt and Cramer, 2008). These concepts are psychology-wide and to be kept in mind as you go through the **Measurement Tools Sections**.

Reliability: This is what we use to assess if something is consistent. For example, the ability of a questionnaire to produce the same results under the same conditions. It asks whether or not the test is measuring something relatively unchanging: are the scores stable over time? Reliability is a necessary but not sufficient condition of a questionnaire.

▶

►
  ■ *Inter-/intra-rater* reliability attempts to assess whether the scores are consistent across/within raters.
  ■ *Test/re-test reliability* assesses whether or not the scores are consistent across time; what about practice effects/mood states? Some test results can be expected to change.

Internal consistency: This asks whether or not the items are inter-correlated. Chronbach Alpha method splits the test into all possible halves, correlates all scores and averages the correlations for all splits. In psychology we generally accept a cut off of 0.7 with anything above **0.8** deemed as reliable.

Validity: This refers to whether or not the questionnaire measures what it intended to measure. Validity is a necessary but not sufficient condition of a questionnaire. We can think of validity as accuracy – does the questionnaire hit the bulls-eye? There are several types of validity. These include:

  ■ *Content/face validity:* How representative are your items? How well do they relate to the construct being measured at face value?
  ■ *Criterion validity*: Is the questionnaire measuring what it intends to measure?
  ■ *Predictive validity:* If we use the questionnaire in a variety of settings, would it predict an appropriate outcome? For example, tests in mathematical ability should predict success in maths examinations.
  ■ *Concurrent validity:* Does it correlate well with other already validated measures of the same construct? Comparison with real world observations?
  ■ *Construct validity:* A higher level concept is applied to a test that fulfils predictions which would be made given the nature of the construct it supposes to operationalize.
  ■ *Convergent validity:* Measures of constructs that theoretically *should* be related to each other are, in fact, observed to be related to each other.
  ■ *Discriminant validity:* Measures of constructs that theoretically should *not* be related to each other are, in fact, observed to *not* be related to each other.
  ■ *Factorial validity:* Is your factor structure valid? Does it make intuitive sense? If items cluster into meaningful groups, factorial validity can be inferred.

Tips on making your own questionnaire:

  ■ Each item should contain only *one* complete thought or idea.
  ■ Items should be succinct, rather than long.
  ■ No complex sentences. The language of the items should be simple, accessible, clear and direct.
  ■ No double negatives.

►

▶
- No items that are likely to be endorsed by almost everyone or by almost no one.
- No items that are ambiguous and may be interpreted in more than one way.
- No items which clearly contain a socially desirable response.
- Item content and language should be suitable for people of different ages, meaningful across the socioeconomic gradient, for men and women and not culture-specific.

Think about it...

What is the value of assessment? What about social desirability? What is your experience with assessments?

The Gratitude Questionnaire-Six Item Form (GQ-6)

McCullough et al., 2002

Directions:

Using the scale below as a guide, write a number beside each statement to indicate how much you agree with it.

1 = strongly disagree
2 = disagree
3 = slightly disagree
4 = neutral
5 = slightly agree
6 = agree
7 = strongly agree

_____1. I have so much in life to be thankful for.
_____2. If I had to list everything that I felt grateful for, it would be a very long list.
_____3. When I look at the world, I don't see much to be grateful for.
_____4. I am grateful to a wide variety of people.
_____5. As I get older I find myself more able to appreciate the people, events, and situations that have been part of my life history.
_____6. Long amounts of time can go by before I feel grateful to something or someone.

▶

▶ ### Scoring:

Add up your scores for items 1, 2, 4, and 5. Reverse your scores for items 3 and 6. Add the reversed scores for items 3 and 6 to the total from Step 1. This is your total GQ-6 score. This number should be between 6 and 42.

Interpretation

If you scored 35, you score in the 25 per cent percentile of a sample of 1224 adults who took the GQ-6 as part of a feature on the Spirituality and Health website. If you scored 38 out of 42, you scored higher than 50 per cent of the people who took it. If you scored 41 out of 42 you scored higher than 75 per cent of the individuals who took it. If you scored a 42 or higher, then you scored among the top 13 per cent.

For more cultural and contextual norms, please refer to www.psy.miami.edu/faculty/mmccullough/gratitude/GQ-6-scoring-interp.pdf.

Review

This questionnaire documents your level of gratitude. It contains six items on seven-point Likert scale. Overall, the scale yields a high internal consistency (0.82) and is positively correlated with positive emotions, life satisfaction, vitality, optimism, empathy, sharing and forgiving. It is negatively related to depression and stress level.

The scale has low-to-moderate correlations with self-deceptive and impression management scales (McCullough et al., 2002).

Notes

1 At this time the Veterans administration 1946 and the National Institute of Mental Health 1947 were established.
2 Contrary to criticisms, positive psychology does not refer to all other disciplines as 'negative psychology'. Positive psychologists use the term 'psychology as usual' instead.

CHAPTER 2

Understanding Emotions

❖ LEARNING OBJECTIVES

This chapter will consider key psychological and social aspects of emotions in general and in relation to positive emotions in particular. The chapter examines the origin and functions of positive affect and positive emotions. Some theorists hold that positive affect is simply a function of people's progress towards goals; other theorists argue that positive emotions have a constructive function such as facilitating creativity and play. These and other theories will be discussed. Another key focus of the chapter is the construct of emotional intelligence, which continues to receive much popular and research attention. Finally, echoing an important recent orientation in the field of positive psychology, the chapter illustrates the case of 'negative emotions' as an equally constitutive element of human growth, learning and success and their typically interdependent dialectic relationship with 'positive emotions'.

Topics include:

- Defining emotions.
- The science behind positive affectivity and neuroscience.
- The broaden-and-build theory of positive emotions.
- The power of the positivity ratio – revisited.

- Emotional intelligence.
- Cultural and moral discourse as constitutive of emotional content, interpretation and subsequent responses.
- Rethinking negative emotions.

MOCK ESSAY QUESTIONS

1 Critically discuss the extent to which positive emotions can be said to have beneficial (and harmful) effects.

2 Critically consider ways in which seemingly negative emotions are beneficial to personal growth and success.

3 Critically discuss the contribution of positive psychology to our understanding of emotional intelligence.

4 Compare and contrast the ability and the mixed models of emotional intelligence.

Defining Emotions

We would like the reader to stop for a minute and reflect upon the last time they felt 'really happy'. As this segment of memory starts to take shape, try to remain mindful of what thoughts come to mind, noting also the accompanying feelings. The intention of the exercise is to prompt reflection about the nature of emotions in general, such as their phenomenology (what does it feel like?), conditions (when do I feel so?), manifestation (what does it do?) and their intimate connection with cognition and interpretation – all of which are longstanding preoccupations, typical of mainstream psychology. In addition, through the lens of positive psychology, the exercise is intended to entice the reader's appreciation of a simple yet crucial feature of positive emotions; namely, their ability to propagate further positive affect (like optimism; joy) and catalyse further beneficial, resourcing action (like expanding our thinking, fuelling our creativity and broadening our options). We will examine positive emotions' binding co-dependent intersection with negative emotions at the end of the chapter. Before we move to explore the interesting area of positive emotions we stop to consider what emotions are. The emphasis will be on delineating commonly agreed understandings of emotions rather than seeking to address or resolve variations in focus or definition among psychologists.

Emotions are notable features of our everyday psychological life and carry often deeply rooted information about our internal worlds, shaping our responses and motivating our actions. As a distinct aspect of being human, all emotions are useful in that they serve a function and are likely to harbour some degree of adaptive advantages. Subsequently, emotions are best attended to rather than minimized or ignored, not least since they are likely to find an outlet anyway, leaking their message and purpose into our conscious or unconscious levels of existence in spite of being neglected, concealed or denied. For instance, researchers studying 'emotional regulation', which involves the repertoire of implicit or explicit techniques that we utilize to increase, decrease or maintain intensity or duration of positive or negative emotional experiences (Oatley et al., 2006), have shown it to be liable to failure: failure in that typical emotion regulation strategies may 'ironically bring about the very emotional outcomes that people hope to avoid' such that we can find ourselves displaying 'unwanted emotions despite [...] best efforts to avoid them' (Koole, 2009: 6).

Affectivity, affective styles and basic human emotions

Emotions tend to focus on a specific event or circumstance across time periods (past, present or future). They are likely to be short lived and, in varying degrees, we are aware of them at the time of occurrence (Keltner et al., 2013). Feelings, and their subjectively experienced cues, are different from, but a dynamic constituent of, emotions. Moreover, the 'level of awareness of an emotion feeling depends in part on its intensity and expression, and after language acquisition, on labelling, articulating, and acknowledging the emotion experience' (Izard, 2009: 5).

Oatley et al. usefully summarize the essential features of an *emotion* as follows:

> 66 (a) a conscious mental state with recognizable quality of feeling and directed towards some object, (b) a bodily perturbation of some kind, (c) recognizable expressions of the face, tone of voice, and gesture, (d) a readiness for certain kinds of action (2006: 415) 99

A *mood*, on the other hand, tends to be an objectless, longer lasting state typically located in the background of our consciousness. It is a 'maintained state of emotion, or a disposition to respond emotionally in a particular way, [...] and perhaps without the person knowing what started the mood' (Oatley et al., 2006: 419). Thus moods, unlike emotions, tend to be unfocused and enduring.

Psychologists have identified and theorized about several distinguishable features for emotion concepts such as *affectivity* – the degree to which an individual experiences positive/negative moods (Peterson, 2006); *hedonic capacity* – our ability to feel good (Meehl, 1975); *positive affect* – the degree to which someone experiences joy, contentment, etc.; and *negative affect* – the degree to which someone experiences stress, anxiety, fear, sadness, etc. Researchers have also aptly established that same event can be experienced differently by people. This difference is termed *affective style*. Affective style is defined as 'a broad range of individual differences in different parameters of emotional reactivity [...] including a) threshold to respond, b) the magnitude of the response, c) the rise time to the peak in the response, d) recovery function of the response and e) the duration of the response' (Davidson, 2003: 657–8). There is also evidence to suggest that same event can generate different emotional reactivity due to individual differences in the brain (Davidson, 2003) and that individual differences in brain activity associated with affective styles tend to remain stable over time. It is interesting to note that research examining the brains of resilient individuals when faced with potential threats have found that more resilient individuals tend to have less activity in the area of the brain that deals with worry (orbitofrontal cortex) (e.g. Waugh et al., 2008). The view of an integrated involvement of our brain and its neurobiological responses as constitutive of all emotional responses (Damasio, 1999) alongside cognition-action interactions is undisputed. What remains under deliberation includes the extent to which emotion feeling is *an outcome* (as Damasio posits) or *a component part* of neurobiological activity (as Izard posits). Dialogues also continue over the various interactions between emotion states, cognition and levels of consciousness required in the ontology of discrete emotions[1] (see Izard, 2009).

Basic human emotions

Paul Ekman's (2003) extensive study of human emotions and expression concluded that there are *six basic human emotions* throughout the world and across gender, age and culture. These include: anger, disgust, fear, joy, sadness and surprise. Another notable theorist Carroll Izard argues that all humans share *ten basic emotions* featuring: anger, contempt, disgust, distress, fear, guilt, interest, joy, shame and surprise. Most of these emotions are identifiable in infants except contempt, shame and guilt, which adds further strength to the view that basic emotions are adaptive responses for our survival or well-being. For instance, the evolutionary benefits of basic negative emotions, which typically 'occur in brief episodes and involve very little cognition beyond minimal perceptual processes' (Izard, 2009: 3), are clear: they channel our thought–action repertoires (i.e. what we think about and the range of actions we are engaged into) to those that had best promoted our ancestors' survival in life-threatening situations. Thus, fear 'makes us' want to run, and anger 'makes us' want to thrash out at the aggressor. The human brain's ability to hone in on real or potential danger is a byproduct of evolutionary and adaptive tendencies. Humans and animals have a stronger tendency or bias towards attending to negative, versus positive stimuli. Thousands of years ago, people survived if they were able to promptly and selectively attend to danger or dangerous situations that could lead to extinction of their genetic line. This selectivity can lead us to consciously narrow our attention to focusing on what is wrong, rather than what is right with ourselves and the world around us. By contrast, research studies are finding that people who score high on self-reported experiences of positive emotions, have an attention bias towards positive information (e.g. Strauss and Allen, 2006).

Positive emotions and why they are important

From decades of research across many populations, the ten so called positive emotions which emerge as most widely researched and experienced in daily life are joy, gratitude, serenity, interest, hope, pride, amusement, inspiration, awe and love. These positive emotions have been found to propagate ways of thinking and acting that are essential for growth and well-being. Barbara L. Frederickson commenced her groundbreaking and widely noted theory of the 'broaden-and-build' functions of positive emotions in the early 1990s (see Fredrickson, 2013 for a review). Since, research demonstrated through numerous controlled experiments that experiences of positive emotions broaden our thought–action repertoires, undo negative emotions, help build resilience and facilitate the kind of psychosocial resources that help us thrive (Cohn and Fredrickson, 2009). Fredrickson's Positive Emotions and Psychophysiology Laboratory (PEP Lab) continues to expand our evidence-based understanding of positive emotions, 'charting their variety, the ways they change how the human mind works, and how, little-by-little, they change people's lives' (Fredrickson, 2013: 3).

The broadening effect

Frederickson's proposal is that when we experience one (or more) of the main positive emotions our minds tend to open up such that we are able to think 'outside the box'. When we broaden our thinking patterns, we tend to get a bird's eye view of our situation which can then help generate alternative understandings and solutions to the tasks at hand. We also become more receptive and more innovative in our approach, with positive emotions being found to enhance verbal creativity tasks and expand our mindset (Fredrickson, 2009).

The building effect

Not only can positive emotions open our mind to different ways of looking at our immediate world and locate alternative strategies, research has shown that the experience of positive emotions coupled with the broadening effect have the ability to build valuable personal resources which we are able to dip into when needed. These resources cut across all realms – intellectual (problem solving; openness to learning; visualizing); physical (increased cardiovascular health; increased coordination); social (maintaining and creating relationships) and psychological (resilience; optimism; sense of identity; goal orientation). As these develop, they induce more positive emotions that continue building the resources in an 'upward spiral' (see Figure 2.1). Importantly, resources accumulated through experiencing positive emotions are long-lasting; their implication and durability 'outlast the transient emotional states that led to their acquisition' (Fredrickson, 2001: 4).

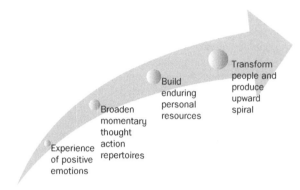

FIGURE 2.1 The broaden-and-build theory of positive emotions (Fredrickson, 2001)

The undoing effect

The next time the reader is faced with a stressful experience or feels stuck in negativity, then they can think about the undoing effect of positive emotions. The undoing effect hypothesis posits that 'positivity can quell or undo cardiovascular after-effects of negativity' (Fredrickson, 2009: 105). Thus, when we feel anxiety or other negative emotions, experiencing positive emotions can help quiet our mind and can help our bodies to return to normal physiological functioning significantly faster than any other types of emotion (Fredrickson, 2013). As Fredrickson (2001: 6) explains, by:

> 66 broadening a person's momentary thought–action repertoire, a positive emotion may loosen the hold that a negative emotion has gained on that person's mind and body by dismantling or undoing preparation for specific action. 99

THE POSITIVITY RATIO – REVISITED

Using an intricate mathematical model based on differential equations drawn from fluid dynamics (a subfield of physics), Frederickson and Losada (2005) proposed ideal positive to negative emotions rations with reference to flourishing. Losada created a nonlinear dynamics model of observed interactions to examine changes in emotions over time and found that business

▶

▶

teams who had a 6:1 positive to negative interaction, used more inquiry than advocacy and discussed more about others than themselves, were high performing. This study then led to the collaboration with Barbara Frederickson, who applied this technique to identify the optimal positive to negative emotion ratio for human flourishing = 3:1 (rounded up). The concept of positivity ratio refers to the proportion of pleasant states, feelings and sentiments vs. unpleasant states, feelings and sentiments, over time. The positivity ratio became widely used to guide predictions about conditions that support flourishing (experiencing 'goodness, generativity, growth, and resilience') or languishing (experiencing a sense of emptiness; not feeling good and so not *doing* good). A positivity ratio of 11.63:1 is associated with flourishing. 2.90:1 is the minimum positivity ratio (i.e. the critical point beyond which the power of positive emotions can unfold) and 1:1 is associated with languishing (Fredrickson and Losada, 2005). In 2013 Brown et al. published a detailed critique of Losada and Fredrickson's (2005) positivity ratio. Brown and colleagues do not oppose the search for such a ratio or the proposition that people who experience a higher positivity ratio would function more optimally. Among other things, their critique challenges the relevance of and demonstrates inaccuracies in the application of the differential equations used in Losada's model. In response, the model has been formally retracted by the authors and declared 'withdrawn as invalid' alongside the model's predictions of positivity ratios of 2.9 and 11.6 in a subsequent erratum (Fredrickson and Losada, 2013). See Fredrickson (2013) for a fuller response to Brown et al. (2013) including arguments and cumulative research studies showing several other elements of the article to remain unaffected by the retraction of Losada's mathematical modelling – such as empirical findings that higher positivity ratios are predictive of a range of beneficial outcomes.

Which positive emotions are important?

In order of occurrence, Fredrickson's top 10 positive emotions include: joy, gratitude, serenity, interest, hope, pride, amusement, inspiration, awe and love. Love however emerges as unique in that it encompasses all other nine emotions and can be elicited through cumulative or variously combined presence of the other main positive emotions. Arguably, love often emerges as the most experienced and most powerful human emotion. Nevertheless, Kirk Schneider (2017) highlights the growing interest in understanding, accommodating and capturing the processes and benefits of the powerfully transformative experience of awe. As Schneider documents in his paper, awe is gaining a strong foothold in arts and literature, social media and increasingly in mainstream psychology and the field of positive psychology. For instance, there are studies showing significant correlations between a sense of awe and pro-social behaviours and involving positive states such as greater altruism, patience and creativity. Relative to 'happiness', awe was also found to have stronger correlations with the lowering of disease-promoting inflammation, levels of stress and a greater overall sense of life-satisfaction (see Schneider, 2017 for a review).

Positive emotions enrich the ways in which we engage with the world around us including our ability to discover and build new knowledge and to cope with adversity. Frederickson (2000: 24) states that by 'opening our hearts and minds' positive emotions enable us to envisage potentiality, see opportunities and expand our capacity to form meaningful connections with others.

Think about it...

Frederickson makes it clear that emotions are individual and can be elicited at different times for different people. Try and think of one of her Top Ten emotions. Try not to overanalyse – just think about it ...

When was the last time I felt this feeling?
Where was I?
What was I doing?
What else gives me that feeling?
Can I think of still more triggers?
What can I do to cultivate this feeling?

(Fredrickson, 2009: 40)

The *circumplex model of emotions* (Russell, 1980; Larsen and Diener, 1992) (Figure 2.2) postulates that emotions exist in a circumplex across two dimensions, highlighting frequency and intensity as the two organizing principles. There are issues with this model, mainly based on the fact that it was created using self-reported data and not mixed with objective markers. Furthermore, have we generalized human emotions to the extent that we can say that these are the only dimensions available?

In addition, in relation to the physiology of emotion, researchers have suggested that there may be two different types of positive affect itself (Gilbert et al., 2008). The first type may be linked to dopaminergic system which controls drive/seeking; the second may be linked to the opiate-oxytocin system which induces soothing/contentment. Gilbert et al. found that positive affect was indeed mediated by three underlying factors: 'activated positive affect, relaxed positive affect and safe/content positive affect' with the latter 'negatively correlating highest with depression, anxiety, stress, self-criticism and insecure attachment' (2008: 182).

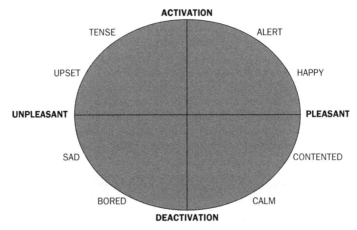

FIGURE 2.2 The circumplex model of emotions (as cited in and adapted from Carr, 2004)

Where do positive emotions come from?

If positive emotions are key to success and well-being, it is important to understand where they come from. There are currently two main theories as to how positive emotions come about:

- via our material brains (Davidson, 2003; Davidson et al., 2003) and
- via our perceived rate of progress towards important goals (Carver and Scheier, 1990).

time out

Mind–body dualism

Greek philosophers, Aristotle and Plato, discussed the human self in terms of three separate entities: the mind, the body and the soul. In the 17th century, René Descartes's postulation 'I think, therefore I am', instigated a longstanding debate between the existence of the immaterial mind (consciousness, self-awareness) and the material body (brain-intelligence) (eventually know as Cartesian Dualism).

The separation debate has been updated by research showing that it is a complex interaction between both – the body and the mind affecting each other (Ratey, 2001).

www.brainpickings.org/?s=self+and+neuroscience

See also this TED-Ed animated exploration of the mind–body relationship and the locus of self within it (with Maryam Alimardani): https://ed.ted.com/lessons/are-you-a-body-with-a-mind-or-a-mind-with-a-body-maryam-alimardani

Looking to our brains

In the last two decades, neuropsychology has made substantial advances in terms of the creation of machinery to access the brain (see Figure 2.3) and its functioning. For example, in order to determine which parts of the brain are being used or which cells are firing, psychologists can access this picture of the brain via functional magnetic resonance imaging (fMRI). This allows scientists to access all parts of the brain, with low invasiveness. Alternatively, if cost and access to such high-tech machinery is limited, psychologists can use an electroencephalography (EEG), which is like a hat with multiple suction caps that people place on their heads, in order to monitor the movement of neurons. Ultimately, these machines allow cognitive and neuro-psychologists access to the brain in an attempt to match other physiological or emotional markers. The fascination with trying to ascertain the brain's relationship with psychological activity continues to capture researchers' efforts and more nuanced understandings are being proposed. In her book *How Emotions Are Made: The Secret Life of the Brain* (2017a) Lisa Feldman Barrett, for instance, emphasizes that the last ten years of neuroscientific research shows the human brain to be a *predictive* rather than a *reactive* organ and that psychological states and phenomena are not merely localized to particular parts of the brain but rather they are constructed with and through complex and multipurpose brain networks.[2]

time out

The brain
Within our wonderful brain there are several systems that are linked to the experience of happiness. The brain can be separated into three categories:

Reptilian: The oldest part of the brain structure, which we share with our ancestors, controls the basic functioning such as temperature regulation, sleeping and waking.

Paleomamillian: This section includes the limbic system, and also deals with controlling movement for survival, as well as some elements of emotions.

Neomamilian: Also known as the cortex, this is the latest evolutionary component to our brain, which enables abstract thinking, planning, and control of lower functioning skills (Ratey, 2001).

Specific areas responsible for the regulation of happiness include:

Reward system: The reward system is responsible for inducing feelings of pleasure and filing the stimulus that has induced the pleasure into memory.

Pleasure system: This is the system that recognizes what the person is doing, seeing or listening to is good.

▶

▶ **Dopamine:** Dopamine is the key neurotransmitter involved in the pleasure centre. Limited levels of dopamine can subdue levels of motivation whereas high levels can cause situations of mania (Ackerman, 2009).

Ventral Tegmental Area (VTA): In collaboration with the substantia nigra, the VTA is the key area of the dopamine system.

Nucleus accumbens: This component of the brain is a very important player in the reward system of the brain. It involves the pleasure centre as it holds the highest concentration of dopamine neurotransmitters. Addictive drugs (e.g. cocaine) target this area.

Prefrontal cortex: This area of the brain is responsible for working memory.

Orbital frontal cortex: This is the area of the brain where decisions are made.

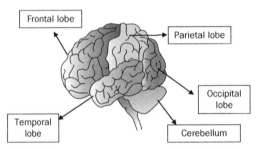

FIGURE 2.3 Basic components of the brain
Source: Original illustration by Howitt (2010).

Electroencephalography and fMRI helped scientists to establish that the two key components in the brain in relation to the experience of positive emotions appear to be the orefrontal cortex (PFC) and the amygdala. The prefrontal cortex is home to emotions and emotional regulation whereas increased activity in the amygdala can predict higher levels of negative affect (Davidson, 2001). The PFC enables the generation of goals as well as pathways for how to achieve them (Davidson, 2003). The PFC monitors daily experiences, in relation to long-term goals, sometimes initiating delayed gratification for the greater good. Individuals who have low activation in the left PFC are therefore are not able to initiate goal-directed behaviour or regulate impulses. Furthermore, people who have increased activation in their right PFC report difficulties in regulating emotions.

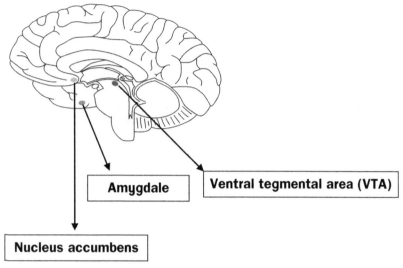

FIGURE 2.4 The pleasure centre
Source: Original illustration by Howitt (2010).

From early research documenting the effects of brain damage (Gainotti, 1972; Sackeim et al., 1982), researchers have discovered the link between the anterior left-sided PFC and positive affect. Specifically, when we experience positive affect, this section of the brain is activated, and vice versa for when we feel anxiety or depression (Davidson et al., 2000b). Our brain is therefore actually divided into two systems – the approach (positive affect) and avoidance (negative affect) systems (Davidson and Irwin, 1999).

These systems and emotions are directly linked to goal attainment. Thus, when we engage in behaviour that is bringing us towards a desired goal, we will feel increased positive affect. However, when we are faced with a threat, we will attempt to remove ourselves from the situation, and likely feel negative affect in response. The behavioural activation system (BAS) is more sensitive and responsive to incentives, making people more extraverted and impulsive, whereas the behavioural inhibition system (BIS) is more sensitive and responsive to threats – arousing anxiety and neurosis.

What is it that makes the brain develop a certain affective style? Several theories exist including: the impact of social influences, activation patterns, neuro-genesis and gene expression (Davidson et al., 2000a). There is mounting evidence for the first theory, via research on plasticity. Specifically, scientists have found that rodents that are raised in a nurturing environment have significant changes to the circuitry of their PFC and amygdala (emotion and emotion regulation areas) in relation to control groups. Furthermore, the evidence also suggests that changes in this area don't have to happen from birth. Enriching environments later on in life can also have a significant impact on the circuitry of our brains within emotions and regulation areas of the brain (Barrett, 2017a).

Emotions, goals and discrepancy theory

Affective neuroscience believes that whether we engage the BAS or BIS will determine affect. Charles Carver and Michael Scheier have spent the past few decades researching goals and self-regulation and their effects on emotional well-being. Their *control-theory* perspective is based on behaviour and self-regulation. When we set ourselves a goal (large or small, physical or mental) this becomes our reference value. We then engage in what is known as a discrepancy loop, trying to minimize the distance between where we are and where we want to be. Carver and Scheier (1990) posit that we are always thinking and behaving in relation to a goal. As we go through the day and experience life events, etc. we are constantly assessing our current state in relation to some standard or desired goal. If there is discrepancy between where the person currently is and where they want to be (reference value), people will adjust their behaviour in hopes of getting closer to the reference value.

Sometimes, however, there are external influences or impediments that stand in the way of attaining our goals. Individuals need to make adjustments, either to their expectancies or environmental circumstances, to override these impediments. It is imperative to note that it is the rate of progress, rather than the progress per se, that determines whether we experience positive or negative emotions. A negative emotion 'comes from inadequate progress towards a goal, whereas positive affect comes from progress towards future success' (Carver and Scheier, 1990: 27).

Positive emotions and other people

When we feel positive emotions, we feel connected to others and able to allow ourselves to open up and include others in our sense of self (Waugh and Fredrickson, 2006). Positive emotions make us feel less as two and more as one. This inclusion side effect has a remarkable impact on personal relationships with others. Not only do we see others as part of our self-concept, but we are more likely to understand other people's complexities and perspectives, which in turn will enhance the relational bond (Waugh and Fredrickson, 2006).

Cross-cultural research shows that having positive emotions is not a selfish endeavour. In fact, by experiencing positive emotions, we are able to take a broader perspective, recognizing others' viewpoints and not just our own, thereby developing stronger relationships with others. This connection to others expands beyond people that we already know. For example, Fredrickson has found evidence that inducing positive emotions can help with combating, and almost eliminating, own-race bias. Own-race bias is the psychological phenomenon that people are not good at recognizing members from other races, which can feed racism and segregation. Furthermore, there is also evidence that supports positive emotions effect on cross-cultural perspective taking, with people who feel higher levels of positive emotions being able to take a larger perspective and exhibit an increase in feelings of sympathy and compassion for someone from dissimilar cultural contexts (e.g. Nelson, 2009; Scollon and King, 2011).

Think about it...

The next time you are feeling a little blue, seek out your favourite person. Research shows that simply by looking at our favourite person, there are several documented immediate physiological and psychological benefits, such as invigoration, enhanced immune system functioning and mood states. So make a date today with your favourite person and get those positive emotions flowing!

(Matsunaga et al., 2008).

Attenuation to positive emotions

It is important to make it clear that people who experience positive emotions and resilience tendencies are both able and liable to feel sadness and anxiety, just as much as anyone else. It appears, however, that they are able to draw on the resources to help them deal with and exit such negative emotion states much faster than those who do not (Fredrickson, 2009).

Positive attenuation is also key in buffering against depressive symptoms. Resilient individuals have a distinct ability to maintain and regulate positive emotions. Dysphoric and non-dysphoric individuals tend to react just the same to emotions as each other; it appears that there is a difference in ability to maintain and regulate these emotions and not the ability to react in the first place (McMakin et al., 2009).

By pursuing positive emotion-eliciting activities, we accrue resources (psychological, social, etc.) that enhance our odds for survival and reproduction. Positive emotions not only mark or signal health and well-being, *but also produce* health and well-being. Individuals who score higher on levels of positive affect tend to report better marriages and job satisfaction, more engagement with physical activity and better sleep patterns. However, we must be wary of such cross-sectional work as we still need to determine what comes first. For example, is it that people sleep better and therefore experience more positive emotions or vice versa? More research is needed to arrive at more nuanced understanding of the causal and interactional relationship between the two types of variables.

It is also useful to reflect at this point in our discussion on the link between the notion of 'positive emotion' and the notion of 'positivity'. In her book *Positivity: Groundbreaking Research to Release Your Inner Optimist and Thrive* (first published in 2009) Fredrickson frequently uses these two terms interchangeably, yet also presents them as distinct. Moreover Fredrickson abundantly illustrates ways in which 'positivity' is both a *phase* and a *consequence* of positive emotions states. It follows that positivity-defined-as-a-mindset can be used as a guiding marker to mitigate against such blurring of conceptual boundaries. It can then be said that *positive emotions are constructive* in that, they spark, amplify and scaffold the 'opening of heart and mind', whereas *positivity is transformative* in that it is a complexly attuned (affect imbued) attitude of embracing that which is unfolding for the benefit of growth.

It is through cultivating positive emotions (time limited) that we acquire wider awareness of and receptivity to internal or external assets – that is, broadened mindsets (long lasting). However, positivity-defined-as-a-mindset can also be conceived as transformative in relation to our engagement with *negative emotions* (angst, sadness, anger, etc.). See the end of this chapter for more on approaching negative emotions positively and their inevitable place in the power of emotional agility leading to new, self-enhancing ways of being.

Personality and positive emotions

The concept of personality is concerned with individuals' differences in how we think, feel and act. Personality can be defined as 'distinctive and relatively enduring ways of thinking, feeling and acting that characterize a person's response to life situations' (Passer and Smith, 2006: 420). Commonly, in psychological studies, researchers use the NEO Big Five traits of personality (see the 'time out' section below) to correlate a range of other concepts with. At present, the literature shows a strong correlation between dispositional global positive affect and the Big-Five personality trait Extroversion (Costa and McCrae, 1980; Shiota et al., 2006).

The two most highly robust relationships with happiness and personality are extraversion and neuroticism, with extraversion predicting well-being up to ten years later. People who are extroverted are more likely to experience positive emotions as well as experience more intense positive emotions. In addition, our attachment style in relationships is likely to have an impact on our ability to feel positive emotions. Not surprisingly, secure attachment has been associated with higher levels of positive affect in romantic relationships versus insecure attachment. Neuroticism, on the other hand, is consistently linked to depression and low levels of well-being.

time out

NEO-Five Personality Traits

According to Costa and Macrae (1992) there are five main personality traits that individuals possess to some degree or another. These include:

1 **Extraversion:** Individuals who score high on extraversion tend to be sociable, talkative, and join in when there is something collective going on. Low scorers tend to be classically considered as more reserved, quiet, shy and prefer to be alone.

2 **Agreeableness**: Individuals who score high on agreeableness tend to be pleasant, compassionate and sympathetic to others needs. Low scorers tend to be untrusting, suspicious, critical and slightly hard-nosed.

3 **Conscientiousness:** Individuals who score high on conscientiousness tend to have high levels of grit, meaning they are industrious, diligent, efficient and reliable. Low scorers tend to be inattentive, idle, unsystematic and sometimes unreliable.

4 **Neuroticism**: Individuals who score high on neuroticism tend to experience high levels of anxiety and insecurity and can be emotionally volatile. Low scorers tend to be more tranquil, steady and composed.

5 **Openness to experience**: Individuals who score high on openness to experience tend to be original and artistic. Low scorers tend to be more conformist and uncreative.

Shiota and colleagues (2006) reviewed correlations between personality traits and the positive emotions known to engage survival fitness: joy, contentment, pride, compassion, amusement and awe. When correlated with the Big Five, each of these positive emotions were found to correlate positively with extraversion. Conscientiousness tended to be correlated with agency-focused emotions such as joy, contentment and pride. Agreeableness correlated with love and compassion. Awe was strongly linked to openness as well as amusement, joy, love and compassion. Neuroticism was negatively correlated with love, contentment, pride and joy. These correlations remained after comparison with peer reports.

Other links to personality traits and enhanced well-being include: optimism, assertiveness, emotional stability, loneliness and self-esteem. However, despite the interesting links, positive psychology has yet to show a clear-cut causal relation between personality and positive life outcomes. Furthermore, the majority of research into personality and positive life experiences/outcomes has been done on adults, thus future research needs to include all ages in order to determine stronger and causal links. Holder and Klassen (2009) argue that understanding personality and well-being will enhance researchers' ability to match interventions to personality type, thereby tailoring the interventions and hopefully achieving maximum potential.

The face and positive emotions

Does smiling have anything to do with our ability to experience positive emotions? The presence of a Duchene smile has been regarded as an objective measure of genuine happiness/positive emotions. There are studies showing positive correlations between Duchene smiling and duration of grief after bereavement, reduced negativity, greater competence, more positive ratings from others and greater well-being in later life (Harker and Keltner, 2001). Also, Johnson et al. (2010) have found experimental evidence that when people smile genuinely (as detected through facial muscular tracking), their thought patterns are immediately broadened.

YEARBOOKS

Did you smile in your yearbook photo? And was it a genuine (Duchene) or a fake smile (Pan American)? This small detail may be important in predicting your future well-being. Dacher Keltner and LeeAnne Harker, researchers at University of California at Berkley, analysed the smiles in the photos of 141 high school seniors (18) from a 1960 yearbook from Mills College. Those that were smiling were contacted at three subsequent time points (age 27, 43 and 52) and questioned on their satisfaction with life and marital satisfaction. Even 30 years later, the females that expressed a genuine, Duchene smile at the age of 18 were more likely to have married and stayed married as well as reporting higher levels of well-being and life satisfaction.

See Harker and Keltner (2001) for the original article.

Emotional intelligence

The capacity to acknowledge, to discern between and to engage effectively with our (and unavoidably other people's) emotions plays a fundamental role in our psychological life. It makes a crucial contribution to orienting our thoughts and actions, shaping our well-being not least through influencing the journey of recovery from negative emotional states (Limonero et al., 2015) and has been strongly correlated with numerous health incidences (Martins et al., 2010). This complex human capacity is captured by the concept emotional intelligence (EI) which Salovey and Mayer (1990: 189) define as the 'ability to monitor one's own and other's feelings and emotions, to discriminate among them, and to use this information to guide one's thinking and action'. At the heart of the concept of EI is the view that emotions serve a function, have a use and are not present for idle purpose (Davidson, 2003). Our emotions carry important information and if we master 'listening' and deciphering their messages we come to know how we feel about events, situations, people and so on. Moreover, emotional suppression can be detrimental to our well-being. Investment in expanding our EI is therefore an important aspect for both personal growth and self-care (Mayer et al., 2004).

After the groundbreaking theory of multiple intelligences (Gardner, 1993), people began to see that intelligence was not simply about IQ, but several kinds of intelligence, including:

- linguistic intelligence;
- logical-mathematical intelligence;
- spatial intelligence;
- bodily-kinaesthetic intelligence;
- musical intelligence;
- interpersonal intelligence;
- intrapersonal intelligence;
- naturalist intelligence.

There are two distinct main groups of models of emotional intelligence: the ability EI models and mixed EI models. The following section will focus on these two types of models with a specific focus on the ability model framework, which we perceive to be the most robust in terms of objective classifications.

The ability model

Pioneers in emotional intelligence testing include John Mayer and Peter Salovey who in collaboration with their colleague David Caruso, developed the Mayer-Salovey-Caruso's EQ[3] Model, which is a 141-item, task-based emotional intelligence test (MSCEIT) (Mayer et al., 2003). Although EI became popular via Daniel Goleman (1996), the theory and research behind EI had been the work of these three men. According to their model, EI is a set of competences or mental skills that include four stages (Brackett et al., 2009). This section will review the branches, and associated types of abilities, outlined from Mayer and Salovey's work, as well as some questions we can ask ourselves that will help enhance our emotional intelligence quotient.

Perceiving emotions

The first branch is 'perceiving' and it pertains to the ability to recognize emotions either in yourself or in others. Questions to ask yourself include: How do you feel? How do others feel? By recognizing these subtle emotional cues, individuals are better equipped to deal with social circumstances.

Using

The second step is entitled 'using emotions', which is the ability to use emotions to facilitate thinking and your mood. Thus if you need to edit your papers or perform surgery, you are able to bring yourself down into a calm, unaroused state in order to narrow your focus. Conversely, if you need to write a creative essay, you can bring yourself up, either by music or self-talk, to enhance positive feeling and thereby facilitate broader thinking patterns (remember broaden-and-build!). Questions to help develop this adaptive use of emotions include: How does you mood influence thinking? How is it impacting on your decision-making?

Understanding

The third branch is 'understanding emotions', and people who are high in this branch are able to understand and analyse emotion-information starting with an appreciation that emotions are highly complex; they don't just come in a nice, neat package. You are not just mad or just hurt; happy or sad, but you can be a mixture of these feelings all at once. They also recognize that emotions can change over time. Thus, when you are angry, you don't always stay angry. They recognize that anger can change into another emotion such as shame or regret. When trying to develop this area, ask yourself: Why are you feeling this? What do these emotions mean? What has caused that for you? Where is that going to go?

Managing

Finally the last branch is 'managing emotions' and this is the ability to manage, or self-regulate, our emotions. Thus, we can identify when and where it is inappropriate to express certain emotions, and wait until the appropriate time. For example, if someone tries to be cheeky during class and this angers us, it would be highly inappropriate to turn round and scream at the student. Highly emotionally intelligent individuals would recognize that there is a time and place for certain emotions and manage them accordingly. Furthermore, this branch deals with managing emotions in others. People who score high in this are able to manage other people's emotions in addition to their own. However, just because someone is able to manage their own emotions does not necessarily mean they can manage others'. In order to develop this area, the reader should ask themselves: What can I do about it? How can these emotions be regulated?

Ultimately, emotional intelligence seems to predict several outcomes such as well-being, self-esteem, more pro-social behaviours, less smoking and alcohol use, enhanced positive mood, less violent behaviour, greater academic eagerness and higher leadership performance (Salovey et al., 2002; Brackett et al., 2009).

Mayer and Salovey's ability model seems to have more support compared to Goleman's model. In addition, ability measures of emotional intelligence seem to be more reliable than self-report measures, which are open to many problems.

Mixed models of EI

According to Goleman, EI is defined as 'the ability to adaptively perceive, understand, regulate, and harness emotions in the self and others' (Goleman 1996; Schutte et al., 2002). Hence, EI mixed models view EI as a combination of perceived emotional skills and personality. According to Goleman, EI matters because of its ability to predict academic, occupational and relationship success better than traditional IQ. However, longitudinal data is needed to confirm any causal relationships between performance and emotional intelligence (Roberts et al., 2001).

According to Goleman's theory of intelligence there are five main areas within the concept:

- managing emotions, where one engages in reframing anxiety and attempting to dismiss feelings of distress;
- using emotion for self-motivation, where one becomes proficient in delaying gratification for future success;
- recognizing emotions in others, where one has the ability to exhibit empathy, which is important for social relationships;
- managing emotions in others, where one is able to help others with their distress or encourage motivation;
- emotional self-awareness, where one is able to understand and identify their own emotions.

In order to measure this type of EI, researchers use the Emotional and Social Competence Inventory, or ESCI (2007). However, a major issue with EI self-reports is that they can be potentially inaccurate, unavailable to conscious interpretation, and vulnerable to social desirability, deception and impression management (Roberts et al., 2001). Furthermore, Goleman's work has been branded as simply pop-psychology (Mayer et al., 2008), which has overshadowed his contribution to the area of EI.

The Bar-ON model of emotional-social intelligence (ESI)

As one further example of a mixed model, the Bar-ON model of emotional-social intelligence views emotional intelligence as the skill of being able to understand ourselves and those around us as well as an ability to interact and connect with others. The Bar-ON is another self-report measurement tool that aims to test individuals' emotional and social skills. Criticisms of this test include reports of high levels of deception (Day and Carroll, 2008; Grubb and McDaniel, 2007).

One big question is whether or not EI is separate from personality traits. This assumption comes from the research within personality traits, which argues that EI self-report measures are too strongly related to several personality traits such as neuroticism, extraversion and agreeableness (Davies et al., 1998). For example someone who is neurotic versus emotionally stable will have issues with trying to identify emotions within themselves and others. Furthermore, their vocabulary and ability to identify emotions will be stunted. Extroverts on the other hand have excellent communication skills and are able to convey their emotions to others well. Likewise, people who are high on agreeableness will be proficient in displaying acts of empathy. Thus a problem with EI is that it may not be unique and may be too highly associated with personality for being seen as a separate construct. Overall, the development of EI, from an ability model perspective, is highly beneficial for an individual's well-being.

Peña-Sarrionandia et al. (2015) call for a greater integration between emotion regulation and EI research traditions. The former is strong in theorizing *how* the person manages their emotions; the latter is strong at theorizing *who* is more optimally utilizing their emotions. In support to this, Peña-Sarrionandia et al. conducted a large meta-analysis and extensive statistical analyses and concluded that high EI individuals are able to regulate their emotions with a higher degree of flexibility and so create space for a wider range of emotions to emerge. They also found that high EI individuals tend to 'shape their emotions from the earliest possible point in the emotion trajectory and have many strategies at their disposal' (2015: 1).

Finally, a move away from a classic neurophysiological view of pre-programmed emotion circuits towards a view that emotions are constructed (Barrett, 2017a) helps strengthen the possibility that we can be more deliberate in altering the necessary conditions for a thriving inner world. In an interview for the British Psychological Society's scholarly publication *The Psychologist*, Barrett reemphasizes how EI can be enhanced by expanding emotional vocabulary since by providing our brain 'new concepts to predict with' we become better equipped and 'deal more flexibly with a broader range of situations' (2017b: 56). Furthermore, by cultivating experiences that yield the acquisition of new concepts, 'our brain's automatic control of future experiences and behaviours' is also altered. As such, in 'a literal, brain-wiring sense, the concepts […] [we] learn today influence […] [our] life tomorrow' (2017b: 56).

Emotions and moral discourse

Emotions represent a fundamental basis for our personal and social existence and as such are always influencing and being influenced by dominant discourses of a local culture, at a given historical time. Let us now turn to the (perhaps surprising) case of boredom to expand on these points.

An emotion we call boredom: its vicissitudes and capacity to promote well-being

Boredom qualifies as a 'negative' emotion in that it is unpleasant, discomforting and tends to be evaded. Boredom state occasions a view of the world that is not, at least at the first glance, compatible with success or the conditions necessary for flourishing. Although characterized by noticeable frustration, weariness and a sense of stuckness, boredom experience is often regarded as trivial and would not impress the (self) observer as much as other related emotions (e.g. anxiety, melancholy, generalized depression) do. The observer may also pass judgement pointing to deficits and shortcomings in relation to the experiencing individual (Tunariu and Reavey, 2007).

In its early research years, boredom was investigated in relation to poor work performance and later through motivational principles such as equilibrium and discrepancy. Notably, in his 1975 book *Beyond Anxiety and Boredom*, Csikszentmihalyi concluded that too low (e.g. monotonous) or too high (e.g. information overload) levels of environmental stimulation produce anxiety respectively manifested as boredom or as worry. Boredom is also a socially constructed object of our consciousness entangled in morality and social functioning and their combined consequences for subjective experience. Representations that people associate with the idea of emotions are relative to a historically and culturally specific set of norms, frames of truth-reference as well as structures and practices that help sustain their validity at subjective, relational, social, institutional or cultural levels (see e.g. the seminal book by Harré, 1986, on the socially constructed nature of emotions). The relevance of cultural discourses to emotional life and subjective realities more broadly has been identified in relation to positive psychology over the recent years. For instance, it has been pointed out that a narrow or blinkered focus on positive thinking would leave the discipline at risk of recycling and propping up the tyranny of positivity-discourse at the detriment of inclusive and mindfully self-authored ideologies about the notion of 'a good life' (e.g. McDonald and O'Callaghan, 2008; see also Chapter 11).

The term most commonly regarded as the ancestor of contemporary boredom is acedia (accidie in Middle English) meaning 'without care' or 'listless depression'. The earliest documentation of acedia can be traced to the

Egyptian desert-priest (circa 345–399 AD) Evagrius of Pontus. Perhaps one of the first prototypes of today's self-help texts, Evagrius's *Practical Treatise* (cited in Sorabji, 2000) offers insights, advice and exercises to monks living in the isolation of the desert to help tackle the threat of the soul being affected by undesirable passions (emotions). Pivotal to Evagrius's thesis of emotions is a differentiation between 'bad thoughts' as the first movement of emotions and 'passions of the souls' (i.e. emotions in themselves) as the second movement. The first movement was envisaged as a perturbation of the mind: thoughts with embodied manifestations that arise without an individual's solicitation. In the mix, there are 'generic thoughts' that a person forms about a situation on the basis of that which appeared to their senses. It posits that since a person had no control over what arises within, a 'bad thought' in itself was not to be conceived as a violation of (institutional) rules and should not be authenticated as carrying fault or blame. Emotions, on the other hand, Evagrius proposed, occurred whenever a person dwelled on or 'lived out' such thoughts, for in providing them with a focus, their readiness-capacity to motivate action is enabled. 'It is not up to us whether any of these disturb the soul or not. But it is up to us whether they linger (*khronizein*) or not, or whether they stir up emotions or not' (Evagrius, *Practical Treatise* 6; quoted in Sorabji, 2000: 359).

Four ways in which this ascetic text anticipates current thinking about emotions

Reflections on Evagrius's observations make apparent his pioneering thinking about the nature of emotions. Ahead of its time, this 345–399 CE text anticipates some of the key tenets of contemporary psychological understandings of emotions – as exemplified below in relation to the emotion today we call boredom.

First, Evagrius's text anticipates the notion that unlike moods, emotion states involve a distinguishable object under conscious focus and mental processing. Second, it suggests that a change in readiness for action is a necessary key condition for emotions coming into being (Frijda et al., 1989). Third, it anticipates the tenet that the process of managing emotions requires attention, selection of information, appraisals and alignment to one's (immediate and/or higher) goals. For instance, Evagrius's monks were invited to exercise particular vigilance in order *to offset* certain emotions from establishing themselves (thus echoing modern 'emotional sensitivity' strategies) and, where necessary, to engage in what we now refer to as 'emotional regulation' (Koole, 2009) in order to reduce duration that their souls were under siege by various emotions and the intensity of that emotion.

Fourth, Evagrius's text makes apparent the importance of historically and culturally situated truth-claims, alongside associated social structures that sustain them, and their constitutive relationship with emotions. As Armon-Jones (1986: 67) puts it 'an emotion may be dependent on the *de facto* features of a situation [but] its warrantness will be largely dependent on the cultural appropriateness of the agent's construal of the situation'. For instance, in the seventh century, Pope Gregory the Great converted Evagrius's *Eight Generic Thoughts* into the *Seven Cardinal or Deadly Sins*. As 'knowledge' became available outside scholastic establishments, it penetrated and transformed public consciousness, reifying truth, value and subject positioning for the language of emotions.

Finally, Evagrius's deliberations about a two-movement conception of emotions can also be understood as setting the scene for a reformulation of 'negative emotions' in the service of personal growth and fulfilment and so resonating current developments within the positive psychology literature.

Rethinking negative emotions

So-called 'negative emotions' such as anger, stress, guilt, self-doubt, embarrassment, boredom, envy and so on are typically experienced as unpleasant or discomforting states. Their aetiology and function has received a good share of attention by researchers but tended to occupy a marginal place within the field of positive psychology. This was partly due to the rapidly propagated emphasis on positive thinking and the power of positive emotions and their demonstrable beneficial domino effects for learning, creativity and well-being. For instance, negative emotions (e.g. anger, fear, contempt) were shown to constrict an individual's immediately at-hand repertoires for thought and action. On the other hand, positive emotions (e.g. joy, interest, love) were found to broaden such repertoires facilitating novel thinking and creative problem solving and helping to undo the restricting effect of negative emotions (see earlier in this chapter). Over recent years, there have been calls for a more refined approach to understanding, accessing and utilizing both 'negative' and 'positive' emotions (Held, 2004).

As part of what tends to be referred to as *the second wave of positive psychology* or *positive psychology 2.0*, negative emotions are being recognized for their inevitable and essential contribution to the everyday order of the human condition (Wong, 2011; Kashdan and Biswas-Diener, 2014; Ivtzan et al., 2016). This recognition retains as valuable the evidence-based proposition that positive emotions represent a fundamental human strength. However, to best tap onto this potentiality, it is also crucial to remain mindful that capacities endowed with 'positivity' could be miscalculated or go 'into overdrive', generating adverse outcomes. For example, pride in overdrive can become self-righteousness; in overdrive optimism can lead to a false sense of reality and potential recklessness; empathy could contribute to self-neglect or depression; and assertive leadership can be experienced by others as overbearing.

A more nuanced engagement with negative emotions (see also Lomas, 2016) could include exploring how by tolerating the unpleasantness of negative emotions, for instance, we stand a better chance to decipher their message and come to appreciate their teaching so expanding our resources for deliberate, optimal living. Likewise, by trusting the process of unfolding (recalling that emotional states are contextualized and time limited), experiences of negative emotions can be rendered as enabling rather than hindering. For they have the potentiality to add depth, genuineness and sustainability to our pursuit for fulfilment, peace of mind and well-being.

Evagrius's two-movement model of emotions delivers to the monks a critical 'permission' to not become entangled in a narrowing mindset of doubt, guilt or self-loading, but instead to take up an agentic stance, which necessitates negotiations with the shackles of taken-for-granted linguistic practices that organize their daily lives. Boredom is often taken as evidence of slackness or indifference and research shows that many senior leaders regard boredom as indicative of lack of 'strong ambition' in their subordinates (Carroll et al., 2010). A common cultural discourse also entangled in our workplace values is the imperative for 'happiness and success' wherein boredom is constructed as a clue to idleness, dryness of grit and enterprise or a failure to fulfil one's duties well (Kashdan and Biswas-Diener, 2014). The emotion we now call boredom therefore has retained its heritage – generating unhelpful and hostile meanings such as fault and blame towards self or other. Employers, for instance, would benefit from considering boredom among their staff as potentially indicative of a mismatch between talents and ability. It may be that bored employees are caught up in a sense of being under- or over-challenged (Vodanovich and Watt, 2016). If so, their re-engagement requires affirming, creative interventions versus a corrective, superficial approach.

By rethinking the generic thought (first movement of emotions) as ordinary components of being, away from a deficit model, we, relative to our moral orders, have the option to pause, reflect and master our affect experiences (second movement). For, if we *cannot* help perturbations of mind and soul from arising, we *can* help how we engage with emotions, in relation to how their content is experienced, expressed and regulated (Tunariu, 2015). The two-movement distinction helps highlight an alternative narrative about 'negative' emotions. By emphasizing agency and choice, one can instil hope and so set the stage for other, subsequent positive emotions such as a sense of grace and contentment.

If we accept that in its applications to real-life settings positive psychology seeks to catalyse a creative momentum in relation to 'the human drama of survival and flourishing in spite of suffering' (Wong, 2010: 1), then a two-movement model of emotions can also be regarded as a broad framework to:

- contribute to challenging a closed-minded or disquieted attitude towards (experiences of) negative emotions;
- engage with negative emotions in ways that not only accommodate but can further amplify the undoing effects of positive emotions;
- engender a mind-quieting appreciation of the dialectic relationship between opposite emotional states.

In relation to the latter, existential positive-psychology-informed activities are conducive to activities that hold effort and initiative alongside stillness and acceptance (Tunariu, 2017). This kind of co-productive intersection of positive and negative is helpfully articulated by Ivtzan et al. (2016: 5): 'the term 'dialectic' does not simply refer to a static relationship between opposites but to the way in which many phenomena change and evolve through a process of dynamic movement between these opposites'.

Chapter Summary

Reflecting on the learning objectives, the reader will have acquired a comprehensive mapping of the major delineators with respect to emotions, as well as the notion of emotional intelligence. In summary:

- Emotions are short lived in our consciousness and concern a specific event; moods are unfocused and can be considerably more enduring.
- The experience of positive emotions can help broaden our thoughts as well as build recourses in order to gain resilience.
- We all have an affective style; that is, an individualized (through habit and rehearsal) and an individualizing tendency to experience more positive or negative moods.
- Neurobiology and personality traits have an influence on our emotional life.
- There are two main types of models within emotional intelligence research: ability and mixed.
- Negative and positive emotions need to be understood for their distinct as well as their intertwined contribution to human flourishing and success.
- The felt texture and subjective significance of an emotion is greatly indebted to our individualized habits of awareness, repertoires of interpretation, emotion management and the values, hierarchy of goals, and life ethics that underpin these.
- Emotional life is indebted to cultural, societal and moral discourse (dominant systems of statements reifying contextual truth/knowledge claims).

Suggested Resources

www.youtube.com/watch?v=Ds_9Df6dK7c

Video published on 26 January 2009. Professor of Psychology Barbara Fredrickson discusses her book *Positivity*, and considers what positivity is and why it needs to be heartfelt to be effective.

www.intelligencesquared.com/events/daniel-goleman-on-focus-high-performance-fulfilment/

Filmed at the Royal College of Music on 25 October 2013. Daniel Goleman on Focus: The Secret to High Performance and Fulfilment.

www.paulekman.com/webisodes/

This is the link to the Paul Ekman Group website to access the Developing Global Compassion: Webisode series, including dialogues between the Dalai Lama and Paul Ekman.

www.paulekman.com/

This is the link to Paul Ekman's website concerned with the application of emotion and facial expression research. See also Ekman, P. (2014) *Moving Toward Global Compassion*. Paul Ekman Group.

www.positivityratio.com/

You could take the positivity test. Your score would provide a snapshot of how your emotions of the past day combine to create your positivity ratio. You may then choose to monitor your ratio for the next month and appreciate how your skills for flourishing expand, effortlessly.

http://uwmlarsonlab.org/projects/

This is the link to the Laboratory for Affective Neuroscience at the University of Wisconsin-Milwaukee. Explore the link to see current projects and publications by researchers who use multimodal neuroimaging, psychophysiological, behavioral, genetic and self-report tools to generate ground-breaking findings.

http://danielgoleman.info/

This is Daniel Goleman's official website with links to his audio or paperback books as well as assessment tools. See also:
Goleman, D. (2004) *Emotional Intelligence* and *Working with Emotional Intelligence*. London: Bloomsbury Publishing.
Goleman, D. (2007) *Social Intelligence: The New Science of Human Relationships*. London: Arrow.

www.evidencebasedpsychology.com/

This is a link to one of the leading businesses in emotional intelligence. If the reader is interested in evaluating and expanding their emotional quotient this is a link worth exploring.

The Twenty-four Hour Mind: The Role of Sleep and Dreaming in Our Emotional Lives

In this book, sleep researcher Professor Rosalind Cartwright highlights the intricate relationship between sleep and mental and physical well-being. Conscious and unconscious thoughts, feelings and emotions continue with their presence from one day into the next, linking wake and sleep and dreaming states. If one of the key functions of sleep is to regulate negative emotions, then the topic potentially holds particular interest to positive psychologists.

Further questions for the reader

1 What type of affective style do you think you have? How do you know this?

2 How important do you think the one negative emotion is in the positive ratio? Why?

3 Do you think you have high emotional intelligence? What if an objective test showed otherwise? What would your reaction be?

4 Are you able to generate emotion when needed and then reason with this emotion?

5 What would you say to someone who rejects the importance of positive emotions?

Personal Development Interventions

The exercises presented below focus on identifying and enhancing your positive emotion ratio and increasing your time in flow. Both have been found to enhance well-being and success across life domains.

1 Positive emotions

We now know that positive emotions are important for our ability to thrive and flourish. We would like you to monitor your positive to negative ratio (aiming for 3:1) over the next two weeks via Barbara Frederickson's free, easy-to-use website that calculates your positivity ratio for you. Document your ratios every day for two weeks. It is important that you do this every day as the more data you have,

▶

▶

the better you will be able to make a judgement on how you are actually feeling across time, rather than just on the day.

Go to www.positivityratio.com to access the test.

2 Emotional intelligence

How would you like to increase your emotional intelligence? The following exercises are aimed to help you expand your EQ through developing each of the four components of the ability model. Try them out over the upcoming week.

Perceiving: The next time you are talking with a friend, make sure you take the time to see if their facial expressions match their conversation. If you are happy all the time, don't assume that others are. Take the time to look and listen.

Using: The next time you go to write an essay, take heed of the scientific findings that positive moods enable creative thinking, whereas neutral moods enhance editing and analytical thinking. Use this knowledge in your writing-up process.

Understanding: The next time you are angry, stop and write down why you feel this is. Try and follow that emotion back as far as it will go. The anger may be an emotion that started out as hurt or sadness. Tackle the chain of emotions to get to the source of the problem.

Managing: The next time you feel like immediately exploding with anger, think about whether or not this is the appropriate emotion to display given the situation you are in. We need to manage our emotions and regulate them so that they are expressed in appropriate social contexts. Reflect on your thoughts and how you actually handled the situation.

Measurement Tools

Positive and Negative Activation Schedule (PANAS)

(Watson et al., 1988)

Directions

This scale consists of a number of words that describe different feelings and emotions. Read each item and then mark the appropriate answer in the space

▶

▶ next to that word. Indicate to what extent you felt this way *in the last week*. Use the following scale to record your answers:

1	**2**	**3**	**4**	**5**
very slightly or not at all	**a little**	**moderately**	**quite a bit**	**extremely**

___ interested	___ irritable
___ distressed	___ alert
___ excited	___ ashamed
___ upset	___ inspired
___ strong	___ nervous
___ guilty	___ determined
___ scared	___ attentive
___ hostile	___ jittery
___ enthusiastic	___ active
___ proud	___ afraid

Scoring

To score this scale, simply add the positive items (interested, alert, excited, inspired, strong, enthusiastic, proud, active, attentive, and determined) and retain a summative score for these. Do the same for the negative items and compare.

Interpretation

Your scores for the PA items should outweigh the negative scores (hopefully in a 3:1 ratio!).

Review

This is a widely used scale developed by Watson and Tellegen in the late 1980s. It is used across psychological and physical activity research. It is based on monitoring 20 emotion adjectives (10 positive and 10 negative). The scale can be administered using different temporal instructions, ranging from 'right now' to 'in the last week/month/year'. The creators believe that when researchers use a shorter time frame, they are tapping into emotional responses, whereas a longer time frame will highlight mood or personality differences. The internal consistency is quite high (0.86–0.90) and the PANAS has acceptable divergent validity, with good correlations between negative affect and measures of distress and psychopathology. Criticism of the PANAS include the argument that several of the items on this tool are not actually emotions (e.g. alert), and that several important positive emotions for well-being are missing from the scale (love, contentment) (Shiota et al., 2006).

Scale of Positive and Negative Experience (SPANE)

(Diener et al., 2009c)

Directions

Please think about what you have been doing and experiencing during the past four weeks. Then report how much you experienced each of the following feelings, using the scale below. For each item, select a number from 1 to 5, and indicate that number on your response sheet.

1. = Very Rarely or Never
2. = Rarely
3. = Sometimes
4. = Often
5. = Very Often or Always

_____ **Positive**
_____ **Negative**
_____ **Good**
_____ **Bad**
_____ **Pleasant**
_____ **Unpleasant**
_____ **Happy**
_____ **Sad**
_____ **Afraid**
_____ **Joyful**
_____ **Angry**
_____ **Contented**

Scoring[4]

To calculate positive feelings (SPANE-P) you need to add the scores for the six items: positive, good, pleasant, happy, joyful and contented. The score can vary from 6 (lowest possible) to 30 (highest positive feelings score).

   To calculate negative feelings (SPANE-N) you need to add the scores for the six items: negative, bad, unpleasant, sad, afraid, and angry. The score can vary from 6 (lowest possible) to 30 (highest negative feelings score).

   To calculate affect balance (SPANE-B) you must now subtract the negative feelings score from the positive feelings score, and the resultant difference score can vary from –24 (unhappiest possible) to 24 (highest affect balance possible).

▶

▶

Interpretation

If you scored 24 or above, this is a very high score which assumes that you hardly, if at all, experience the negative feelings mentioned and very often or always have all of the positive feelings.

Review

This is a scale developed by some of the authors of the Satisfaction with Life Scale (SWLS) (Diener et al., 1985b). It contains 12 items, which are argued to focus on a broad range of both positive and negative emotions equally (Diener et al., 2009c).

Notes

1 For example, research revealed that discrete emotion experiences 'emerge in ontogeny well before children acquire language or the conceptual structures that adequately frame the qualia we know as discrete emotion feelings' (Izard, 2009: 2).

2 Barrett postulates our emotions, among intrinsically unique personal histories and particularities of environment, do involve neurophysiology but are not pre-programmed to the extent that they exist objectively in nature. Emotions, as Barrett highlights, are made; that is, they are constructed by us as mindful agents rather than built in by our biological makeup.

3 EI refers to emotional intelligence whereas EQ refers to emotional quotient – both used here interchangeably.

4 This is adapted from http://s.psych.uiuc.edu/~ediener/SPANE.html. Please go to the website for further information regarding this tool.

CHAPTER 3

Happiness and Subjective Well-being across Nations

❖ LEARNING OBJECTIVES

Happiness is not a superficial topic; it has a real benefit for those who experience it in balanced ratios. This chapter will focus on the notion of happiness, specifically on the concept of subjective well-being (SWB), how we measure well-being and the most recent findings on the correlates and predictors of happiness within cultures from around the world.

Topics include:

- Definitions of happiness and subjective well-being (SWB).
- How we measure SWB.
- Global happiness polls.
- Highest and lowest SWB-scoring countries.
- Hedonic adaptation and the hedonic adaptation prevention model.
- The burden of choice and its role in influencing our well-being.

MOCK ESSAY QUESTIONS

1 Critically evaluate available research evidence on the correlates and predictors of subjective well-being.

2 Critically evaluate the merits and shortcomings of the concept of subjective well-being as a way of conceptualizing and measuring happiness.

3 Do we always return to our set point of happiness following positive or negative events?

Introduction

Misguided critics of positive psychology often refer to it as a so-called 'happiology'. As the reader will hopefully see, by the end of this textbook and throughout, this is not the case. Positive psychology openly accepts the importance of negative emotions and does not attempt to deny their existence. Just as mainstream psychology became too negatively focused, so must positive psychology be aware of the potential danger of polarization. Having said that, let's focus on the area of happiness and what positive psychology has discovered, over the past few decades, about what makes us happy.

The concept of 'happiness'

Since the dawn of ancient civilization, humans have grappled with pinning down a clear and all-encompassing definition of well-being (Aristotle, Nicomachean Ethics, Book 1, Chapter 4). Although there is no consensus on the definition of 'well-being', there are several synonyms used throughout the literature to describe it such as: happiness, flourishing and subjective well-being. As indicated in Chapter 1, within psychological literature the term 'happiness' is seen as a common-sense, lay representation of well-being. The second meaning of this term refers to a so-called hedonic or pleasure-centred aspect of well-being. 'Flourishing', on the other hand, refers to an aspect of well-being concerned with growth and self-transcendence (going beyond oneself in pursuit of a meaningful action). 'Well-being' itself is an umbrella term for a number of concepts related to human wellness. It encompasses a number of specific psychological definitions, such as *subjective well-being*.

Think about it...

Pause for a few minutes and consider how you would define well-being. What is it for you? Is it about feeling good? Is it about feeling contented? Could it be something to do with achieving what you really want in life? How about happiness? Is it any different from well-being? How do you know when you are happy? Write all your thoughts down before proceeding further. As you read through the next section, compare your own definition with the research one. This will help you to establish a bridge between scientific and common-sense understanding of the same concepts.

Subjective well-being (SWB)

As discussed in Chapter 1, it has been a long road to establishing a scientific science of the concept of happiness. In this section, we will focus on the hedonic concept of happiness as the attainment of subjective well-being (SWB). The notion of SWB is the currently dominant conception of well-being in psychological literature. It is considered a multidimensional construct. A multidimensional construct refers to several distinct but related aspects treated as a single theoretical construct. Subjective well-being encompasses how people evaluate their own lives in terms of both affective (how we feel) and cognitive components (what we think) of well-being (Diener et al., 1999) and can be represented in the following way:

SWB = satisfaction with life + high positive affect + low negative affect

Life satisfaction encompasses the cognitive component of happiness where the individual rates the way their life turned out to be. Diener argues that it refers to discrepancy between the present situation and what is thought to be the ideal or deserved standard. One is satisfied when there is little or no discrepancy between the present and what is thought to be an ideal or deserved situation. On the other hand, dissatisfaction is a result of a substantial discrepancy between present conditions and the ideal standard. Dissatisfaction can also be a result of comparing oneself with others.

Affect refers to the emotional side of well-being, including moods and emotions associated with experiencing momentary events (Diener et al., 1999). There needs to be a balance between the experiencing of positive and negative affect as well as an acknowledgement of the difference in frequency versus intensity of positive affect (Diener et al., 1991). Ultimately, people who report higher levels of SWB tend to demonstrate higher levels of creativity, increased task persistence, multi-tasking, being systematic, optimism, attending to relevant negative information, longevity, less vulnerability to illness, sociability, trust and helpfulness, and less hostility and self-centeredness[1] (Diener, 2000).

The role of pleasure

One of the criticisms of SWB is that it fixates too heavily on the experience of pleasure and positive affect, rather than what is meaningful (more on this in the next chapter. On average, humans seek pleasure and try to avoid pain, due to activations in what is known as the brain's 'pleasure centre' (see the 'time out' section on 'The Brain' in Chapter 2).

RATS

James Olds and Peter Milner conducted an experiment where they placed an electrode into the hypothalamus of rats. When the rat pressed a bar, they would stimulate the electrode. Olds and Milner observed that the rats would press the bar up to 4000 times an hour, forgoing eating, sleeping, engaging in sexual behaviours and taking care of themselves, similar to individuals with extreme addictions. The researchers believed they had found the brain's 'pleasure centre'. Since then, we know that the area they found is one of several areas related to wanting and needing of a certain stimulus, to the point where nothing else matters (e.g. nucleus accumbens).

See Olds and Milner (1954) for the original article.

However, pleasure is not enough to make humans happy and fulfilled. Furthermore, when given the chance, individuals would rather exist in a real world, with the potential to experience both pleasure and pain, than a world that provides only pleasure and positive stimulation (Nozick, 1974).

Think about it...

Imagine a machine that was able to induce only positive experiences, due to cutting-edge research completed by neuroscientists. You would not be able to tell that these experiences were not real. If you were given the choice, would you choose the machine over real life?[2]

Measuring SWB

Subjective well-being encompasses how people evaluate their own lives in terms of affective and cognitive explanations (Diener, 2000) and there are multiple SWB scales (SWLS, Positive and Negative Activation Schedule (PANAS)). The majority of tools are single occasion, self-report tools such as the Satisfaction With Life Scale (SWLS) (Diener et al., 1985b) and Subjective Happiness Scale (Lyubomirsky and Lepper, 1999; Lyubomirsky, 2006).[3] These scales have reported very high levels of validity and reliability (good internal consistency), and are sensitive to change in life circumstances. Furthermore, the tools converge with mood reports, expert ratings, experience sampling measures, reports of family and friends, and smiling.

Considerations of the scales used point to the itemization of the scales (very short) and the time frame. For example, the questions are very basic and non-situation specific. Furthermore, researchers argue that moods can have a heavy influence over how we determine our satisfaction with life at any given moment. However, researchers argue that their research is not affected by the change in current moods and that life satisfaction is indeed stable enough to fight through the influence of a person's current mood.

Other methods of research into satisfaction with life (SWL) and SWB include comparing in-person interviews with anonymous questionnaires in order to contain impression management (Diener, 2000). Experience sampling methods have been employed in order to reduce memory biases. Finally, objective measurements (physiological markers) are used in tandem with self-reports, reducing subjective biases. The future of SWB measurement will rest on the reduction of questionnaires and cross-sectional surveys and include more experience sampling or daily diaries' methods, qualitative descriptions, measures of cognitive and physiological aspects, as well as the use of longitudinal and experimental designs.

Major global and national studies

The increase in funding for major global and national polls has enabled scientists to collect data from 95 per cent of the world population, from urban Manhattan to the remote plains of Kenya. The following polls/surveys have been around the longest and are currently the most influential and all encompassing:

1 *Gallup World Poll.* The *Gallup 2017 Global Emotions Report* (Gallup, 2017) presents the results from Gallup's latest measurements of people's positive and negative daily experiences based on nearly 149,000 interviews with

adults in 142 countries. A key finding reported is that the 'Positive
Experience' Index remained relatively stable (around 70) in 2016 (the
figure was 69 in 2012 and 71 from 2013 to 2015). The report found that
more than 70 per cent of people worldwide said 'yes' they had experienced
'enjoyment, smiled or laughed a lot, felt well-rested, and felt treated with
respect' the day before the interview. While the Positive Experience Index
was 'remarkably consistent at 70', the worldwide Negative Experience
Index was high (at 28) in 2016; so it remained unchanged since 2015 and
'on the higher end of the trend since 2006'. The report highlights that one
in three 'people said they experienced a lot of worry (36 per cent) or
stress (35 per cent)'; three in ten people 'experienced a lot of physical
pain (30 per cent)'; and one in five 'experienced sadness (22 per cent) or
anger (20 per cent)'. Notably, physical pain is identified as 'the only item
that changed from the previous year, rising two percentage points from
28 per cent in 2015'.

2 *World Database of Happiness.* The database contains information and
results from nearly 30 years of scientific research on happiness across the
globe.

3 *World Values Survey.* Since 1981, this survey has collected information on
changing values within 97 countries around the world.

4 *World Happiness Report.* The *World Happiness Report* is a measure of
happiness from over 150 countries published annually by the United
Nations Sustainable Development Solutions Network. The *World
Happiness Report* is edited by John F. Helliwell, Richard Layard and Jeffrey
Sachs (2017).

5 *Eurobarometer.* In Europe, the European Commission issues the
Eurobarometer, which is used to measure citizens' perceptions of quality
of life.

6 *European Social Survey (ESS).* Another European social survey, funded by
the European Commission's framework programme, is the ESS, which aims
to collect data from over 30 countries on their citizen's beliefs, attitudes and
behaviours (including well-being).

7 *LatinoBarometro.* In Latin America, the LatinoBarometro surveys
over 400 million Latin Americas, from 18 countries, on several
topics including trust in government and opinions (as cited in Buettner,
2010).

8 *UK ONS (Office for National Statistics) Personal Well-Being Report.* Since
2011 four personal well-being questions were asked to adults in the UK to
understand how they feel about their lives, capturing SWB, as well as
eudaimonic functioning.

time out

Gallup

George Gallup, the founder of what is now one of the world's leading poll companies, started his organization during the 1930s. From 1960 to 1980, the Gallup organization conducted extensive research into well-being. During the 1990s, the company began to look across the globe at satisfaction, until 2005, when they conducted a groundbreaking, unprecedented global study on well-being, representing over 98 per cent of the world adult population in over 150 countries. Within these major global studies the following seven areas are targeted, including: 'Law and order, food and shelter, work, personal economy, personal health, citizen engagement and well-being' (Rath and Harter, 2010: 139). Well-being is separated into two categories: objective (GDP, health, employment, literacy, poverty) and subjective (evaluative – how they rate their own life – and experienced – what they experience in daily life).

Since then, Gallup has created the Well-being Finder, an instrument based on these initial findings. After several pilot studies, including qualitative and quantitative inquiries, they concluded that five elements were essential for overall well-being (as discussed earlier):

1 Career well-being
2 Social well-being
3 Financial well-being
4 Physical well-being
5 Community well-being

They have also created a daily experience tracker, which can be used to help individuals track their 'experiencing self', thereby highlighting, in real terms, 'good' versus 'bad' days. From their research, they concluded that a good day includes ten circumstances, which are to be ranked on a scale from 1–10:

■ Feeling well rested
■ Being treated with respect
■ Smiling or laughing
■ Learning or interested
■ Enjoyment
■ Physical pain
■ Worry
■ Sadness
■ Stress
■ Anger

The Well-being Finder needs further research to increase reliability and validity, however, is an interesting addition to Gallup's enormous database on happiness.

For more information, see: Rath and Harter (2010: 137–52)

Who is happy?

Now that we are clear on how we are defining happiness within this chapter, we will move onto the data that we currently have on who in the world is happy. The majority of people on earth score in the 'somewhat satisfied' set-point. This means that at any given time point, the majority of people view stimuli and circumstances as positive. Thus, a common assumption that most people view themselves as unhappy appears to be false (Myers, 2000). For example, most people (more than two-thirds) in most samples (across age, race, sex, measures) view themselves as 'above average' in happiness. The exceptions to this appear to be those that are 'hospitalized, alcoholics, newly incarcerated inmates, new therapy clients and students living under political suppression' (Myers, 2000: 57).

Furthermore, the good news is that, as individuals, we have a lot of sway in whether or not we become happy. Researchers postulate that after genetics (50 per cent) (Tellegen et al., 1988) and life circumstances (10 per cent) we have control over approximately 40 per cent of our happiness levels (also called the '40 per cent solution') (Lyubomirsky, 2006, 2008; Sheldon and Lyubomirsky, 2004, 2006a, 2007, 2009).

The happiest places on Earth

So who are the current happiest countries? Denmark, for example, has consistently scored within the highest ranking countries in happiness levels across the globe (8.0).

Rank	Country
1	Norway
2	Denmark
3	Iceland
4	Switzerland
5	Finland
6	Netherlands
7	Canada
8	New Zealand
9	Australia
10	Sweden

TABLE 3.1 Happiest places on earth (*World Happiness Report*, Helliwell et al., 2017)

time out

The Sun

If you take a closer look at the table, you will notice that the majority of the happiest countries are situated in the northern part of the hemisphere, where there is not a lot of sun and limited light. This is interesting, as research has shown that when comparisons are made, people who live in colder climates also tend to have a higher suicide rate than warmer climates.

There are several explanations for this; for example, people in colder climates may be more diligent and open in reporting suicides. Another explanation is what scientists call the 'sun bonus'. A lack of sunshine can result in lower level of vitamin D, which is directly related to serotonin in the brain. When people do not see light or sun for long periods of time, they can experience seasonal affective disorder (SAD) or depression from the lack of sunlight. This may explain the correlation between suicide, as well as the findings that people who experience higher levels of sunshine and daylight hours experience a boost of happiness via their proximity to the equator.

Rank	Country
1	Central African Republic
2	Burundi
3	Tanzania
4	Syria
5	Rwanda
6	Togo
7	Guinea
8	Liberia
9	South Sudan
10	Yemen

TABLE 3.2 Unhappiest places on earth (*World Happiness Report*, Helliwell et al., 2017)

The power of five

Two major studies have revealed similar findings from their research endeavours. The Foresight Report (a collation of already completed pieces of research) and Gallup's World Poll (150+ countries) suggest five necessary elements for well-being. The next section will review these two reports before going into more detail on the specific facilitators of well-being.

Five Ways to Well-being

The Foresight Report was commissioned to the New Economics Foundation (NEF) to review all evidence-based research on ways to well-being. After reviewing over 400 pieces of well-being scientific research from around the world, Aked et al. (2008) suggested five consistent findings throughout the research that would increase well-being. Based on scientific evidence the five ways to well-being include:

1 *Connect.* Research constantly shows that when we build connections with people around us, we experience higher levels of well-being as well as stronger resilience in the face of adversity. The report suggests identifying the influential and important people in our lives and investing time and energy into building those relationships.

2 *Be active.* As discussed in more detail within Chapter 9, an important part of well-being is taking care of the body as well as the mind. The NEF found that activity is an important part of enhancing well-being. Simply moving the body can have a massive effect on mood and cognitive functioning.

3 *Take notice.* Following from the exciting research on savouring, this element refers to research that demonstrates that 'stopping to smell the roses' actually can enhance our well-being (more on savouring in Chapter 8).

4 *Keep learning.* By engaging the brain and challenging themselves to keep learning, a person can enhance levels of well-being.

5 *Give.* As seen in results from random acts of kindness research, people experience high levels of well-being when they give something or their time to others.

Five essential elements for well-being

Based on new research from the Gallup organization, Rath and Harter (2010) reveal 'five essential elements for well-being'. Although they do not cover what may be morally important in life, these elements are, in order of importance:

1 Career well-being: this represent where someone spends most of their time during the day.

2 Social well-being: this represents their relationships and experiences of love.

3 Financial well-being: this represents how well they can manage their finance situations.

4 Physical well-being: this represents their ability to have good health and energy.

5 Community well-being: this represents their role and participation within the community they live in.

The authors note that all five are essential and the pursuit of one over the others will hinder a person's well-being levels. The presence of all five is what distinguishes individuals from those who thrive versus those who suffer. Indeed, the five elements are all things that are within a person's control.

So from two very different types of studies, and two very different types of results, what actually makes us happy? The next section will take the reader through the wonderful work of SWB research, which will show that what we think will bring us happiness actually isn't always the case.

What makes us happy?

The next section will review several proposed correlates and causes of happiness from the recent work polls (Gallup-Healthways Well-being Index and World Values Survey).

time out

The Ladder of life

The Cantril Self-Anchoring Striving Scale (Cantril, 1965) has been included in several Gallup research initiatives, including Gallup's World Poll of more than 150 countries, representing more than 98 per cent of the world's population, and Gallup's in-depth daily poll of America's well-being (Gallup-Healthways Well-being Index; Harter and Gurley, 2008).

The Cantril Self-Anchoring Scale developed by pioneering social researcher, Dr. Hadley Cantril, taps into happiness of the here and now (experiencing self) and the future (reflecting self).

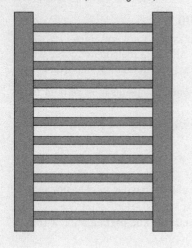

10: Best Possible Life

9

8

7

6

5

4

3

2

1

0: Worst Possible Life

▶

► When taking part, participants are asked the following:

Please imagine a ladder with steps numbered from zero at the bottom to 10 at the top similar to the one below (using a visual makes it easier to use cross culturally, where language is a barrier).

The top of the ladder represents the best possible life for you and the bottom of the ladder represents the worst possible life for you.

On which step of the ladder would you say you personally feel you stand at this time? (ladder-present)

On which step do you think you will stand about five years from now? (ladder-future)

Scoring

Thriving: Individuals who score (7+) on their present life and (8+) on their future life are considered to be thriving. This means that they are experiencing high levels of well-being on a daily basis. Thrivers tend to report significantly fewer health problems, fewer sick days, less worry, stress, sadness and anger, and more happiness, enjoyment, interest and respect.

Struggling: Individuals who score 5 and 6 are considered 'struggling', meaning that they hold moderate views on their current and or future life situations. People who are struggling tend to report more daily stress and worry as well as claim double the amount of sick days in comparison to their thriving peers.

Suffering: Individuals who score 4 and below are considered suffering, which means that they rate their life as very poor and do not see it changing in the future. Gallup have found that in comparison to their thriving peers, individuals who are suffering tend to lack satisfaction of basic needs, and experience more physical pain, increased stress, worry, sadness and anger.

Think about it...

What do you think of the ladder of life? Is it a reliable tool to use when researching happiness? If not, why not? Where would **YOU** point to on the ladder of life?

Income and SWB

> ### Think about it...
>
> Bhutan, a tiny country in Asia, has rejected the concept of gross national product (GNP) as the measurement of its country's success, and introduced gross national happiness (GNH). Do you think this is a better way to measure a country's wealth?

In the Gallup World Poll in 2016 of 142 nations and a representative sample there were striking disparities in health and consequences of income. Ultimately, income is linked to the satisfaction of basic biological needs (e.g. food, shelter) in poor nations, with social welfare programmes protecting against adverse effects of poverty in rich nations. Plus there is greater income inequality (variability) in poor nations. The positive correlation between income and SWB in poor nations seems to be more apparent when assessing one's life in general versus immediate affective experiences (Diener et al., 2009b). Income may also influence well-being since wealthier nations appear to have more human rights, lower crime, more democracy, more equality, more literacy, more longevity and better health. However, these countries with higher income tend to have more competitiveness, more materialism and less time for socializing and leisure.

> ### FORBES
>
> In 1985, Ed Diener and his colleagues had the fortunate opportunity to access 100 individuals on the *Forbes* richest Americans' list. An interesting survey asked several groups of people within several continents their rating of happiness. The results show that Forbes magazine's 'richest Americans' (net worth over $125 million) scored only slightly above (5.8) the random control group. Furthermore, 37 per cent of the rich list scored lower on happiness levels than the average American.
>
> **See Diener et al. (1985a) for the original article.**

The high income in these countries correlates significantly with: lighter prison sentences for the same crimes, better physical and mental health, greater longevity, lower infant mortality, reduced risk of being the victim of violent crime, reduced likelihood of experiencing stressful life events, reduced likelihood of being diagnosed with DSM depression, greater chances of a child completing school and not being pregnant as a teenager and greater interpersonal trust. Furthermore, income tends to correlate modestly but significantly, even controlling for education, with marital status, occupation, employment, age and gender (Blanchflower, 2001; Blanchflower et al., 2001).

Interestingly, income is correlated with happiness in men, not so much in women and low personal income is related to depression for husbands and not so much for wives. Low income is related to depression for single but not married women and people with high income are perceived as more intelligent and successful but also as more unfriendly and cold (see Diener and Biswas-Diener, 2008; Kesebir and Diener, 2008; Biswas-Diener, 2011).

There are several cons to incurring and maintain higher levels of income such as spending more time at work and having less time for leisure and social relationships. Most importantly is the effect of 'The hedonic treadmill', which undermines happiness by forcing wealthy people to adapt to their conditions, raising their expectations and desires thus making it difficult for them to be happy with their current status. Ideally, research suggests that in order to maintain balanced levels of well-being, individuals must take home approximately $5000 (the equivalent of £3000) per month (these figures are subject to annual inflation of course, but the principle proposed here stands); anything more will do little to enhance happiness. Indeed, an extra $10,000 per annum will only bump up happiness levels by approximately 2 per cent (Christakis and Fowler, 2009).

Think about it...

Does money make you happy? Based on evidence from multiple studies, Rath and Harter (2010) suggest five tips for enhancing 'financial well-being':

1 Be happy with what income you do have.
2 Live within these means.
3 Spend wisely and save wisely (by thinking long term and well as short term).
4 Spend on experiences and not just materials (experiences create memories which can then be savoured at a later date).
5 Spend your money on others and not just yourself.

Relationships and SWB

One of the greatest predictors and facilitators of SWB is social relationships. We need other human beings and we like being around them. Whether we are introverted or extraverted, spending time in social settings enhances our levels of well-being (Froh et al., 2007). The World Happiness Report 2017 emphasizes the importance of the social foundations of happiness. This can be seen by comparing the differences between the top and bottom ten countries in the happiness rankings. There is a four-point happiness gap between the two groups of countries, of which three-quarters is explained by the six variables, half due to differences in having someone to count on, generosity, a sense of freedom and freedom from corruption (all social variables).

Friends and acquaintances

People feel happiest when they are with friends, followed by being with family and being alone. The Well-being Indexes show that people tend to need to spend six to seven hours per day in social settings, and up to nine if their job is stressful, to enhance or maintain well-being.

PEOPLE

Daniel Kahneman conducted a study that employed the experience sampling method, which takes snapshots of people's happiness throughout their day. When people were buzzed, they were asked to write down what they were doing, whom they were with and how happy they were. The results showed that people were happiest when they were with others and unhappiest when alone. The order of most happiness-inducing activities to least is as follows:

Socializing after work, relaxing, dinner, lunch, watching TV, socializing at work, talking on the phone at home, cooking, child care, housework, working, commuting from work, commuting to work (as cited in Buettner, 2010: 197).

See Kahneman et al. (2004) for the original article.

Furthermore, it appears that happiness is contagious, meaning that people who interact on a daily basis with happy people, in small, large, direct or indirect networks, are happier (Fowler and Christakis, 2008). Not only do friends and wider social networks influence our SWB, they can influence our likelihood of engagement with detrimental health behaviours (e.g. smoking) (Fowler and Christakis, 2008 as cited in Rath and Harter, 2010).

Children and well-being

Despite what society may have told us about children as an infinite source of joy, research demonstrates an opposite effect. Specifically, individuals who have children have lower scores on well-being measurement tools than those who do not. Furthermore, any additional children after the first born tend to reduce the well-being of parents involved. The relationship between children and marital satisfaction appears to have a curvilinear relationship, with high levels of life satisfaction at marriage ceremony, and dropping significantly at the birth of the first born, followed by a continued drop throughout childhood and adolescence, where it hits bottom, and then returning to higher levels after the children have left. Nelson et al. (2014) question the above conclusions, suggesting that the relationship between parenthood and well-being is more complex. If parents encounter negative emotions, magnified financial problems, more sleep disturbance and troubled marriages, having children makes them indeed less happy. However, if parents experience greater meaning in life, satisfaction of their basic needs, greater positive emotions and enhanced social roles, children actually contribute to their overall happiness.

Work/employment and SWB

The Gallup International Labour Organization (ILO) Report: *Towards a Better Future for Women and Work* (Ray et al., 2017) shows that in 2016 58 per cent of women who were not in employment would like to hold jobs that involved paid work; and 41 per cent would like to be able to both hold a paid job and care for their families. Moreover, while a top challenge for both men and women employees is striking a good balance between work and rest, and work and family time, women are more likely to also encounter challenges related to opportunities for fair pay and/or access to 'decent work'. The ILO's core tenets of decent work are 'productive work for women and men in conditions of freedom, equity, security and human dignity' (Ray et al., 2017: 10).

Work can have a tremendous effect on our overall well-being. Specifically, research has shown that how we perceive our job and our career orientation can further influence our happiness levels. It is not only professions such as being a doctor or nun (or something that a society may deem as a 'meaningful' job at a given historical time) that involve a special kind of calling and so create happiness. Indeed, manual labour workers do report high levels of well-being in their work life. In fact, approximately a third of employees in any sector or area of employment perceives work as a 'calling orientation'. So what is a calling orientation and how does it differ from other types of jobs?

First of all, people who have a *job orientation* view their job in terms of a means to an end. The job equals money and is not important to their overall life. *Career orientation* (although a little more engaged) is concerned with building a career and perceiving the job they are in as a way to progress forward. Furthermore, this person is focused on the extrinsic rewards that can come with progressing in their career. Finally, a *calling orientation* is when a worker is immersed healthily in what they do. They do the job not for the money or the fame, but because they believe it is worthy in its own right (Diener and Biswas-Diener, 2008).

Think about it...

What orientation did you adopt in previous jobs you've had? If you have had more than one, try to think about how it made you feel to start and end the day. If you dreaded getting up and heading to work, or felt relieved by the end of the day, you were most likely working in a job orientation.

Extensive research has been conducted on the relationship between happiness and success at work. The dangers of having a job orientation are that individuals who are simply waiting to punch out at the end of the day have higher levels of disengagement and stress and lower levels of reported happiness (except towards the end of the work day) (Rath and Harter, 2010). Since work is a place where we tend to spend over a third of our day, we must ensure that we create a place where we want to be, like to be and feel engaged while present (Harter, 2009; Biswas-Diener, 2011).

Researchers have found that certain personality characteristics are more predominant in certain occupational settings, and when personal and professional profiles are aligned, this can enhance satisfaction at work. Researchers have specifically looked at the interactions between the 'Big Five' and six occupations: teachers, managers, service workers, crafts persons and manufacturing (blue collar) home workers (Winkelmann and Winkelmann, 2008). They found that a mismatch between personality profile and occupation led to reduced life satisfaction. Teachers scored the highest in life and job satisfaction; however the mix of personality traits in teachers explains some of this. It appears that the most important character trait for satisfaction with work is the character strength of vitality.

Think about it...

Do you like what you do each day? Rath and Harter (2010: 15) state that only 20 per cent of us will respond with a resounding 'Yes'.

Health and SWB

Diener and Biswas-Diener (2008: 33) separate the research on SWB and our physical condition into three health categories: 'a) the likelihood a person will contract a specific illness; b) how long a person lives after contracting a life-threatening illness and c) how long a person's lifespan is'. Within the first category, longitudinal research has shown that people who experience higher levels of positive emotions are protected from various illnesses including heart disease.

COLDS

Positive emotions may be the key to protecting against those pesky winter colds. Sheldon Cohen, PhD, of Carnegie Mellon University, conducted a groundbreaking experiment on the beneficial effects of positive emotions on immune system functioning. For two consecutive weeks, 334 volunteers were assessed on their day-to-day experience of positive and negative emotions (vigour, well-being and calm; depression, anxiety and hostility). Once their data had been collected, the experimenter squirted a rhinovirus (otherwise known as the common cold) up participants' noses. The experimenters then kept the participants under observation, for five days, in a hotel specifically cleared for the experiment. The researchers were interested in whether or not the participant caught the cold, and to what degree they showed any symptoms. The results showed that individuals who experienced higher levels of positive emotions were more resistant and showed less severe symptoms than those that displayed less positive emotions. Thus, we could say a smile a day keeps the doctor away!

See Cohen et al. (2003) for the original article.

The second category, surviving after the diagnosis of a life-threatening illness, is slightly more complicated. When someone has balanced levels of positive emotions and optimism, their health can be positively influenced. However, when people adopt a 'positive viewpoint', which hinders the adoption of medical advice and treatment, high levels of happiness can be detrimental. Researchers argue this is because happier people are more likely to be too optimistic and delay seeking medical advice for potentially cancerous symptoms.

Finally, when defining health in terms of longevity, the research shows that, quite simply, happier people live longer. Danner et al. (2001) accessed some happiness data collected from young nuns at age 22 on average. Decades later, they found that happier nuns lived about 10 years longer than their less happy colleagues. Because the nuns all had similar diets, housing and living conditions, this finding could not be attributed to external causes.

PSYCHOLOGISTS

As a follow up from the famous nuns study, Sarah Pressman analysed the autobiographies of 96 famous psychologists. The results echoed the latter study, with psychologists who used more positive feeling words living on average six years longer than those that used more negative feeling worlds.

See Pressman and Cohen (2007) for the original article.

Religion and SWB

People who report themselves as being spiritual or religious tend to report slightly higher levels of well-being, in addition to higher scores on hope and optimism (Ciarrocchi et al., 2008). But do all religions make us equally happy, and if so, what elements of religion? Is it the belief in organized religion or just a sense of spirituality? The belief in something higher? The concept of the afterlife? The attendance of religious ceremonies and adherence to religious practices? Research in America shows that people who identify with any of the above forms of 'religiosity' score mildly happier than those who do not. This effect is not present however cross-culturally and is dependent on the type of religion followed. Researchers expect that this is due to the unique elements found within different religious beliefs and their links to anxiety, guilt and oppression. Furthermore, religions that isolate and denigrate other religions and members outwith the community can cause unhappiness.

In order for a religion to enhance well-being, researchers Diener and Biswas-Diener (2008) propose that the elements needed are:

- *comforting beliefs* in what awaits us on the 'other side';
- *cocial support* from a community;
- *connecting to something permanent and important* which can give comfort, meaning and a sense of identity;
- *growing up religiously* which may influence a solid upbringing with clear set of values and morals to abide by;
- *experience of rituals* that excite, amaze and involve the congregation and its followers.

Think about it...

If you were an atheist, how could you adopt the principles of religion for a happier life?

Age, gender and education

Again, contrary to popular belief, scientists have found that elderly individuals are as happy as their younger counterparts. With regards to gender, there appears to be no significant differences between the happiness levels of men and women (Nes et al., 2008; Biswas-Diener, 2011). Finally, people who score high on well-being tend to hold higher educational attainment than those lower on the scales.

Think about it...

A re there any other correlates that you expected to be on the list (e.g. climate)?

Theories of SWB

So now that we know the potential correlates and the outcomes of SWB, why does it occur? We are still searching for answers as to what are the causes and/or consequences of well-being. Diener (1984) proposed two approaches to understanding causation within SWB research: *bottom up* approaches which attempt to find which particular variables (genetics, personality plus demographics, age, sex, ethnicity, etc.) cause SWB, and *top down* approaches which attempt to understand SWB as producing certain outcomes.

Genetics, personality traits and SWB

There appears to be a strong genetic influence on an individual's well-being. Furthermore, there is evidence indicating predictive variability in life satisfaction according to personality traits (Magnus et al., 1993). *Dynamic equilibrium theory* states that personality determines baseline levels of emotional responses; events may impact us in the short term. However, over time, we eventually revert to our genetic set-point. Furthermore, people who are happy in their home life tend to be happy at work, thus displaying consistency across situations (work/leisure). These categories of findings appear to support the set-point theory, that is, the notion of a stable personal baseline of happiness to which we return as a default regardless of changes for the better that our lives might have encountered. Yet there are also findings (see e.g. Headey and Muffels, 2017) that challenge the view of long-term SWB as stable due to a tight dependence on personality traits and genetic makeup. Headey et al.'s (2008) research, for instance, provides longitudinal findings about 'the effects of consciously chosen life goals, including religious ones, on SWB' which challenge the set-point theory, adding strength to the notion of authentic happiness as a key player in our experiences of SWB. Debates and discussions about the extent to which happiness can change continue to take place (see Headey, 2008; Sheldon and Lucas, 2014).

Epigenetics is the area of biological research that looks at the causal interactions between genes and their environment (Curley and Keverne, 2009). More specifically, research has started to show that the environment can have an influence on gene expression and behaviour, especially in the mother–infant relationship during key developmental phases, thereby influencing 'brain development, behaviour as well as risk and resilience to health and disease' (2009: 347).

Adaptation theory

Humans have a unique evolutionary tendency to react strongly to recent events; however this diminishes over time (approximately three months). Following multiple studies, researchers have suggested that humans tend to have natural happiness set-points, which, following good and/or bad news/events, we tend to revert to after approximately three months. This evolutionary adaptation process, *hedonic adaptation theory* (otherwise known as hedonic treadmill) (Lykken and Tellegen, 1996) is linked to 'zero-sum theory', which posits that happy periods in our life are inevitably followed by negative periods, which cancel each other out; therefore any attempt to increase happiness will be unsuccessful.

LOTTERY

Do you play the lottery? If so, why? Do you believe it will make you happier? Unfortunately, Brickman's monumental study on happiness among lottery winners suggests otherwise. In a longitudinal experiment, some of the impact of winning the lottery versus surviving an accident with severe impairment was compared. Twenty-two Lottery winners who won amounts ranging from 50,000 to one million US dollars were interviewed on basic demographic variables and asked questions pertaining to how their life had changed since winning. The lottery winners related everyday events as less pleasurable than the control groups and were no happier than reports on how happy they were before winning.

In relation to 11 paraplegics and 18 quadriplegics, the lottery winners scored the same on happiness levels. This does not mean that paraplegics were happy about their conditions. In fact, they tended to have a positive

▶

reflection on their past, with a low satisfaction with everyday present life. Ultimately, this experiment supports the theory of hedonic adaptations: that bad or good, we have a natural set point that we will inevitably return to.[4]

See Brickman et al. (1978) for the original article.

The proposed antidote to this adaptation is *variety*, hence individuals must continually change their approach and happiness interventions in order to counteract any adaptation mechanisms (Tkach and Lyubomirsky, 2006) as reflected in the *hedonic adaption prevention* (HAP) model. Research, for instance, has shown that an individual's number of positive events directly affects the number of experienced positive emotions which helps sustain well-being, all moderated by surprise and variety as well as intrinsic desire for change (Lyubomirsky et al., 2009).

Think about it...

Recall a time in your life when you were up for promotion, expecting an exciting event or bought a new item. How did you feel when this happened? How did you feel a week later? A month later? Reflect on the impact that moment has on you right now.

Similar to our evolutionary tendency to revert to our happiness set-point Daniel Gilbert (2007) focuses on the concept of *affective forecasting* and how this impacts on our ability to be happy. With the unique ability of humans to be able to think and imagine the future come interesting and powerful consequences (Wasko and Pury, 2009). *Impact bias* is an evolutionary quirk that distorts our perception of the hedonic impact of future events. We may think that two outcomes, such as passing a test or failing a test, will have distinct intensity and durational differences on us; however, this rarely turns out to be true (Wasko and Pury, 2009).

TENURE

Linked to affective forecasting, Gilbert et al. (1998) conducted six studies that aimed to assess the discrepancy between how people forecast the impact of negative and positive news, as well as their subsequent emotions after achieving or failing to receive tenure. The results showed that those who

▶

had been denied tenure overpredicted how negative they would feel whereas assistant professors who were given tenure overpredicted how happy they would feel. For both groups, their long-term happiness level forecast was deemed accurate.

See Gilbert et al. (1998) for the original article.

The only life experiences that have been found to have a longer-lasting negative impact on our happiness is the death of a spouse and long-term unemployment.[5] Bereavement is one of the most devastating life events and has a significant impact on individuals' well-being, and researchers propose that it takes approximately five to seven years to return to previous levels of well-being. The damaging effects of unemployment, on the other hand, are harder to recover from. In the same study, Clark et al. (2008) followed over 130,000 individuals over several decades. They found that men who were unemployed for a long period of time (more than one year) did not return to their previous levels of well-being.

Furthermore, according to Gilbert (2007) humans synthesize happiness. Natural happiness is what we feel when we get what we want; however, *synthetic happiness* is what we make when we don't get what we want. Gilbert argues that synthetic happiness is just as real and beneficial as the other type of happiness, and that perceptions of synthetic happiness as an inferior kind of happiness are incorrect. The reason we developed this evolutionary ability to synthesize happiness is argued to be due to the belief that we need to keep going and get what we want, otherwise we'd give up if we knew we would be just as happy as if we didn't.

Discrepancy theories

The 'American paradox' (Myers, 2000) refers to the phenomenon that despite an increase in wealth across the globe over the past 50 years, happiness levels have stayed the same. There are several explanations for this. The first is the *Relative Standards Model*, which is reasonably well supported. Subjective well-being is primarily a function of comparison processes (social comparison, with past self, with internalized standards).

When we interact with others, we cannot help but compare ourselves to them on many levels. Otherwise termed as *social comparison*, we can compare our situation, attractiveness and wealth to others either in an upward or downward spiral. Ultimately, we tend to seek out and interact with people who make us feel good about ourselves and not people who make us feel bad. Thus, our brand new designer handbag is only great until we see a bigger, more expensive and new season one on a friend. On the other hand, it we see a friend with a less expensive handbag, we will feel better about our status and ourselves.

Our personality may influence whether or not we use downward versus upward social comparison and how we use it (e.g. cancer). Cancer patients, for example, have been known to use it in both ways, but on a positive scale. They use upward social comparison to look up to or see cancer patients who have finished chemotherapy and think 'someday that will be me'. Alternatively, they will look around at fellow patients, some who are younger, with children, and think 'well at least I got it now, rather than when I was young, like them'. Thus, social comparison is only detrimental if we use it to negatively evaluate ourselves with others.

Think about it...

Taken from a well-known economic query (Solnick and Hemenway, 1998) to test the rationality of individuals and finance, please answer the following questions:

Would you rather earn £50,000 a year while other people make £25,000, or would you rather earn £100,000 a year while other people get £250,000? Assume for the moment that prices of goods and services will stay the same.

What did you say? Would it surprise you to know that the majority of people who are asked this question would prefer the latter? Why do you think this is?

Previous beliefs were that striving for material goods does not meet basic human needs (see the discussion of self-determination theory – SDT– in Chapter 4) and that materialistic goals may be unattainable. Furthermore, unhappiness and low social support might lead to compensatory materialism. However, an argument against the detrimental effects of materialism is that materialism is only bad if you cannot afford it. Thus, those that report being higher on materialism with higher incomes report higher well-being (Crawford et al., 2002). As long as you live within your means, and can afford what you like without the financial strain, materialism is not as detrimental.

Linked to discrepancy theory is the *paradox of choice* (Schwartz and Ward, 2004). As nations become richer and consumers become more demanding, our world is packed with choice, alternatives and variations to almost everything for sale. Freedom of choice has become replaced with the 'tyranny of freedom', where more choice is not necessarily a good thing (Schwartz et al., 2002).

Think about it...

Can you recall a time when you wanted to buy a specific item, a new computer for example? How many choices were there? Did this make things easier or harder on your final decision?

An abundance of choice has led to three leading problems for consumers and citizens of Western societies. These include:

1 Information problems: We are swamped with information, which leaves us in a precarious position; how can we possibly gather all we need to know in order to make an educated choice?

2 Error problems: If we are not able to access all information about all the possible choices, we are likely to encounter and engage in more errors of judgement.

3 Psychological problems: The stress and anxiety caused by excess choice and the above issues can create lowered levels of psychological well-being.

Of course, introducing choice isn't necessarily the issue here; it is introducing too much choice that seems to affect one's levels of happiness.

JAMS

The supermarket is riddled with choice. We can have any type of food, any way we want it and packaged how we like it. However, the jams experiment showed that sometimes we can get too much of a good thing. Taking place in an ordinary grocery store, researchers set up a stand to allow shoppers to taste test a selection of jams. The demonstration had two conditions. One had six types of jams, whereas the second had 24. The results of observation analysis showed that more shoppers stopped in front of the extensive-selection display of jams (60 per cent) than in front of limited selection (40 per cent). Furthermore, both stands experienced similar sampling statistics (1.5 flavours). However, when it came to actually choosing and purchasing a jam, shoppers who confronted the display of 24 jams were less likely to purchase any than when they encountered the display of six (3 per cent vs. 30 per cent). Researchers suggest that too much choice can cause anxiety and decreased well-being.

See Iyengar and Lepper (2000) for the original article.

When it comes to decision-making, Schwartz has separated individuals into two categories: *satisficers* versus *maximizers*. Satisficers are individuals who are able to choose items that meet their minimum criteria and go for 'what's good enough'. Maximizers, on the other hand, are individuals who fixate on searching for all the possible options and look for the best possible choice. Accordingly, maximizers have a more difficult time making choices, as they need to make sure they have covered all options.

Furthermore, researchers have identified that there are several pitfalls associated with being a maximizer, including:

- *Regret* at not getting the best choice or anticipating regret in the future.
- *Opportunity costs.* Inevitably, when we choose one thing, we automatically reject the other. Each choice has a cost in itself.
- *Escalation of expectations.* As the choices available to us rise, so do people's expectations.
- *Self-blame.* Since we have so much choice available to us, we believe it is our own fault if things go wrong.
- *Time.* The hours people spend sifting through the multitude of choice takes away from the time spent on more worthwhile pursuits.

There is some financial gain in being maximizers (on average they obtain starting salaries $7000 higher than satisficers). However they are also unhappier, experiencing higher levels of regret, perfectionism, depression, upward social comparison and neuroticism.

Think about it...

What type of decision maker are you when it comes to choices? Do you like to research all the options before you make a final decision or do you tend to go for the option that suits what you need?

Goal theories and SWB

Everyone needs goals. Some researchers believe that, without them, we wouldn't be able to survive, 'Commitment to a set of goals provides a sense of personal agency and a sense of structure and meaning to daily life' (Diener et al., 1999: 284). Thus, happiness is the direct result of the process of attaining valued and self-congruent goals, and it is the quality of goals one chooses to pursue that influences well-being. Of course, this is culturally dependent; however, as long as people are engaged in meaningful goals to a quality destination, and receive positive feedback in their attainment of the desired outcome, they are happy.

AIM approach

Diener and Biswas-Diener (2008) propose an 'AIM approach' for creating a 'happy mindset'. According to Diener and Biswas-Diener, there are three basic components to a positive attitude and happy mindset that we need to engage: attention, interpretation and memory.

Attention refers to the ability to look at the entire picture when going through daily life; both the good and the bad. People who attend to only the negative will shut out the positives in life and live in what Diener and Biswas-Diener (2008: 188) term 'an ugly world'.

Interpretation refers to the tendency for humans to put together a story when all the facts are not yet presented. When people interpret events and situations in a negative light, it tends to spill over into their moods. According to Diener and Biswas-Diener (2008) there are six main destructive thinking patters that individuals tend to default to when interpreting events:

1 *Awfulizing.* Exaggerating a negative event or person beyond what is objectively true.

2 *Distress intolerance.* The perception an individual adopts which tells them that they will not be able to recover or withstand potentially traumatic events.

3 *Learned helplessness.* Stemming from Seligman's work, this is when people adopt a mentality that they have no control over their negative situations and give up.

4 *Perfectionism.* Individuals who use this tend to fixate on the minutiae details and only accept excellence.

5 *Negative self-fulfilling expectancies.* The phenomenon of eliciting negative responses from others via a person's previous communications with others.

6 *Rejection goggles.* This is when people identify and fixate on rejection, even when it may not exist in the situation. (Adapted from Diener and Biswas-Diener, 2008: 193–4).

Finally, *memory* is based on the ample research backing memory, recalling past positive events and experiences and savouring, leading to enhanced well-being.

COLONS

Nobel Prize winner Daniel Kahneman (see Redelmier et. al., 2003) proposed the 'peak end rule' or peak end experience, where individuals judge their experiences on how they were at their peak (either pleasant or unpleasant)

▶

as well as how they ended. One slightly uncomfortable experiment demonstrating the peak end rule involves several hundred participants and an intrusive colonoscopy. After finding contradictory reports on patients' actual experience and reported experience of colonoscopies, 652 patients were randomly assigned to either a control or experiment group. The control group simply went through the colonoscopy as planned. The intervention group however, had the colonoscopy left in for an extra 60 seconds. Although leaving the apparatus in place for an additional minute was mildly discomforting, it was less so than the actual procedure. Thus, ending on a mildly discomforting, rather than painful, note significantly affected the recollection of the entire procedure. This also supports the theory of duration neglect, as it isn't the length of the occurrence that is important for recollection, but how the event ends.

See Redelmeier et al. (2003) for the original article.

Overall, when we attend to positive things around us, use clear rather than negatively biased interpretation for events and interactions, as well as engage in positive reminiscence, we can set ourselves up for creating a more positive attitude and happier existence.

Chapter Summary

Reflecting on the learning objectives the reader will now understand SWB across cultures and more specifically:

- There are several definitions of happiness, with the most prolific in research being the concept of subjective well-being (SWB).
- One of the reasons suggested as to why some humans are never satisfied is hedonic adaptation.
- The hedonic adaptation prevention model is currently being used to counteract this evolutionary tendency to revert to our happiness set points.
- Subjective well-being is traditionally measured via self-report measurement tools, such as the SWLS, since happiness is a subjective phenomenon.
- Currently, there are several global happiness polls that enable us to look at countries' populations and their current happiness levels.
- Sometimes choice is not a good thing, especially if we tend to lean on the maximizing side.

Suggested Resources

www.gallup.com/home.aspx
> To find out more about the Gallup World Polls or to access books written by the organization, go to this website.

www.youtube.com/watch?v=HH0sssQzQGg
> Watch positive psychology with Martin Seligman. Talk recorded at an Action for Happiness event in London on 9 May 2016.
>
> *Stability of Happiness: Theories and Evidence on Whether Happiness Can Change.*
> Book edited by Kennon M. Sheldon and Richard E. Lucas.

Further questions for the reader

1 Do you agree with the research findings on children and well-being? Honestly argue for or against these findings.

2 What would your life be like if you never had to worry about money?

3 What do you think is missing from the area of subjective well-being? Discuss.

Personal Development Interventions

The exercises presented below focus on identifying and enhancing your subjective well-being.

1 AIM approach

We would like you to try our Diener and Diener's (2008) AIM approach at creating a positive attitude. Make sure you attempt each one!

Attention: Tomorrow, make a concerted effort to attend to the positive experiences, events, people and environments around you. Write down what you witnessed and reflect.

Interpretation: Challenge your interpretations. Refer to the list of six types of destructive thinking patterns and the next time you make a sweeping negative statement, reframe the sentence to use more constructive wording.

▶

Memory: As you attend to the positives tomorrow, bank these memories so that you can reflect on them, savour them and replay them for future enjoyment.

2 Intensely positive experiences

Similar to the 'M' (memory) in the AIM approach, we invite you to take reminiscence one step further. We would like you to engage in writing about an *intensely positive experience* (Burton and King, 2004). This is an experience characterized by intense positive emotions such as awe, wonder and ecstasy in context such as a momentous achievement (e.g. graduation), sharing an occasion with significant others (e.g. birth of a child), being close to nature, and so on.

We would like you to think of an IPE and write about it for 15 minutes, for three consecutive days. Keep track of how you feel during, after and at the end of the week.

Measurement Tools

Satisfaction With Life Scale (SWLS)

(Diener et al., 1985b)

Directions

Below are five statements with which you may agree or disagree. Using the 1–7 scale below, indicate your agreement with each item by placing the appropriate number in the line preceding that item. Please be open and honest in your responding.

1 = Strongly Disagree
2 = Disagree
3 = Slightly Disagree
4 = Neither Agree or Disagree
5 = Slightly Agree
6 = Agree
7 = Strongly Agree

_____ 1. In most ways my life is close to my ideal.
_____ 2. The conditions of my life are excellent.

_____ 3. I am satisfied with life.

_____ 4. So far I have gotten the important things I want in life.

_____ 5. If I could live my life over, I would change almost nothing.

Scoring

Simply add your scores to attain one final score.

Interpretation

31 – 35 Extremely satisfied
26 – 30 Satisfied
21 – 25 Slightly satisfied
20   Neutral
15 – 19 Slightly dissatisfied
10 – 14 Dissatisfied
 5 – 9 Extremely dissatisfied

Review

The SWLS is five questions on a 7-point Likert scale. It has high internal consistency (0.87) and good test-retest reliability (0.82) (over two months). Furthermore, the research shows us that it has strong correlations with other mental well-being measures (around 0.7) and between self-reported scores and experimenters.

Critiques of this test come from the confusion surrounding whether or not life satisfaction is a result of personality dispositions or current moods and current life circumstances. Pavot and Diener (2008) argue it is the summation of both sets of factors, and should be used in conjunction with more focused tools when assessing change. Furthermore, current mood has been shown to have little to no effect on our overall judgement of life satisfaction (bar long-term unemployment and widowhood) (Pavot and Diener, 2008).

Subjective Happiness Scale (SHS)

(Lyubomirsky and Lepper, 1999)

Directions

For each of the following statement and/or questions, please circle the point on the scale that you feel is most appropriate in describing you.

▶ 1. In general I consider myself

1	2	3	4	5	6	7

Not a very happy person

A very happy person

2. Compared to most of my peers, I consider myself

1	2	3	4	5	6	7

Less happy

More happy

3. Some people are generally very happy. They enjoy life regardless of what is going on, getting the most out of everything. To what extent does this characterization describe you?

1	2	3	4	5	6	7

Not at all

A great deal

4. Some people are generally not very happy. Although they are not depressed, they never seem as happy as they might be. To what extent does this characterization describe you?

1	2	3	4	5	6	7

Not at all

A great deal

Scoring

You are required to add each item's score. Item 4 is reverse coded, thus if you scored 1 then give yourself 7. Your scores will range from 1 to 7.

Interpretation

The world adult population scores, on average, between 4.5 and 5.5.

Review

This scale is even shorter than the SWLS, including only four items on a 7-point Likert Scale. This scale does not explicitly discriminate between cognitive and affective dimensions, like the SWLS; however, it does have good internal consistency 0.79–0.96 (M = 0.86) as well as concurrent validity (0.7) with SWLS and convergent validity with self-esteem, optimism and extraversion scales.

The Maximizing Scale

(Schwartz et al., 2002)

Directions

Below are fifteen statements with which you may agree or disagree. These statements concern your past, present, or future. Using the 1–7 scale below, please indicate your agreement with each item by placing the appropriate number on the line following that item. Please be open and honest in your responding. The 7-point scale:

1	2	3	4	5	6	7
Strongly disagree	Disagree	Slightly disagree	Neither agree	Slightly agree	Agree	Strongly agree

_____ **1.** Whenever I'm faced with a choice, I try to imagine what all the other possibilities are, even ones that aren't present at the moment.

_____ **2.** No matter how satisfied I am with my job, it's only right for me to be on the lookout for better opportunities.

_____ **3.** When I am in the car listening to the radio, I often check other stations to see if something better is playing, even if I am relatively satisfied with what I'm listening to.

_____ **4.** When I watch TV, I channel surf, often scanning through the available options even while attempting to watch one programme.

_____ **5.** I treat relationships like clothing: I expect to try a lot on before finding the perfect fit.

_____ **6.** I often find it difficult to shop for a gift for a friend.

_____ **7.** Renting videos is really difficult. I'm always struggling to pick the best one.

_____ **8.** When shopping, I have a hard time finding clothing that I really love.

_____ **9.** I'm a big fan of lists that attempt to rank things (the best movies, the best singers, the best athletes, the best novels, etc.).

_____ **10.** I find that writing is very difficult, even if it's just writing a letter to a friend, because it's so hard to word things just right. I often do several drafts of even simple things.

_____ **11.** No matter what I do, I have the highest standards for myself.

_____ **12.** I never settle for second best.

_____ **13.** I often fantasize about living in ways that are quite different from my actual life.

▶

▶ **Scoring**

Please add the items and average to find your total score.

Interpretation

The authors consider people whose average score is higher than a 4 as *maximizers*. If you scored higher than 5.5, you are classified as an 'extreme maximizer' (along with approximately 10 per cent of the population), however if you score lower than 2.5, you are classified as an 'extreme satisficer' (again with approximately 10 per cent of the population). The rest fall between scores higher than 4.75 (approximately 33 per cent) and lower than 3.25 (approximately 33 per cent).

Review

Although the undertaking of this scale can be quite eye-opening, researchers have begun to question whether or not this measurement tool is effective in measuring the construct of maximization, arguing that what Schwartz is measuring is not actually maximization in its truest from. Furthermore, there are issues surrounding the multidimensionality of the scale, whereas the concept should be placed on a uni-dimensional scale (Diab et al., 2008).

Notes

1 Thus criticisms of positive psychology and the pursuit of understanding happiness do not seem to stand in the research data as people who have higher SWB tend to be more altruistic and help others more; thus, positive psychology is not a self-centred, individualistic discipline.

2 Most people answer no, that they would prefer reality and glimpses of true happiness to a lifetime of simulated reality.

3 These tools are located for your convenience at the end of this chapter.

4 This study has recently been contested following the findings of another longitudinal research study on medium-sized lottery winners (£1000–£120,000). Gardner and Oswald (2006) found that these winners had enhanced psychological health and well-being when compared to controls (no wins) or a smaller lottery win (less than £1000). All in all, the Brickman et al.'s (1978) study is repeatedly mentioned throughout positive psychology, and it is a good one for the reader to know about.

5 Divorce and chronic disability are close behind bereavement and unemployment in terms of their long-term negative effect on overall well-being (Lucas, 2007; Lucas et al., 2003).

CHAPTER 4

Eudaimonic Well-being

❖ *LEARNING OBJECTIVES*

Is happiness enough for a good life? Is merely feeling good an adequate measure of someone's quality of life? Do we really know what it means to be *subjectively well* when we assess someone's subjective well-being? This chapter will review some answers to these questions and introduce the notion of eudaimonic well-being, as well as some corresponding theories.

Topics include:

- The definition and historical roots of eudaimonia.
- The concept of psychological well-being (PWB).
- Self-determination theory (SDT).
- The three basic psychological needs.
- The concept of flow and its nine characteristics.
- The importance of meaning and purpose in life.
- The links between existential psychology and positive psychology.
- Positive death and meaning.

MOCK ESSAY QUESTIONS

1 Compare and contrast the concepts of subjective and psychological well-being.

2 Based on our current knowledge of the subject, to what extent it is possible to arrive at a common definition of eudaimonic well-being?

3 'I would rather wake up unhappy than without meaning in my life.' Discuss.

The other side of happiness

As discussed in the previous chapter, there are two camps of thought about what makes people happy and/or experience well-being. The previous chapter discussed the concept of subjective well-being (SWB), which is a person's satisfaction with their life and the experience of positive affect and low negative affect. Ryan and Deci (2000) argue that SWB is simply a definition of hedonism and that the types of activities and goals theorized to promote well-being may be misleading. Vittersø (2004) criticized SWB as ignoring the complexity of philosophical conceptions of happiness with a complete failure to explain the dimension of personal growth, while Ryff (1989) argued that there was a failure to answer the question of what it actually means to be well psychologically. Ultimately, and what appears to be very important for a balanced sense of well-being, the concepts of meaning and purpose are ignored (King and Napa, 1998; McGregor and Little, 1998). As you have seen in the previous chapter, the preferred mode of measuring well-being is also firmly grounded in this (hedonic) paradigm.

An alternative approach is the *eudaimonic* paradigm, where well-being is construed as an ongoing, dynamic process (rather than a fixed state) of flourishing, personal growth, self-actualization or self-transcendence by means of engagement in an activity which utilizes one's resources and is subjectively meaningful. Researchers within the eudaimonic framework argue that happiness and 'the good life' are not simply the experiences of feeling good. There has to be more to life than just pleasure and satisfaction. Eudaimonic well-being proposes that true happiness is found in the expression of virtue and doing what is worth doing. Thus, the realization of human potential is an ultimate goal (Aristotle). Individuals must therefore seek and pursue happiness through prudence (John Locke) and self-discipline (Epicurus). Eudaimonism is defined as fulfilling or realizing one's daimon or true nature. This occurs when people's life activities are: mo/st congruent with their deep values (Waterman, 1993); handled by a fully functioning person (Ryff and Singer, 2008); self-determined (Ryan and Deci, 2000); authentic (Seligman, 2002a); challenging and complex (Vittersø, 2004; Vittersø et al., 2009a); reflecting broad goals and purpose (Steger et al., 2013);

congruent with one's true self (Huta and Ryan, 2010); and flow like (Csikszentmihalyi, 2002; Delle Fave et al., 2011a; Fullagar and Delle Fave, 2017).

Views differ, however, as to how the experiences of eudaimonic and hedonic well-being relate to each other. On the one hand, it may be that eudaimonic well-being always includes hedonic well-being to some extent. On the other hand, it is not impossible that they are largely independent dimensions (Boniwell and Henry, 2007. Finally, Kashdan et al. (2008) point out the difficulty of identifying distinct phenomenological experiences associated with eudaimonic well-being and thus consider hedonic and eudaimonic well-being to be identical.

The question also arises as to whether eudaimonic well-being is a process or an outcome, or whether both exist. The prevailing discourse is to construct it as a state (e.g. Waterman et al., 2008), but some researchers have suggested that it may be more appropriate to view it as a process (e.g. Vittersø et al., 2009b; Huta and Waterman, 2014).

Finally, researchers have started to look into whether or not there is a relationship between eudaimonic well-being and personality differences, or if eudaimonic well-being in itself can be seen as a personality trait. More specifically, research intends to discover whether or not there is such a thing as a hedonic or eudaimonic orientation (Vittersø et al., 2009b) that gives a greater propensity to experience eudaimonic well-being.

As Boniwell (2008) pointed out at the early stages of positive psychology development, the area of eudaimonic well-being appears, at best, in a state of untidiness. However, with the active development of research in this area, substantial advances are being made in discussing conceptual and operational definitions (Huta and Waterman, 2014). Table 4.1 summarizes different theories that fall under the eudaimonic umbrella, highlighting their main eudaimonic themes, as most of these theories propose a multi-factorial (rather than a singular) definition. The next section will review selected theories from this list.

Psychological well-being

The concept of PWB (Ryff and Singer, 2006) consists of six components: self-acceptance (positive evaluation of oneself and one's life), personal growth, purpose in life, positive relations with others, environmental mastery (the capacity to effectively manage one's life and environment) and autonomy. There is some empirical support for the six-factor model with moderate associations between two subscales of PWB (self-acceptance and environmental mastery) and SWB (the other dimensions correlated weakly or inconsistently with these indicators). Ryff argues that this pattern demonstrates that traditional measures ignore the key aspects of well-being (Ryff, 1989). A number of researchers, however, are critical of these dimensions. Vittersø (2004) notes several findings suggesting that Ryff's six dimensions can be accounted for by two factors corresponding to hedonic and eudaimonic well-being.

Definitions	Waterman	Ryff	Ryan and Deci	Seligman	Vitterso	Steger	Huta	Delle Fave
Growth	x	x	x	x	x	x	x	x
Meaning	x	x	x	x	x	x	x	x
Authenticity autonomy	x	x	x	x		x	x	
Best one could be	x	x	x	x	x	x	x	
Relatedness		x	x			x		
Competence		x	x		x			
Engagement flow			x	x	x			x
Awareness			x			x		
Acceptance		x						
Effort	x				x			x
Physical health			x					

TABLE 4.1 Mapping of eudaimonic theories onto eudaimonic definitions (adapted in a simplified form by Huta and Waterman, 2014)

Keyes et al. (2002) hypothesized that SWB and PWB, although conceptually related, are empirically distinct conceptions of well-being. Factor analysis of data from over 3000 respondents confirmed that SWB and PWB are two correlated but distinct factors and that they show a different pattern of relationships to demographic and personality variables. In her later work, Ryff builds on her work to conceptually define eudaimonia in terms of trait psychological well-being, that is, to be fully functioning, and to succeed in the face of life's existential challenges (Ryff and Singer, 2008).

Self-determination theory (SDT)

Self-determination theory theory argues that similar to Maslow's hierarchy of needs, there is an evolutionary adaptive function of basic psychological needs. *Autonomy* is the tendency to self-regulate one's behaviour in accordance with personal volition (rather than external control). It is also the tendency to resist coercion, pressure and control; to regulate one's behaviour in accordance with one's own needs (and situational affordances) which promotes better survival than organizing behaviour to meet external demands. Thus, autonomy is the volition and the desire to freely choose actions consistent with one's integrated sense of self, feeling that one is voluntarily engaging in a behaviour, regardless of whether the behaviour is dependent on others or not.

Competence is the tendency to be interested and open, to seek learning/mastery opportunities (it promotes acquisition of new skills). The need for competence manifests in early motor play, manipulation of objects and exploration of surroundings. It is the tendency to experience satisfaction from learning for its own sake – and the tendency to explore and seek challenges. This need is shared to some degree with other mammals. Thus, competence is the ability to affect the environment and attain desired outcomes.

Relatedness is the tendency to feel connection and caring with group members (it promotes group cohesion and mutual protection). It is similar to Baumeister and Leary's 'need to belong' and has overlap with Bowlby's attachment need. This need can at times conflict with need for autonomy, but normally it is complementary.

Besides the above-mentioned needs (autonomy, competence and relatedness) are there any other basic needs that must be met for psychological well-being? In their 2017 volume on self-determination theory, Ryan and Deci (2017) put forward three more candidate needs of meaning, self-esteem and security, yet argue that there is not yet sufficient evidence for their inclusion. Let's consider these in turn.

Meaning, or making sense of one's life, is the basic psychological need that has been put forward by Dan Pink in his TED talk (one of the most watched in the history of TED), and is seen as the central concept in the SDT, yet not a need.

Why not? This is actually because meaning is viewed as an outcome of the basic needs satisfaction, rather than a basic need in its own right.

Safety/security appears as a basic need already in Maslow's hierarchy of needs (which is strangely not as well supported empirically as one would think), yet not recognized as one of the basic psychological needs because of its deficit nature; that is, this need only appears when a person is threatened or made to feel insecure in any other way. The same applies to *self-esteem*: it's a safety need of the self, a need to feel worth while. It surfaces only when the sense of self is thwarted.

Authentic happiness

Seligman (2002b) argued that there are *three routes to happiness*: 1) the pleasant life, which enables high levels of positive emotion and gratification; 2) the good life, which enables constant absorption, engagement and 'flow'; and 3) the meaningful life when one uses one's strengths in the service of something greater than one's self. The latter concept falls under the umbrella of eudaimonia. Eudaimonia is defined as identifying one's unique virtues and strengths of character, developing them, and then using them in the service of the greater good, particularly the welfare of humankind. The important thing to note from this area of research is that people who engage in hedonic, pleasant activities experience higher levels of positive affect in the short term; however, eudaimonic pursuits may give meaning and value in the long term.

Flow

Think about it...

Have you ever started an assignment or essay only to find that five hours have gone by without you even noticing it? Have you ever played a football game, or a rugby match, or completed a dance routine where you were so absorbed in what you were doing you didn't notice anything or anyone else around you? And you played your best? This feeling of 'being in the zone' is what researchers describe as *flow*. Think about your experiences of flow as we go through the next section of the textbook.

Flow theory was created by Mihaly Csikszentmihalyi after his fascination in the 1960s with artists and their unwavering concentration. He noticed that all rewards of painting came from painting itself – a theory now known as intrinsic motivation. During this time, researchers such as Maslow, Deci and Ryan began to look at why and how people were led to intrinsic behaviours (later, these same researchers would create what is now known as self-determination theory (SDT), discussed above and in Chapter 7). However, Csikszentmihalyi wanted to go further and return to the subjective experience: how did flow actually feel? He entered into the realm of phenomenology, which focuses on the lived experience of psychological phenomenon.

The main point here is that Csikszentmihalyi's early work was to focus on and understand what it was like (the lived experience) when things were going well and when people were performing at their best. After several experiments across a range of participants (artists, dancer, rock climbers), Csikszentmihalyi noticed that there were 'a common set of structural characteristics was found to distinguish those patterns of action that produced flow from the rest of every day life' (Csikszentmihalyi and Csikszentmihalyi, 1988: 8).

Flow[1] is defined as 'the intense experiential involvement in moment-to-moment activity, which can be either physical or mental. Attention is fully invested in the task at hand and the person functions at her or his fullest capacity' (Csikszentmihalyi, 2009: 394). Flow has direct ties with consciousness and psychic energy where it is posited that when people feel *psychic entropy* (chaos and anxious thoughts) they will experience depression and stress. However, the attainment of *psychic negentopy* or *flow* (exclusion of any negative thought) is ideal for enhancing the experience positive affect (Csikszentmihalyi, 2009).

There are several conditions required to facilitate the flow experience. These include:

- *Structured activity with clear goals and immediate feedback.* This means that activity must have rules and a clear outline in order to help orientate the person. As the person continues through the activity, they must be able to get a sense of feedback that they are on the right track towards the desired goal. Without feedback, confusion and consciousness will creep in.

- *Balance of challenges versus skills.* As the model of optimal experience shows (Figure 4.1), in order to reach and maintain positioning within the flow channel, a person must have a delicate balance between their skills level and the challenges at hand. If the challenge is too high above their current skill level, then this will produce anxiety. If it is too low, this will produce boredom. Furthermore, if a person has no skill and there is no challenge (such as TV watching) then they will exist in a channel of apathy.

- *Complete concentration (merging of action and awareness).* The activity must initiate a complete merger of the activity and all consciousness. All attention is within the activity and there is no room for consciousness. Also, the person loses a sense of 'themselves' and becomes one with the activity they are completing. There is no time or room to be self-conscious. Furthermore, attention is placed in the task at hand and onto all task-relevant stimuli. Everything else but the activity is irrelevant at that point in time.

- *Sense of control.* This stems from the activity's ability to allow the person to lose self-consciousness, thereby gaining a sense of control over what they are doing. This also ties in with the perception of skill versus challenge; thus if someone perceives the skill and challenge to match, they will feel a better sense of control.

- *Transformation of time.* This element is the unique experience of where time speeds up, and before we know it, we've been engaging in the activity for hours when it felt like minutes. Or, as in dance, time can slow down, where a minute feels like hours, seconds like minutes. There is a definite distortion of time from the reality of the clock.

- *Activity for the sake of activity (and a wish to repeat!).* This component refers to the activity's ability to make us want to do it all over again. No rewards, no external forces. Simply, we like doing it and want to repeat it again.

- *Your personality.* Finally, there is another potential facilitator of the flow experience and that is personality. Perhaps the reader knows someone that enjoys life and appears to be intrinsically led in their daily endeavours. They have skills that enable them to have an innate general curiosity in life, persistence, low self-centredness and ability to be motivated by intrinsic rewards (Nakamura and Csikszentmihalyi, 2005). These people would be described as having an *autotelic personality* and are more susceptible to experiencing flow.

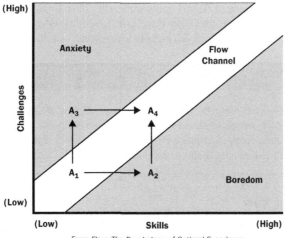

From *Flow: The Psychology of Optimal Experience*
by Mihaly Csikszentmihalyi (1990: 74)

FIGURE 4.1 Flow

Demographics of flow

This next section will review who, when, where and with whom we are most likely to experience flow.

Who's in flow?

It is approximated that around 10–15 per cent of US and European populations have never experienced flow but 10–15 per cent of the same population report experiencing flow every day. Research has shown that we tend to experience flow in different measures and intensities throughout the lifespan.

Using the experience sampling method (ESM), Csikszentmihalyi and his colleagues can assess real-time occurrences of flow, across people from varied social demographics and countries. The ESM (Csikszentmihalyi and Csikszentmihalyi, 1988) was created specifically for counteracting the detriments of conventional retrospective measurement within psychology. Now widely used in other areas of psychology, the ESM is a beeper that people are asked to carry for any length of time (usually a week). The beeper will randomly go off throughout the day and people are asked to answer a number of questions related to flow and the context they are in (work, leisure, alone, with friends, etc.).

Csikszentmihalyi and Larson (1984) found that teenagers tend to feel their most happy, strong and motivated when with friends, and the opposite when alone.

The activities in which we are most likely to experience flow are: sports and activity, dance participation, creative arts, sex, socializing, studying, listening to music, reading and, paradoxically, working. However, many other activities can produce the experience of flow (Csikszentmihalyi, 2002; Delle Fave and Massimini, 2004; Fullagar and Delle Fave, 2017). Activities that tend to inhibit flow (and induce apathy and boredom) include housework, watching TV and being idle.

> ### Think about it...
>
> Could the relationship between flow and the activities listed above be due to cultural influences? Research conducted in Iran, Romania, Nepal and several other countries contradict traditional Western findings with regards to housework, watching TV and raising children (Delle Fave and Massimini, 2004).

Benefits of flow

Ultimately, there are several consequences in attaining flow. Within the sport domain, athletes and coaches report peak performance and enhanced skill acquisition. Those who experience flow in play and leisure report increased positive emotions (after the fact). Education systems arranged in order to induce flow can bring about higher grades, levels of commitment and achievement in education within their students. Finally, occupational settings can experience greater engagement and leadership development.

Although there has been a lot of research done on flow, there are still a few avenues that are yet to be expanded. For example, what about micro flow (those little spates of time that we appear to be in flow, albeit for seconds, not minutes)? What are the elements needed for this? How can we create it? Is it flow? Also, and importantly within the sport and occupational domains, is the concept of 'group flow', where people report being in flow in tandem with their fellow teammates. The dynamics between people and this phenomenon are yet to be fully understood.

Dangers of flow

In class, we get asked quite a lot 'is flow a morally good phenomenon?' This is an interesting question which challenges the assumption that flow equals peak performance. The answer is that flow can be found in activities that are both morally good and bad (e.g. gambling). Research has also demonstrated a potential to become addicted to flow-inducing activities (e.g. rock climbing, video game playing), where the activity becomes necessary for daily functioning (Csikszentmihalyi, 1992). Overall, engaging in flow-inducing activities that challenge and stretch us as a person can, within reason, have a tremendous positive affect on overall well-being.

Applying flow theory

Flow doesn't just happen by chance (Csikszentmihalyi, 2002). Two approaches for applying flow have been suggested: 1) change environments to facilitate flow; and 2) help others find flow (Csikszentmihalyi, 2009). Through the first facet, managers/workers can shape activity structures and environments to foster flow or obstruct it less (see e.g. Rathunde and Csikszentmihalyi, 2005). Secondly, therapists can help assist individuals in finding flow, which in turn can lead to higher levels of performance and increased positive affect (Fullagar and Delle Fave, 2017). Therapists can also help clients identify activities that get them into flow, working together to increase the difficulty or complexity of these activities (ensuring that these are matched by growing skills). It is important for clinicians to encourage re-allocation time away from apathetic activities (e.g. TV) to flow-inducing activities.

Later work on flow

Delle Fave, a disciple of Csikszentmihalyi, who continues to be the leading flow researcher, identifies two core components of eudaimonia (Delle Fave et al., 2011a;

Fullagar and Delle Fave, 2017). The first, understandably, pertains to flow (optimal experience) as originally conceptualized by Csikszentmihalyi (1975). The second component of eudaimonia involves the establishment of long-term meaning-making as discussed below.

Think about it...

Write a critical reflection on the similarities and differences of the following sectors of eudaimonic well-being:

- PWB
- authentic happiness
- STD
- flow and autotelic personality

Which happiness do you subscribe to?

Meaning and purpose in life

Throughout several areas of research and practice, the issue surrounding the meaning of life and meaning within life is essential to fulfilled individuals (Steger, 2009; Wong, 2009). Meaningless in life has been proposed to be akin to the existential fear of death. Researchers argue that when one is faced with meaninglessness, one can encounter several negative experiences. Thus, researchers would argue that the search for meaning and purpose is more relevant than the search for happiness (Wong, 2009). Researchers also argue that not only should we be measuring meaning in life, but the structural properties of personal meaning systems, such as 'differentiation (how diverse the sources of meaning are), elaboration (how people construct their own links and connections between events to give life purpose) and coherence (how well do all the features fit together) measures' (Pöhlmann et al., 2006: 111). These measures enhance mental and physical health/well-being as well as predict life satisfaction (Pöhlmann et al., 2006).

A superb figurehead for both the positive psychology and existential areas, Frankl's work on meaning still persists today. His concept of 'will to meaning' proposed three benefits of living a meaningful life: creative, experiential and attitudinal value. Since Frankl's contribution, researchers have identified seven major sources of meaning, found cross-culturally: achievement; acceptance; relationship; intimacy; religion; self-transcendence and fairness.

King and Napa (1998) argued that it was a combination of both happiness (SWB = SWL, PA, NA) and meaning (such as connectedness, purpose and growth akin to eudaimonia) that created overall well-being. Furthermore, those that rate high on meaning have been found to be given the highest liking ratings in their samples.

McGregor and Little (1998) analysed a diverse set of mental health indicators and concluded that the concept of well-being should be conceived as consisting of two elements: happiness (satisfaction with life, positive affect, negative affect) and meaning (connectedness, purpose and growth). Compton et al. (1996) supported this combination, they however changed the second component to personal growth. Their work identifies two main factors out of 18 indicators of well-being, one representing happiness/SWB, and another – personal growth. Measures of happiness/SWB related to a factor different from that of personal growth construct (including maturity, self-actualization, hardiness and openness to experience). The factors themselves were moderately correlated.

Developing a purpose in life and identifying reasons to live help mediate between stress, coping and suicidal behaviour (Mei-Chuan et al., 2007). Individuals who report enhanced levels of depression, hopelessness and suicidal thoughts are much more likely to use emotion-oriented coping strategies. Avoidance coping strategies, when used in a healthy way, can be a positive approach to well-being, as they can channel negative thoughts into other areas of life, thereby potentially creating reason for living (Mei-Chuan et al., 2007).

Meaning as the central definition of eudaimonia has been proposed by several theories outlined in Table 4.1, but, as we can see from the section above, the topic has a long research tradition from before and outside of positive psychology.

Existential thought and positive psychology

Another philosophical and research tradition that raises similar questions as the ones discussed in this chapter, yet not originally identified as eudaimonic, is existential psychology. As we will see, the two can be perfectly integrated.

Traditionally existential thought seen in the context of general psychology has been deemed to be fixated on the darker side of human life (such that 'happiness is derived from accepting suffering as the essence of the human condition' Wong, 2009: 364) and overlooked within positive psychology research. Since the two focus on the same fundamental questions – such as, what is a good life and what makes life worth living? (Wong, 2009: p. 361) – not to examine their insights in collaboration would be a remarkable missed opportunity.

Something that can be termed existential positive psychology takes into account the unavoidable contribution of the core tenets of the human condition (confrontations with death, freedom and choice, isolation, meaninglessness, authentic sense of self) to understanding the human capacity to transcend and to experience 'mature happiness' and the wisdom that underpins it. Three types of mature happiness have been distinguished:

- authentic happiness (arising from being and living authentically; that is, attempts to congruently and deliberately embrace one's freedom to choose and the responsibility for acting on/living out this freedom);
- eudaimonic happiness (arising from doing virtuous deeds); and
- chaironic happiness (a spiritual gift of happiness that is bestowed and independent of our abilities and circumstances especially within suffering).

Happiness is best seen as a process – not an-end-result – as ongoing and the result of forgoing self-interest and serving something higher than the self. This formulation of happiness also acknowledges the complementary importance of both negative and positive elements of human functioning as essential for personal growth. The duality hypothesis posits that 'positives cannot exist apart from negatives and that authentic happiness grows from pain and suffering' (Wong, 2009: 364). As an illustration, Wong connects the issue of identity crises and authenticity by proposing that generational issues via consumerism and capitalism are crippling today's society in their search for 'the self'. Poignantly, Wong argues that authenticity does not always lead to happiness, but can give rise to contentment which, in existential terms, is typically associated with the commitment and 'risk' (or existential courage) to being who one feels best represents the self. It is also worth highlighting that this contentment accommodates the knowledge that authentic living often requires dismantling comforting attachments with the norms or with material provisions and the goals (and standard of achievements) that these delineate as worth striving for. An individual's confrontation with subsequent confusion or discontentment is the ultimate enabler of personal growth. Pursuing happiness may not be the aim of life; however pursuing meaning and authenticity will along the way yield happiness – at least in the sense of 'happiness' as feeling 'at home' in oneself (Tunariu et al., 2017a).

Death and positive psychology

Humans have developed the capacity to think, be conscious and anticipate the future. This insight and powerful mechanism is also an anxiety-inducing mechanism that allows us to recognize that at some point we will die. However, even death, the most feared concept within human existence, is a potential avenue for growth and development. 'Positive death', or 'good dying', should be seen as an integral part of a good life (Wong, 2009). Meaning management theory posits that death can have either a negative or positive effect on us, depending on how we view it. By embracing death, we can live more authentically, thereby enhancing the likelihood of self-actualization. Transforming death anxiety into a productive energy force is a positive viewpoint on a traditionally 'negative' component of the life process.

Researchers propose that there are three distinct attitudes towards death:

1 neutral death acceptance, when one accepts that death is a part of life and attempts to live life to the fullest;

2 approach acceptance, when one accepts that there is an afterlife which will be pleasurable; and

3 escape acceptance, which perceives death as the preferable option to a miserable life.

Terror management theory

Another theory linked to realization of death is terror management theory (TMT). This theory suggests there is an innate, biological need to survive and deals with the management of the evolutionary cognitive realization of inevitable death (Pyszczynski et al., 2002). The mortality salience hypothesis suggests that when a person is reminded of the inevitability of death, their worldview defence strengthens and the individual seeks to conform to the accepted beliefs and behaviours of their culture (Harmon-Jones et al., 1997). Thus, a traumatic and life-threatening event, paired with the lifelong reminder of a person's close encounter with death (physical scars, deformity) creates a mortality salient environment. The person will have a conscious reminder of the inevitability of their own death and, according to Pyszczynski et al. (2002), utilize proximal defences and distraction to defend themselves from death-related reminders.

Integrating hedonic and eudaimonic well-being

So how do we reconcile the debate within the field over what constitutes a good life: hedonic or eudaimonic well-being? We know that those who follow their eudaimonic pursuits score highly on SWL (Huta et al., 2003). Eudaimonic measures tend to correlate much better with growth, development, challenges and efforts (Waterman, 1993). Examples of widely used eudaimonic well-being scales include the Personally Expressive Activities Questionnaire (PEAQ; Waterman, 1993), the Questionnaire for Eudaimonic Well-being (QEWB, Waterman et al., 2010), the Scales for Psychological Well-being (Ryff, 1989), the Basic Psychological Needs Scales (Gagné, 2003), the Orientations to Happiness subscales (Peterson et al., 2005), the Flow Simplex (Vitterso et al., 2001), the Personal Growth Composite (Vitterso et al., 2009), Meaning in Life Questionnaire (Steger et al., 2006), and the Hedonic and Eudaimonic Motives for Activities

(HEMA) (Huta and Ryan, 2010). We envisage that with such a variety of measures, more and more answers will be emerging with further research.

The criticisms of the hedonic paradigm stem from the lack of clarity on what types of positive affect are important for well-being. Is it Frederickson's 12 emotions? Should SWL be viewed as a component of hedonism? Satisfaction with life is an independent evaluative element and perhaps there needs to be a re-evaluation of the concept of dedonic well-being. For example, what do we really mean by happiness and well-being (Galati et al., 2006)?

Furthermore, within the eudaimonic paradigm, there is a lack of conceptual unity. For example, what is being understood under personal growth: is eudaimonic well-being more about the development/growth or transcendence/meaning? Or all of them? Ultimately, the way forward includes the undertaking of exploratory research to define and develop appropriate definitions of eudaimonic well-being. Qualitative approaches can offer intricacy and depth and capture complexity of phenomena. They can be extremely useful in mapping out the field, developing conceptual clarity and formulating an overarching framework. However, most existing studies have employed a top-down approach to data analysis. Furthermore, many studies focused on what lay people believe makes them happy rather than exploring the meanings attributed to happiness. 'Qualitative common-sense knowing is not replaced by quantitative knowing. Rather, quantitative knowing has to trust and build upon the qualitative' (Campbell, 1979: 66). Important progress in this direction has been achieved by Delle Fave et al. (2011b), who combined qualitative and quantitative methodologies to see how people from different cultures understand the concepts of meaning and happiness.

Chapter Summary

Reflecting on the learning objectives the reader would now understand the concept of eudaimonic well-being and more specifically that:

- Eudaimonia is defined as the area of happiness concerned with following the good life and achieving actualization.
- Psychological well-being consists of six components considered to be neglected by traditional hedonic paradigm.
- Meaning and purpose in life is essential for well-being.
- Purpose in life can reduce suicidal behaviours.
- Flow occurs when someone engages with an activity that is intrinsic and matches their skill level.
- Self-determination theory includes three psychological needs imperative for well-being: include autonomy, competence and relatedness.

Suggested Resources

www.ted.com/talks/angela_lee_duckworth_grit_the_power_of_passion_and_perseverance

TED Talks Education, April 2013. Angela Duckworth studies self-control and grit to determine how they might predict both academic and professional success.

www.meaning.ca

This website links to Paul Wong and his meaning website. The reader will find all they need to know about existential and positive psychology as well as references to leading existential articles/books from across the decades.

http://qlrc.cgu.edu/about.htm

This is the link to the Quality of Life research centre, based at Claremont University, under the supervision of Csikszentmihalyi. Use for links regarding flow, optimal experience and general positive psychology.

http://ppc.sas.upenn.edu/resources/questionnaires-researchers

This is the link to the Positive Psychology Center. Professor Martin E.P. Seligman is the Director of the Center. Questionnaires that can be downloaded and/or links provided to sources include: Adult Hope Scale; Curiosity and Exploration Inventory; Gratitude Questionnaire; Inspiration Scale; Meaning in Life Questionnaire; Mindful Attention Awareness Scale; PERMA-Profiler; Psychological Well-Being Scales; Satisfaction With Life Scale; Silver Lining Questionnaire; Subjective Happiness Scale; and links to the VIA Survey of Character Strengths.

Further questions for the reader

1 Should positive affect and the current version of SWL be used as the outcome measures for studies of eudaimonic well-being?

2 How should eudaimonic well-being be defined?

3 Is flow always a good thing? What dangers can you think of?

4 Is flow the only optimal experience you can think of? List any additional experiences. You do not need to know the exact name for them.

Personal Development Interventions

1 Flow

Flow is a wonderful thing. Think about and write down three activities that you consistently experience flow in. This could be going to the gym, painting, socializing or reading, in fact any activity that meets Csikszenmihalyi's nine criteria for flow. Over the next week, try to incorporate at least one of these activities into your routine. Document how you felt immediately after the event. Continue to list and incorporate flow-inducing activities into your weekly agenda.

2 Meaning

You don't need a therapist or counsellor to help you find meaning in your life. Try and align your behaviours with your values and regulate the following throughout your daily life:

P urpose and life goals
U nderstanding the demands of each situation and life as a whole
R esponsible actions and reactions consistent with your purpose and understanding
E valuation of your life in order to ensure authenticity and efficacy
                              (PURE Model, adapted from Wong, 2009: 366)

Measurement Tools

Meaning in Life Questionnaire (MLQ)

(Steger et al., 2006)

Directions

Please take a moment to think about what makes your life and existence feel important and significant to you. Please respond to the following statements as truthfully and accurately as you can, and also please remember that these are

▶

▶ very subjective questions and that there are no right or wrong answers Please answer according to the following scale:

Absolutely Untrue	Mostly Untrue	Somewhat Untrue	Can't Say True or False	Somewhat True	Mostly True	Absolutely True
1	2	3	4	5	6	7

_____ **1.** I understand my life's meanings.

_____ **2.** I am looking for something that makes my life feel meaningful.

_____ **3.** I am always looking to find my life's purpose.

_____ **4.** My life has a clear sense of purpose.

_____ **5.** I have a good sense of what makes my life meaningful.

_____ **6.** I have discovered a satisfying life purpose.

_____ **7.** I am always searching for something that makes my life feel significant.

_____ **8.** I am seeking a purpose or mission for my life.

_____ **9.** My life has no clear purpose.

_____**10.** I am searching for meaning in my life.

Scoring

Presence = 1, 4, 5, 6 and 9 (reverse-coded)
Search = 2, 3, 7, 8 and 10

Interpretation

Scores above 24 for both presence and search indicate life value and meaning.

If you scored above 24 on presence and below 24 on search, this implies that while you may feel that your life has value and meaning, you are not actively exploring that meaning at the present time.

Review

Research on the MLQ has shown good reliability and test-retest stability. Presence is positively related to well-being, intrinsic religiosity, extraversion and agreeableness, and negatively related to anxiety and depression. The presence subscale positively correlates to multiple measures of well-being while negatively correlating with depression and anxiety. The search subscale is positively correlated to scales such as neuroticism and depression and negatively correlated to well-being.

Flourishing Scale

(Diener et al., 2009c)

Directions

Below are eight statements with which you may agree or disagree. Using the 1–7 scale below, indicate your agreement with each item by indicating that response for each statement.

7   Strongly agree
6   Agree
5   Slightly agree
4   Mixed or neither agree nor disagree
3   Slightly disagree
2   Disagree
1   Strongly disagree

____ I lead a purposeful and meaningful life.
____ My social relationships are supportive and rewarding.
____ I am engaged and interested in my daily activities.
____ I actively contribute to the happiness and well-being of others.
____ I am competent and capable in the activities that are important to me.
____ I am a good person and live a good life.
____ I am optimistic about my future.
____ People respect me.

Scoring

Add the responses, varying from 1 to 7, for all eight items.

Interpretation

The possible range of scores is from 8 (lowest possible) to 56 (highest PWB possible). A high score represents a person with many psychological resources and strengths.

Review

This scale attempts to address the many variables proposed to co-exist with human flourishing (e.g. positive relationships, competence and meaning). Originally, the authors called the scale 'Psychological well-being' but have since renamed it the Flourishing Scale to better reflect the items.

Flow Experience Questionnaire

(Csikszentmihalyi and Csikszentmihalyi, 1988: 195)

Directions

Please read the following and answer the questions below:

> My mind isn't wandering. I am not thinking of something else. I am totally involved in what I am doing. My body feels good. I don't seem to hear anything. The world seems to be cut off from me. I am less aware of myself and my problems.

_____

> My consternation is like breathing. I never think of it. I am really oblivious to my surroundings after I really get going. I think that the phone could ring and the doorbell could ring or the house could burn down or something like that. When I start I really do shut out the whole world. Once I stop I can let it back in again.

_____

> I am so involved in what I am doing. I don't see myself as separate from what I am doing.

_____

Have you had experiences like those described in the three quotations?
How often have you had such experiences?
What were you doing when you had these experiences?
What started the experiences?
What kept them going?
What stopped them?

   For these experiences, indicate the degree to which you agree or disagree with the following statements:

1	2	3	4	5	6	7	8
Strongly disagree						**Strongly agree**	

_____ **1.** I get involved.
_____ **2.** I get anxious.
_____ **3.** I clearly know what I am supposed to do.
_____ **4.** I get direct clues as to how well I am doing.
_____ **5.** I feel I can handle the demands of the situation.

▶

▶ | _____ **6.** I feel self-conscious.

_____ **7.** I get bored.

_____ **8.** I have to make an effort to keep my mind on what is happening.

_____ **9.** I would do it even if I didn't have to.

_____**10.** I get distracted.

_____**11.** Time passes more slowly or more quickly.

_____**12.** I enjoy the experience and the use of my skills.

Scoring

The first section is analysed via qualitative analysis, whereas the second section is simply a summative score (reverse scoring for 2, 6, 7, 8, 10).

Interpretation

Within the second section, the higher the score, the higher the frequency of flow.

Review

The Flow Experience Questionnaire (Csikszentmihalyi and Csikszentmihalyi, 1988) consists of three vignettes with six questions and a Likert scale. However, present-day flow research primarily uses experience sampling methods to ensure accurate and immediate recollection of flow within everyday life.

Note

1 Originally termed _autotelic experience._

CHAPTER 5

Optimism, Explanatory Style and Hope

❖ **LEARNING OBJECTIVES**

People sometimes attribute miraculous powers to positive future-oriented thinking. To what degree is it beneficial to have a positive, optimistic or hopeful outlook? Why and in which ways do optimism and hope confer their beneficial effects? This chapter discusses recent literature pertaining to optimism, hope and related 'positive future-thinking' constructs.

Topics include:

- Definitions of hope, optimism and explanatory style.
- A brief history of optimism.
- Differences and similarities between these constructs.
- Positive thinking and its effects on well-being.
- Defensive pessimism and positive illusions.
- Hope theory.

MOCK ESSAY QUESTIONS

1 Discuss the strengths and limitations of Snyder's cognitive formulation of hope.
2 Is seeing a glass as half full always beneficial?
3 Compare and contrast the theories of dispositional optimism and explanatory style.

The history of optimism

Optimism has been described as a 'Velcro construct' (Peterson, 2006: 119) as it has many correlates including happiness, heath and achievement (Carver and Scheier, 1998). But what exactly is optimism and is it always good to 'look on the bright side of life?'

In the early days of philosophy and psychology, optimism was thought of as naïvety or a superficial denial of suffering. Health practitioners regarded positive mental health as the absence of naïve optimistic illusions (optimism). Based in part of this logic, mental health experts, from the 1930s to the 1960s, often defined mental health as intact 'reality testing', such that the person holds only modest expectations about the future and has a more accurate or balanced view of the world (as reviewed in Peterson, 2000). However, since then, researchers have found mounting evidence to suggest that optimism isn't just a form of denial, but a necessary component to resilient and happy individuals.

Of course, in psychology, nothing is ever straightforward, thus within positive psychology there are two main schools of thought surrounding the definition and conceptualization of optimism: *dispositional optimism* and *explanatory style*.

Dispositional optimism (Scheier and Carver, 1987) is defined as a personality trait[1] relating to generalized outcome expectancies. Thus *optimists* are characterized by their broad expectancy that outcomes are likely to be positive whereas *pessimists* are characterized by the future anticipation of negative outcomes.

Leading researchers Carver and Scheier (2009) posit that optimism is tied into their self-regulatory model, which states that all human activity is based on goals. In order to reach our goals, we need to self-regulate our actions and behaviours. As such, when hardship experiences occur while trying to reach these goals, people who are optimists will continue and push through in order to reach their goal, whereas pessimistic people will be more likely to give up (see also Carver et al., 2009).

The two main elements of dispositional optimism are the concepts of expectancy and confidence. *Expectancy* is the most crucial element as it has a direct link with expectancy value theories of motivation, which posit that all behaviour is a result of a person's desire to obtain their values or goals. Thus, in order to achieve a goal, it must have value and spark motivation to continue (Scheier and Carver, 2009). *Confidence*, the second competent, is highly influential on optimism. If confidence is high that the goal can be achieved, then the person is more likely to act. If there is doubt, then the person will disengage. Scheier and Carver define optimism and pessimism as 'simply broader versions of confidence or doubt, operating to most situations in life rather than one or two' (2009: 657).

Psychologists measure dispositional optimism via the LOT-R, a short ten-item questionnaire that focuses on differentiating optimists from pessimists (Scheier et al., 1994). We have included this measurement tool at the end of this chapter for the reader to try and find out what type they are!

Think about it...

Do you know anyone who is an 'eternal optimist' or a 'thundering pessimist'? Have they always been this way? Are you this way? Do you think you can learn to become more optimistic?

On the other hand, *attribution style* (*explanatory style*) (Seligman, 1998) refers to the way in which one explains the causes and influences of previous positive and negative events in order to create expectancies about the future. Research has shown that attributions for negative events are more important than those for positive events. Pessimists explain negative events by inferring internal, stable and global causes: the event was caused by myself (internal), by something that is chronic (stable), and by something that is pervasive and will affect other situations as well (global). Optimists, however, explain negative events by inferring external, unstable and local causes: the event was caused by something/someone other than myself (external), by something that will likely not persist (unstable), and by something that is likely limited to only this specific circumstance (local). Optimists adopt unstable, external (leaving one's self-esteem intact) and specific (depending on circumstances) explanations for bad events. Currently, literature has shown that the 'internal/external' component to explanatory style is not as important as stability and globality.

PRESIDENTS

Researchers in the USA were interested in whether or not the optimistic content of a presidential candidate's speech could influence the voting

▶

▶

results. Peterson and his colleagues looked at speeches from 1900 to 1984 and found that individuals who used more optimistic wording (and less focus on the negative) won 85 per cent of the US presidential elections.

See Zullow et al. (1988) for the original article.

Psychologists measure attribution styles via the *Attributional Style Questionnaire* (ASQ), which presents vignettes (scenarios) to people, and they have to choose which of several explanations for the event most seems likely (some explanations being more internal, global and stable, etc.).

Think about it...

The *Pollyanna principle, the* name of which was taken from the protagonist in the classic novel Pollyanna (Porter, 1913), supposes that the subconscious human brain is wired to have a positivity bias towards situations and other people. How do we know this? Numerous studies have shown that the Pollyanna principle is more pervasive than we would believe. For example, people overestimate their interaction with positive stimuli more than they do with negative. Can you think of a time when this occurred to you?

The main difference between the two schools of thought is that attributional style – based on Seligman's early work with Learned helplessness' as model of depression (Abramson et al., 1978) – recognizes optimism as a learned skill and not a stable personality trait. Similar to cognitive behaviour therapy (CBT) techniques, Seligman recommends monitoring our automatic thoughts and attitudes and disputing pessimistic explanations. The key to learned optimism is *reframing.* In order to achieve this, we must learn how to identify our beliefs about certain situations and recognize how these beliefs can have a detrimental effect on our emotions and subsequent behaviours.[2]

SELL, SELL, SELL

Optimistic attributional style has been associated with sales success. Researchers assessed an independent insurance company's sales persons on their optimistic explanatory style. Those sales persons who were in the top 10

▶

▶

per cent of scorers for optimistic explanatory styles sold 88 per cent more insurance than the bottom 10 per cent scorers.

See Seligman and Schulman (1986) for the original article.

However, dispositional researchers have argued whether or not attribution style really is optimism. Attributional style is concerned with the question of *why* good and bad events happened whereas dispositional optimism focuses on what will likely happen in the future. Despite this difference, Peterson (2006) reports that the measurement tools for both schools of thought have similar correlates and have some levels of convergence.

time out

Learning optimism ... Learning your ABCs
The first step in learning your **ABCs** is to negotiate the acronym:

A dversity
B elief
C onsequence

Adversity: The straight, non-judgemental facts of the situation. For example: who, what, when, where.

Belief: Your immediate patterned belief (why it happened; what will happen next).

Consequence: Your feelings and behaviours related to these beliefs.

Ultimately, when we identify our beliefs and recognize their effects on emotions and behaviours (beliefs have consequences) we can challenge and change them to more productive thought patterns.

(Seligman, 1998)

Benefits of optimism

Over the past few decades, research has provided convincing evidence on the benefits of an optimistic outlook, especially within the areas of depression and stress, health and psychological trauma. We will go through the areas in more detail regarding the evidence to date.

Optimism, depression and stress

Optimists tend to experience less distress during adversity then pessimists, according to cross-sectional and prospective data reports (Carver and Scheier, 2009). Optimism does not simply mean that you lay down and wish for things to happen in a positive manner. Contrary to this, optimism prospectively predicts active coping with stress (e.g. planning, social support seeking), whereas pessimism predicts avoidant coping (e.g. distraction, denial). These differences in coping tend to then predict changes in psychological/physical adjustment. So, developing an optimistic trait may help lead to the engagement of active, constructive coping, such as acceptance, positive reframing and use of humour, whereas pessimism has been linked with disengagement and denial among breast cancer patients. Extreme forms of pessimism (hopelessness about the future) have also predicted an extreme form of disengagement coping, found to be moderated by the pathways dimension of hope (Lopes and Cunha, 2008).

With regards to depression, several studies have found that optimism prospectively predicts psychological and physical well-being (e.g. perceived stress, depression, loneliness, social support) among college students, even when controlling for alternative predictors, such as self-esteem, locus of control and desire for control. Optimism can also prospectively predict incidences and levels of postpartum depression, even when controlling for initial depression severity. Optimism is suggested to protect mothers against developing depression following the birth.

Optimism and health

Diseases which attack the immune system such as cancer and HIV/AIDS can show researchers objective markers with regards to self-reported optimism. For example, people who score higher on optimistic traits during early stage breast cancer diagnosis report higher levels of well-being. Furthermore, researchers have even discovered association between pessimism scores predicting early mortality among young patients with recurrent cancer. This correlation remained even after controlling for cancer site and symptom severity (Schulz and Mohamed, 2004).

There is also evidence to suggest that optimism is associated with living longer. Patients who engage in 'realistic acceptance' of the inevitability of death had a shorter survival time in a sample of 78 men with AIDS (Reed et al., 1994; reviewed in Taylor et al., 2000). In that study, those who scored high on 'realistic acceptance' died an average of nine months earlier, even controlling for many other potential predictors of death such as AIDS-related symptoms, number of CD4 T helper cells, medication, distress and overall health status. These researchers concluded that unrealistic optimism (or positive illusions) rather than realistic acceptance was actually a more effective predictor of survival. These findings fit with Taylor's general position that positive illusions can be beneficial when confronted with severe illness because such positive illusions help the person to find meaning even amid extreme adversity (Taylor, 2009).

HEARTS

Before going into their operation patients were asked to fill out a questionnaire regarding how optimistic they were about their upcoming coronary bypass surgery. Results showed that prior to surgery, optimists experienced less hostility and depression and greater relief, happiness, satisfaction with medical care, and perceived emotional support post-surgery. Most interestingly, optimism significantly predicted rate of recovery, including behavioural milestones (sitting up in bed, walking) and staff member ratings. These effects remained six months post-surgery, and even five years later, optimists were more likely to be working and less likely to be re-hospitalized. On objective measures of physical health, optimistic patients were less likely to develop problematic enzymes and heart problems than pessimists. Also, pessimists were more likely to suffer a heart attack during surgery even when controlling for relevant disease parameters.

See Scheier et al. (1989) for the original article.

One way in which optimism appears to mediate these effects is the facilitation of positive affect, since optimism is associated with positive affect. It may be the interaction between these factors such as good mood and immune functioning that mediates the effect. Furthermore, optimistic patients with HIV practised better health habits than their more pessimistic counterparts (better health behaviours in general: more medication compliance, less smoking/ drinking, better diet, more exercising, fewer anonymous sexual partners, etc.). Optimists tend to be unrealistically optimistic about their ability to control their own health, but this can lead them to persist with health-promoting behaviour such as eating lower fat food, taking vitamins or enrolling on a cardiac rehabilitation programme. For instance, the benefits of optimism have been found to be mediated by health-related cognition such as lowering experience of pain sensations through active dissociation from the stressor or through decreasing pain catastrophizing (Hanssen et al., 2013). Optimism has been shown to be potentially enhanced through positive future techniques (Meevissen et al., 2011) and although longitudinal research is needed to appraise the sustainability of such techniques, a mindset characteristic of optimism can, as Seligman suggested, be learnt.

Overall, researchers in optimism would argue that optimists are not simply people who stick their heads in the sand and ignore threats to their well-being.

For example, they attend to health warnings and usually discover potentially serious problems earlier rather than later. Pessimists, on the other hand, are far more likely to anticipate disaster – and as a result, are more likely to give up.

Think about it...

Researchers suggest that we can have 'big optimism', which focuses on generic, grander positive expectations, whereas 'little optimism' focuses on more immediate and specific positive experiences. Can you give an example of each? (Peterson, 2006).

Optimism as positive illusions

Positive illusions (Taylor, 1989) are predicated on the belief that most people are biased towards viewing themselves in an optimistic way, thus they see their past behaviour, personal attributes and themselves in an enhanced light; they have an unrealistic sense of personal control and they have an unfounded sense of optimism that the future will be better than the facts suggest. Like positive illusions, self-deceptive strategies (Taylor and Brown, 1994) are used to manage 'negative information' (limited control over an unpredictable world, our future is bleak; losses and death). These arguments have some backing following research that shows that we are not good at accurately identifying reality.

Optimism and locus of control

What is it about control that makes us happy? This section will review the concepts of locus of control and perceived control. Perceived control relates to a person's self-assessment of their ability to exert control, which interestingly we humans frequently overestimate. Thompson proposes that there are three main strategies of maintaining control:

- changing to the goals that are reachable in the current situation;
- creating new avenues for control; or
- accepting current circumstances. (Thompson, 2002)

PLANTS

Langer and Rodin, both Yale professors, argued that nursing homes are decision-free environments for those who live there. They conducted a study that gave patients some control over small decisions in their lives.
The researchers split the members of the nursing home into two groups: the

▶

▶

responsibility-induced group (RI) and the control group. At a floor meeting, the RI residents were told they had choices on the arrangement of furniture, visiting hours and entertainment and they were given a small plant to care for. The other group (control group) had a floor meeting where they were told that the nurses would take care of their every need, what entertainment to expect, what visiting hours were set, how room layouts were arranged and that nurses would care for their plants. They tested the floors on several pre-post measures and the RI group reported better moods, enhanced alertness and were more active. However, the disturbing results came 15 months after the intervention was finished. Pre-intervention, the nursing home reported a 25 per cent mortality rate in any 15-month period. This time, they found that the participants who were in the RI group had a 50 per cent lower mortality rate than the control group (15 per cent vs 30 per cent). The difference in mortality between groups as well as to previous baseline measures was believed to be the result of giving control and choice to the participants.

See Langer and Rodin (1976) for the original article.

Locus of control (LOC) was developed as a concept in 1966 by Rotter and since then has been examined by many studies against hundreds of diverse dependent variables. People with a strong internal LOCl believe that the responsibility for whether or not they succeed ultimately lies with themselves. Internals believe that success or failure is due to their own efforts. Externals, on the other hand, believe that the reinforcers in life are controlled by luck, chance or powerful others. Therefore, they see little impact of their own efforts on the amount of reinforcement they receive. Researchers have been studying whether or not LOC was a stable personality dimension; however, it is now agreed that LOC is not a fixed personality trait and can vary according to situation. Rotter (1966) challenged the oversimplified conceptualization of LOC that implied that internality is associated only with positive consequences, while externality is only associated only with negative consequences. Rotter argued for the unidimensionality of the locus of control scale, while acknowledging the presence of some sub-factors. A substantial body of research, however, supports the multidimensional characteristics of the majority of locus of control scales, varying from two to three factors with several sub-factors.

Think about it...

How is it possible that both internal LOC and optimistic explanatory style for bad events contribute to functioning well (tip: consider the internality dimension)? How would you work on increasing internal LOC and self-efficacy, bearing in mind the difference between these two concepts?

Defensive pessimism

So, with all the positive evidence behind it, is optimism always a good thing? Well, as in all psychology, this data is based on averages and some evidence suggests that optimism can be detrimental in certain circumstances and for certain individuals. So what good is it being a defensive pessimist and are there any benefits? Well, thankfully, yes there are.

Defensive pessimism is based on the ability to think of, and plan, for the worst-case scenario of a situation; hence defensive pessimists like to be prepared and cover all angles. It is a cognitive strategy to set low expectations for upcoming performance, despite having performed well in previous similar situations (Norem and Cantor, 1986). This thinking style has been found to cushion the potential blow of failure, motivate reflection and rehearsal and can be used as a strategy to 'harness' anxiety for motivation. Defensive pessimists set their sights unrealistically low and think about how to solve potential problems in advance of a daunting task (Held, 2004). Trying to change defensive pessimists into optimists is counterproductive (and vice versa) but positive psychologists try to explain away the benefits of defensive pessimism. In fact, defensive pessimists tend to be more anxious and deliver poorer performance if they are 'not allowed' to engage in pessimistic rehearsal. This is opposite to optimists who are more anxious if they are 'made to think about' possible failure. Defensive pessimists have also been found to show significant increases in self-esteem and satisfaction over time, perform better academically, form more supportive friendship networks, and make more progress on their personal goals than equally anxious students who do not use defensive pessimism (Norem and Chang, 2002).

Unrealistic optimism

Unrealistic optimism, wishful thinking or relentless optimism can have negative consequences on individuals. They tend to perceive risk as lower than average. There tends to be an optimistic bias in risk perception, with optimists viewing themselves below average for such occurrences such as cancer, heart disease, failure and heartbreak (Peterson and Vaidya, 2001). Furthermore, in the case of serious traumatic events (e.g. death, fire, flood or violent rape) optimists may not be well prepared (although optimists might be better equipped to rebuild than pessimists).

Engaging in blind optimism may be unhealthy for long-term physical and psychological well-being. Introducing *positive realism* or *flexible optimism* into our thinking will allow us to avoid 'wishful thinking', while realistically assessing the likelihood of positive and negative outcomes in any given situation. This cautionary observation is also supported by neuroscience. Schacter and Addis (2007) discuss studies involving functional magnetic resonance imaging scans from participants asked to relive (positive, neural, negative) past experiences or to pre-experience their future and which concluded that the human brain is biased towards promoting an optimistic, rosy picture of the future. Collectively the 'optimistic brain' findings provide 'clues concerning the neural underpinnings of optimistic bias by showing that areas involved in emotional processing selectively reduce their activity when people think about negative future events and coordinate activity when people think about positive future events' (Schacter and Addis, 2007: 1346).

The two (limbic areas) regions of the brain identified are the rostral anterior cingulate cortex (rACC – a strip of cortex surrounding the corpus callosum) and the amygdala. Both areas showed a reduction in activity when participants contemplated negative future outcomes more than when they imagined positive future events or recalled positive or negative past experiences (see also Sharot et al., 2007, page 1 who suggest 'effective integration and regulation of emotional and autobiographical information' as a key mechanism for mediating this optimism bias). It is beneficial to hold a positive outlook in life yet this needs to be balanced such that we remain motivated enough (and our brain wiring primed enough) to act preventively and not be caught off guard (Schacter and Addis, 2007).

Think about it...

Is it better to think things are going to turn out well, and avoid worrying? Or should we expect the worst, and not be disappointed? Which is more valuable in our lives: do we want to know the truth, even when that makes us unhappy? Or is it sometimes better to look on the bright side, despite the evidence?

The three 'selves' in optimism: self-confidence, self-esteem and self-efficacy

The three selves (self-confidence, self-esteem, self-efficacy) are used interchangeably within everyday linguistic life. So what exactly are these concepts and how do they relate to optimism and well-being?

Think about it...

When you think of yourself and your qualities, do you tend to think in a more abstract or detailed perspective? Researcher have found that how we perceive our self has a significant impact on our overall well-being (Lucas et al., 1996). More importantly, research shows that happier people report thinking about themselves with a higher level of abstraction than less happy individuals (Updegraff and Suh, 2007).

The most notorious of the three is *self-confidence*. Self-confidence has had some nastier, narcissistic connotations, with inducing an inflated sense of self among one of them. Carol Craig, founder of the centre for confidence and well-being in Glasgow, Scotland, researches Scotland's 'crisis of confidence' and attempts to enhance levels of confidence within schoolchildren. Typically, confidence can be thought of as: 'being certain in your own abilities ... and about having trust in people, plans or the future' (Craig, 2007: 2). As discussed earlier in the chapter, confidence in the self and the situation is important for perseverance towards goals.

Self-efficacy on the other hand, is the belief a person has that they can reach their goals or a desired outcome (Bandura, 1997). To avoid getting confused by the concept of the 'self' we would suggest thinking of self-efficacy as 'the power of I can'. Simply put, it is the expectation that one can master a situation, and produce a positive outcome based on beliefs about our personal competence or effectiveness in a given area. Ultimately, self-efficacy is a person's belief about their chances of successfully accomplishing a specific task (Maddux, 2009).

Self-reflection is one of the core features of agency and is expressed in the concept of self-efficacy. Self-efficacy beliefs provide the foundation for human motivation, well-being and personal accomplishment. This is because unless people believe that their actions can produce the outcomes they desire, they have little incentive to act or to persevere in the face of difficulties. People's level of motivation, affective states and actions are based more on what they believe than on what is objectively true. For this reason, how people behave and their accomplishments can often be better predicted by the beliefs they hold about their capabilities than by what they are actually capable of accomplishing. People who regard themselves as highly efficacious act, think and feel differently from those who perceive themselves as inefficacious. They produce their own future, rather than simply foretell it.

It is important to note that self-efficacy is not a perceived skill; it is what an individual believes they can do with their skills under certain conditions. Self-efficacy beliefs are not predictions of behaviour (what I can rather than what I will do), nor are they causal attributions. Furthermore, self-efficacy is not the same as self-concept or self-esteem, although it can contribute to them. Self-efficacy is not a motive, drive or need for control. Self-efficacy beliefs are not outcome-expectancies, but a belief that I can perform the behaviour that produces the outcome. Finally, self-efficacy is not a personality trait; it is domain and situation specific.

So where does self-efficacy come from? Bandura (1977; 1986; 1997) posits that self-efficacy derives from our mastery/performance experiences: our own direct attempts at control (most powerful source). It can also be developed through vicarious experiences, by watching someone else's accomplishments and behaviours. The closer we identify with the model, the greater the impact on self-efficacy. We can also develop self-efficacy by verbal persuasion, which is encouragement from outside sources meant to increase efficacy. Maddux (2002) suggests that we can develop self-efficacy via *imaginal experiences*, which is imagining ourselves or others behaving effectively in hypothetical situations.

time out

Social cognitive theory

Conceptualized by eminent psychologist Albert Bandura, self-efficacy derived from his work within social cognitive theory (SCT) (Gomez, 2009). Social cognitive theory consists of: personal factors in the form of cognition, affect and biological events; and behaviour and environmental influences which create interactions that result in a *triadic reciprocality*. It differs from biological and behaviourist theories as it views people as self-organizing, proactive, self-reflecting and self-regulating. Individuals are agents proactively engaged in their own development and can make things happen by their actions (Lent and Hackett, 2009).

Observational learning is another component of SCT discovered via a set of well-known experiments, called the 'Bobo doll' studies. Bandura showed that children (aged 3 to 6) would change their behaviour by simply watching others. Bandura and his colleagues also demonstrated that viewing aggression by cartoon characters produces more aggressive behaviour than viewing live or filmed aggressive behaviour by adults. Additionally, they demonstrated that having children view pro-social behaviour could reduce displays of aggressive behaviour (Bandura et al., 1961; Bandura, 1977, 1986).

Implications of self-efficacy

People with high levels of self-efficacy demonstrate a high quality of functioning, resilience to adversity and reduced vulnerability to stress and depression (Maddux, 2002), such that low self-efficacy expectancies are an important feature of depression, dysfunctional anxiety and avoidant behaviour.

Self-efficacy is critical to the adoption and success of healthy behaviour changes including exercise, diet, stress management, safe sex, smoking cessation, overcoming alcohol abuse, compliance with treatment regimes, etc. Furthermore, research has shown that self-efficacy affects the body's physiological response to stress, including the immune system, while also playing a part in the activation of catecholamines and endorphins (Maddux, 2002). When people have high levels of self-efficacy, they tend to engage more with goal setting and self-regulation, influencing choices of goal-directed activities, expenditure of effort, and persistence in the face of challenges and obstacles. Since people regarding themselves as efficacious attribute their failures to insufficient effort, they tend to try more things and pick themselves back up again.

Collective efficacy (Maddux, 2002) is defined as a group's shared belief in its conjoint capabilities to organize and execute the courses of action required to produce given levels of attainment. It involves identifying the abilities of others and harnessing these to accomplish a common goal. High levels of collective efficacy have been linked to marital satisfaction, athletic team success in competitions, academic achievement of pupils and effectiveness and group brainstorming among teams.

Think about it...

School performance is improved and efficacy is increased when students adopt short-term goals, learn specific learning strategies and receive rewards based on engagement and not just achievement. Write down your short-term academic goals and reward yourself for your engagement with the material once you've hit those targets.

But can we really distinguish self-efficacy from other related constructs? Judge et al. (2002) conducted four studies to determine discriminant validity of self-esteem, neuroticism, locus of control and generalized self-efficacy. The measures of all four traits were strongly related, with a single factor explaining the relationships among the four constructs, thus these constructs may be markers of a higher order construct.

In conclusion, self-efficacy impacts the choices we make; the effort we put forth/level of motivation; how we feel about ourselves, others and the task; and how long we persist when we confront obstacles (especially in the face of failure).

Self-esteem

Over the decades, there have been several definitions proposed for the concept of *self-esteem*. For example, Rosenberg defined it (also known as self- appraisal) as the 'totality of the individual's thoughts and feelings with reference to himself as an object' (1965). Today, we would define self-esteem as 'the disposition to experience oneself as competent to cope with the basic challenges of life and as worthy of happiness' (Branden, 1994a: 27).

There have also been several proposed types of self-esteem such as:

- global and specific (Rosenberg et al., 1995);
- trait and state (Crocker and Wolfe, 2001);
- contingent and true (Deci and Ryan, 1995);
- explicit and implicit (Karpinski and Steinberg, 2006).

We need to distinguish between being conceited, narcissistic and defensive, on the one hand, and accepting oneself with an accurate appreciation of one's strengths and worth, on the other. The effects of self-esteem are often enmeshed with other, correlated variables such as high subjective well-being, low neuroticism and high optimism. Moreover, a study conducted by Derrick Wirtz and colleagues exploring the extent to which people perceive self-control or self-esteem as moderators of a good life concluded that self-control was given less importance in comparison with self-esteem which was 'strongly associated with lay concepts of the good life' (Wirtz et al., 2016: 572).

Individuals with high levels of self-esteem tend to report greater perseverance in situations where they deem themselves likely to succeed. They also tend to self-report higher levels of intelligence and happiness. Low levels of self-esteem have been linked to several negative outcomes such as: depression in times of low stress; smoking in young women; increased bulimia risk; body dissatisfaction; perfectionism; a tendency to experiment with drugs/alcohol (also sexual initiative) and aggression.

However, high levels of self-esteem are not always a good thing. People who score high but have unstable self-esteem tend to be particularly anger and aggression prone. They appear confident and secure but in reality are highly sensitive to evaluative feedback. To protect themselves from ego challenges, they become angry and deny the legitimacy of the perceived injustice.

Think about it...

Write a character sketch of yourself, but in the third person, as it might be written by a friend who knows you well. Reflect on both your positive and negative characteristics.

(Branden, 1994b)

Models of self-esteem

According to the *sociometer model* of self-esteem, self-esteem generally correlates strongly with the belief about whether one is included or excluded by other people (Leary et al., 1995). Children and adolescents who feel more accepted by their parents have higher levels of self-esteem (Litovsky and Dusek, 1985). Low self-esteem and depression often follow social exclusion (e.g. divorce, relationship break-ups, failing to be admitted into a group, not being accepted by one's peer group). Hence, aggression among low self-esteem individuals can be better explained by social rejection than low self-esteem per se. Children who are ostracized are more hostile, aggressive and disruptive (and have lower self-esteem).

The *terror management model* of self-esteem perceives self-esteem as a function to shelter people from deeply rooted anxiety inherent in the human condition (Goldenberg and Shackelford, 2005; Pyszczynski et al., 2004). Self-esteem is a protective shield designed to control the potential for terror that results from awareness of the horrifying possibility that we humans are merely transient animals groping to survive in a meaningless universe, destined only to die and decay. However, Deci and Ryan (2000) would argue against this, claiming people typically engage with life; that is, they seek challenges, connections, authentic meaning and significance, not because they are trying to avoid the scent of death, but because they are healthy and alive.

It is probably misguided to assume that interventions aimed at boosting self-esteem will produce positive outcomes. High self-esteem is often a product rather than a cause of high competence/good performance. High self-esteem can also sometimes be illusory and leads people to conclude that they are doing better than they are.

Think about it...

How are your levels of self-esteem? Researchers would argue that merely reciting boosters or affirmations is likely to result in an inflated sense of worth. Thus, to boost self-esteem, try to engage in realistic and accurate self-appraisal, reflecting on your meaningful accomplishments and situations where you have overcome adversities.

Hope

Hope is defined as the determination to achieve goals (agency) plus believing that many pathways can be generated. *Agency* is the belief that one can begin and sustain movement along the envisioned pathway towards a given goal. Agency thoughts serve to motivate the person. *Pathways* thinking reflects an individual's perceived ability to formulate plausible goal routes (Snyder, 2002). This explanation of hope is very different from the dictionary definition of 'hope' (i.e. positive expectation, desire, longing). Hope is thought to energize goal-directed striving, particularly when the attainability of goals is at least somewhat in doubt and when the goal is viewed as very important (similar to all expectancy-value theories). People with high levels of hope often set more difficult goals, but are more likely to achieve them. They probably break the goals down into smaller sub-goals. This is used in CBT where therapists facilitate both agency thoughts (efficacy thoughts) and pathways thoughts (breaking down complex goals into achievable steps). Remoralization, the facilitation of hope, is the common pathway in therapy.

High scores on hope correlate with self-esteem, positive emotions, effective coping, academic achievement and physical health (reviewed in Peterson, 2000; Snyder, 2002). Hope also buffers against interfering, self-deprecatory thoughts and negative emotions and is critical for psychological health. People who are hopeful focus more on the prevention of diseases (e.g. through exercising) and have higher levels of success in their performance and academic achievement.

Overall, the explanatory style model of optimism and Snyder's hope model suggest that we can change to a greater extent than the dispositional model of optimism. Explanatory style gives most explanation for the mechanism through which we are optimistic. It is also least focused on the future and all models have cognitive and emotional elements, and all address motivation. Its focus on causality and how goals can be achieved is similar in concept to agency within hope theory.

Future research is focusing on clarifying the structure of optimism: are optimism and pessimism direct opposites of each other along the same continuum? Does having one automatically mean we can't have the other? Recent research suggests that the polarization is not as clear-cut as this; whether optimism is the opposite side of pessimism, or the two are distinct constructs, remains debatable (Scheier and Carver, 2009). Furthermore, more research is needed to understand the developmental antecedents of optimism, especially within a child environment. Research has shown that there is a clear link between childhood socioeconomic status and later optimism, even if the adult's socioeconomic status changes. So what is it about the early environment that is so crucial for optimism development? Parent transmission (modelling, teaching coping styles) is a hot topic for future research as is the development of more interventions targeted at increasing optimism, in early and adult life, are imperative for development of the area (Scheier and Carver, 2009).

Chapter Summary

Reflecting on the learning objectives the reader would have acquired knowledge about the concept of optimism, explanatory style and hope. In summary:

- We have explored definitions of hope, optimism and explanatory style.
- Until the last few decades, optimism was seen as a deficit, rather than a good thing.
- The main difference between the two concepts of optimism is that which surrounds the argument of trait versus learned ability.
- There are many health benefits from engaging in optimistic thinking as well as positive illusions.
- Pessimism isn't always a bad thing (e.g. defensive pessimism).
- Hope theory posits that people need agency and pathways to experience hope.

Suggested Resources

https://thepsychologist.bps.org.uk/volume-25/edition-2/self-control-%E2%80%93-moral-muscle
'Self-control – the moral muscle'. British Psychological Society – The Psychologist, 25: 112–15. Psychologist Roy F. Baumeister outlines research into willpower and ego depletion.

www.brainpickings.org/2013/11/27/the-psychology-of-self-control/
'The Psychology of Self-Control' by Maria Popova at Brain Picking. 'Everyone's self-control is a limited resource; it's like muscle strength: the more we use it, the less remains in the tank, until we replenish it with rest.'

https://itunes.apple.com/us/app/itunes-u/id490217893?mt=8
Check out the iTunesU app for free psychology lecture downloads.

http://c.r.snyder.socialpsychology.org/
Leading positive psychologist Richard Snyder tragically passed away in January 2006. Thanks to colleagues of his at the social psychology network, the reader can access his profile with links to his work at the above address.

Further questions for the reader

1 What type of 'IST' are you? An optimist? A pessimistic? A defensive pessimist?

2 Which theory of optimism do you relate to? Why?

3 Is it better to think things are going to turn out well, and avoid worrying? Or should we expect the worst and not be disappointed?

4 Is hope always a good thing?

Personal Development Interventions

1 Cultivating optimism

One of the ways that we can start to build and cultivate optimism is by engaging in the 'best possible selves' exercise (Sheldon and Lyubomirsky, 2006). This exercise requires you to sit, undisturbed, in your favourite writing space, alone and away from the madding crowd. You are asked to do this exercise for 20 minutes on three consecutive days:

▶

Think about your life in the future. Imagine that everything has gone as well as it possibly could. You have worked hard and succeeded at accomplishing all of your life goals. Think of this as the realization of all of your life dreams. Now, write about what you imagined ...

Now reflect on your future goals and then list several ways that you could achieve them. These larger goals can be broken down into smaller, more achievable sub-goals. Keep motivating yourself to pursue your goals and reframe any obstacles you meet as challenges to be overcome (adapted from Boniwell, 2008: 23).

2 Increasing self-esteem

This exercise is designed to help enhance your self-esteem. Based on Nathan Branden's sentence completion exercise, you are asked to conduct the following exercise for the next week. If you relate to this task check out Branden's 31-week self-esteem programme in his book, *The Six Pillars of Self-esteem* (1994b).

For this task, we would like to you to set aside 2–3 minutes in the morning, before you head off to your daily routine and when you are alone, to complete the following sentences. Make sure you do them quickly, without thinking too much and try and come up with no less than six endings, and no more than 10.

If I bring more awareness to my life today ...
If I take more responsibility for my choices and actions today ...
If I pay more attention to how I deal with people today ...
If I boost my energy level by 5 per cent today ...

At the end of the week, reflect on the endings and try and see what patterns emerge. Once you have done this, complete the following:

If any of what I wrote this week is true, it might be helpful if I ...

(Branden, 1994b: 310–11)

Measurement Tools

Life Orientation-Revised (LOT-R)

(Scheier et al., 1994)

Directions

Please be as honest and accurate as you can throughout. Try not to let your response to one statement influence your responses to other statements. There

► are no 'correct' or 'incorrect' answers. Answer according to your own feelings, rather than how you think 'most people' would answer.

A = I agree a lot
B = I agree a little
C = I neither agree nor disagree
D = I disagree a little
E = I disagree a lot

1. In uncertain times, I usually expect the best.
2. It's easy for me to relax.
3. If something can go wrong for me, it will.
4. I'm always optimistic about my future.
5. I enjoy my friends a lot.
6. It's important for me to keep busy.
7. I hardly ever expect things to go my way.
8. I don't get upset too easily.
9. I rarely count on good things happening to me.
10. Overall, I expect more good things to happen to me than bad.

Scoring

Items 2, 5, 6, and 8 are fillers and therefore should be excluded. Please add the remaining items to receive one final score.

Interpretation

There are no 'cut-offs' for optimism or pessimism. Higher scores reflecting higher levels of optimism.

Review

The LOT-R is a revised version of the original LOT, which focused on differentiating optimists from pessimists. The newer version includes more explicit items regarding an individual's prediction about the future. This test is quick, easy to use and good for research purposes, hence many studies have used this scale.

Generalized Self-Efficacy Scale (GSE)

(Schwarzer and Jerusalem, 1995)

Directions

Below are 10 statements about yourself, which may or may not be true. Using the 1–4 scale below, please indicate your agreement with each item by placing the appropriate number on the line following that item. Please be open and honest in your responding.

1	**2**	**3**	**4**
Not at all true	**Hardly true**	**Moderately true**	**Exactly true**

_____ **1.** I can always manage to solve difficult problems if I try hard enough.

_____ **2.** If someone opposes me, I can find the means and ways to get what I want.

_____ **3.** It is easy for me to stick to my aims and accomplish my goals.

_____ **4.** I am confident that I could deal efficiently with unexpected events.

_____ **5.** Thanks to my resourcefulness, I know how to handle unforeseen situations.

_____ **6.** I can solve most problems if I invest the necessary effort.

_____ **7.** I can remain calm when facing difficulties because I can rely on my coping abilities.

_____ **8.** When I am confronted with a problem, I can usually find several solutions.

_____ **9.** If I am in trouble, I can usually think of a solution.

_____**10.** I can usually handle whatever comes my way.

Scoring

Please add the item scores and divide by the number of items to retain a final score.

Interpretation

The range of scores fall between 10 and 40 points, with the average score equalling 29 (when averaged). There is no cut off; however, you can calculate where your participant falls in relation to the group/median.

Review

This scale is translated into 30 languages and has thousands of data behind its use.

Notes

1 Research into genetic factors and optimism demonstrates that 25–30 per cent of the variability is due to genetics.
2 We will go through the ABC technique in more detail in Chapter 6.

Resilience, Post-traumatic Growth and Positive Ageing

❖ LEARNING OBJECTIVES

Challenging situations, disappointments, limitations, stress, loss, hurt and suffering, significant life changes like getting older and even death – all these are inevitable features of being human. Although on the surface these features sound like nemeses of positive psychology, many researchers maintain that positive psychology would benefit from studying their place within the richness of the human condition and how to respond and manage them so as to assist their contribution to a life well lived. This chapter will focus on the topics of resilience and growth as well as visiting the process of ageing from a positive perspective.

Topics include:

- Common psychological responses to trauma.

- Defining resilience.

- The phenomenon of post-traumatic growth.

- Sense of coherence and its effects on health and well-being.

- Resilience, existential thought and reframing.

- Wisdom and its place in the developmental process.

- Components to positive ageing.

MOCK ESSAY QUESTIONS

1 That which does not kill us makes us stronger. Critically discuss.
2 Discuss relative benefits and shortcomings of these two terminologies: 'growth through adversity' and 'growth after adversity'.
3 Evaluate available research evidence that ageing can be associated with positive outcomes.

Responses to stress and trauma

Prolonged, stressful living can cause havoc on our physical, emotional and psychological well-being. However, research suggests that stress can be good and useful – when it is experienced in small and infrequent doses. Intermittent stress, or allostasis (Charney, 2004), is important in helping us keep prepared for better response (vs succumbing) to possible future stressors. An experience of adversity/stressors, if not chronic, can equip a person with what is known as 'psychological preparedness', enabling them to become stronger in the face of future stressors. Encounters with adversity and time-limited forms of stress or 'suffering' (frustration; disappointments; challenges; drawbacks; existential angst) can serve as 'stress inoculation' (Janoff-Bulman, 1992, 2004). For instance, active coping (facing one's fears and using the fear to catalyse and orient action) is associated with resiliency; whereas avoidance of fears (denial; collusion) is associated with the maintenance of fear and the stress it inflicts on the mind and body (Feder et al., 2010)

Trauma tends to be experienced as a result of a sudden or ongoing system of stressors. It creates a high degree of emotional distress and affects the whole person 'substantially interrupt[ing] [an individual's] personal narrative' (Tedeschi and Calhoun, 1995: 16). Life-threatening situations that involve events such as natural disasters – but more so, man-made inflictions such as victimization through violence, psychological or sexual assault – are profoundly distressing and tend to generate long-lasting problems for the experiencing individual and encompass complex journeys of recovery towards a satisfactory adaptation. The negative consequences of trauma experienced in childhood, for instance, can continue through adulthood. This is partly due to neurological development being adversely affected (Read et al., 2014) and a brain wiring potentially priming responses to new situations that 'replicate the experience of loss of power, choice, control and safety in ways that may appear extreme, or even abnormal, when a history of past adverse events is not taken into account' (Sweeney et al., 2016: 1). On the other hand, research also found that those who have experienced trauma, adversity or risk often also develop a stronger self-belief, grit and flexibility in approaching resources for self-regulation (e.g. Lerner et al., 2003; Bonanno, 2004; Mancini and Bonanno, 2010). This trend of engaging with processes and outcomes encompassed by the concept of resilience (see later in this chapter) occurs across cultures, wherein their ontology and success are greatly entrenched in cultural mores and practices (Ungar, 2008), and across ordinary as well as extraordinary challenges across the lifespan (Masten and Wright, 2010) or, in case of young people, normative as well as non-normative developmental transitions (e.g. Liebenberg et al., 2013). New, positive psychology informed early and/or preventive interventions to foster resilience continue to be designed and their effectiveness evaluated (e.g. Springer et al., 2014; Pluess et al., 2017).

Inquiries into the human condition's potentiality for healing following an adverse experience have led to the development of new approaches to understanding and working with trauma. There is debate however as to what constitutes a traumatic event.

There are consistent features across a *traumatic experience*. It tends to entail an occurrence that is *out of the ordinary* and one which somehow the individual would need to try to come to terms with so as to restore a view of the world, and of self within it, as coherent and meaningful once again. Also a common feature is that the experience demarcates an intense felt sense of *before and after* against a background where fundamental tenets of regular and high-order frameworks for meaning-making have been challenged and profoundly destabilized, with the upshot that a suitable adjustment to a traumatic experience seems to be intricately 'dependent on developing a way to understand the trauma and its aftermath *in personal terms*' (Calhoun and Tedeschi, 1999: 320, italics added).

A common belief is that after trauma, such as an illness diagnosis, a person becomes severely stressed. Research shows that only 5 to 35 per cent of individuals succumb to and sustain an emotional negative state and the downward-spiral ways of thinking that it initiates (Cordova, 2008; Kangas et al., 2002). Thus, as positive psychology asks: what about the other 65 to 95 per cent? What happens to them? This will be discussed further on in the chapter.

In summary, when individuals are faced with trauma or distressing change, three main possible psychological responses tend to emerge:

- succumbing to the stressor (also referred to as post-traumatic stress *disorder* or PTSD[1]) or displaying a state of survival with impairment;
- resilience focused on recovery – bouncing-back from stress, regaining equilibrium and relatively quickly returning to baseline level of functioning and state of health;
- post-traumatic – sustaining the process of recovery such that the recovery trajectory becomes a resilient adaptation that leads to growth and enhancement.

Defining resilience

Resilience is a multi-fold construct. It is both a capacity and an active process encompassing a person's 'flexibility in response to changing situational demands, and the ability to bounce back from negative emotional experiences' (Tugade et al., 2004: 1169). Some researchers see resilience as more multifaceted than this. Lepore and Revenson (2006) for instance distinguish three facets of resilience: *recovery, resistance* and *reconfiguration.*

1 Recovery is that facet of resilience which refers to the return back to normal, pre-stressor, level of functioning (health and psychosocial well-being).

2 Resistance as a facet of resilience is said to occur when a person displays minimum or no signs of disturbance (low distress, normal functioning) following a traumatic event.

3 Reconfiguration is said to occur when a person returns to homeostasis in a different formation: key aspects about that individual have changed (either positively or negatively) as a result of their traumatic experience.

Reconfiguration shares similarities with the concept of post-traumatic growth including, for instance, in that it occasions transformations, which unlike recovery or resistance, entail travelling beyond simply maintaining or returning to baseline functioning. According to Lepore and Revenson, people exhibit this form of resilience 'when they are able to reconfigure their cognitions, beliefs, and behaviours in a manner that allows them to adapt to traumatic experiences and, possibly, withstand future traumas' (2006: 27).

Think about it...

Think of a time when you ...

a overcame a difficult period of time;

b bounced back from a tough situation;

c got through a difficult time with relative ease;

d challenged yourself and went out of your 'comfort zone'.

(Adapted from Reivich and Shatte, 2002)

Components of resilience

The human capacity for positive developmental outcomes under and following adversity is an important personal as well as social asset. Notwithstanding the need to take into account nuances demanded by cultural, contextual, developmental and individual relativity, a number of factors have been identified by researchers as important facilitators of resilience. These include: a) reframing; b) harvesting the resourcing 'power' of positive emotions; c) participation in physical activity; d) active engagement with trusted social support networks; e) recognizing and using (authentic) strengths; and f) deliberate optimism in crafting new and positive future perspectives.

One of the biggest obstacles to healthy psychological function is negative, as in pessimistic, ruminative thought. A decisive pathway to a more resilient self is altering the hold of the negative or pessimistic thinking patterns and developing an *optimistic explanatory style* (Reivich and Shatte, 2002; Seligman, 2002b). Through the application of popular methods from CBT (Beck, 1976), positive psychology research has shown that when we are faced with a challenging situation, employing the *ABCDE* technique, where A /Adversity (the issue or event); B/beliefs (automatic pessimistic beliefs about the event); C/Consequences (of holding that belief); D/Disputation (your conscious arguments against your pessimistic belief); and E/Energization (what you feel when you've disputed your B effectively), can increase resilience and decrease depression levels (Gillham et al., 2007; Gillham et al., 1995). Since pessimistic rumination is a precursor and maintainer of depression (Papageorgiou and Wells, 2003), this technique acts as a buffer to stress reactions and is imperative for challenging destructive thoughts and creating more resilient skills and repertoires for thought and action. An increased sense of coping competence has also been negatively correlated with depression, neuroticism and stress (Schroder and Ollis, 2013).

When faced with a difficult situation, individuals often engage in one of several *thinking traps* such as: jumping to conclusions; tunnel vision; magnifying the negative and minimizing the positive; personalizing or externalizing blame; overgeneralizing small setbacks; engaging in mind reading and using unhelpful emotional reasoning (Reivich and Shatte, 2002). (For full review, see Reivich and Shatte, 2002: 95–122.) Individuals need to identify which thinking traps they tend to succumb to and then construct a more realistic view of the adversity.

time out

Resilience Interventions

There are several resilience programmes throughout the world; one of the most notable is the Penn Resilience Programme (PRP). This was developed based on the work of resilience experts Reivich and Shatte and Seligman's work on learned optimism. The approach follows a cognitive behavioural angle and focuses on teaching students at a young age, to identify pervasive negative/pessimistic thinking and test/challenge these thoughts. The programme runs over 18 to 24 one-hour sessions on the main principles found to increase resilience and well-being topic matters. The results are promising, with two-year follow ups showing that interventions groups have less depression, higher well-being and increased grades (see Springer et al., 2014; Boniwell et al., 2016).   ▶

> ▶ See also Christine Padesky and Kathleen Mooney's (2012) strengths-based CBT model for building and strengthening personal resilience. Its four-step design features the use of client-generated imagery and metaphor to identify personal strengths and delineate a bespoke model of personal resilience.

Resilience and our sense of coherence

The holocaust was one of the twenty-first century's greatest horrors. After the slaughter of six million people, the survivors and those left behind have shown tremendous resilience (low PTSD) and growth in the face of the most heinous adversity. Not only have we seen psychological growth, research has shown that even all these decades later, survivors from the prison camps show significant physical health functioning (salutogenic) versus illness-inducing (pathogenic) outcomes (Cassel and Suedfeld, 2006). Disclosure to others, marital history and religious observance have been proposed as mediators to both positive and negative long-term consequences (Lev-Wiesel and Amir, 2003).

Salutogenesis means 'the origins of health', and is conceptually defined as the process of movement towards the health end of a health–disease continuum. There are several implications of adopting a salutogenic orientation such as: rejecting a dichotomy in favour of a continuum conception of health disease; focusing on movement towards health rather than movement towards disease; preferring an interest in the overall spectrum over expertise and compartmentalization; interest in what pushes us towards health (anti-risk factors); and search for salutary factors (strengths, compensatory mechanisms, significant social roles, self-images other than that of the sick role).

Salutogenesis is implicitly linked to *sense of coherence* (SOC). Antonovsky (1979) originally developed SOC in an attempt to understand why some people are less likely to be affected by stressful environments than others. At the point of its discovery, SOC represented a departure from a pathological perspective dominant in medical and social sciences. Sense of coherence is defined as:

> 66 a global orientation that expresses the extent to which one has a persuasive, enduring though dynamic feeling of confidence that (1) the stimuli deriving from one's internal and external environments in the course of living are structured, predictable, and explicable; (2) the resources are available to one to meet the demands posed by these stimuli; (3) these demands are challenges, worthy of investment and engagement.
>
> *– (Antanovsky, 1987)* 99

In other words, it is the extent to which one is confident that internal and external environments are predictable and there is a high probability that life situations will work out as well as can be expected:

1 *Comprehensibility* refers to a person's insight into their achievement and difficulties. We can hardly judge whether appropriate resources are at our disposal to cope with a task unless we believe that we have some understanding of its nature. Seeing and confronting stimuli as an integral part of sense-making aids comprehensibility in that they will be expected, or if unexpected they will be ordered or explicable.

2 *Manageability* refers to a high probability that things will work out as well as can be reasonably expected: the extent to which someone perceives that the resources at their disposal are adequate to meet the demands posed by the stimuli that are bombarding them. Manageability has some similarity to Bandura's concept of self-efficacy. Of course, this element is not sufficient on its own, as cognitive and motivational components are no less essential.

3 *Meaningfulness* refers to the motivational belief that it makes emotional sense to cope; that, though life may have its pains, one wishes to go on. People have areas of their life that are important to them that they very much care about and that make sense to them. Thus, people with a weak SOC give little indication that anything in life seems to matter particularly to them.

So how does one accrue an SOC? Researchers would argue that an SOC usually develops by around age 30. The more one's experiences are characterized by consistency, participation in shaping outcome, and balance of stimuli (rather than overload or underload), the more one is likely to see the world as coherent. Antonovsky believed the SOC remains relatively stable as long as 'radical and enduring changes in one's life situation' do not occur. Some studies appear to confirm this, although in one large study, SOC was significantly lower in the youngest age group and increased with age. It is possible to conceive of SOC as a personality characteristic or coping style (Antonovsky and Sagy, 2001). Sense of coherence is a rich concept and includes the elements of hardiness, self-efficacy and locus of control (Linley, 2003). It is, however, seen as more universally meaningful than the abovementioned constructs (Antonovsky, 1993). There exists substantial empirical and theoretical support for its nature as a unitary construct (Antanovsky, 1993). Sense of coherence has also been linked to high associations with well-being and life satisfaction and reduced fatigue and loneliness. Some research findings show significant negative correlations with anxiety and depression; moreover, a strong SOC protects against depression, predicts low suicidal thoughts in depressed patients and predicts lower (30 per cent) mortality from all causes (Antonovsky, 1993). Furthermore, low SOC predicts musculoskeletal symptoms (neck, shoulder and low-back) in later life, and is a predictor of response to pain management programmes for chronic pain sufferers. It is linked to pain levels in cancer patients. In arthritis patients, lower SOC is linked to pain levels, as well as greater difficulty in performing daily activities and general health.

Resilience and coping styles

Lazarus and Folkman's transactional model of stress appraisal is the most widely known and used model within coping research. Coping is defined as 'constantly changing cognitive and behavioural efforts to manage specific external and/or internal demands that are appraised to be taxing or exceeding the resources of the person' (Lazarus and Folkman, 1984, as cited in Cheavens and Dreer, 2009: 223). Primary appraisal is the extent to which an individual perceives their situation to be threatening. Secondary appraisal is an individual's perception of whether or not they have the resources available to them to deal with the stressor.

There are two main coping strategies that individuals use when faced with stressful or adverse situations. *Problem-focused coping* is when people identify the stressor and take active steps to engage with and tackle the issues at hand. *Emotion-focused coping* is when individuals tend to focus on dealing with the emotions surrounding the situation, rather than attempting to change or deal with the situation. Emotion-focused coping tends to consist of turning to others and seeking social support. This type of coping includes avoidance, which is when an individual ignores the situation at hand and avoids any interaction with solving the issue (Thornton and Perez, 2006; Urcuyo et al., 2005). Earlier research posited that problem-focused coping was the better form of coping; however, newer research shows that emotion-focused coping can indeed have positive consequences as well. For example, avoidance was seen as a negative copping strategy, although we now know that in the short term, engaging in healthy distractions can be a good thing for people who have experienced significant trauma.

Post-traumatic growth

Resilience (the returning to 'normal' functioning) is typically accompanied by a sense of growth and even thriving following an adverse event. In many ways, the phenomenon captures the German philosopher Friedrich Nietzsche's well-known observation that can be paraphrased as: 'That which does not kill us makes us stronger' (1844–1900).

Resilience, existential thought and reframing

Scholars tend to agree on the pivotal place of subjective realities and experience in understanding trauma. Indeed, whether an individual exposed to traumatic events 'experiences an existential shattering or not' it is vital for our conceptualizations about trauma 'to address the implications of the deconstruction or shattering of one's world view' in their own terms. Individualized narratives are an inherent feature of trauma and represent a vital 'source of sustaining [present and future] meaning and resilience' (Hoffman et al., 2013: 1). Particular sensitivity to the linguistically and culturally mediated values and practices to fashioning the texture of personal resiliency through and after adversity is therefore crucial to the endeavour (see also Ungar, 2008, 2011).

A common theme throughout humanity is the notion of self-sacrifice and suffering for a greater good (Jimenez, 2009). Suffering for the benefit of self-actualization is present within religious teachings and philosophical and psychological literature, with an emphasis on apprehending high-order knowledge, peace of mind and development of the self (authentic living); transcending life's limitations through tolerating and learning from existential angst and adversity. See for instance Rollo May's *Man's Search for Himself*, first published in 1953; Friedrich Nietzsche's *Thus Spoke Zarathustra*, first published in full in 1891; and Søren Kierkegaard's *The Concept of Anxiety*, first published in 1844 pointing out (before Freud did) anxiety/angst as inherent and key to the dynamics of the human condition. A shift in perspective lies at the heart of resilience as post-traumatic growth; that is, a shift from framing an adverse event as hurtful, destabilizing or indeed potentially a justified grievance to conceiving it more and more in terms of it representing a challenge which, when mastered, can yield an opportunity to expand and accrue knowledge and develop the self as a result. It is a subjective and highly individualizing process. Whether seen as growth through or after adversity, the process cannot be rushed. And its profound embeddedness in the human condition cannot be underestimated either (see also Wong, 2010).

Writing about anxiety from an existential perspective Danish philosopher Søren Kierkegaard (1813–1855) proposes it as the best teacher for he/she 'who has learnt to be anxious in the right way, has learnt the ultimate'. The emphasis is on seeing the time when we most grapple with angst/anxiety as the time that is most critical for 'tasting' and seizing our existential freedom. This tends to require tolerating the angst and exercising one's choice to choose what next for oneself. Choice is not to be confused with option: options are there in front of me. Choice in the existential sense refers to acknowledging the responsibility (we have towards ourselves) to own our freedom to choose. The choice of 'not choosing' (seen as denying the freedom to choose which ultimately rests only with the individual) is still a choice albeit, in existential terms, a 'self-deception' (see also Jean-Paul Sartre's (1905–1980) notion of 'bad faith' in his *Essays in Existentialism*). Successful confrontations with basic existential givens (including freedom; meaninglessness; mortality; existential guilt) tend to bring forth a return to self; and a liberating hope coupled with the 'courage to be' – to live authentically versus divided within (see e.g. Macquarrie, 1974). At the crossroad that follows a traumatic event, there is choice for the self-in-becoming: who I am? What I am to be? What would be a life that is well lived?

Reframing: from a grievance to a challenge

Instigating and maintaining a shift in perspective benefits from a *habit of resourcing*; that is, engaging in activities that resonate on a personal level in ways that help energizing action towards the desired direction of travel. Boniwell and Ryan (2012); for instance, worked with the resilience as a muscle metaphor to anchor resourcing activities in their SPARK intervention. They indicate *I am; I can; I like; I share with others* as types of resilience muscles as resourcing platforms for enhancing personal resilience. Tunariu (2015) added another, *My choice and choices*, as part of a new resilience and well-being intervention designed to facilitate the formation of positive identities through the acquisition of skills for growth and flourishing; namely, the iNEAR programme.

iNEAR is informed by existential positive psychology, coaching and counselling psychology. It comprises several themed lessons organized around/as a mindful social agent developing:

- new knowledge about myself;
- emotional resources and emotional intelligence;
- awareness of values, of options, of choice; and
- responding with growth 'in spite of ...'.

Philosophically oriented dialogues on ethics, dilemmas and their resolutions scaffold curiosity and positive future perspectives. An important experiential goal, implicitly running throughout the programme, is amplifying the drive for self-actualization through exposure to 'aha' moments. It also aims to expand young people's tolerance to uncertainty and contradiction for the benefit of coping repertoires of skills, emotional mastery and growth. As it integrates key resilience ingredients, iNEAR helps equip its participants to better cope with adversity in general and perceive adverse events as potential opportunities for learning (for the first wave of iNEAR findings see Tunariu et al., 2017b). The expanded version of iNEAR includes further activities to address negative beliefs and dislike of ambiguity aimed at normalizing life contradictions and lowering anticipation of adverse consequences (such as a sense of 'not being in control'). This helps expand an individual's capacity to 'stay' with *existential uncertainty* by promoting readiness and tendency to engage in the dialectical rhythm of effort and acceptance. Similarly, it also broadens one's repertoire of self-soothing strategies useful for 'staying' with ordinary, *everyday uncertainty* by promoting acceptance of multiplicity and relativity in worldviews, and openness to innovative solution-finding.

time out

There is a field of study within positive psychology that looks at how, through dealing with (and not the direct result of) trauma, a person can become better, stronger and operate at higher levels of functioning than those that existed before the traumatic event occurred. Previously studied under the terminologies of benefit finding, positive changes, growth from adversity, thriving and psychological growth (Tennen and Affleck, 2004; Lechner, 2009), this phenomenon is now known as post-traumatic growth (PTG). Post-traumatic growth has been found to exist within sample of survivors from 'war, bereavement, breast cancer, mastectomy, bone marrow disease, heart attack, rheumatoid arthritis, spinal cord injury, MS, shipping disaster, tornado, plane crash, rape, childhood sexual assault, incest, shooting, HIV, infertility, chemical dependency, military combat and bombing' (Joseph et al., 2005: 263–64; Ai et al., 2007).

time out

Viktor Frankl

Readers who have come across the wonderful and powerful book *Man's Search for Meaning* will be well aware of the name Viktor Frankl (Frankl, 1963). Frankl was an Austrian psychiatrist who was imprisoned in Theresienstadt, Auschwitz and Turkheim during the years 1942–1945. Throughout his incomprehensible ordeal in the Nazi concentration camps, Frankl lost his wife, children and family. During his incarceration, Frankl watched his fellow inmates to discover a theory of survival and human drive: the will to meaning. Frankl proposed that those that had a will to meaning, those that had something to live for, even in the direst circumstances, survived. Frankl's theory was later translated into a form of psychotherapy, entitled logotherapy, with the main school still in operation in Vienna. His story and theories are a triumph to the human spirit and a testament to his belief that when everything is taken away from a man, they still have the ability to choose their reactions.

Post-traumatic growth across five main domains

Calhoun and Tedeschi (2004) proposed that PTG can be usefully divided into five main domains.

Personal strength (or perceived changes in self) is apparent when trauma survivors report becoming stronger, deeper, more authentic, confident, open, empathetic, creative, more alive, mature, humanitarian, special, humble, and the list goes on. Many describe themselves as a 'better person' now that they have undergone this wake up call. *Relating to others* is apparent where people report becoming closer with their immediate and extended families. People report that friendships bind tighter and that people who were acquaintances/strangers/neighbours before the event become prominent positive features in their daily life. Camaraderie and friendship among survivors of the same trauma is common. A downside of this is that many trauma survivors report that their friends go missing and are not supportive during their adversity. Although painful at the time, people report that this is a bonus as it allows them to identify their true friends and spend time (which is now much more precious) with those that count.

The third domain encompasses ***appreciation for life*** (or increased existential awareness). As one would expect, many people undergo a change in life philosophy. When trauma highlights our vulnerability and that we are not invincible, we start to reflect on deeper issues such as mortality, spirituality, the meaning of and purpose in life, and so on. Many survivors report that the trauma allowed them to 'see clearly', to understand what matters in life and allow them to make changes to their priorities, from how and with whom they decide to spend their day, to the importance of nature, health, life and the importance (or unimportance) of physical appearance and monetary goods.

The ***new possibilities*** domain covers an individual's desires to change their life goals, re-enrol in schooling to learn a new subject, get a degree or obtain new skills. Overall, there is a keen focus on the 'here and now' with a new appreciation of life and their time here on earth. Finally, ***spiritual change*** occurs where people may decide to return to their previous (or alternative) faith. They begin to actively participate (attend church, pray) and their belief in a higher being is strengthened via gratitude to that being.

Criticisms of the concept of PTG

One of the major criticisms of PTG is whether or not it 'truly' exists. Some researchers believe that what trauma survivors are actually experiencing is a form of cognitive dissonance (Festinger et al., 1956/2008) or positive illusions (Taylor, 1989). In both cases, the individual is protected from the overwhelming confusion and devastation of the trauma. Cognitive dissonance is a psychological reasoning in which reality is actually so different from what one believes that in order to understand, the person rationalizes the occurrence in order to maintain equilibrium within the psyche. Thus, for someone who loses a loved one, accepting the death is too much for one person to bear so the individual creates or rationalizes the death in order to keep going (Festinger et al., 1956/2008).

Positive illusions, on the other hand, can actually be good for us. While not necessary or sufficient conditions for mental health, positive illusions have been shown to promote mental health and are often 'directly responsive to threatening circumstances' (Taylor and Brown, 1994: 28). Like cognitive dissonance, people create positive illusions about their traumatic situation in order to rationalize and move on. Again, if someone is diagnosed with cancer, afterwards they create positive illusions that the experience taught them something, in order to comprehend the trauma as not happening in vain. These theories postulate that we can't have trauma happen for the sake of happening; humans need to find a reason for it, otherwise it would be too hard to comprehend.

Furthermore, criticisms have come in the form of the *tyranny of positive thinking* (Held, 2004). Thus, not only are people required to recover, but they now have the added pressure to find something positive out of the experience as well. This can cause an overwhelming sense of pressure, depression and disappointment in the self if positivity is not found immediately or at all. Ultimately, PTG does not push this, but rather highlights that alongside deep sadness, hurt and distress, people (but not all) can find something beneficial out of their struggle with adversity. Simply knowing that this is possible can have a profound positive effect on current trauma survivors.

Whether or not PTG is actually real, the argument appears counterproductive, as it is simply 'the subjective sense of being bettered' (Thornton, 2002: 162). Thus, if there is no obvious psychopathology, nor is there any detriment to themselves or others, and the presence appears to be beneficial on both psychological and physical levels, then researchers within the domain believe that it is important to study in its own right. Furthermore, if PTG is simply an illusion or a socially desirable bias, the critics have not yet created a measurement tool or agreed upon definitions for identifying illusions or distortions (Calhoun and Tedeschi, 2008).

Facilitators of PTG

Research has shown correlations between variables and higher scores on PTG tools; however the results are mixed. People who are more wealthy and educated and younger tend to experience higher levels of growth. This could be for several reasons. First of all, people who are higher in socioeconomic status tend to be more educated and therefore have fewer financial worries after trauma. Thus, when diagnosed with cancer, someone who struggles day to day with financial worries has the added stress of providing for their family, as well as the time and physical toll of chemotherapy.

With regards to the existence of PTG personalities, the evidence is not clear-cut and, although certain personality traits such as optimism and extraversion tend to appear (Antoni et al., 2001), there are similar numbers of studies suggesting otherwise. This is a good thing, we think, as it means that anyone is capable of experiencing this phenomenon. Not surprisingly, researchers have suggested that people who experience more positive emotions will be better equipped to deal with adversity (broaden-and-build) as well as experience PTG (Linley and Joseph, 2004). Again, certain personalities are more prone to experiencing higher levels of positive emotions, thus, personality may play a factor within this facilitator.

Time and type

Again, PTG researchers are currently trying to understand whether time and the objective severity of a trauma matter in the attainment and valence of growth. This is not easy; for example, objectively, stage 3 cancer is worse than stage 1; however, depending on the individual, stage 1 might be enough to shatter their previous beliefs and send them into a pit of despair. The person with stage 3 may have had several earlier traumas that prepared them for this and thus not experience PTG due to their current levels of resilience. Indeed, those that are more resilient tend not to experience higher levels of growth. This is reasoned because they may not see the trauma as 'traumatic' due to the fact that they are resilient in the face of adversity. Furthermore, in terms of time since severity, researchers believe that there needs to be enough time to contemplate the tragedy and work through the survivor's cognitive beliefs before it can be incorporated; however, research has shown that those who are able to report immediate benefits have lower levels of stress several months/years later. It appears that the reaction and attainment of growth is quite individual (see e.g. Cordova, 2008).

Coping styles

There are some links between coping styles and PTG (Urcuyo et al., 2005). For example, people who use approach-focused coping (active and problem-focused coping) are able to engage in positive reappraisal, acceptance, seeking social support and contemplating reason for the tragedy. Furthermore, emotional approach coping is highly beneficial as greater emotional expression in the immediate aftermath has been linked to PTG. Despite the beneficial effects of approach-oriented coping, the use of avoidance coping can be beneficial depending on the individual, the trauma and the length of use. As discussed earlier, escape, avoidance and healthy distraction can be quite necessary when dealing with trauma. As long as it is not continual and the only form of coping, these can be used to enhance PTG. Overall, the use of dynamic coping is ideal for the experience of PTG to exist. Moreover, the presence of social support remains one of the most important facilitators we know within PTG research (see Lechner et al., 2008; Sabiston et al., 2007).

How do we measure PTG?

The majority of PTG research is measured through quantitative assessment. Major tools include the Stress Related Growth Scale (SRGS) (Park et al., 1996), the Post-Traumatic Growth Inventory (PTGI) (Tedeschi and Calhoun, 1996) the Benefit Finding Scale (BFS) (Antoni et al., 2001) and the Changes in Outlook questionnaire (Joseph et al., 1993). The tools tend to ask questions surrounding cognitive shifts in thinking since and related to the trauma. For example, within the PTGI (Tedeschi and Calhoun, 1996), individuals are asked to think about the trauma they experienced and respond to the following questions on a Likert scale from 0 (I did not change as a result of the event I described above) to 5 (I changed to a very great degree as a result of the event I described above)[2]:

1. My priorities about what is important in life   0   1   2   3   4   5

2. An appreciation for the value of my own life   0   1   2   3   4   5

3. I developed new interests   0   1   2   3   4   5

4. A feeling of self-reliance   0   1   2   3   4   5

5. A better understanding of spiritual matters   0   1   2   3   4   5

The tools mentioned above have very high internal consistency and reliability. Since quantitative measurement tools are numerically restrictive and can lack access to the entire phenomenon, we also use qualitative research strategies, which allow the participant to speak freely about the phenomenon in their own words. The data is typically accessed via semi-structured interviews, written response, focus groups and/or diaries.

How does PTG happen?

There are several leading models within the area of PTG, including: shattered assumptions theory (Janoff-Bulman, 1992); organismic valuing theory (Joseph and Linley, 2005) and the transformational model (Tedeschi and Calhoun, 2006). *Shattered assumptions theory* assumes that we all have an inner world in which we harbour fundamental assumptions of a sense of safety and security. Trauma occurs when these assumptions are tested and our sense of security is 'shattered'. Post-traumatic growth is the process of rebuilding around the traumatic experience and thus acknowledging the trauma in a non-anxious way.

Organismic valuing theory of growth through adversity (Joseph and Linley, 2008) is a person-centred approach with growth akin to fully functioning. This theory assumes that a person must overcome obstacles in their social environment and not necessarily their pre- or post-trauma personality in order to obtain PTG. Known as the *completion tendency*, a person must incorporate the trauma into their worldview via accommodation or assimilation. *Assimilation* is when a person keeps their old worldview and initiates self-blame. Hence there is no reordering of their previous schemas. *Accommodation*, on the other hand, modifies pre-existing schemas in order to accommodate the new information. A person can do this one of two ways: either positively or negatively. Negative accommodation leaves a person susceptible to depression and helplessness, whereas positive accommodation leads to growth (Joseph and Linley, 2008).

This theory goes beyond discussing outcomes and attempts to clarify the cognitive processes following trauma (assimilation, positive accommodation and negative accommodation). Furthermore, it attempts to explain the reasoning for why people can become more vulnerable and not resilient in the aftermath of crisis (Joseph and Linley, 2008). Thus, by assimilating the trauma into their cognitive functioning, the person returns to baseline with feelings of being more vulnerable to future traumas. A person can experience accommodation and assimilation within differing components of the self-structure; a person is not limited to either/or.

The Transformational Model (Tedeschi and Calhoun, 1995) remains a widely used model of growth. It posits that PTG is the result of excessive rumination (or cognitive processing) following a seismic event (Tedeschi and Calhoun, 2003). Following the seismic event, the person is presented with challenges (e.g. management of emotional distress). They must then engage in managing excessive rumination in three stages. First, they experience automatic and intrusive thoughts; over time, the individuals will learn to manage these automatic thoughts until they engage in what is called 'deliberate rumination'. Throughout their grappling with these thoughts, the person is engaged in self-disclosure as they attempt to reduce emotional distress. By doing so, the person commences their disengaging from previous goals, resulting in changed schemas and narrative development. Once these processes have been completed, the person is able to achieve PTG in addition to wisdom or 'preparedness'. Importantly, this model acknowledges that distress can co-exist alongside PTG (Tedeschi and Calhoun, 2008).

Think about it...

Have you personally experienced PTG or has someone close to you? Have you seen it modelled? What were the mechanisms that brought you to experience growth? Which model do you relate to?

In conclusion, when tragedy strikes, there are threee main *psychological responses* to trauma. Resilience is important for protective and reactive functions. The phenomenon PTG is amply reported by people and by researchers as something that generates – subjectively as well as objectively – real psychological and physical benefits.

Wisdom

One of the proposed benefits of surviving a traumatic experience is the attainment of wisdom (Tedeschi and Calhoun, 1995; Haidt, 2006). But what is this 'wisdom'? The values in action strengths approach defines wisdom as

❝the ability to take stock of life in large terms, in ways that make sense to oneself and others. Perspective is the product of knowledge and experience, but it is more than the accumulation of information. It is the coordination of this information and its deliberate use to improve well-being. In a social context, perspective allows the individual to listen to others, to evaluate what they say, and then to offer good (sage) advice. Directions back to the interstate do not qualify as wisdom, unless the highway is the metaphorical route to the life well-lived.

– (Peterson and Seligman, 2004: 106).❞

The kind of wisdom that positive psychology is seeking to theorize about is best seen a higher form of knowledge; one that affords wider perspective and the ability to adjust to new challenges, contractions and if needed to paradoxes that characterize coming to terms with 'life' from a vantage point of expanded awareness and insight.

Think about it...

Can you give an example of someone you consider wise? Why is this? List their wise attributes and reflect upon them.

There are several approaches to wisdom in psychology. For example, developmental psychologist Erickson noted wisdom as the final stage of personality development (60 years and up), while Piaget described as wisdom the product of the final stage of cognitive development (i.e. the application of dialectical thinking to solving complex problems). However according to researchers specializing in this area of study, wisdom has little to do with age, with levels of wisdom levelling into young adulthood. It is experience and the amassed encounters with life complexities that create wisdom (Baltes et al., 1995). Sternberg, for instance, conceptualized wisdom as a balance between practical intelligence and tacit knowledge applied to solving problems to achieve the greater good for all (Sternberg, 2009). According to Sternberg in order to achieve wisdom, one must balance several competing interests as across the intra-personal (own), inter-personal (others) and extra-personal (communities and environment) realms. When faced with a challenging situation, an individual can respond in one of three ways: a) *adapt* to it; b) *shape it* so the situation adapts to us; or c) *select* to change one's environment to something more advantageous to our needs. Overall, Sternberg's Balance Theory of Wisdom posits that wisdom is apparent when an individual is problem solving in a way that is taking other people into account, is using multiple responses strategies, and is aiming for the result to serve the common good of all.

Think about it...

What prevents us from thinking and acting in a wise manner? What ways can you think of that would help to increase wisdom in action?

Positive ageing

Since the 1990s, the global population has expanded and so has global life expectancy. In response to this socioeconomic fact, leading ageing researcher, George Vaillant pointed out that researchers and policy makers alike should focus their attention on ways to 'to add more life to years, not just years to life' (Vaillant, 2004: 561).

'Life expectancy equals the average number of years a person born in a given country is expected to live if mortality rates at each age were to remain steady in the future'.[3] The *United Nations World Population Prospects 2015 Revision* indicated that for 2010–2015 worldwide, the average life expectancy at birth was 71.5 years (68 years and 4 months for men and 72 years and 8 months for women).

According to the 2015 World Health Organization (WHO) data, global life expectancy at birth in 2015 was 71.4 years. Women on average live longer than men across all major regions and this gap (4.5 years in 1990) remains almost the same by 2015 (4.6). Global average life expectancy however has increased by five years between 2000 and 2015, which is 'the fastest increase since the 1960s'.[4]

Year	1990	2000	2007	2015
Males	62	64	66	69.1
Females	66	68	70	73.8

TABLE 6.1 World Health Organization global life expectancy

There are several implications of living longer; one in particular is retirement. Statutory retirement at 65 and the state pension were introduced when the average length of life was around 50. Since then, and due to tough economic times, countries like France are extending the retirement/pension age as their population grows older. As the average length of life is now around 80, the post-retirement period may occupy a quarter of our life. Possible solutions to the retirement paradox have included (adapted from Boniwell, 2008):

- creating age-friendly work environments and valuing diversity;
- continuing career development and introducing phased retirement schemes; enhancing and enabling a better work–life balance before retirement.

Any way we look at it, the human race is living longer and the majority of us can look forward to a long and healthy old age. Our chances of extended physical and mental health can be further improved by the lifestyle choices we make.

Ageing well

There are several negative myths about the ageing process which lead society to begrudge and fear this inevitable and natural process (Lupien and Wan, 2004). Two of the most important myths include a) loss of neurons and b) irreversible deterioration of cognitive abilities. However, this is certainly not the case. Modifying lifestyle habits can prevent the deterioration of cognitive functioning. Numerous studies have found that higher levels of physical, mental or social activity reduce risk of cognitive impairment or dementia five or more years later. Furthermore, research has found links between age of dementia onset and strength of social ties.

Think about it…

What do you think are the key ingredients for healthy ageing? How important do you rate:

- diet
- exercise;
- genetics;
- family environment;
- wealth?

How to age 'healthily'

From a longitudinal study spanning several decades, Valliant and his colleagues discovered six factors that *do not* predict healthy ageing (Vaillant, 2004):

1 Ancestral longevity.
2 Cholesterol level at 50.

3 Parental social class.

4 Warm childhood environment (stability of parental marriage, parental death in childhood, family cohesion).

5 Stable childhood temperament (rated by parents).

6 Stress.

These findings were in direct contradiction of what research believed to be major determinants of whether or not a person aged healthily. Interestingly, factors that did predict healthy ageing (Vaillant, 2004) included:

1 Not being a heavy smoker or stopping smoking young (by about the age of 45).

2 Mature adaptive defences.

3 Absence of alcohol abuse (moderate drinking is perfectly fine).

4 Healthy weight.

5 Stable marriage.

6 Exercise (burning more than 500 kilocalories per week).

7 Years of education (the more, the better).

The good news is that the list of predictive healthy ageing factors includes many aspects that are under our own control. Inspired by the work of George Vaillant's *Aging Well* work, Lisa Allred highlights several positive actions for growing old with grace (Allred, 2015):

1 Caring about others and remaining open to new ideas.

2 Showing cheerful tolerance of the indignities of old age.

3 Maintaining hope.

4 Maintaining a sense of humor and capacity for play.

5 Taking sustenance from past accomplishments while remaining curious and continuing to learn from the next generation.

6 Maintaining contact and intimacy with old friends.

Benefits of ageing

One major benefit of ageing is the significant reduction in depressive episodes and anxiety disorders, with the prevalence of common mental disorders dropping around statutory retirement age (Carstensen and Charles, 2002; Vaillant, 2004). Older adults tend to experience fewer negative emotions but a similar number of positive emotions and develop greater emotional complexity (e.g. joy and sadness can be intermixed at the same moment). Studies show that with age come more contentment and the formation of deeper and closer bonds with people, thereby deriving more satisfaction from relationships. Similar to

PTG, time becomes more meaningful, and older people select contacts more carefully and strategically. Older people tend to have an intact memory for emotionally important material and an increased ability to see interpersonal problems from multiple perspectives.

So in order to engage in successful ageing, Lupien and Wan (2004) offer several tips for successful ageing. We should: 1) engage with life and maintain activities that are personally meaningful to us; 2) create environments where we are able to feel in control and able to make choices; 3) maintain a positive attitude (associated with good memory, longevity, good health, well-being and a will to live); and 4) always believe that we can keep learning and remember. See also Ardelt et al.'s (2018) study which explores the complementary intersections between growth, adjustment and sense of accomplishment across life, and wisdom and well-being in old age. For instance, their findings show that 'openness to experiences in early adulthood predicted wisdom 60 years later, whereas greater emotional stability and extraversion predicted subjective well-being' (2018: 1514).

STEREOTYPES

Becca Levy and colleagues at Yale University have conducted a series of experiments comparing the effects of positive and negative age stereotypes on memory, numerical ability, self-confidence and cardiovascular responses to stress (Levy, 2009). They used positive (wise, astute, enlightened, sage) and negative (confused, dying, dependent, senile) age stereotype words for subliminal priming. Results showed that stereotypes exerted a powerful effect on performance and the attitudes of older adults, whereby negative stereotypes impaired capability, confidence and recovery from stress and positive stereotypes improve memory, numerical ability, confidence and the will to live. Levy (1996) concluded that positive stereotypes minimize the adverse physiological effects of stress in older adults, while having no effect on the performance or attitudes of young adults.

See Levy (1996) for the original article.

Living longer

Adopting positive attitudes has been linked to increase in longevity, such that positive self-perceptions held at 50 years of age can add up to 7.5 years of life (Levy et al., 2002) regardless of gender, socioeconomic status, loneliness and health. In addition, the will to live is an important influence on longevity.

In conclusion, people are living longer, healthier, more productive lives and social structures and social attitudes lag behind the new realities of ageing.

Thus, research shows that negative age stereotypes are outdated and dangerous, impairing performance, confidence and physiological functions on the receiver, thereby reinforcing negative stereotypes. Positive attitudes to ageing reflect the new reality and reinforce health and capability. Encouraging positive attitudes is a matter of urgency as is communicating the benefits of age and the ways of improving functioning through exercise and activity can all contribute to creating a positive ageing culture.

Chapter Summary

Reflecting on the learning objectives the reader would have acquired knowledge about the concept of resilience, PTG and positive ageing. In summary:

- A traumatic experience tends to be *out of the ordinary* and demarcates an intense felt sense of *before and after*.
- The three main psychological responses to a traumatic event are: resistance, recovery and reconfiguration.
- The reconfiguration form of resilience shares similarities with the concept of PTG. It occasions transformations beyond simply maintaining or returning to base-line functioning.
- Resilience is a complex concept, defined in several ways. It is both capacity and process of engendering an adaptive response with multiple positive outcomes.
- Resilience (the returning to 'normal' functioning) is often accompanied by a potentiality for growth and even thriving following an adverse event. Although perhaps undetected, it tends to involve degrees of existentially embedded confrontation with the freedom to choose manifested in a shift of perspective and reframing of 'suffering'.
- Sense of coherence is important for well-being. The more our experiences are characterized by consistency, participation in shaping outcome and balance of stimuli (rather than overload or underload), the more we are likely to see the world as coherent.
- There are five main components within PTG: personal strength; relating to others; appreciation for life; new possibilities; and spiritual change.
- Wisdom can be seen as one of the final stages of personality development. However, it has little to do with age.
- The human race is getting older, but we can enhance well-being by positive ageing.

Suggested Resources

www.youtube.com/watch?v=uwg4Lr7o2fQ
Recording of George E. Vaillant's lecture 'Happiness is the cart: love is the horse'. Published on 12 May 2015.

www.brainpickings.org/2014/10/15/nietzsche-on-difficulty/
Blog by Maria Popova on Friedrich Nietzsche exploring 'Why a Fulfilling Life Requires Embracing Rather than Running from Difficulty'. Published on 15 October 2010.

www.youtube.com/watch?v=l0q2F7axxsM
Death and Existentialism – video of interview Irvin Yalom. Prometheus Unchained. Published on 20 January 2014. Existential Psychotherapist Irvin Yalom discusses existence, states of mind and key principles of existentialism in general and in relation to 'change/transcendence' in existential psychotherapy in particular. Yalom is also the author of numerous books of therapy tales (*Love's Executioner* and *Momma and the Meaning of Life*) and teaching novels (such as *When Nietzsche Wept* and *The Schopenhauer Cure*).

www.thepositiveencourager.global/george-vaillants-work-on-positive-aging-3/
The Positive Encourager website. A range of useful and interesting resources to encourage the application of positive psychology to everyday life organized by Mike Pegg, the founder of *The Positive Encourager* website.

Further questions for the reader

1 When it comes to resilience interventions, whom should we be targeting? Children or adults? Vulnerable populations or 'normal' functioning population?

2 What do you think of Nietzsche's paraphrase?

3 What do you think about PTG? Is it 'real'? Does it matter?

4 Are you persuaded by the view that existential philosophy is unavoidably connected with and strengthens the endeavours of positive psychology?

5 How do you intend to 'age well'?

Personal Development Interventions

1 Expressive writing

As demonstrated by the powerful work on expressive writing by Texan Professor James Pennebaker (1997; 2004), you can try, if you feel you are ready, to engage in expressive writing. Pennebaker has shown that writing can organize thoughts and emotions and help find meaning in tragic experiences. If you have experienced an adversity, and would like to try the following exercise, then please do so. However, if the tragedy is too raw, then you are advised to wait until you are emotionally ready to take part.

You are asked to choose and then write about a painful, distressing experience in detail. Please take the next 15 to 30 minutes to write anything about this specific traumatic experience. You are then asked to continue for three consecutive days. You may choose to write about the same experience or another one if you wish.

Measurement Tools

Changes in Outlook Questionnaire (CiOQ)

(Joseph et al., 1993)

Directions

Below are printed some statements about your current thoughts and feelings following the event you described above. Please read each one and indicate, by circling one of the numbers beside each statement, how much you agree or disagree with it at the present time using the following scale.

1	2	3	4	5	6
Strongly disagree	Disagree a little	Disagree	Agree a little	Agree	Strongly agree

	1	2	3	4	5	6
1. I don't look forward to the future anymore	1	2	3	4	5	6
2. My life has no meaning anymore	1	2	3	4	5	6
3. I no longer feel able to cope with things	1	2	3	4	5	6

4. I don't take life for granted anymore	1	2	3	4	5	6
5. I value my relationships much more now	1	2	3	4	5	6
6. I feel more experienced about life now	1	2	3	4	5	6
7. I do not worry about death at all anymore	1	2	3	4	5	6
8. I live everyday to the full now	1	2	3	4	5	6
9. I fear death very much now	1	2	3	4	5	6
10. I look upon each day as a bonus	1	2	3	4	5	6
11. I feel as if something bad is just waiting around the corner to happen	1	2	3	4	5	6
12. I am a more understanding and tolerant person now	1	2	3	4	5	6
13. I have a greater faith in human nature now	1	2	3	4	5	6
14. I no longer take people or things for granted	1	2	3	4	5	6
15. I desperately wish I could turn back the clock to before it happened	1	2	3	4	5	6
16. I sometimes think it's not worth being a good person	1	2	3	4	5	6
17. I have very little trust in other people now	1	2	3	4	5	6
18. I feel very much as if I'm in limbo	1	2	3	4	5	6
19. I have very little trust in myself now	1	2	3	4	5	6
20. I feel harder towards other people	1	2	3	4	5	6
21. I am less tolerant of others now	1	2	3	4	5	6
22. I am much less able to communicate with other people	1	2	3	4	5	6
23. I value other people more now	1	2	3	4	5	6
24. I am more determined to succeed in life now	1	2	3	4	5	6
25. Nothing makes me happy anymore	1	2	3	4	5	6
26. I feel as if I'm dead from the neck downwards	1	2	3	4	5	6

Scoring

The scale is simply a summative score. Please reverse score the following items: 1, 2, 3, 4, 9, 11, 16, 17, 18, 19, 20, 21, 22, 25, 26

Interpretation

The range of scores fall from 26–150, with a higher number indicating greater levels of change.

▶ | **Review**

Currently the CiOQ and the PTGI are the most used tools within PTG research. The CiOQ is a retrospective self-report measurement tool that assesses two dimensions of both positive and negative change following trauma. The measurement tools and methodologies for assessing PTG have come under scrutiny in the past few years (Ford et al., 2008) and the field must create less fallible modes of inquiry (Linley and Joseph, 2009).

Notes

1 Post-traumatic stress disorder is characterized as the hyper-arousal of the autonomic nervous system where individuals are exposed to constant re-experiencing of the trauma and the need to avoid all things associated with trauma (Rothschild, 2000).
2 For the full 21-item PTGI scale, please contact the original authors.
3 https://en.wikipedia.org/wiki/List_of_countries_by_life_expectancy
4 www.who.int.

CHAPTER 7

Values, Motivation and Goal Theories

❖ LEARNING OBJECTIVES

This chapter focuses on the relevance of motivation and goal theories for understanding optimal adjustment and well-being. This includes, for example, differences in well-being between people who are intrinsically versus extrinsically motivated. Some of these researchers have examined whether it is psychologically better to strive for wealth and fame versus meaning and personal growth. We will also reflect upon the role of values and time perspectives in motivation and goal achievement.

Topics include:

- The importance of goals and goal setting.
- The role that values play in our decision-making.
- Intrinsic versus extrinsic motivation theories.
- Self-determination theory SDT continuum.
- Psychological needs (autonomy, competence and relatedness).
- Time perspective and time use.

MOCK ESSAY QUESTIONS

1 Critically discuss the importance of psychological need satisfaction for intrinsic motivation.

2 Discuss the contribution of SDT to our understanding of human motivation.

3 Drawing on available research evidence, compare and contrast different time perspective profiles with reference to well-being (broadly defined).

Goals

Goal-theorists argue that human subjective well-being cannot be explained purely in terms of either objective external conditions or stable internal traits. They claim that it depends on the human ability to reflect, to choose a direction in life, to form intentions and to direct oneself towards a certain path or goal (Schmuck, 2001).

Life goals (also called core goals, personal striving, personal projects, life tasks, future aspiration) are motivational objectives by which we direct our lives. They are deemed long-term goals as they direct someone's life for an extended period of time. When we consciously attempt to understand our goals, why we are pursuing them and if they match our values, we can enhance our well-being (Sheldon et al., 2010).

Goals and making lists of short-term and life goals are important for our well-being and even daily survival (Cantor and Sanderson, 1999). People make lists for many reasons; however research has shown that goals are important for several reasons. First of all, goals give us a sense of purpose, a reason for being. We would be lost without goals. It is also the actual progression towards the goal, and not necessarily the attainment of the goal that creates well-being (the journey not the destination). Furthermore, goals add structure and meaning to our daily life, helping us learn how to manage our time. Thus, as we go through our day, and meet smaller sub-goals, we can enhance our self-esteem and self-efficacy (Lyubomirsky, 2008). For example, people with aspirations and dreams that are in progress or achievable and are personally meaningful are happier than those that do not have them.

Within *goal theory*, there are two research traditions: 1) focus on the process of goal pursuit (how well an individual is doing) and 2) focus on the content and quality of life goals (what and why). The process of goal pursuit was discussed in Chapter 2 (linked with positive emotions) therefore we will now focus on the second element of goal theory.

Content-related goal theories focus on the following aspects of goals:

- *What* goals are pursued, for example personal growth or money? Love or attractiveness?
- *Why* goals are pursued, for example because I want to or because I have to?
- *How congruent* are one's activities with their values, for example value-as-a-moderator model?

What goals are descended from Fromm's (1976) 'having orientation' (obtaining wealth and status) versus 'being orientation' (self-actualization). Other researchers have also defined the same concepts in several ways, for example: self-focused versus others-focused goals (Salmela-Aro et al., 2001); extrinsic (financial success, image, fame) versus intrinsic aspirations (personal growth, relationships, community involvement (Kasser and Ryan, 2001); self-enhancement versus materialist values (Schmuck, 2001).

Think about it…

Do you have a 'bucket list'? These tend to be lists that are done under the assumption that there is a race against death. This could be a death that is imminent or a 'to-do list' before you die. Either way, there is an implicit challenge against time and mortality. Furthermore, 'bucket lists' or 'life lists' can be lists that are set 'to do' before a specific or momentous change in a person's life (e.g. turning 50, getting married, having a baby). Again, there is a challenge to achieve against the clock. Take a moment to reflect and write your own bucket list.

Remember, goals are varied, not all goals are equal, and the kinds of goals that aid happiness (Lyubomirsky et al., 2005b; Sheldon and Lyubomirsky, 2007) tend to be:

- *Intrinsic* (do it for the sake of doing it) versus *extrinsic* (do it for the sake of something else. Feel driven by something other than pure motivation, e.g. work and money). If we engage with and enhance intrinsic motivation, we can become more authentic and self-fulfilled (Deci and Ryan, 2000; Schmuck et al., 2000).
- *Authentic/self-concordant:* match our values which are our deep-set beliefs that can change and they form the basis of why we do what we do. Values help us prioritize. Value as a moderator model: not the content but how the congruence between the person values and their goals (Oishi et al., 1999).
- *Approach oriented*: do something rather than avoid something.
- *Harmonious*: Sometimes goals can be conflicting – try to maintain harmonious goals that compliment rather than contradict each other (Oishi and Diener, 2001).

- *Flexible and appropriate*: change with age and time.
- *Activity goals*: joining a club, volunteering, new experience and new opportunities.

Also goals are linked with *challenge*. When challenges match our skill levels or just push/stretch us a little beyond what we are used to, we can enter into the psychological domain of flow. Flow is the total absorption in the task that leads to an engaged life and enhanced positive emotions (see Chapter 4 for more about flow).

So when making a life list we need to choose wisely and make sure the list includes all the above. If we stay flexible we will be open to more opportunities.

Motivation and self-determination theory

Self-determination theory (SDT) is a positive psychology theory of motivation which posits that humans strive to be self-governed, where their behaviour is 'volitional, intentional and self-caused or self-initiated' (Wehmeyer and Little, 2009: 869). SDT is the most recognized motivation theory today (Fenouillet, 2016). Originally, Ryan and Deci wanted to understand the conditions that promote intrinsic motivation. Over the decades, they concluded that the social environment has a powerful influence in promoting intrinsically healthy, self-determined development and satisfying our three basic needs: autonomy, relatedness and competence. When intrinsically motivated, people *want* to engage in the activity; they need no external prompts, promises or threats to initiate action. Being intrinsically motivated also enhances well-being, engagement and success. Extrinsic actions, on the other hand, offer a reward separable from the behaviour itself.

Think about it...

In general, are your goals more extrinsic versus intrinsically based? Does it depend on the goal? Write down your current goals and reflect on whether you are striving for intrinsic versus extrinsic rewards.

We cannot be intrinsically motivated all the time; we cannot sustain action at all times based on intrinsic motivation alone. What happens then? Ryan and Deci's self-determination continuum (see Figure 7.1) tackles this conundrum, proposing six types of motivations applicable in the quest for becoming self-determined. The first type is *amotivation* – this is applicable when an individual has absolutely no motivation to do what is asked and will most likely not do it. *External regulation* is a type of motivation resourced and mediated by external forces; under these conditions an individual will most likely do what is asked because someone is 'making them do it'. *Introjected regulation* occurs when someone is motivated to do something based on guilt and other similar types of emotions. This is more an internalized 'ought to, should do' rather than a 'want to' type of motivation.

Identified regulation marks the starting point for increasing self-determination. This is when an individual is motivated by the knowledge that the goal is personally meaningful and valuable. The actions are carried out because the person recognizes that it is in their best interest. *Integrated regulation* is evident when an individual engages with a goal that they find consistent with who they are, yet there is still some outcome at the end. Finally, *intrinsic regulation* is when someone engages in a goal or activity that is fully intrinsic and done because it is interesting in itself. Deci and Ryan (2000) argue that although we can't be intrinsically motivated all the time, the further to the right end of the continuum we are, the greater levels of autonomy we will begin to feel.

Let us apply this continuum to work, in order to make better sense of it. Motivation in work is determined by circumstances. The individual may be working without having any reasons to either continue or to stop. When externally motivated, the person works in order to earn money and satisfy his basic physical needs – for food, shelter, and so on. Introjected regulation means the person perceives their job as an obligation, in order to keep a good image of themselves (as a good head of the family, for example) or not feel ashamed. With identified motivation, work is seen as a career progression towards important and personally chosen goals. Integrated motivation means the work is perceived as a calling, a chance to contribute something to life. Finally, intrinsic motivation simply means a person loves what they do, just because.

Think about it...

What activities do you have to do that you feel are governed by extrinsic motivation?

In order to enhance your intrinsic motivation, and move towards achieving integrated regulation, try to enhance your autonomy, competence or related-ness. For example, if your activity is studying, looking at the entire textbook can be daunting. Separate it into sections, creating smaller sub-goals. Each time you finish a section, and achieve your sub-goal, you will move towards building your levels of competence and thus move towards becoming more intrinsically motivated.

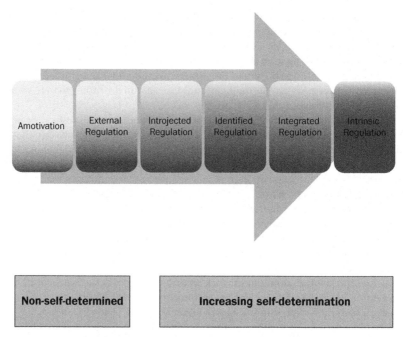

FIGURE 7.1 The process of organismic integration

Building self-determination

There are several benefits of promoting autonomous versus controlled behaviour. For example, actions that are autonomous and thereby have an internal locus of causality have been found to promote greater creativity; cognitive flexibility and depth of processing; higher self-esteem; enhanced positive emotions; satisfaction and trust as well as physical and psychological well-being (see Deci et al., 1989). Furthermore, people who perceive their actions as autonomously regulated tend to enjoy and achieve higher levels of satisfaction from school, increased behavioural persistence, effective performance, and better mental and physical health (Black and Deci, 2000; Deci and Ryan, 2000).

Individuals who report as having identified regulation in religious attendance, relationship status, weight loss and addiction programmes, are associated with better mental health, better adjustment, better attendance, better weight loss maintenance and increased positive affect. Not surprisingly, external and introjected motivation reduced well-being and success in all three cases (Ryan et al., 1995; Williams et al., 1996).

Children of parents who use a controlling versus autonomy-supportive parenting style have been found to be less likely to be intrinsically interested in play. Researchers propose that controlling parenting styles spoil children's fun and interest in play. Ultimately, a lack of basic need satisfaction (e.g. cold, controlling parenting) can lead to the development of extrinsic need substitutes. Adolescents with mothers who were rated as cold and non-nurturing were more oriented towards compensatory aspirations (wealth) and the emotional coldness of mother at the age of 4 has been linked to predicted extrinsic aspirations 12 years later (Kasser et al., 1995).

Think about it...

Intrinsically motivated behaviours have internal locus of causality (feeling self-determined). So what would happen if we were to introduce extrinsic rewards for the same activity? For example, what if we said that we would give you £5 for reading the rest of this chapter,[1] when you already intrinsically enjoy reading it? Research has found that the activity would feel controlled by external rewards, your intrinsic motivation would decrease and the activity would be pursued less when the reward is withdrawn. The implication of this is: don't turn play into work by conveying that the activity should only be done for external rewards.

The quickest way to undermine motivation is to threaten negative consequences, conduct surveillance and evaluation of performance and introduce deadlines. But wait a minute... does not this look like the entire education system? Unfortunately, it does. However, if parents, teachers and other figures of authority want to facilitate intrinsic motivation they can adopt several methods of practice. First of all, providing choice is an excellent way to engage the fundamental need of autonomy. Secondly, they can provide positive informational feedback that acknowledges competence and is not viewed as controlling. Finally, fostering secure relatedness provides a secure base of a warm/caring relationship that encourages safe exploration of the environment.

Self-determination can be enhanced by supporting autonomy, competence and relatedness needs. Here is the summary of relevant principles informed by research (see Ryan and Deci, 2017; Deci et al., 2017):

Supporting autonomy needs:

- Provide reasonable choices.
- Renounce to the 'reward-and-punishment' approach.
- Introduce rules and make requests, if necessary and *always* clarify the reasons or values used to establish them.

- Take the perspective of others, listening to and respecting different opinions and points of view.
- Support initiative, give freedom for improvization.
- Replace the language of control by language of autonomy: for example 'it must be done', 'you should' ' to 'it would be good if …'

Supporting competence needs:

- Provide tasks of optimal difficulty.
- Provide suggestions and support, address issues.
- Give informative, non-negative feedback.
- Compliment successes.
- Suggest mastery goals, not performance-based goals.

Supporting relational needs:

- Invest time.
- Give attention.
- Take care of others.
- Do things together.

Values

We will now shift to look at congruence of values and goal pursuit in the attainment of well-being. Values are different from needs in that they are ideas that are dear to us and that implicitly or explicitly govern our lives. Similar to emotions, researchers have identified a list of 10 universal values (Schwartz, 1994). This list was updated by Schwartz et al. in 2012 to include:

- Power – dominance
- Power – resources
- Achievement
- Hedonism
- Stimulation
- Self-direction – thought
- Self-direction – action
- Universalism – concern
- Universalism – nature
- Universalism – tolerance
- Benevolence – dependability
- Benevolence – caring

- Tradition
- Conformity – rules
- Conformity – interpersonal
- Security – personal
- Security – societal
- Face
- Humility

The value-as-a-moderator model predicts that people gain a sense of satisfaction out of activities and goals congruent with their values (Oishi et al., 1999). Furthermore, research suggests that when people engage in activities that are congruent with their goals, they will derive a sense of satisfaction from their day, regardless of whether or not they are extrinsic values (such as power) or intrinsic values (e.g. benevolence, self-direction). People exhibit more intense positive and negative affect in response to daily events, if these events are coherent with their personal strivings (Oishi et al., 1999) .

Finally, Sheldon and Kasser (1995) have researched whether or not *congruence* and *coherence* are essential for personality integration. *Vertical coherence* refers to the consistency between lower and higher levels of goals. *Horizontal coherence* involves consistency between goals at the same level. Lastly, *Congruence* refers to the pursuit of goals for self-determined reasons and through intrinsic motivation. Both congruence and vertical coherence have emerged as predictors of various well-being outcomes. Thus, research shows that we must try to maintain harmonious goals that compliment rather than contradict each other (Oishi and Diener, 2001).

Failing to reach our goals

If the pursuit of goals is so fundamental for well-being, why do people so often fail to pursue goals that are important to them? There are many proposed reasons for this. Many times it is simply due to logistical reasons, as we need to put our effort into less important, but more immediate goals. Furthermore, finding and maintain that passion and desire can be difficult over sustained periods of time, thus sometimes we just 'run out of steam'. Finally, research has shown that when people follow 'the wrong goals' (e.g. money, fame and other extrinsic goals), people tend to disengage with them sooner and give up. Thus, choosing the right goals, maintaining passion (by reminding ourselves of the immediate drudgery's importance for future success) and making time for our valued goals are important for successful outcomes and well-being. Interestingly, writing goals down and discussing them with others makes us more likely to commit (Lyubomirsky, 2008).

The next section will focus on an important influence on goal attainment and motivation: *time*. In addition, the next section will explain how the perspective we take on time can have a massive impact on our overall well-being.

Time

Time. It is the one thing that we can't buy, make or sell and in today's world, we often come across the problem of time crunch. The area of 'time research' focuses on *time perspective* (TP) and time use as important contributors to well-being.

According to philosophers, time can be seen as objective or subjective: time as an objective phenomenon (geographical, 'clock' time) versus time as an internal phenomenon (psychological time, time as it is processed by the human mind, subjective time, the inner time of the mind, lived time). When talking about time research, two substantial lines of research can be contrasted: approaching time use objectively, that is through calculating daily time expenditure, and subjectively, that is relying on a person's own perception of their time use. While the so-called objective time use research, such as time diary studies widely used in social science, provide multiple insights, other empirical examples demonstrate that the focus solely on objective time and its expenditure, rather than subjective time, gives an insufficient representation of a) objective outcomes of activities (e.g. achievement of a desired outcome); b) psychological states; c) the meaning people assign to the ways they spend their time; and d) the relationship of time use with constructs such as well-being (Boniwell, 2009). Subjective time use domain deals with what people think and feel about their time use (whether they experience time pressure, time anxiety, feeling in control, satisfied or dissatisfied with their time), not only with what they actually do, and includes constructs such as time affluence, subjective time use, time perspective, time personality and time urgency. *Time perspective* is defined as an individual's cognitive way of relating to the psychological concepts of past, present and future. Thus, *subjective time use* is a person's own perceived representation of their own time use. Individuals are proposed to have a *time personality* with dimensions including punctuality, planning, leisure-time awareness, impatience and time congruity. *Time urgency* refers to time-urgent individuals who are more time-aware and chronically hurried, trying to fulfil their ambitions, quite efficient, prioritize tasks and use deadlines as measures of time remaining (Boniwell, 2008).

A TP can also be thought of as a preferential direction of an individual's thoughts towards the past, present or future, which exerts a dynamic influence on their experience, motivation, thinking and several aspects of behaviour (De Volder, 1979). The formation of a TP is influenced by many factors learned in the process of socialization, including cultural and religious background, education, belonging to particular social class and family modelling.

Although situational forces, such as inflation, being on vacation or under survival stresses, can affect TP, it can also be seen as a relatively stable dispositional characteristic. Zimbardo's theory of time perspective proposes that there are five factors:

1 *Future TP*. This is when an individual tends to work for future rewards, engages in delayed gratification and is often linked with success. A focus on the future is fundamental to well-being and positive functioning (see Boniwell, 2008). Bohart (1993) proposes that the ability of humans to be future oriented is fundamental for human development, because it allows the sense of possibility, of being agentic, of taking responsibility and of making choices. Furthermore, future time perspective, and especially possession of long-term goals, positively correlated with virtually all aspects of well-being, especially a meaningful life, social self-efficacy, and realism/persistence (Zaleski et al., 2001).

2 *Present hedonistic TP*. This is when an individual exhibits little concern for the consequences of their actions. Their behaviour is determined by physical needs, emotions, strong situational stimuli and social input. This TP is at risk of giving in to temptations, leading to addictions, accidents and injuries, and academic and career failure.

3 *Present fatalistic TP*. This is when an individual is characteristically hopeless, with a belief that outside forces control one's life (e.g. spiritual or governmental forces).

4 *Past positive TP*. This is when an individual has a warm, pleasurable, often sentimental and nostalgic view of their past. They maintain relationships with family and friends, continue traditions and history and hold a continuity of self over time. Furthermore, past-positive TP has been linked to higher levels of meaning and satisfaction with life (Foret et al., 2004).

5 *Past negative TP*. This is when an individual focuses on previous personal experiences that were aversive or noxious.

Researchers have found that there is a strong tie between the TP we adopt and our well-being. For example TP has been found to be related to many attitudes, values and status variables, such as: educational achievement, health, sleep and dreaming patterns and romantic partner choices. Furthermore, TP is indicative of choice of food, health choices, parental marital state, desire to spend time with friends and perceived time pressure (Zimbardo and Boyd, 1999). Time perspective is also predictive for a wide range of behaviours, including risky driving, delinquency and sexual behaviours (Zimbardo et al., 1997) as well as substance abuse of beer, alcohol and drugs (Keough et al., 1999).

Time perspective even predicts the extent to which unemployed people living in shelters use their time constructively to seek jobs (future-oriented), or waste time watching TV and engaging in other non-instrumental activities and avoidant coping strategies (present-oriented) (Epel et al., 1999). Researchers have found significantly shorter time horizons in pathological versus social gamblers (Hodgins and Engel, 2002).

Time perspective is influenced by cultural biases. Protestant nations tend to be more future-oriented than Catholic nations, and that is correlated with gross national product indices. Within countries, those living in southern regions tend to be more present-oriented than those in northern regions. Cultures with more individualistic focus tend to be more future-oriented than do those emphasizing collectivism. Western ways of life have become predominantly goal-focused and future-oriented.

Balanced time perspective

As there are problems associated with an excessive orientation towards any one perspective, a balanced time perspective (BTP) has been proposed as the ideal mode of functioning. A blend of temporal orientations can be considered as the most adaptive, depending on external circumstances and optimal in terms of psychological and physiological health. The construct of BTP was initially proposed by Zimbardo and Boyd (1999) at the time of the introduction of the final version of Zimbardo Time Perspective Inventory (ZTPI): 'In an optimally balanced time perspective, the past, present, and future components blend and flexibly engage, depending on a situation's demands and our needs and values' (Zimbardo, 2002: 62).

People with a balanced TP are capable of operating in a temporal mode appropriate to the situation in which they find themselves. When they spend time with their families and friends, they are fully with them and value the opportunity to share a common past. When they take a day off work, they get involved in recreation rather than feel guilty about the work they haven't done. However, when working and studying, they may well put on their more appropriate future TP hat and work more productively. Indeed, when work is to be done and valued, the balanced TP person may get into the flow of enjoying being productive and creative – a present-hedonistic state for a future-focused activity. That is when work becomes play as the worker becomes engaged with the process of the activity and not only with a focus on the product of their labours.

Although Zimbardo and Boyd (2008) did not develop any direct indicator of BTP, they proposed an interesting starting point for its empirical operationalizations by formulating a description of an optimal mix of time perspectives. The authors proposed that the optimal TP profile consists of:

- high on past positive TP;
- moderately high on future TP;

- moderately high on present hedonistic TP;
- low on past negative TP;
- low on present fatalistic TP.

Based on these theoretical foundations, several attempts have been made to operationalize the BT construct. Current literature distinguishes between four different approaches to measuring balanced TP: the 33rd percentile cut-off approach (Drake et al., 2008), resulting in selecting about 5 per cent of respondents with a BTP; the cluster analysis approach (Boniwell et al., 2010) resulting in a larger proportion of respondents selected as BTP (10 to 23 per cent); the Deviation from Balanced Time Perspective method (Stolarski et al., 2011; Zhang et al., 2013) resulting in a linear and normally distributed variable; and a combined approach proposed by Wiberg et al. (2012), also confirming the BTP as a normally distributed trait.

Individuals with a BTP have been shown to be happier on both hedonic and eudaimonic indicators, suggesting that learning to achieve a BTP may be one of the keys to unlocking personal happiness (Boniwell et al., 2010). It is easy to understand why. Operating in past-positive and present-hedonistic modes enhances individuals' chances of developing happy personal relationships, which is a key factor in enhancing their well-being, according to research on exceptionally happy people. Also future TP shows some positive associations with life satisfaction, as well as optimism, hope and internal locus of control.

Think about it...

Try to understand your TP profile and evaluate whether your dominant TP is serving you well. Remember a future TP does not have all the answers. Make sure you pay attention to past negative TP. Try to work on the development of a balanced TP.

Time use and time management

We know that how we perceive time can have an influence on our overall well-being; however, does this hold the same for how we manage and use our time? There is no apparent relationship between objective time use (amount of time) and global well-being; however there is a relationship between activity time allocation and experienced happiness, and a relationship between satisfaction with time use and well-being. While higher income is associated with higher life satisfaction, it is not related to happiness in the moment, since people with greater income tend to devote relatively more time to work, commuting, compulsory non-work activities (shopping and childcare), and active leisure, and less of their time to passive leisure pursuits. Work/commute and compulsory activities are associated with higher tension and stress.

In 2007, the very first review of empirically based time management literature looked at 35 papers between 1954 and 2005 on time management, time use, time and structuring on academic and work performance (Claessens et al., 2007). The effects of time management programmes (based on eight studies) showed mixed results with regard to self-reported engagement in time management behaviours and performance improvement; however, time management programmes provided positive supervisor ratings in one study and increases in feelings of control of time. The effects of time management (self-perceptions) was also found to improve college grades but had no effect on job performance.

Think about it...

Focus on psychological aspects of time use (congruence, responsibility, anxiety) but don't get overly enthusiastic about time management tricks (planning, clearing, organizers). Remember, knowing *why* can make an activity worth while. It's important to achieve something on a daily basis.

Chapter Summary

Reflecting on the learning objectives the reader should now understand the concepts of goals, motivation and values. More specifically, they should know:

- Goals are important to our sense of well-being.
- It is the what, why and congruence of these goals that can enhance or inhibit our well-being.
- Motivation to continue goals must be developed into intrinsically motivated goals to enhance well-being.
- Self-determination theory employs the organismic integration model, which suggests that as we move from one end of the scale to the other, we become more self-determined and authentic.
- Time perspective research provides useful pointers for a well-functioning life.

Suggested Resources

www.youtube.com/watch?v=A3oIiH7BLmg
The RSA. Published on 24 May 2010. Philip Zimbardo explains how our individual perspectives of time affect our work, health and well-being.

www.worldvaluessurvey.org/
This is the most comprehensive, up-to-date survey regarding value changes across the globe. The World Value Survey (WVS) is currently undertaking new research.

www.thetimeparadox.com/
Visit The Time Paradox website to complete your Zimbardo Time Perspective Inventory and get the results in real time. You may also want to read the associated book on the mysteries of time.

Further questions for the reader

1 What makes you achieve your goals? Do you have any that you would like to achieve in the next month? Year? Five years?

2 What values do you relate to and why do they influence your daily life and the decisions you make?

3 Are you time-spent? Do you constantly find that you run out of time to finish papers, study or socialize? What are the reasons for this? Where might you be able to save time?

Personal Development Interventions

1 Values

Integrity has been associated with increased levels of happiness (Branden, 1994b). Values and behaviour need to exist in equality for happiness. Make a list of the activities that you find most pleasurable and meaningful – that make you happy. Place beside it how much time you spend per week/month engaging in those activities. Does the maths reflect harmony between your values and your behaviour? Take a look in the mirror – are you living your life the way you really want to?

▶

2 Intrinsic motivation

For the next week, we would like you to try to increase your intrinsic motivation when it comes to studying for exams. Make sure you give yourself as many choices as possible (e.g. when to study, for how long to study for, etc.). Once you've made these choices, reflect on how you feel about them. Do they differ from how other people choose to study? By increasing your choice selection, you will enhance your level of autonomy, thereby hopefully moving towards the self-determined end of the SDT continuum.

Measurement Tools

Self-Determination Scale (SDS)

(Sheldon and Deci, 1995)

Directions

Please read the pairs of statements, one pair at a time, and think about which statement within the pair seems more true to you at this point in your life. Indicate the degree to which statement A feels true, relative to the degree that statement B feels true, on the 5-point scale shown after each pair of statements. If statement A feels completely true and statement B feels completely untrue, the appropriate response would be 1. If the two statements are equally true, the appropriate response would be a 3, and so on.

1. A. I always feel like I choose the things I do.
   B. I sometimes feel that it's not really me choosing the things I do.

   Only A feels true   1   2   3   4   5   **Only B feels true**

2. A. My emotions sometimes seem alien to me.
   B. My emotions always seem to belong to me.

   Only A feels true   1   2   3   4   5   **Only B feels true**

3. A. I choose to do what I have to do.
   B. I do what I have to, but I don't feel like it is really my choice.

   Only A feels true   1   2   3   4   5   **Only B feels true**

4. A. I feel that I am rarely myself.
   B. I feel like I am always completely myself.

   Only A feels true   1   2   3   4   5   **Only B feels true**

▶ 5. A. I do what I do because it interests me.
   B. I do what I do because I have to.

   Only A feels true   1   2   3   4   5   **Only B feels true**

6. A. When I accomplish something, I often feel it wasn't really me who did it.
   B. When I accomplish something, I always feel it's me who did it.

   Only A feels true   1   2   3   4   5   **Only B feels true**

7. A. I am free to do whatever I decide to do.
   B. What I do is often not what I'd choose to do.

   Only A feels true   1   2   3   4   5   **Only B feels true**

8. A. My body sometimes feels like a stranger to me.
   B. My body always feels like me.

   Only A feels true   1   2   3   4   5   **Only B feels true**

9. A. I feel pretty free to do whatever I choose to.
   B. I often do things that I don't choose to do.

   Only A feels true   1   2   3   4   5   **Only B feels true**

10. A. Sometimes I look into the mirror and see a stranger.
    B. When I look into the mirror I see myself.

    Only A feels true   1   2   3   4   5   **Only B feels true**

Scoring

Items 1, 3, 5, 7, 9 need to be reverse scored. Calculate the scores for the Awareness of Self subscale (items 2, 4, 6, 8, 10) and the Perceived Choice subscale (items 1, 3, 5, 7, 9) by averaging the item scores for the five items within each subscale.

Interpretation

The subscales can either be used separately or they can be combined into an overall SDS score. Higher scores indicate a higher level of self-determination.

Review

This scale is a short, easy-to-administer test that assesses self-determination levels within individuals' personalities.

Note

1 Which of course we will not do.

CHAPTER 8

Positive Psychological Interventions

❖ LEARNING OBJECTIVES

Within psychology, theory is just half of the puzzle. We need to know how the topics we research can be used to help people change to become happier, more fulfilled and to flourish. This chapter will review recent research on positive psychology interventions (PPIs) and how we can begin to change our behaviours.

Topics include:

- Mindsets.
- Trans-theoretical model of change.
- Grit and perseverance.
- Self-regulation to keep the change going.

- Evaluating interventions.
- Positive psychology interventions (PPIs).
- Examples of validated interventions.

MOCK ESSAY QUESTIONS

1 'Grit explains academic achievement over and above our IQ.' Discuss.
2 What are some of the concrete interventions by which positive psychologists might try to enhance well-being, and what is the evidence that such procedures are effective?
3 Critically discuss the contribution of the mindset theory to our understanding of change processes.

First comes your set of mind

The reader should think about their role models from childhood, or, even better, their role models now. Chances are these role models were/are someone who has achieved something in an area of life that the reader finds admirable. So how do these people become so good at what they do? Are they born like that? Or do they develop, with hard work, into the achievers we eventually come to know? And, if they develop through hard work, what is it that keeps them going through the difficult times? Researcher Carol Dweck would argue that 'the view you adopt for yourself profoundly affects the way you lead your life' (Dweck, 2006: 6). This view is also known, in the research world, as someone's *mindset*.

Mindset involves how we perceive basic abilities and qualities such as: intelligence, parenting, business, relationships, musicality and creativity. There are two main types of mindsets: the *fixed* and *growth* Mindset. The *fixed mindset* believes that qualities are carved in stone. They are either present naturally or not at all, therefore we are either good at maths or not; we can play sports or we cannot. Things must come naturally to people with a fixed mindset or else they perceive the ability to be out of their grasp. People with a fixed mindset tend to focus more on success as winning and achieving, rather than about developing as a person. People with a *growth mindset*, on the other hand, believe that with experience, effort and engagement, people can grow.

We may find that we have tendencies in different areas and that is normal. For example, we may have a fixed mindset when it comes to maths but hold a growth mindset regarding learning an instrument. Different people may naturally prefer to adopt different mindsets in different contexts. This section of the chapter examines the proposal that adopting a growth mindset can have several beneficial consequences for happiness, satisfaction and performance success in the long run.

Understanding mindsets

So what do these mindsets look like when they are in action? The first difference relates to how each mindset views goals: either *performance-oriented* or *learning-oriented*. Someone with a fixed mindset views goals in terms of a successful outcome. For the fixed mindset, the goal is validation from others and achievement, for it is believed that potential can be measured (e.g. low marks equals not smart). Unfortunately for this mindset, both success and failure cause anxiety since the person now has to keep up the standard they have created and becomes afraid of failure. The growth mindset, on the other hand, focuses on *learning goals*, where the focus is on mastery and competence, and not simply winning. The growth mindset recognizes that scores and marks reflect how people are doing *now* and do not measure a person's potential. People who have a growth mindset have been found to increase their performance and enjoyment of skills and tasks, as well as decrease negative emotion.

Think about it...

Have you ever been hampered by a fixed mindset? Where and when does this usually occur?

Why mindsets matter

So, why does it matter whether we see things through a fixed or growth mindset? Well, researchers argue that when people come up against tough times, the type of mindset they default to will either enable or hinder them towards attaining their desired goal. This process involves how someone's mindset responds to setbacks, views effort in tackling the situation and how the person eventually develops strategies to overcome their difficulties. Let us take a closer look at the fixed mindset.

When a person who harbours a fixed mindset is confronted with a difficult situation, it tends to elicit a 'helpless response'. This means that when faced with failure or challenge, people with a fixed mindset do not pay attention to learning information. They can get depressed, become de-energized and lose self-esteem. They also denigrate their abilities and under-represent past successes and over-represent failures. Ultimately, they explain the cause of events as something stable about them.

In addition, 'effort' is akin to a curse word to the fixed mindset. Those with a fixed mindset view effort as a reflection of low ability, since hard work and effort mean they were never really good at it anyway. Simply put, effort equals a lack of ability. Since the fixed mindset is so against effort, they move on to develop strategies that hinder any progression from their current status. Fixed mindsets continue to use the wrong strategy when faced with a problem. When this eventually does not work, they then disengage from the problem and finally, they give up.

Now let us take a closer look at how the growth mindset responds to adversity or challenging situations. They tend to use a 'mastery response', which enables them to pay attention to learning information. The growth mindset tries out new ways of doing things, as they are not afraid of failing in the process. When faced with tests which are impossible to pass they will factor in other reasons for their lack of success and not blame their ability (e.g. this test was beyond my ability for now). To the growth mindset, effort is a good word. They view effort as a necessary part of success and try harder when faced with a setback. Simply put, effort equals success. Finally, the strategies the growth mindset uses focus on generating other ways of doing things. Thus, if one route does not work they will try others. They tend to think 'outside of the box'. Thus, as we can see, there are several benefits of adopting a growth mindset, especially in the face of challenge and setbacks.

Where do mindsets come from?

Dweck (2006, 2017) argues that mindsets are socially constructed and are therefore learned within the home and classroom environments. The development of mindsets is influenced by the messages we pick up, especially in relation to praise and how we internalize validation and affirmations from other people in general. Praise, as demonstrated by several large experiments, can have a detrimental impact on children. Of course, good feedback is important and constructive criticism is necessary to develop and learn. Praise is not a villain, however – praising for effort and process, rather than outcome, will help the person become more motivated to persevere and ultimately more resilient.

Praise

Mueller and Dweck (1998) performed a succession of six experimental conditions to make one of the strongest cases for the 'perils of praise'. It can get a bit confusing, so try and follow along …

Children in late grade school and kindergarten were given a first series of easy problems to solve. Following completion, children were offered one of three types of praise:

Intelligence praise – 'You must be really smart!'

Process praise – 'You must have worked really hard!'

Factual praise – 'You got 8 out of 10 right. Well done!'

▶

The students were then, on purpose, given a set of much harder problems to solve (beyond their comprehension level). No matter what they scored, they were all told that they got 5 out of 10. The students that were given the *intelligence praise* attributed their failure to the fact that they 'weren't good enough'. They reported that their fun declined significantly, and when asked if they would like to take the games home to practise, their future likelihood to play the game again declined significantly. This was directly in opposition to the results of the *process praise* group. These students attributed their low mark to the fact that they 'didn't work hard enough'. They also reported having the same amount of fun as the first set and were more likely to take the games home with them.

The next stage of the experiment asked all students to choose their next task. They had to choose between one that would challenge them or one that was based on designing not to fail. They were also offered the choice to receive a new set of challenges or to receive a review of where they scored in relation to other students. Finally, they were asked to write to a student in another state and tell them how they did on the problem-solving tasks. As you may already guess, the intelligent praise group chose the problems that were easy, they chose to see where they fit in relation to others, and in the letter task over 40 per cent lied! In the process praise group, they chose their next problem designed on learning more and when they were asked to tell others how they did only 1.3 per cent lied!

The interesting results came when the researchers reviewed the real scores for each group. Remember how we said that the first set was easy. Well most did well on those (all equal at baseline). Of course, the students all did worse on the second set because the problems were for a few levels higher than where they were. However, on the third set, the problems were readjusted to be the same level of difficulty as the first set (easy). Theoretically, they all should have done better. But this didn't happen. The process praise group did significantly better on the easy problem tasks in the third set than the intelligent praise group.

See Mueller and Dweck (1998) for the original article.

In summary, as parents, teachers or any figurehead in a child's life, Dweck and colleagues (1983; 1995) argue that we need to tune into the messages we are sending and praise for strategies, effort and process rather than the final outcome. We can also try to be a role model to others, showing that we are not fixed, but can grow.

Next comes the change

After we have worked through perceptions of abilities, how do people actually change and can they change long term? For any of us who have decided (usually around 1 January) to take on lifestyle change, we will know how hard it is to maintain that alteration.

The first question we need to ask ourselves is whether or not we are actually ready for change. James Prochaska and his colleagues at the University of Rhode Island have done fantastic work in the area of negative behaviour changes. Specifically, they have worked and documented decades of research on how people give up unhelpful behaviours such as smoking, drinking, tanning, unhealthy diets, and so on. Mainly, Prochaska was interested in why and how people change of their own volition, in other words intentional self-changers versus therapy-seeking changers. His work has had a significant impact on addiction research and continues to mount evidence for explaining such complex human behaviour (Prochaska and Velicer, 1996; Prochaska et al., 1994).

Prochaska's transtheoretical model (TTM) of change contains five stages of change:

1 Pre-contemplation
2 Contemplation
3 Preparation
4 Action
5 Maintenance

Within these stages, there are processes of change that can help the person move from one stage to the other. The processes include: consciousness raising, counter conditioning, dramatic relief, environmental re-evaluation, helping relationships reinforcement management, self-liberation, self-re-evaluation, social liberation, and stimulus control.

As the person progresses through the stages, they shift how they think and feel. At first, they consider the costs versus benefits of change, creating a *decisional balance*. The TTM predicts that when in the pre-contemplation stage, the cons are more salient than pros. The decisional balance will be reversed as the person gradually moves through the stages (Prochaska et al., 1994). So how then do we change for good? And is this even possible? Prochaska posits that it takes, on average, five attempts at the model before someone reaches long-term maintenance (termination). Of course, termination means different things for different maladaptive behaviours; however, it is usually the absence of the negative behaviour for six months plus a day (Prochaska and Prochaska, 2009).

Although we recognize that the TTM is not the only model available to help us try to understand behaviour change – for example *theory of reasoned action* (TRA) (Ajzen and Fishbein, 1980) and *theory of planned behaviour* (Ajzen, 1988; 1991) – there is huge support for the TTM model within unhealthy behaviour change research (e.g. smoking, alcohol and dieting).

Keeping the change going

So once we have changed our behaviour, how do we keep it up? There is a family of closely related concepts, a) self-discipline, b) grit and c) self-regulation) that we believe is important for understanding how and why people persevere with lifestyle changes.

Self-discipline

We all know it's good for us, and it's good to have plenty of it, but how often do we work on enhancing self-discipline? Indeed, self-discipline, defined as the ability to choose successfully among conflicting impulses, is frequently the within the bottom five strengths in global polls (Peterson, 2006). Critics have argued that positive psychology offers too readily the ability to give into impulses; that in order to be happy we need to give up some things in life (Van Deurzen, 2009). In response to this, we just have to read the research on grit, self-discipline, delayed gratification and self-regulation (conducted by researchers within the realm of positive psychology), which shows links between these impulse control mechanisms and well-being (see e.g. Duckworth and Steinberg, 2015).

Grit

Grit is defined as perseverance and passion for long-term goals. Perseverance is especially important when we are looking at what is making people happier. In this definition, perseverance accounts for 'the intentional continuation or re-application of effort towards a goal despite a temptation to quit' (Pury, 2009: 678). Thus, a person can persevere in terms of how long they stick at a project or how many times they attempt to change. Research has continued to show that scoring high on assessment tools pertaining to grit can predict final grades, school attendance, test score achievement, selection into competitive high-school programmes, hours doing homework and hours spent watching TV better than IQ in teenagers. In other words, many teenagers do not reach their intellectual potential based on failure to exercise grit and not on their overall intelligence levels (Duckworth and Seligman, 2005, 2006).

Self-regulation

Self-regulation (SR) is the process by which we can seek to have control over thoughts, our feelings and impulses. Scoring high on measurements of SR demonstrates increased flexibility and adaptability to circumstances as it enables people to adjust their actions to a remarkably broad range of social and situational demands. It also allows us to change ourselves to live up to social standards and facilitates our interaction with the outside world (Maddux, 2009).

MARSHMALLOWS

Imagine you are a kid again. You are invited into a room and told to sit down. In front of you is a nice, sweet, fluffy marshmallow just waiting to be eaten. Except there's a catch. The experimenter says that you can either have this one marshmallow now, or wait and receive two. It's up to you. What would you do? Take the one right away, or wait patiently in order to receive a second marshmallow? In the 1970s, Walter Mischel, a professor at Stanford University, found that not many children were able to delay gratification (approximately 30 per cent), as demonstrated by the famous marshmallow experiment. Years later, Michel re-contacted the 650+ participants (then teenagers) and found a link between the children's early ability to resist temptation and success in later life. Specifically, children who were unable to resist the marshmallow (less than 30 seconds) had increased behavioural problems, lower academic achievements and problems maintaining social relationships. On the other hand, those that were able to resist had significantly higher academic achievement scores (SATs). Who knew a marshmallow could tell so much about a person's future!

See Mischel et al. (1989) and Shoda et al. (1990) for the original articles.

So what do we need to attain SR? There are several ingredients needed for the acquisition and maintenance of SR. These include:

- *Standards.* In order to initiate SR, we need clear, well-defined standards. If the standards that we are trying to aspire to are ambiguous, inconsistent or conflicting then we will have severe difficulty in engaging in self-regulation. Carver and Scheier (1998) proposed their feedback loop model to understand goal-directed SR maintenance. First of all, a person performs a test by comparing their current state to the desired standard. If the person falls short of the standard, SR requires initiating some operation to change the self in order to bring it up to what it should be.

- *Monitoring.* A person must be able to monitor and keep track of their progression to the goal, and monitoring must be done in a positive, and not destructive, fashion.

- *Strength/willpower.* SR appears to depend on limited resources that operate like energy and can become temporarily depleted (see ego depletion below). Studies have shown that there may be links to glucose in the blood (the brain's principal source of fuel) as an important component of this resource. Research shows that acts of self-control (as part of our SR system) consume large amounts of glucose, resulting in lower levels in the bloodstream (Gailliot et al., 2007).

- *Motivation.* Above all, even if the standards are clear, monitoring is fully effective and resources are abundant, someone may still fail to self-regulate if they do not care or have no motivation to reach the goal.

Ego depletion

Baumeister, a leading researcher on the topic area, has completed several studies in order to understand the complex behaviour of SR (Baumeister, 2003; Baumeisteret al., 2000). It appears that when people engage in a task that requires effort, and then engage in an SR-depleting exercise, their ability to self-regulate weakens (Vohs et al., 2008). Thus, our capacity to self-regulate is impeded by depletion.

Apart from being aware of it and planning for it, what else can we do to mitigate for the effects of ego depletion? Research shows that SR is actually like a muscle and can be built up like a bicep. The more we work it, the stronger it gets (Baumeister et al., 2006). Performing non-taxing exercises (e.g. keeping food diaries, monitoring posture, following a budget) can help build SR, which then spills over into other areas of our life. Self-regulation is a core capacity; when we use it in one area it is likely to have a domino effect and positively affect other areas such as healthy eating, study habits, chores completion, alcohol, tobacco and caffeine consumption, emotional control and financial budgetary.

Thus, developing grit, engaging in delayed gratification and enhancing self-regulatory practices can have an immense impact on our ability to persevere and achieve our goals. See also Duckworth and Steinberg's (2015) examination of the concept of self-control in a developmental context and their proposals for understanding, cultivating and measuring self-control in children.

Think about it...

How self-regulated are you? Try building up your SR muscles. For the next week, write down everything you spend, to the last penny.

Positive psychology interventions

As with psychology in general, the application of theory is paramount to thoroughly understanding any phenomenon. Over the past few years, the notion of a 'positive intervention' has risen to prominence, as it was discovered that certain intentional actions can be effective in increasing and sustaining happiness and other positive states, as well as in reducing depression and anxiety. The next section of the chapter will focus on these *PPIs* and how they differ from other psychological interventions. We will review some of the mounting major evidence-based interventions and try exercises out along the way.

Definition of PPIs

Postive psychology interventions are best defined as:

> 66 Treatment methods or intentional activities that aim to cultivate positive feelings, behaviours or cognitions … [Moreover] [p]rograms, interventions, or treatments aimed at fixing, remedying, or healing something that is pathological or deficient – as opposed to building strengths – do not fit the definition of a PPI.
> – *(Sin and Lyubomirsky, 2009: 468)* 99

Although this definition appears divisive, it enables researchers to conceptualize the differences between PPIs and *psychology as usual* interventions.

Think about it...

What is YOUR definition of a PPI?
What makes it different from mainstream psychology iInterventions?
Who should PPIs be used with?
When should we employ PPIs?
Can PPIs be delivered online versus face to face? Can online PPIs be effective? If so, when are they effective?[1]

What works (and how do we know it)?

Do mental well-being interventions work? Well yes, actually, and quite significantly so. Sin and Lyubomirsky's (2009) meta-analysis demonstrated that in a sample of 4000+, both normal and depressed populations benefited from participation in PPIs. There were however several important factors for impact. Depression status influenced results, with those reporting higher levels of depression at baseline reporting the greatest impact. Also, as found in other studies, people who self-selected for the studies had higher levels of improved well-being. The age of participants was influential, with the younger experiencing more benefits. Whether the PPIs were delivered in individual or group therapy or self-administered had an impact with individual therapy having greatest impact. Finally, PPIs that were longer than four weeks, but shorter than 12, tended to have better results.

time out

Qualitatively evaluating PPIs

Evaluating PPIs is a very complex, time-consuming and expensive endeavour. There is also a very large difference between evaluating a large-scale versus small-scale study. In a perfect world, all interventions would use proper assessment tools and neat research designs. They would recruit appropriate sample sizes and conduct proper statistics with everyone on the research team having the relevant education. In reality however, we may not have access to hundreds of participants or to software (SPSS). We may not have access to or knowledge of statistics or the money to buy in people to analyse statistics. However, we still want to know: did it work? By how much? For whom? Why? How? What worked best? What didn't?

Qualitative evaluation

One major criticism of positive psychology, from a European perspective, is that it has fixated itself on the 'scientific method' and less on using methodologies that enable researchers to access the entire human participant. Accessing the person as a whole falls under the realm of qualitative methodology. Conducting this type of research is an important piece of the jigsaw that can give us information we would never have got from quantitative inquiry alone. Researchers, and you students, can use interviews (structured, semi-structured or unstructured) to collect data on the experiences of the PPIs. It is best to use qualitative enquiry for small sample sizes as it focuses on in-depth, exploratory analysis of interventions (Robson, 2004). Questions should be open and non-directive and focus on one concept at a time. Try not to use double negatives, using 'what' or 'how' instead. Examples of intervention evaluation questions could be:

1 What was your experience of the programme?
2 What was your favourite part of the programme? Least favourite?
3 What would you change about it?
4 Would you recommend this programme to others? (Why or why not?)

Birth of the first PPI

Michael Fordyce (1977) was one of the pioneers in implementing PPIs. In fact, he piloted several experimental conditions over several years, on hundreds of college students, to create his programme, *14 Basic Happiness Principles* (Fordyce, 1981; 1983). The theoretical underpinning of the programme is that if people can try to enhance these 14 characteristics found in very happy people, they too will become happy. The 14 principles are:

1 Be more active and keep busy.
2 Spend more time socializing.
3 Be productive at meaningful work.
4 Get better organized and plan things out.
5 Stop worrying.
6 Lower your expectations and aspirations.
7 Develop positive, optimistic thinking.
8 Get present-oriented.
9 Work on a healthy personality.
10 Develop an outgoing, social personality.
11 Be yourself.
12 Eliminate negative feelings and problems.
13 Close relationships are the number one source of happiness.
14 Value happiness.

Since Fordyce's work, some of these principles have been upheld via scientific research. Unfortunately, Fordyce's work has been overlooked by many new 'positive psychologists' and a return to the beginning is necessary to paint the whole picture of intervention research.

The Positive Activity Model

Sonia Lyubomirsky is the positive psychologist widely known for developing and validating the largest number of PPIs. Her early book *The How of Happiness* (2008) has assembled together all of the major PPIs existing at this moment. However, not being quite satisfied with the how, she went on to also comprehend the what, when and why of PPIs. Drawing upon theory and multiple empirical studies Lyubomirsky constructed and tested a new model – the *Positive Activity Model*, which provides an overview of activity features and person features (see Figure 8.1). This model aims to explain how and why performing positive activities makes people happier. Positive activities operate as such for individuals only if they increase positive emotions, positive thoughts, positive behaviours and need satisfaction (these are mediating variables), all of which in turn enhance well-being. Features of positive activities (e.g. dosage, variety and social support) and of the person themselves (e.g. motivation, effort, efficacy beliefs, demographics, baseline levels of well-being) influence the degree to which the activities improve well-being. An *optimal person-activity fit* (i.e. the overlap between activity and person features) further predicts increases in well-being. The latter three constitute the moderators of the positive activity-well-being relationship.

Typically, a psychological intervention works well when it 'reaches' and resonates with its beneficiaries; that is, when its intended *theory of change* is well aligned with needs and readiness to engage with the proposed change at both individual (inner lifeworld) and systems (social and structural) levels that surround the recipients at that given time. The notion of 'readiness' is complex and implicates the intersection of just the right kind of competences, resources (especially psychological resources and worldviews), opportunities and willingness to buy in (Tribe and Tunariu, 2017). Similarly, researchers using PPIs informed by certain theoretically and empirically justified standards and activities found that 'individuals tend to select and use a subset of the techniques' (Schueller, 2014: 387). This selectivity is also mediated by the participants' cultural heritage and the worldviews and dominant values that it promotes – a point which positive psychology practitioners and researchers need to take into account when designing interventions or interpreting subsequent evaluation results (Pedrotti, 2014)

Could any PPI work for anyone? In a word – no. This is a very important point to emphasize. As we are all individuals, with our own idiosyncratic tendencies and habits of thinking, each intervention will not suit everyone. This point was highlighted by Lyubomirsky and her team as result of their systematic attempt to understand why some worked for some but not for others (Lyubomirsky et al., 2005a; Lyubomirsky, 2006). They concluded that there has to be a good 'fit' with the interventions and three main criteria:

1 Fit with the source of your unhappiness.
2 Fit with your strengths.
3 Fit with your lifestyle.

The Person–Activity Fit Diagnostic (Lyubomirsky, 2007) asks participants to consider 12 activities that they judge on whether or not they would feel natural or forced. Lyubomirsky's team have found a significant correlation between 'person fit' scores and their adherence to interventions as well as well-being scores following the intervention. Another contribution from Lyubomirsky concerns the importance of variety. Following several research studies, the team concluded that people who included variety into their interventions had greater increases in well-being. The researchers explain these findings as a result of hedonic adaptation theory. Thus, if we are going to take up any of these, it is best to shake things up.

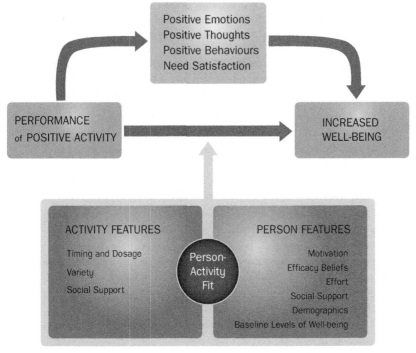

FIGURE 8.1 Model of psychological mediators and moderators underlying the efficacy of positive activity interventions (adapted from Lyubomirsky and Layous, 2013)

How many PPIs are out there?

Seligman et al.'s (2005) review of the literature yielded over one hundred that classified as a PPI. In retrospect, this number had not been supported by subsequent meta-reviews and meta-analyses. Using the above-mentioned definition, Sin and Lyubomirsky (2009) found 51 PPIs studies. Applying somewhat stricter criteria, Bolier et al. (2013) managed to identify only 39 PPIs. Weiss et al. (2016) found 27 articles looking at the impact of PPIs on psychological well-being and Weis and Speridakos (2011) identified a further 27 hope interventions positively affecting well-being outcomes.

Could physical activity interventions be considered as 'treatment methods or intentional activities that aim to cultivate positive feelings, behaviours or cognitions'? Sonia Lyubomirsky herself seems to believe so, positioning physical activity as one of her 12 HOWs to happiness (2008). Indeed, multiple meta-analyses provide compelling evidence that different forms of physical activity lead to increased well-being outcomes (see Reed and Ones, 2006; Wang et al., 2010; Knobben, 2013; Josefsson et al., 2014; Koch et al., 2014; Hanson and Jones, 2015) and are therefore considered to satisfy the definition.

Boniwell (2017) proposes the ACTIONS acronym as a useful way of characterizing and differentiating between major types of PPIs. Subsequently, the seven categories that PPIs can be organized into are as follows:

1 A stands for *Active interventions* – concerned with sport and physical activity.

2 C is for *Calming interventions* – concerned with mindfulness and meditation.

3 T is for *Thinking or taking stock* – working through and integrating past events, whether negative or positive, into our present situation.

4 I is for *Identity-related actions* – concerned with personal strengths and one's representation of oneself.

5 O is for *Optimization* – concerned with actions that enable goal setting, looking to the future, and potentially improving the current situation.

6 N is for *Nourishing* – actions concerned with self-soothing, taking pleasure and care of oneself.

7 S is for *Social actions* – concerned with establishing and maintaining positive relationships.

Using the meta-analyses cited above Boniwell (2017) identified 64 distinct interventions as successfully impacting a positive variable and, using the ACTIONS acronym, has indicated their distribution in Table 8.1 below. As a caveat, the size of the intervention is often difficult to define, with mindfulness or positive psychotherapy often considered as a single intervention, despite consisting of multiple exercises, at a par with a brief 'Three Good Things' exercise, necessitating only about eight minutes, and repeated in the same form for a week. In order to provide actual parity, Boniwell (2017) attempted to break larger packages into manageable and comparable exercises or chunks (i.e. mindful breathing, mindful body scan), while always indicating whether the available evidence relates to the package or individual exercises.

Intervention category	Interventions
Active (6)	Aerobic exercise, dance, tai chi, walking together, yoga, health check
Calming (8)	Mindful breathing, mindful body scan, mindful listening, mindful non-judging, mindful observation, loving-kindness meditation, mindful acceptance, the serenity prayer
Thinking (11)	Discussing beliefs, your worst life experience, benefit-finding, one door closes, another opens, positive reminiscence, your best ever life experience, three good things, capturing happiness, three funny things, life review
Identity (6)	Positive introduction, strengths identification, using strengths in a new way, identity groups, best possible self, job crafting
Optimizing (14)	Mental time travel, your life course journal, positive bibliography, positive statements, optimism, resilience, psychological capital, hope quest, goal setting, coaching, the miracle question, obituary, good enough, bar at the right height
Nourishing (7)	Massage, self-compassion meditation, cultivating sacred moments, savouring, rest-breaks at work, nourishing happiness, me time
Social (12)	Socializing, family strengths tree, strengths date, grateful thoughts, forgiveness, kindness day, counting kindnesses, active communication, compassionate action, active-constructive responding, gratitude visit, gift of time

TABLE 8.1 Positive psychology interventions clustered using the ACTIONS acronym

Examples of PPIs

The following is a list of those interventions/theories that have underpinned the positive psychology research discipline and shown promising results. According to the ACTIONS acronym, the section is divided into the main mechanisms that seem to channel the positive outcomes of the intervention.

Active interventions

As the subsequent chapter will discuss, a mere 10 minutes could boost mood, though 30 to 35 minutes three or more times per week is optimal. The effect of exercise is greater for people who do not feel very happy to start with, and with low-intensity exercise. High-intensity exercise improves well-being only for people who are fit. It is also important not to overdo it: after 75 minutes happiness levels start to decrease.

Other types of positive activity include dance, tai chi, walking (preferably with others) and yoga. Activity evaluation interventions, such as a health check-up (measuring one's smoking, alcohol intake, height, weight, BMI, body fat, grip strength, urinalysis, blood pressure, peak expiratory flow rate, stress, cholesterol, stamina, flexibility and current physical activity levels) are also positive for well-being, probably because of the additional impetus that these may have for our physical activity rates (Weiss et al., 2016).

Calming interventions

Calming interventions are mainly derived from mindfulness approaches and acceptance and commitment therapy (ACT). Mindfulness, otherwise defined as a receptive attention to, and awareness of, present events and experience (Brown and Ryan, 2003), is one of the major interventions promoted by positive psychology. It is also a practice that has been around for many thousands of years, is a common element of Eastern religions and is typically associated with Buddhism. It entails the skills of paying attention purposefully, in the present moment and without judgement. Neuro-psychological studies demonstrate that mindfulness meditation produces changes in brain activation associated with reductions in negative affect and increases in positive affect. They also reveal a clear link between meditation and immune function, and between changes in brain function and immunity among meditators. For instance, participants in an eight-week long meditation course were compared with participants on a waiting list in terms of brain and immune system activity. It was found that those in the meditation course showed increased left-hemisphere activity (associated with positive emotions) as well as increased production of antibodies in response to an influenza vaccine (Davidson et al., 2003). Both trait (a personality predisposition) and state (the actual experience of mindfulness) are predictors of different aspects of affective well-being (Brown and Ryan, 2003). The meta-analysis of the effects of mindfulness meditation intervention across 20 controlled and 27 observational studies concluded that it is also an effective intervention for a range of chronic diseases in a variety of samples (Grossman et al., 2004).

In order to get into a mindful state, individuals are instructed to practise focusing their attention on the present moment, observing the world and their own thoughts and feelings in a patient, non-judgemental way, without getting caught up in the past or future, or any single line of thinking or preconceived notion (Langer, 2009).

Two group approaches based on mindfulness techniques have been extensively investigated. The first, mindfulness-based cognitive therapy (MBCT) is a group intervention designed to train recovered, recurrently depressed patients to disengage from thinking that may mediate relapse recurrence. It is based on an integration of cognitive behaviour therapy (CBT) for depression with mindfulness meditation. Mindfulness-based cognitive therapy has the goal to reduce relapse and recurrence for those who are vulnerable to episodes of depression and has also been used for other disorders such as stress, anxiety and chronic pain. Based on Jon Kabat-Zinn's practical techniques, MBCT includes simple breathing meditations, body scans and yoga stretches to help participants become more aware of the now, including getting in touch with moment-to-moment changes in the mind and the body. In addition to learning mindfulness meditation techniques, participants are also introduced to simple CBT principles underlying constructive thinking. Supported by several randomized controlled trials, MBCT emerges as a powerful approach to mood regulation (Teasdale et al., 2000) and relapse prevention (Shapiro, 2009). The second approach, mindfulness-based stress reduction (MBSR) (Kabat-Zinn) focuses on the management of alterations in body functionality, image and so on while accepting physical changes and attempting to reach mastery over body. Mindfulness-based stress reduction has been found to enhance management and reduction of pain, psychological distress and control and acceptance of body. It has even been found to reduce stress and depression similar to the effects of cognitive behavioural stress reduction, in addition to enhanced mindfulness, energy and reduced pain beyond treatment as usual (TAU).

A new version of meditation currently being tested within positive psychology is loving-kindness (LK) meditation (Fredrickson et al., 2008). Preliminary results have shown significant increase in positive emotions and subsequent building of personal resources through the participation in LK meditation.

Think about it...

Try out a little mindfulness right now by following the personal intervention at the end of the chapter; but remember:

1 Mindfulness means paying attention in a particular way: on purpose, in the present moment, and non-judgementally ...

2 It does not involve trying to change your thinking. It involves watching thought itself ....

3 It's not to be confused with positive thinking ...

Thinking interventions

Thinking, or taking stock, is about working through and integrating past and present events, whether negative or positive, into our present situation. Many of these interventions stem from CBT, acceptance and commitment therapy (ACT) and expressive writing paradigm, but were evaluated not only for their effectiveness around reducing depression and anxiety, but also around enhancing well-being (broadly defined).

To offer some examples of thinking actions, the expressive writing interventions stem from the results of trauma research where scientists found that trauma survivors were able to find meaning through expressive writing (Pennebaker, 2004; see Chapter 7). Many, many studies replicated and extended the expressive writing design where survivors are asked to write about a painful, distressing experience in detail for 15 to 30 minutes, for three consecutive days. Some research (Burton and King, 2008) has shown that even two minutes of writing can enhance individuals' health and well-being. Individuals who write expressively about past traumatic events make fewer visits to doctors, have enhanced immune functioning, and report less distress and depression than individuals who do not. Pennebaker admits that although they know that the intervention works, they do not understand why and for whom. One reason proposed is the *catharsis hypothesis,* which dictates that the exercise allows people to write freely without judgement or restraint on paper, and can help organize thoughts and emotions. Writing about even the worst life experiences results in the increase of well-being, psychological well-being and even health (Bolier et al., 2013).

Research has tried to separate the difference between systematically analysing happy moments (increasing interest) versus replaying them (increasing positive affect). They have found that while systematically analysing can increase interest it does not induce further pleasantness, whereas simple mental replay can induce both interest and pleasantness (Vittersø et al., 2009b).

As far as current daily events are concerned, robust research surrounds interventions focused on expressing gratitude. Gratitude is the underlying concept for many PPIs as it promotes the savouring of positive events and may counteract hedonic adaptation. Common techniques instruct participants to look back at their day just before they go to bed and find three things that went well for them during the day or three things that they feel grateful for. Several conceptually related studies have taken a different take on how gratitude can increase well-being.[2] The timing of this exercise is significant. Studies have shown that the well-being of those who carried it out three times a week for six weeks actually decreased slightly, which suggests that there is such a thing as too much, while the well-being of those who carried out this exercise once a week for six weeks or every day for a week increased substantially. This finding co-exists with the fact that people who continue 'counting their blessings' occasionally after the intervention demonstrate the best outcomes. The most likely conclusion is that it is important to notice the good things in life now and then, yet not allow this practice to become a chore (Boehm and Lyubomirsky, 2009).

In another prominent study, people who engaged in counting their blessings (vs burdens) tended to also experience more joy, energy, attentiveness and pro-social behaviour. As gratitude and blessings bring up different associations (due to religious connotations), this intervention has been renamed as 'three good things' (Emmons and McCullough, 2003) and 'spot the positives' (Boniwell, 2017). Seligman puts another twist on this intervention, asking people to write down three good things that happened to them that day, and their role in bringing about the events. This taps into positive internal explanatory styles, highlighting how a person can control their daily positive experiences (Seligman et al., 2005).

Identity interventions

Identity interventions are concerned with defining our core selves, identifying and developing strengths, where we are at our best, and also about achieving a match between our identity and our professional activity.

Research shows that simply taking the strengths test (VIA online) and identifying your Top 5 signature strengths can significantly enhance your well-being levels (Seligman et al., 2005). From there, you can do many things with this information to create a strength-based approach to life. For instance when you are deciding on what career to follow or what job to take as you decide on the future, try to match your Top 5 strengths with your job as the most valued jobs, relationships and hobbies are the ones congruent with people's strengths. Thus, if your top strength is kindness, then try to source a job with some form of mentoring elements. Alternatively, the intervention of job crafting offers a systematic way of adjusting your work tasks to your strengths.

Finally, you can try using your signature strengths in a new way every day, for at least one week. Infusing your daily life with variety in how you express your strengths has a lasting effect on increased happiness and decreased depressive symptoms for up to six months (Seligman et al., 2005).

Taking the idea of strengths one step further, King (2001) created a well validated intervention entitled *best possible self*. The best possible self is a narrative description of you as your best possible self, when everything you wish to have come true has. Again, after 15–30 minutes, for three to four consecutive days, results showed that the intervention group had increased subjective well-being, decreased illness for five months and enhanced insight into motives and emotions, optimism, self-regulation and confidence. This exercise has been repeatedly shown to enhance positive emotions (Sheldon and Lyubomirsky, 2006b) and by extending to include listing main goals and sub-goals, the exercise can help highlight and restructure priorities.

Optimizing interventions

If identity interventions are about realizing who you are and who you would like to be, then the optimizing category is all about getting closer towards the desired future. It includes many interventions related to goal setting, touching on optimism, hope, psychological capital and coaching.

Typical instructions for such interventions would be as follows: Write down several tasks you would like to accomplish that are realistically challenging, applicable to the workplace and personally valuable. Now, choose one of these goals and break it down into more manageable smaller sub-goals. Next, write down multiple ways in which you could accomplish your goal and think of contingency plans for overcoming potential obstacles and problems. Think of any resources you could leverage to accomplish your goal. Think of success stories you know of and how similar goals were obtained. You might also want to talk to someone about additional pathways to your goal that could be utilized, as well as additional obstacles to expect (Boniwell, 2017).

Importantly, making it to a desired future does not always require setting the hardest goals or pushing ourselves to do our best. In Chapter 3 we introduced the concepts of maximizing and satisfying and associated personality profiles (Schwartz et al., 2002). Satisficers are people who make a decision or take action once their criteria are met. That does not mean they'll settle for mediocrity, but as soon as they find the car, the hotel or the pasta sauce that has the qualities they want, they are satisfied. Maximizers want to make the optimal decision. So even if they see a bicycle or a photographer that seems to meet their requirements, they cannot make a decision until they have examined every option, so they know they are making the best possible choice. Satisficing leads to happiness and satisfaction, where maximizing is associated with perfectionism and being frequently dissatisfied. One PPI developed by Rashid (2015) helps individuals identify some ways to increase satisficing (or getting to that 'good enough' feeling) in their life and devise a personal satisficing plan.

Nourishing interventions

Nourishing actions are concerned with self-soothing, taking pleasure and taking care of ourselves. Most of them contain an element of *savouring*. The reader may have already heard of savouring or its other synonyms (e.g. basking, rejoicing, enjoying, relishing, luxuriating, cherishing); however, leading experts in the area, Bryant and Veroff (e.g. 2007) argue that the latter concepts are much narrower, and that savouring actually encompasses these synonyms.

Savouring is defined as 'the capacity to attend to, appreciate and enhance the positive experiences in one's life' (Bryant and Veroff, 2007: xi). It is important to distinguish savouring as a process and not as an outcome, thus it is something we do and not something that happens, and it requires active engagement on the person's behalf. Therefore, savouring requires a person to slow down and attend intently to their surroundings, feelings, experiences – to stretch out the experience so to speak.

Bryant and Veroff propose that savouring can be done in terms of three time orientations, four processes and ten strategies. How a person decides to savour is entirely up to their own preference. In terms of time orientation, people can engage in savouring through a) the past (reminiscing); b) the present (savouring the moment) or c) the future (anticipating). Bryant and Verroff propose four savouring processes: 1) thanksgiving (gratitude); 2) basking (pride); 3) marvelling (awe); and 4) luxuriating (physical pleasure).

There are 10 identified strategies that can be employed in order to enhance savouring across time orientation and process. We now review these strategies and how to employ them in daily life.

1 Sharing with others

Sharing positive experiences with others is the single, strongest predictor of level of enjoyment. This of course is more so with extroverts than introverts. Sharing with others may foster bonding and reinforce healthy relationships for several reasons. First of all, it is nice to be with loved ones and watch them enjoy themselves. Also, others may point out pleasurable aspects that we may have not noticed and we may become more playful in the presence of others. A desire to share the pleasure makes us more attentive to all the pleasurable details of the experience.

2 Memory building

When we experience positive events, we can engage in memory building, which is simply actively taking vivid mental photographs for future recall. This strategy is correlated with a desire to share with others.

3 Comparing

Comparing is a difficulty strategy to employ. Research shows us that people who engage in downward social comparison can indeed enhance their own well-being; however, when people engage in upward social comparison, they may dampen their enjoyment if comparing to someone better off than them.

4 Sensory-perceptual sharpening

This strategy asks us to intensify pleasure by focusing on certain stimuli and blocking out others.

5 Self-congratulation

Sometimes, we just don't have someone beside us or in our life to help us celebrate our accomplishments. This strategy can sometimes be inappropriate yet it must not be confused with boasting, but an acknowledgement of an effort well spent that simply requires telling ourselves how proud we feel while maintaining perspective.

6 Absorption

This can be described as allowing ourselves to get totally immersed in the moment, akin to self-induced flow.

7 Behavioural expression

When we smile, can we actually induce positive emotions/feelings? Can laughing, giggling, jumping up and down, dancing around change our mood? There is lots of evidence that outwardly expressing positive feelings can intensify them.

8 Temporal awareness

This strategy asks us to acknowledge fleeting moments of time and to engage in carpe diem.

9 Counting blessings

Of course, we now know the importance of reminding ourselves of our good fortune and thinking about how lucky we are. Take some time to count your blessings at the end of the day or the week.

10 Killjoy thinking

The tenth strategy is actually a 'how not to' strategy in the 10 ways of savouring. It highlights that fact that if we engage in worry, ruminative thought or killjoy thinking, there will be no room for savouring experiences.

Think about it...

Ok – now it's practice time! Find a friend, classmate of family member to practise savouring with. Get one person to be the coach and one to be the 'savourer'. Take them through one of the nine savouring processes.

Activity debrief

- Anything surprise you about this exercise?
- What was challenging for the coach or savourer?
- What did you learn?

Social interventions

The well-known *random acts of kindness (RAK)* intervention asks participants to engage in kind acts towards others (e.g. holding the door open for a stranger, doing roommates' dishes). These interventions are thought to bolster self-regard, positive social interactions and charitable feelings towards others. The importance of this exercise is to vary the types of acts and also to do them all on the same day. Reasons for this are that when we repeatedly do the same thing for others, the novelty will wear off and the altruistic act becomes a chore. Likewise, if someone is asked to commit five acts of kindness on the same day, they will see and feel a reinforced reaction to their kindness. Researchers have discovered that pro-social behaviour can lose its impact if spread out over the week. Overall, these kindness interventions, and many others (e.g. Otake et al., 2006), suggest that happiness can be boosted by behavioural intentional activities and that the timing and variety of performing such intentional activities significantly impacts interventions' effectiveness. As the researchers say, 'Variety is the spice of life', and in PPIs there is no exception (Lyubomirsky et al., 2005a).

Think about it...

When was the last time you bought something nice for someone else? New research has shown that individuals benefit more from spending money on others than they do spending it on themselves (Dunn et al., 2008). So when you get that birthday money or bonus you were waiting for, think about how and on whom you can spend it!

One of the most powerful (albeit relatively fleeting) positive impacts on well-being is the *gratitude visit* (Seligman et al., 2005). The gratitude visit (or gratitude letter) requires writing a letter to someone we never properly thanked. We can either read the letter aloud in person or send the letter through the mail (though the first format is ideal). Even more interesting is that this exercise works even when the letter isn't sent (Lyubomirsky et al., 2006)!

Ultimately, gratitude is an imperative component for well-being, which forces people to step back and reflect upon what and whom they have in their life, as well as counteracting complacency and 'taken-for-grantedness'.

Active constructive responding

It goes without saying that when tragedy strikes, we need people around us. But what about when things are going well? Gable et al. (2004) decided to look at not how people react to others when they receive bad news, but to how they react when someone comes to them with good news. Active constructive responding (ACR) requires a person to respond with genuine excitement, outwardly displaying their excitement and capitalizing on their success (prolonging discussion of the good news, telling people about it, suggesting celebratory activities). Interestingly she found that relationships in which each member engages in ACR tend to flourish as opposed to the other relationships where individuals employ passive constructive, active destructive and passive destructive methods of response (see the Think about it ... section below).

Think about it...

When someone approaches you with good news, how do you respond? Are you:

- happy for them, but tend not to make a big deal about it (passive constructive)?
- sceptical, and point out why the good news isn't so good at all (active destructive)?
- or more of an indifferent reactor (passive destructive)?

The next time a friend comes to you with good news, try to engage in ACR and notice the subsequent interactions.

In conclusion, we believe that positive psychology needs to continue its work on replicating and advancing PPIs, as well as think outside the box when it comes to actual exercises for implementation. Parks and Schueller's (2014) handbook of PPIs, for instance, identified interventions that have not yet made it into a meta-analysis, such as *creativity, patience, courage* and *flow* interventions that show promising results. Furthermore, new directions in PPIs include the use of tangible tools in positive psychology coaching and training that integrate clear hands-on elements in administering interventions. Such tangible tools can include creating a poster-based *best possible self* exercise, the *integrated well-being dashboard* (Boniwell, 2016), *Positive ACTIONS Cards* (Boniwell, 2017), *Strengths Cards* (Boniwell, 2013), *The Happiness Box* (Boniwell and Reynaud, 2015) and *HEX* (Bab and Boniwell, 2016). These are based on sound theoretical and empirical foundations and are now subject to research trials on their effectiveness.

Chapter Summary

Reflecting on the learning objectives the reader would have acquired knowledge about the concept of positive psychological interventions. In summary:

- People can choose to adopt either a fixed or growth mindset, with the latter creating more chance for success.

▶

- Prochaska's trans-theoretical model of change demonstrates an interesting perspective on human behaviour modification.
- Grit and perseverance are imperative for success at attaining goals.
- Self-regulation is important to keep the change going and can be strengthened via corresponding exercises.
- There are several ways to evaluate PPIs, with qualitative inquiry enabling a more in-depth understanding.
- The number of validated PPIs is growing, with recent meta-analyses showing that they are helpful in increasing well-being and supporting personal growth.
- The positive activity model proposes four mediating variables (positive emotions, positive thoughts, positive behaviours and need satisfaction) and two categories of moderating variables (characteristics of the positive activity and characteristics of the person), as well as the importance of person-activity fit for optimal positive activity success.
- Positive ACTIONS is a useful acronym for organizing and recalling PPIs.

Suggested Resources

www.youtube.com/watch?v=DbC18wFkHNI
Educating For Happiness and Resilience with Dr. Ilona Boniwell. TEDx Talk published on 20 May 2013.

www.positran.eu
To access information regarding ACTIONS cards and multiple ways to use them, follow the link above. They represent the largest collection of evidence-based PPIs.

https://itunes.apple.com/us/app/live-happy/id1036216178?mt=8
Use iTunes to download Sonja Lyubomirsky's 'LIVE HAPPY' App for the iphone.

Further questions for the reader

1 Can you think of an example of where you changed your mindset?
2 Of these interventions, how many do you already use?
3 What are your reactions to your Fit scores?
4 Will you engage in any that are not in your top four? Why or why not?

Personal Development Interventions

The exercises presented below ask you to engage with several interventions that have been scientifically shown to enhance your well-being. We have tried both of these exercises with our undergraduate and MSc students.

1 ACTIONS Lab

Alone or with a friend or a coach/helper, look through the interventions presented in this chapter and identify actions that you are using at the moment or have tried in the past. How did/do they make you feel? Have you noticed any changes in yourself as a result of their implementation? If so, what were they? Would you like to continue or re-start using any of these actions? If so, which ones, why and how?

2 Portfolio

For the next month, try to incorporate as many PPIs as possible into your daily routine to assess their feasibility and effectiveness. Keep a 'scientific diary' so that you can record your thoughts and experiences and reflect once you have finished the four weeks. How do the results compare to the original research? Did they work? Why or why not?

You can take this further and collate the exercises you completed throughout the textbook (e.g. your answers to the Think about it … sections), as well as the questionnaires, and put them into the portfolio for a scrapbook of your personal experiences and journey over the course of the semester.

Measurement Tools

Person-Activity Fit Diagnostic

(Lyubomirsky, 2007)

Directions

Consider each of the following 12 happiness activities. Reflect on what it would be like to do each one every week for an extended period of time. Then rate each activity by writing the appropriate number (1–7) in the blank space next to the terms *Natural, Enjoy, Value, Guilty and Situation.*

▶

People do things for many different reasons. Please rate why you might keep doing this activity in terms of each of the following reasons. Use the scale provided:

1	2	3	4	5	6	7
not at all			somewhat			very much

NATURAL: I'll keep doing this activity because it will feel 'natural' to me and I'll be able to stick with it.

ENJOY: I'll keep doing this activity because I will enjoy doing it; I'll find it to be interesting and challenging.

VALUE: I'll keep doing this activity because I will value and identify with doing it; I'll do it freely even when it's not enjoyable.

GUILTY: I'll keep doing this activity because I would feel ashamed, guilty, or anxious if I didn't do it; I'll force myself.

SITUATION: I'll keep doing this activity because somebody else will want me to or because my situation will force me to.

1. Expressing gratitude: Counting your blessings for what you have (either to a close one or privately, through contemplation or a journal) or conveying your gratitude and appreciation to one or more individuals whom you've never properly thanked.

___ NATURAL ___ ENJOY___ VALUE ___ GUILTY ___ SITUATION

2. Cultivating optimism: Keeping a journal in which you imagine and write about the best possible future for yourself or practising to look at the bright side of every situation.

___ NATURAL ___ ENJOY ___ VALUE ___ GUILTY ___ SITUATION

3. Avoiding overthinking and social comparison: Using strategies (such as distraction) to cut down on how often you dwell on your problems and compare yourself with others.

___ NATURAL ___ ENJOY ___ VALUE ___ GUILTY ___ SITUATION

4. Practising random acts of kindness: Doing good things for others, whether friends or strangers, either directly or anonymously, either spontaneously or planned.

___ NATURAL ___ ENJOY ___ VALUE ___ GUILTY ___ SITUATION

5. Nurturing relationships: Picking a relationship in need of strengthening, and investing time and energy in healing, cultivating, affirming and enjoying it.

___ NATURAL ___ ENJOY ___ VALUE ___ GUILTY ___ SITUATION

▶ **6. Developing strategies for coping**: Practising ways to endure or surmount a recent stress, hardship or trauma.

___ NATURAL ___ ENJOY ___ VALUE ___ GUILTY ___ SITUATION

7. Learning to forgive: Keeping a journal or writing a letter in which you work on letting go of anger and resentment towards one or more individuals who have hurt or wronged you.

___ NATURAL ___ ENJOY ___ VALUE ___ GUILTY ___ SITUATION

8. Doing more activities that truly engage you: Increasing the number of experiences at home and work in which you 'lose' yourself, which are challenging and absorbing (i.e. flow experiences).

___ NATURAL ___ ENJOY ___ VALUE ___ GUILTY ___ SITUATION

9. Savouring life's joys: Paying close attention, taking delight and replaying life's momentary pleasures and wonders, through thinking, writing, drawing or sharing with one another.

___ NATURAL ___ ENJOY ___ VALUE ___ GUILTY ___ SITUATION

10. Committing to your goals: Picking one, two or three significant goals that are meaningful to you and devoting time and effort to pursuing them.

___ NATURAL ___ ENJOY ___ VALUE ___ GUILTY ___ SITUATION

11. Practising religion and spirituality: Becoming more involved in your church, temple or mosque, or reading and pondering spiritually themed books.

___ NATURAL ___ ENJOY ___ VALUE ___ GUILTY ___ SITUATION

12. Taking care of your body: Engaging in physical activity, meditating, and smiling and laughing.

___ NATURAL ___ ENJOY ___ VALUE ___ GUILTY ___ SITUATION

Scoring

For each of the 12 activities, subtract the average of the GUILTY and SITUATION ratings from the average of the NATURAL, ENJOY and VALUE ratings.

In other words, for each of the 12 activities:

Fit score = (Natural + Enjoy + Value)/3 − (Guilty + Situation)/2

Interpretation

The four activities with the highest fit-scores are those that will work best for you. Write down the four activities. Park the list for now and keep it in mind as we go through the interventions in detail. ▶

▶ **Review**

This tool was created in order to determine your best fitting activities/
interventions. Our classes report mixed, even polarized, reactions to the results of
this test. Either the test tells them what they already know, or else it highlights an
activity that they would never have thought of doing themselves. Overall, it's an
interesting awareness exercise to get you thinking about what interventions you
could incorporate easily into your life.

Notes

1 See Bolier and Martin Abello's (2014) useful synthesis on current state of
   art and future directions for defining, designing, enhancing effectiveness
   and carrying out research evaluations suitable for online PPIs.
2 Froh et al. (2009) summarize nine published studies testing the effects
   of gratitude interventions.

CHAPTER 9

Physical Activity and Positive Psychology

B. Grenville-Cleave and A. Brady

❖ LEARNING OBJECTIVES

Positive psychology has been criticized for focusing primarily on 'the neck up'. This is changing with the acknowledgement of mind–body links and the accumulation of multidisciplinary research into the role of physical activity in well-being.

This chapter will focus on the links between physical activity and psychological well-being. It will explore how positive psychology can help develop a deeper understanding of physical activity experiences.

Topics include:

- What physical activity (PA) is and is not.
- Differences between types of PA such as sport and exercise.
- Characteristics of PA.
- Benefits of PA.
- The role of positive psychology in understanding PA.
- Interventions for enhancing engagement in PA.

MOCK ESSAY QUESTIONS

1 Are all types of PA equally good for psychological well-being?
2 Critically discuss how positive psychology can help increase our understanding of PA experiences.
3 Select two or three well-known PPIs mentioned elsewhere in the book (e.g. gratitude visit; best possible self) and discuss how these might be adapted or applied in your chosen PA setting.

The body in psychology

'Mens sana in corpore sano', attributed to the Roman poet Juvenal (55–c.138 A.D.) and translated as 'a healthy mind in a healthy body', aptly describes the position that most psychologists adopt, even though the first two decades of positive psychology research have focused primarily on the psychological to the exclusion of the physical. The dualist separation of the mind and body has been entrenched in academia and medicine for many centuries through the creation of discipline-informed knowledge and practice.

Think about it...

The psychosomatic principle (that the mind can influence the body) has existed in the medical field for millennia, with scientific research as far back as the 1970s linking psychological and physical health. Why, therefore, has society generally been so slow in recognizing these links? What role might positive psychology play in addressing this issue?

One answer could be related to the 'parity of esteem' principle, which states that mental health must be given equal priority to physical health. In the UK, this was enshrined in law by the Health and Social Care Act 2012. Despite considerable advocacy from high-profile academics such as Lord Richard Layard, mental health services continue to receive far less funding than physical health services.

It could be argued that early attempts within positive psychology to acknowledge mind–body links have been clumsy, and to a certain extent, justified early criticism for example inferring that mere 'positive thinking' could overcome physical illnesses such as cancer (Held, 2002). At the same time, positive psychology has also been criticized by others, such as the humanistic movement, for not fully acknowledging mind–body links and holism in particular.

While lack of space prevents us from exploring the theory in depth in this chapter, it is worth noting that studies of holism – and related topics such as embodiment and identity – and their relationship to well-being, are beginning to emerge, for example in high performance and professional sport (e.g. Jolley et al., in press). Embodiment is the felt sense of our physical self which influences how we experience everyday life. Though we may sometimes consider our body only as a physical vehicle, 'we are beings who live with and through bodies' (Kim, 2001: 69). A person's experience of their physical self can dramatically influence their well-being (Hefferon, 2013) and offers much potential for development within positive psychology. In a study of older women's experiences of embodiment and yoga, Humberstone and Cutler-Riddick (2015) found that yoga techniques used by the women supported the integration of body and mind, and challenged a dualistic body–mind way of viewing the body, and ideas about physical constraints in older age.

As this chapter will show, despite the many benefits associated with PA, the widespread acknowledgement that health and well-being are holistic and the reciprocity established between mind and body, there is surprisingly little reference to PA in positive psychology or theories of well-being. One articulation of well-being that does account for PA is the five ways to well-being (Aked et al., 2008) which has been adopted by many health organizations in the UK (see the 'time out' section in Chapter 3).

Knowledge of how PA is related to health and well-being has developed considerably over the past 40 years through the increasingly specialized disciplines of sport and exercise psychology. As with mainstream psychology, it has been argued (Brady and Grenville Cleave, in press) that, historically, sport psychology's approach has been characterized by understanding and researching strategies to enhance competitive sports performance by reducing or reframing problematic experiences and behaviours such as anxiety, choking and overtraining, rather than to increase or optimize positive experiences or behaviours. Exercise psychology has developed valuable knowledge about how participating in PA influences psychological well-being and mental health. In both sport and exercise psychology there is an opportunity to embrace positive psychology through topics such as gratitude, passion, character strengths and enjoyment. As with other disciplines, viewing PA through a positive psychology lens extends the vocabulary with which to understand and examine the effects, as well as individual experience, of PA. Hefferon (2013), for instance, provides a comprehensive account of the roles of the body and PA in supporting psychological well-being, whether short-term experiences of pleasure (hedonic well-being) or long-term experiences of meaning and personal growth (eudaimonic well-being).

What PA is and is not

Physical activity is often confused with physical exercise; however physical exercise, like sport, is a subset of PA, an umbrella term which has been defined as 'any bodily movement produced by skeletal muscles that results in energy expenditure' (Caspersen et al., 1985: 126). Physical exercise refers to types of PA which are structured or organized, often aimed at improving physical health, such as attending weekly gym sessions with a personal trainer or participating in organized yoga or Pilates classes. Sport is distinguished from exercise because it is rule bound, involves competition and often requires learning techniques and training to achieve competence and mastery.

Thus PA is a more general term encompassing physical exercise as well as more traditional sport activities (which may occur at different levels of ability from novice to elite, at amateur, professional or elite levels), as well as day-to-day activities such as doing household chores, walking the dog, using the stairs at work rather than taking the lift, and participating in a community cycling club. PA may be formal or informal, structured or unstructured, prescribed as a therapy or volitionally undertaken, competitive or non-competitive, group or individual, leisure or work. The breadth of activity covered by PA, and the many reasons for participating, suggest that it may be useful for researchers to distinguish between types of PA such as sport and exercise in order to better understand the experience of PA, its benefits for participants' physical and mental health and the potential issues arising.

Characteristics of PA

In the latest guidance for developing and maintaining cardiorespiratory and muscular fitness, and flexibility in healthy adults, the American College for Sports Medicine (ACSM) states, 'The scientific evidence demonstrating the beneficial effects of exercise is indisputable, and the benefits of exercise far outweigh the risks in most adults' and 'exercise training beyond activities of daily living to improve and maintain physical fitness and health is essential for most adults' (Garber et al., 2011: 1334). As research evidence about the health-related effects of PA has progressed, so too has guidance for daily and weekly exercise (see Table 9.1). Contemporary guidance from the ACSM recommends that to achieve optimal health outcomes, structured exercise programmes should include components that address cardiorespiratory, resistance, flexibility and neuromotor dimensions. International and national guidelines for achieving physical and mental health through PA now exist for different age groups including babies, toddlers, children and adolescents, adults and older adults (e.g. DHSC, 2011; Public Health England, 2016; WHO, 2010).

Year	1978	1995	2011
Frequency of activity	3–5 times a week	4–7 times a week (ideally daily)	≥5 day/wk moderate intensity OR ≥3 days/wk vigorous intensity OR a combination of both on ≥3–5 days/wk
			PLUS 2–3 days/wk – resistance exercises for each of the major muscle groups, and neuromotor exercise involving balance, agility and coordination
			AND ≥2 days/wk – flexibility exercises for each of the major muscle-tendon groups to maintain joint movement range
			ALSO Intersperse frequent, short bouts of standing and physical activity between periods of sedentary activity, even in physically active adults
Intensity of activity	Vigorous	Moderate	Moderate, vigorous or combination
Duration of activity	20 minutes	A total of 30 minutes of activity daily (in bouts of at least 10 minutes)	Moderate intensity ≥30 mins/day ≥150 mins/wk Vigorous intensity ≥20mins/day ≥75 mins/wk Plus time for resistance and conditioning activity
Activity type	Aerobic	Aerobic	Aerobic, resistance (strength), neuromotor, flexibility and anti-sedentary

Source: Adapted from Carron et al., 2003; Pate et al., 1995; and Garber et al., 2011.

TABLE 9.1 A comparison of past and present guidelines for physical activity for adults

Though guidelines have been updated outlining the frequency, duration, intensity and type of PA recommended to gain optimal health, Berger et al. (2015) note the importance of acknowledging individual preferences for PA type and mode, as well as preferred exercise intensity in understanding and designing or prescribing PA for psychological benefits, because in most cases enjoyment of the activity is related to adherence. The four characteristics of acute PA associated with mood enhancement and psychological benefits are that the activity: 1) should promote rhythmical abdominal breathing (linked to stress management); 2) be relatively non-competitive (as competitive outcome can influence mood); 3) be temporally and spatially certain and predictable (as these activities allow the mind to wander and/or connect with the body) and 4) involve rhythmical and repetitive movements (may encourage introspection and creative thinking) (Berger et al., 2015).

In a worldwide survey of PA levels of adults and young people from 122 countries (105 countries for young people data) findings show that less than a third (31 per cent) of adults met the guidelines for vigorous exercise on three or more days a week (Hallal et al., 2012). Large differences were found between regions (see Table 9.2).

WHO region	Percentage of adult population who meet the requirement of vigorous exercise on 3 or more days/week	Percentage of adult population who report walking for at least 10 mins consecutively on 5 or more days per week	Percentage of adult population who are physically inactive	Overall, the percentage of adults spending 4 or more hours per day sitting
Africa	38.0	57.0	27.5	37.8
The Americas	24.6	65.6	43.3	55.2
Eastern Mediterranean	43.2	66.9	43.2	41.4
Europe	25.4	66.8	34.8	64.1
Southeast Asia	43.2	67.2	17.0	23.8
Western Pacific	35.3	65.0	33.7	39.8
Worldwide average	31.4	64.1	31.1	41.5

TABLE 9.2 Worldwide PA and inactivity information for adults in World Health Organization (WHO) regions

Within every age group, data reflects that males are more likely than females to participate in vigorous-intensity PA. Participation decreases with age and estimates of insufficient PA for young people were much higher than were those reported in adults. The proportion of adolescents not achieving 60 minutes per day was equal to or greater than 80 per cent. The worldwide figure for physical inactivity among adults is 31.1 per cent, ranging from 4.7 per cent (4.3–5.1 per cent) in Bangladesh to 71.9 per cent (31.0–87.2) in Malta. Inactivity rises with age, is higher in women than in men, and is increased in high-income countries.

Bucking the gender-related trend that, worldwide, women do less vigorous PA, are more physically inactive and have higher levels of sedentary behaviour compared to men, is the finding that there was hardly any difference between men and women regarding walking for 10 minutes continuously for five or more consecutive days per week. Evidence shows that active transportation, such as walking, has a range of health benefits and can increase PA levels of whole populations (de Nazelle et al., 2011).

Benefits of PA

If exercise were a pill, it would be one of the most cost-effective drugs ever invented' (UK NHS Choices). The potential benefits of PA and exercise for the mental health of clinical and non-clinical populations have been categorized (Mutrie and Faulkner, 2004) as follows:

1 preventing mental illness;
2 treating existing mental illness;
3 improving the quality of life for people with mental illness;
4 improving the psychological well-being of the general public (i.e. non-clinical population).

For an extensive account of contemporary research about the effects of PA on psychological well-being in clinical and non-clinical populations readers are advised to access texts by Faulkner and Taylor (2005) and Biddle and Mutrie (2008). Presented below in Table 9.3 are just some examples of evidence from these texts about the effect of PA in particular domains of psychological well-being.

time out

The Daily Mile

The Daily Mile is a primary school initiative, spearheaded by one headteacher in Scotland in 2012, and now backed by the Scottish Government and taken up by over 3000 schools in over 25 countries. The Daily Mile programme is very simple: primary school children are encouraged to take a break from their lessons to run a mile together every day. It only takes 15 minutes out of the core teaching/learning time, and requires no equipment, no kit (children run in the clothes they wear to school) and no training. A three-month pilot study at Coppermill School in London found increased pupil attainment, improved behaviour and attention as well as increased well-being and physical fitness. The Daily Mile programme is currently being researched by Dr Craig Moran at the University of Stirling, Scotland, where undergraduate students are being encouraged to run their own Daily Mile.

Domain	Selected findings
Anxiety and stress	• Exercise has a low-moderate anxiety-reducing effect • Regular PA can reduce trait anxiety • A single bout of PA can reduce state anxiety and stress reactivity and recovery from brief psychosocial stressors
Depression	• Evidence supports a causal link between exercise and decreased depression • Epidemiological evidence demonstrates PA is associated with a decreased risk of developing clinically defined depression • Both aerobic and resistance exercise can be used to treat moderate and more severe depression • The antidepressant effect of PA can be of the same magnitude as found for other psychotherapeutic interventions
Emotion and mood	• PA in many forms is consistently associated with positive affect and mood • Large-scale epidemiological studies using varied measures and indices of psychological well-being have confirmed a positive relationship with PA and psychological well-being • Evidence from meta-analyses shows that adopting goals in exercise and sport that focus on personal improvement and effort are moderately-highly associated with positive affect • Meta-analytic evidence shows that environments/group climates in sport and exercise settings that encourage focus on personal improvement, effort and mastery are moderately-highly associated with positive affect

Self-esteem and self-perceptions	• PA can be used to promote physical self-worth and other physical self-perceptions such as positive body image
	• Positive effects of PA on self-perceptions are found with both aerobic and resistance training, though the latter shows greater effectiveness in the short-term
	• The positive effects of PA on self-perceptions can be experienced
	  ○ by males and females
	  ○ across all age groups, though the strongest effect evidence is in children and young people
	  ○ the impact on positive affect of PA is likely to be greater for those with low levels of self-esteem initially

Cognitive functioning	• Fit older adults display better cognitive performance than unfit older adults • Fitness and cognitive functioning findings are task dependent with pronounced effects for activities related to attention and reaction time • PA is inversely related to cognitive decline • Meta-analytic evidence shows that there is a significant positive relationship between PA and cognitive functioning in children and young people with good health across all ages (i.e. 4–18 years of age) and in those with and without physical disabilities as well as among those with learning impairments (Sibley and Etnier, 2003, cited in Biddle and Mutrie, 2008: 186)

Source: Adapted from Faulkner and Taylor, 2005; Biddle and Mutrie, 2008.

TABLE 9.3 Examples of some of the benefits of PA for psychological well-being

Complete State Model of Mental Health

One of the potential limitations with understanding the benefits of PA for mental health is the assumption that the absence of illness, or the treatment and curing of illness, automatically lead to the presence of good health and good functioning. In other words, good health, ill health and ability to function are understood as a single continuum, thus the further one moves away from mental ill health, the closer one gets to good mental health and functioning (see Chapter 1). The limitation of the single continuum model has been highlighted by the work of Keyes and Lopez (2002) in their Complete State Model of Mental Health, which explores mental health and functioning along two continua, being low to high well-being and low to high mental ill-health symptoms. This produces the following quadrants:

1 High well-being/low mental illness symptoms = Complete mental health or flourishing
2 Low well-being/low mental illness symptoms = Incomplete mental health or languishing
3 Low well-being/high mental illness symptoms = Complete mental illness or floundering
4 High well-being/high mental illness symptoms = Incomplete mental illness or struggling

Keyes and Lopez's (2002) model illustrates the complexity of the connection between mental health, ill health and ability to function. It is not simply that one's ability to function is not wholly dependent on one's mental health. Keyes and Lopez posit that, with or without a diagnosis of mental illness, one may or may not exhibit indicators of flourishing. This model emphasizes the danger of labelling individuals with mental health difficulties, since it is possible that those with diagnosed conditions may, at the same time, display signs of flourishing.

How positive psychology can help contribute to our understanding of PA

This section outlines some of the key areas within positive psychology that have been researched in the PA discipline, namely positive emotions, relationships, meaning, passion and achievement.

Positive emotions and PA

A task facing scientists, researchers and practitioners is to build on the substantial evidence base showing that acute and chronic PA are positively associated with many dimensions of psychological well-being and mental health, and establish an understanding about the causal mechanisms, that is how and why PA is beneficial psychologically as well as physically. A number of explanations (possibly related or concurrent or sequential) for the psychological benefits have been proposed including biological (biochemical and physiological) as well as psychological (cognitive and psychosocial) and these are summarized in Table 9.4.

Mechanism	Proposed process of mechanism
Thermogenic hypothesis	PA leads to elevated core body temperature which is associated with decreased muscle tension, relaxation, enhanced mood and reduced anxiety and stress reactivity
Monoamine hypothesis	PA facilitates neurotransmitters such as dopamine and serotonin and/or neurotransmitter systems which serve as chemical messengers for cognitive functions (e.g. memory, attention) and mood states. Associated with relationships between both PA-reduced depression and PA-increased cognitive functioning
Endorphin hypothesis	Increased production of endorphin-peptide production after exercise which can facilitate reduced feelings of pain and heightened feelings of euphoria. Often presented as the explanation for the 'runner's high' and positive mood effects of PA
Opponent-process hypothesis	The brain is primed to oppose any stimuli (pleasurable or aversive) and respond by regaining homeostasis. When PA is experienced (as pleasurable or not) it stimulates the sympathetic nervous system (SNS) which induces an activated state and the brain responds possibly by stimulating the parasympathetic nervous system which serves to reduce activation and induce a calm state
Cerebral change hypothesis	Moderate to vigorous PA produces large increases in cerebral blood flow bringing increased essential nutrients which are reflected in improved cognitive functioning
Expectancy hypothesis	The placebo effect – that is people expect to feel better and so they do
Distraction hypothesis	Time away from the stresses and routines of everyday life leads to the benefits associated with PA. Comparison of quiet time out versus PA found the psychological effects of PA exceed mere time out
Environmental mastery hypothesis	Enhanced self-worth or self-esteem linked to feeling of control, learning and mastery of the physical activity or associated behaviours
Identity development hypothesis	Psychological benefits derived from viewing oneself in a new or expanded way, becoming aware of using or developing personal qualities/strengths and experiencing personal growth

Source: Adapted from La Forge, 1995; Carron et al., 2003; Biddle and Mutrie, 2008

TABLE 9.4 Proposed mechanisms to explain the psychological benefits associated with physical activity

Both amateur and professional athletes experience the positive emotions associated with 'runner's high' commonly described to feature 'pleasantness,' 'inner harmony,' 'boundless energy,' or even druglike 'orgiastic' sensations' (Boecker et al., 2008: 2523). Although the extent of mood change resulting from engaging in physical exercise varies considerably from person to person (Dietrich and McDaniel, 2004), it is commonly accepted that most people benefit from an increase in positive emotion to some degree. Importantly, the fact that experiencing negative emotions prevents many people from engaging in PA, yet PA promotes positive emotions, appears to support Wilson and Gilbert's (2003) research which suggests that people are not very good at forecasting how they will feel in the future. Physical exercise programmes (such as gym membership or sessions with a personal trainer) and PA programmes (such as group gardening or walking) are increasingly appearing 'on prescription' in the UK and elsewhere, not just for the physical health benefits but for the therapeutic and psychological benefits. Within sport and physical exercise psychology specifically, participating in PA has been linked for some considerable time to enhanced positive emotions (see e.g. Boecker et al., 2008).

As proposed by Fredrickson's 'broaden-and-build' theory of positive emotions (see Chapter 2), research provides evidence that experiencing frequent positive emotions can build additional physical, social, intellectual and psychological resources, such as physical strength, coordination, balance, cardiovascular health, ability to connect with others, problem solving and optimism. In turn, these additional resources enable us to develop greater resilience to cope with, and even undo, the negative emotion that arises from experiencing disappointment and adversity. Although lay understanding suggests that the PA must be high intensity to produce the runner's high, research is not conclusive on this point. An early meta-analysis of acute aerobic exercise suggests that a lower intensity PA produces higher well-being than moderate to high intensity (Reed and Ones, 2006); however a more recent study suggests that both lower and higher intensity PA results in higher well-being (Reed and Buck, 2009; see also von Haarena et al., 2015). Regarding the link between the duration of PA and positive emotions, Reed and Ones (2006) posit that between 40 and 60 minutes of PA increases well-being, whereas over 75 minutes reduces it, and for sessions of between 7 and 35 minutes there are no differential effects.

Pre-dating positive psychology but in line with the broaden-and-build theory referred to earlier, research within the field of sport and exercise psychology suggests that enjoyment resulting from experiencing flow during participation in elite sport is a significant factor in developing athletes' commitment, motivation and performance excellence within sport (Jackson and Roberts, 1992). Hogan et al. (2015) posit that positive emotions, such as enjoyment resulting from flow experiences, could mediate increased motivation for training. It is unsurprising therefore that scholars such as Kimiecik et al. (in press) and Côté et al. (2007) emphasize the role that positive emotion plays in elite athlete development – in other words, experiences of positive emotion linked to informal and deliberate play as a child (e.g. backyard soccer and family softball) encourage continued participation in sports as an adult.

Participation in exercise during adolescence has been found to be a significant predictor for exercise and also positive mood in adult life (even controlling for adults' current level of exercise) (Rasmussen and Laumann, 2014). Hence, health benefits aside, it is somewhat short-sighted for schools to curtail the amount of time devoted to recess in favour of formal curriculum teaching time (Mallen and Grenville-Cleave, in press). Importantly, it would appear that early and over-specialization as well as highly structured physical activities for children (e.g. regular tennis or cricket lessons or swimming coaching), which are common in the USA and UK, may not be conducive to well-being. In contrast, Vealey and Chase (2016) suggest that diversification, that is, participating in different physical activities in a less structured way (informal football game this week, tennis match with friends of different abilities the next, etc.) is related to enjoyment and psychological well-being.

Despite the many physical, psychological and social benefits of regular participation in PA, large-scale survey data (Eurobarometer, 2010; World Health Organization, 2010) show that low participation in regular PA among most adults means that these benefits are not realized (Stenseng et al., 2015). Among recreational participants a factor influencing regular engagement in PA is the experiential quality of the sport or exercise experience with more enjoyment and satisfaction reported from those who take part regularly (Stenseng et al., 2015).

With considerable potential to provide insight in sport and exercise settings, emerging research from positive psychology recognizes that there is a two-way relationship between positive affect and successful outcomes; in other words positive affect contributes to success in performance and is not just an outcome of successful performance. Findings from varied disciplines and contexts (e.g. neuroscience, education, health, work settings and many sub-disciplines of psychology) have established that positive affect is causally related directly or indirectly to performance success (see Davidson and Schuyler, 2015). Findings demonstrate that positive affect fosters a range of desirable behaviours, skills and resources linked with success in PA including sociability, creativity, altruism, liking of self and others, resilience, strong bodies and immune system, adaptivity and effective conflict resolution skills.

Examining relationships between the role of positive affect and achievement success in PA remains a relatively unexplored area. To date attention has tended to focus on the study of negatively valenced negatively charged emotional affect and its impact on performance, and positive affect has tended to be examined as post-participation outcome (McCarthy, 2011; Brady and Grenville Cleave, in press).

There are situations during particularly challenging types of PA when awareness of one's emotional state is undesirable and may impair attentional and decision-making processes that support performance. In accounts of experiences of flow states (see Chapter 4), PA participants describe being totally absorbed in the task at hand in the present rather than being aware of particular past or current emotions (Seifert and Hedderson, 2010). This may support the idea that while we want to enjoy PA, when it is challenging and absorbing, our experience of positive emotion and enjoyment may emerge at particular intervals or after the activity rather than during or throughout the activity.

Relationships and PA

In the 1930s, scholars suggested that engaging in play (a form of PA) is not only enjoyable but helps children work out the rules for social interaction and develop relationships with others. Not only is the ability to form and maintain healthy relationships an important life skill, research from many areas of psychology including clinical, social and health as well as positive psychology suggests that there are many other benefits related to psychological well-being, for example: companionship, affection, intimacy and emotional security (O'Connell et al., 2016). Studies also suggest that individuals who maintain more and varied social ties (such as friendships, family relationships, intimate relationships and being a part of social, political and religious groups) are more likely to live longer than those who have fewer (Cohen and Janicki-Deverts, 2009). Within sport psychology particularly, most research into relationships has taken a deficit-reduction approach rather than benefit-enhancement. Emerging evidence from the field of positive psychology regarding the benefits of building and maintaining social ties suggests an opportunity for new areas for exploration within PA.

It is interesting that most psychological research within sport and exercise has focused primarily on the individual athlete rather than their relationships with others (e.g. coach or team mate) or how these relationships can contribute to enhanced performance in or experience of sport and PA (Grenville-Cleave et al., in press). Within positive psychology, the study of relationships and their contribution to psychological well-being (as opposed to ill-being, conflict or aggression for example) is gaining ground. Given their significance in PA experiences (and particularly for children and young people), more research is required to understand the importance of other social agents, such as peer group members or friends.

> ### Think about it...
>
> When have others had a positive impact on your experience of PA? How? When have you helped someone else stick to some personal PA project and how did you do this? When have you been part of an effective group or team in PA, and why was it effective?

There are several evidence-based interventions aimed at developing and maintaining strong and supportive relationships with others (see Chapter 8). Gratitude, defined as 'a felt sense of wonder, thankfulness and appreciation for life' (Emmons and Shelton, 2002: 460), for instance, is a well-known intervention shown to enhance well-being and the formation of good social ties. Gratitude has also been explored in the sport and PA arena in relation to performance and well-being by Chen and colleagues (e.g. Chen and Wu, 2014), as well as in relation to the athlete's ability to develop strong and supportive relationships with others, such as their coach, team mates and even other competitors (Grenville-Cleave et al., in press). Overall, expressing gratitude is associated with relationship formation and relationship maintenance behaviours (Algoe et al., 2008; Lambert and Fincham, 2011), promoting trust, encouraging reciprocal, pro-social behaviour between a benefactor and recipient (Emmons and McCullough, 2003), and building team cohesion (Chen et al., 2015; see also Chen and Wu, 2014).

Meaning and PA

As described earlier, PA can be experienced through many forms and it can have diverse and significant meaning at personal and varied collective levels. Meaning in life in (MIL) is considered a core element in some key theories of well-being (e.g. Seligman, 2011). As a construct MIL is characterized as having a coherent appreciation of one's self, one's life experiences and a sense of a lifelong purpose (Steger, 2012). PA does not need to be one's occupation, as in the case of professional or elite athletes, to hold a high level of meaning. Regardless of cultural background, personal characteristics or physical ability, PA can be highly meaningful and a central part of one's identity and life. In the longitudinal Evergreen Project in Finland, Takkinen et al. (2001) examined the role of PA in life for a group (n=198) of elderly people born between 1904 and 1913, and found that PA predicted a sense of meaning in life as well as self-rated health and functioning. Meaning in life is positively linked with a range of objective and subjective physical health indicators and has a positive relationship with health-promoting lifestyle factors such as physical exercise (see Steger et al., 2015).

PA programmes can be designed to support meaningful activity in life and to enhance many dimensions of psychosocial development and well-being. One such programme is that called LifeMatters (Hanrahan, 2018) which is a 10-week programme that uses physical games and psychological skills to benefit disadvantaged youth. LifeMatters was designed around basic needs theory (BNT, Deci and Ryan, 2000), which proposes that people have an innate drive to fulfil three basic needs of competence, autonomy and relatedness. Experiences that support fulfilment of these needs are associated with enhanced self-motivation, mental health and well-being, and inversely, activities or experiences that deny or thwart the satisfaction of these needs are associated with diminished well-being and motivation (Ryan and Deci, 2000). LifeMatters is a programme of ten 90-minute sessions and it has engaged a range of young participants including orphans, teenagers living in poverty, inner city youth and and former gang members in a range of countries such as Mexico, USA and Argentina. Rather than taking a deficit perspective and trying to stop unwanted behaviours such as aggression, helplessness, drug use or criminal activity associated with the young people, LifeMatters successfully adopted a strengths-based approach to promote an increase in desirable personal and pro-social behaviours. In impact studies LifeMatters was shown to significantly increase young people's life satisfaction, global self-worth, self-concept, resilience, competence, confidence and connection (Hanrahan, 2018).

Passion and PA

Examining the construct of passion can highlight how, among people who seem highly engaged in exercise and sport, differences in the meaning associated with their activity can lead to stark differences in behaviours and well-being experiences. Many people who participate in sport and exercise are passionate about the activity because it is highly personally important, it is immensely enjoyable and satisfying, they invest considerable time and energy in it and it may be self-defining (Vallerand et al., 2008). The construct of passion is described as having a strong inclination, love and high value for an activity. Pursuing a passion for PA may lead to positive emotional experiences via mastery and personal growth, self-regulation and task engagement, and contributing to a fulfilling and purposeful life. Passion may be influenced by different regulatory processes according to how the focus activity is integrated into the person's identity, which lead to different affective and behavioural outcomes. Vallerand (2015) proposed the Dualistic Model of Passion to describe two distinct types of passion as harmonious passion (HP) in which we take part in the activity for its own sake, that is for intrinsic reasons, and obsessive passion (OP) in which the activity is both central to our sense of self, and a way of gaining extrinsic benefits such as social status or approval.

In a series of reviews in PA contexts, compared with OP, HP has been linked with greater well-being and optimal functioning via a range of interpersonal (e.g. relationships) and intrapersonal adaptive outcomes (e.g. health, motivation, concentration, identity congruence, flow, vitality, coach–athlete relationship quality) (Stenseng et al., 2015; Vallerand, 2015). By contrast, OP predicted or was positively associated with maladaptive outcomes such as ill-being, socially prescribed perfectionism, lower self-esteem, anxiety, life conflict, interpersonal conflict, rumination and burnout. Because HP was either unrelated or negatively related to the maladaptive outcomes, it was proposed that in those who regularly exercise, HP may confer a protective effect when experiencing negative outcomes (Chichekian and Vallerand, 2018). A study by Rousseau and Vallerand (2008) found that in older adults HP predicted positive affect experienced after PA, which led to increases in psychological well-being. By contrast, OP predicted negative affect after PA and a decrease in well-being. Stenseng et al. (2015) note that in competitive sport, because obsessive passion may generate high effort, commitment and lead to success and satisfaction, under conditions of performance success, the relationship between OP and well-being may not be so straightforward. It may be that when athletes with OP are experiencing failure the deleterious consequences of OP become more evident.

time out

Dual career development and successful athlete transition

Emerging literature recognizes that sports people with a less well-developed sense of self (e.g. those who identify exclusively as a 'professional footballer' or 'elite athlete') and/or those who have not completed any other significant development during their time in sport are most at risk of failing to transition successfully within sport or out of sport on retirement through age, injury or non-selection (Park et al., 2013; Pink et al., 2015). Importantly the concept of 'dual career development' (Aquilina, 2013) posits that taking a more holistic approach to development through dual career activities and/or other meaningful pursuits also supports performer well-being, which benefits athletic performance in the present as well as in the future after sport (Pink et al., 2015). Within elite youth football, the My Future Today programme, which is grounded in positive psychology principles, encourages young footballers on the brink of a professional contract to identify other strengths, skills and abilities alongside the obvious footballing talent (Jolley et al., in press).

As our relationship with particular forms of PA may change over time, so too may the meaning and experience we derive from it. For example, research demonstrates that when people retire from elite or professional sport, because it has been such a large part of their life, they will transition more effectively with pre-emptive and sometimes specialist support to develop other interests and skills through other achievement domains (Ashfield et al., in press).

Achievement and PA

Whether framed as accomplishment (PERMA, Seligman, 2011), competence (basic needs theory, Deci and Ryan, 2000), environmental mastery or personal growth (psychological well-being), experiencing progress and personal development through learning and achievement is acknowledged as an essential component of well-being. There are many ways to view achievement in PA and some may be objective, highly visible and tangible and may involve winning, competition or cooperation with others and recognition of gaining particular standards or targets. There are also many subjective, intrinsic and personal dimensions of accomplishment in PA such as experiencing excitement, risk, heightened vitality, positive emotions, flow and enjoyment, satisfaction from trying one's hardest, overcoming challenges in the activity, reaching a personal milestone, and being with or helping others.

An individual's beliefs about their ability and how they can experience achievement and success in a particular domain can have considerable short- and long-term consequences for their aspirations, motivation, resilience and the enjoyment and satisfaction they experience (Dweck, 2017). Eminent positive psychologists acknowledge the topic of mindset (see Chapter 8) as making an important contribution towards understanding human achievement behaviours (Biswas-Diener, 2010). An individual's mindset refers to the implicit beliefs about the stability or malleability of personal attributes and behaviours (Dweck, 2017) and it is particularly pertinent in sport and exercise contexts where many myths and misconceptions exist about ability in PA contexts. For example, pervasive beliefs exist about the need to be naturally talented or 'the sporty type' to take part in or gain benefits from PA. In reality, almost everyone can gain many of the benefits from involvement in appropriate PA. Research supports the idea that in achievement situations people have tacit alignment either to an entity (fixed mindset) or an incremental (growth mindset) self-theory. People with a fixed mindset view their physical ability and attributes as innate and relatively stable (regardless of environmental or other personal factors) and by contrast, those with a growth mindset believe their physical ability is malleable and can be developed through both environmental factors such as feedback, and personal factors such as wanting to learn and investing effort (Dweck, 2017).

Findings across diverse contexts show repeated distinctions and adaptive or maladaptive consequences associated with holding a fixed and/or growth mindset (Dweck, 2017). Findings in sport and exercise contexts specifically highlight how a growth mindset either predicts or is positively associated with a range of desirable and adaptive outcomes such as positive affect and enjoyment, interest and persistence, resilience, heightened self-efficacy, task (rather than outcome) orientation, skill acquisition and performance (Biddle et al., 2003; Jowett and Spray, 2013). While Olympic hopefuls described how to be successful as involving some talent and innate physiological qualities, to be successful required more emphasis on hard work via practice and learning to develop the necessary physical and psychological qualities (Jowett and Spray, 2013). These high-performing athletes explained how they found ways of reframing setbacks such as poor performance or injury as they believed the 'adversity was teaching them the vital skills and attributes needed for their psychological development within the sport' (2013: 152). Our own consultancy experiences echo the calls to encourage understanding about mindsets among leaders, coaches, trainers and physical education teachers (Vella et al., 2011; 2013).

Chapter Summary

Reflecting on the learning objectives, the reader now understands ways in which PA contributes to psychological well-being. More specifically, the reader will know the following:

- PA may take many forms, not all of which are equally associated with psychological (or physical) benefits.
- Recommendations for PA levels to optimize health in adults.
- Mechanisms proposed to explain how psychological benefits of PA are realized.
- The key findings about the psychological benefits of PA.
- Selected insights from positive psychology regarding PA and positive emotions and enjoyment, relationships, meaning and achievement.

Suggested Resources

http://thedailymile.co.uk
Website for the Daily Mile primary school PA programme, including resources and information about how to set up your own Daily Mile, as well as details of a preliminary study on the benefits to children, which

included increased attainment, class behaviour, focus and concentration, self-esteem and fitness.

www.who.int/dietphysicalactivity/en/
The World Health Organization's (WHO) global strategy on diet, PA and health.

http://neweconomics.org/2008/10/five-ways-to-wellbeing-the-evidence/
New Economics Foundation's Five Ways to Wellbeing, including PA.

www.gov.uk/government/publications/uk-physical-activity-guidelines
UK Government PA guidelines.

www.nhs.uk/livewell/fitness/pages/fitnesshome.aspx
The UK's National Health Service (NHS) website with up-to-date information about the benefits of physical exercise; guidelines for PA for babies and children under five; children and young people, adults, the elderly, those with disabilities and wheelchair-users; ideas for strength, balance, flexibility and sitting exercises; information about nutrition; easy and gym-free exercises and ways to exercise for free.

The Growth Mindset Coaching Kit by Jeremy Frith and Rachel Sykes. Frith Sykes Ltd, Guernsey, UK.
A great resource for developing and applying ideas to develop a growth mindset in sport and exercise.

Further questions for the reader

1 Could you think of an instance when you took up PA that led you to experience little or no psychological benefits?

2 Would you argue that harmonious passion and obsessive passion can co-exist?

Personal Development Interventions

Interventions for enhancing engagement with PA

Five ways to well-being bingo

How do you get physically active? Do you spend Saturday afternoons on the golf course, or with your kids in the park? Do you walk the dog every day? See a

▶

personal trainer at the gym? Dance round the house while doing the chores? Choose a couple of your favourite ways of getting physically active and see how they deliver any or all of the Five Ways to Well-being (Aked et al., 2008). We have completed a bingo card for one of our favourite physical activities below (see Table 9.5).

Your PA of choice	1. Connect	2. Be active	3. Take notice	4. Keep learning	5. Give
e.g. working on my allotment	Yes: talking to fellow allotment holders; sharing gardening tips; swapping plants and seeds	Yes: digging; weeding; hoeing; planting; watering; harvesting; applying compost, etc.	Yes: noticing the weather; when is the right time to plant; when to water; what is ready to eat, etc.	Yes: growing new fruit and vegetable varieties; trying new planting techniques	Yes: sharing fruit, vegetables, plants and seeds with neighbours, family and friends
?		Yes	?	?	?
?		Yes	?	?	?
?		Yes	?	?	?

Source: Based on Aked et al., 2008

TABLE 9.5 Five Ways to Well-being Bingo

Walking our way to clearer thinking and feeling good

Linked to the many sources of evidence for psychological benefits of PA and supported by many mechanisms for gaining these benefits (see Table 9.4), getting up and walking continuously (and ideally briskly) for as little as 10 minutes indoors or outdoors can be a great strategy to change your mood and improve your thinking. This can be at any point in the day and since there is no time like the present, why not put this book down and go now? Before you go and after you return, why not complete the PANAS Scale (Watson et al., 1988, see Chapter 2) but with the time frame of how you feel 'right now' and see whether you notice any changes?

Measurement Tools

Physical Activity Enjoyment Scale (PACES)

(Kendzierski and DeCarlo, 1991)

Directions

Please rate how you feel at the moment about the physical activity you have been doing using the scale below.

1.	I enjoy it	1	2	3	4	5	6	7	I hate it
2.	I feel bored	1	2	3	4	5	6	7	I feel interested
3.	I dislike it	1	2	3	4	5	6	7	I like it
4.	I find it pleasurable	1	2	3	4	5	6	7	I find it unpleasurable
5.	I am very absorbed in this activity	1	2	3	4	5	6	7	I am not at all absorbed in this activity
6.	It's no fun at all	1	2	3	4	5	6	7	It's a lot of fun
7.	I find it energizing	1	2	3	4	5	6	7	I find it tiring
8.	It makes me depressed	1	2	3	4	5	6	7	It makes me happy
9.	It's very pleasant	1	2	3	4	5	6	7	It's very unpleasant
10.	I feel good physically while doing it	1	2	3	4	5	6	7	I feel bad physically while doing it
11.	It's very invigorating	1	2	3	4	5	6	7	It's not at all invigorating
12.	I am very frustrated by it	1	2	3	4	5	6	7	I am not at all frustrated by it
13.	It's very gratifying	1	2	3	4	5	6	7	It's not at all gratifying
14.	It's very exhilarating	1	2	3	4	5	6	7	It's not at all exhilarating
15.	It's not at all stimulating	1	2	3	4	5	6	7	It's very stimulating
16.	It gives me a strong sense of accomplishment	1	2	3	4	5	6	7	It does not give me any sense of accomplishment
17.	It's very refreshing	1	2	3	4	5	6	7	It's not at all refreshing
18.	I felt as though I would rather be doing something else	1	2	3	4	5	6	7	I felt as though there was nothing else I would rather be doing

▶

► **Scoring**

To get a total score add all scores for question numbers 2, 3, 6, 8, 12, 15 and 18. Then reverse the score for all other questions. Thus a score of 7 becomes 1, 6 becomes 2, 5 becomes 3, 4 stays the same, 3 becomes 5, 2 becomes 6, and 1 becomes 7. The higher the number the more enjoyment was experienced. A maximum score is 126, so convert your score to a percentage, divide your total by 126 and multiply by 100.

Interpretation

The higher the total PACES score, the greater the level of enjoyment.

Review

Eleven of the items are reverse scored and the higher the total PACES score, the greater the level of enjoyment.

CHAPTER 10

Applying Positive Psychology

❖ LEARNING OBJECTIVES

How can psychotherapists and other clinicians facilitate optimal functioning and psychological well-being? Since the strengths-based approach is utilized within most areas of applying positive psychology, this chapter commences by reviewing different approaches to conceptualizing and classifying human strengths, focusing specifically on the values in action (VIA) and strengths profile inventories. The rest of the chapter discusses some of the recent advances on the interface between psychotherapy, coaching and positive psychology. Finally, the chapter considers the applications of positive psychology to educational and organizational settings.

Topics include:

- The concept and application of strengths.
- 'Positive therapy', its siblings and cousins.
- Positive psychology coaching (PPC).

- Positive education curricula.
- Positive psychology in organizations.
- Enabling institutions and their place in society.

MOCK ESSAY QUESTIONS

1 From what is wrong to what is strong. To what extent could the focus on strengths (as opposed to weaknesses) contribute to functioning well?

2 Discuss how positive psychology's empirical research can be used in one-to-one environments.

3 Discuss how research findings from positive psychology can inform other areas of applied psychology, such as educational and organizational psychology.

Character strengths and virtues

So what exactly are strengths and how can they be used to enhance and maintain 'the good life'? Studying strengths of character is a difficult notion at the best of times. Science is supposedly predicated on the basis of 'fact and objective truths', whereas values and characters are fluffy, philosophical notions, seemingly impossible to pin down. Some researchers argue that psychology should maintain its focus on the study of character, whereas other researchers believe that character is a philosophical matter rather than a psychological one. Christopher Peterson and Martin Seligman, however, believe otherwise (Peterson and Seligman, 2004). Following an extensive review of thousands of pieces of literature, science and text, from across the world and centuries, they identified 24 character strengths that are organized into six virtues[1] (see Table 10.1). The VIA classification of strengths and virtues is widely recognized and used by psychologists as a reference guide in relation to strengths and positive functioning.

As positive psychology advocates, good character is more than bad character negated or minimized. Furthermore, human strengths are not secondary to weaknesses. Through the pioneering work of Peterson and Seligman, human strengths are now amenable to scientific assessment and understanding.

Strengths versus talents

Within psychology, terminology is never straightforward. Thus, some researchers study *strengths* whereas others study *talents*. Strengths are argued to be distinguishable from talents as talents can be considered to be more innate, not necessarily with moral implications and can be wasted (e.g. someone may have a talent for football or singing but decides not to develop or use that talent).

Wisdom and Knowledge	• Curiosity and interest • Love of learning • Judgement, critical thinking, open-mindedness • Practical intelligence, creativity, originality, ingenuity • Perspective
Courage	• Valour • Industry, perseverance • Integrity, honesty, authenticity • Zest, enthusiasm
Love	• Intimacy, reciprocal attachment • Kindness, generosity, nurturance • Social intelligence, personal intelligence, emotional intelligence
Justice	• Citizenship, duty, loyalty, teamwork • Equity, fairness • Leadership
Temperance	• Forgiveness, mercy • Modesty, humility • Prudence, caution • Self-control, self-regulation
Transcendence	• Awe, wonder, appreciation of beauty and excellence • Gratitude • Hope, optimism, future-mindedness • Playfulness, humour • Spirituality, sense of purpose, faith, religiousness

TABLE 10.1 The VIA classification of strengths and virtues

Think about it…

What do you think of this distinction? Are we ever really born with talent, or do we develop talent with hard work and effort?

Definition of a strength

In order to be classified as a character strength, Peterson and Seligman set out several inclusion criteria, some of which are as follows (adapted from Boniwell, 2008):

- It must be present in a range of the individual's behaviours, thoughts, feelings and actions, generalizable across situations and times.
- It must contribute to fulfilment of the good life for self and others.

- It must be morally valued in its own right, irrespective of the beneficial outcomes it can lead to.
- Displaying the strength does not diminish others, but may benefit them.
- It can be measured.
- It can be distinguished from other character strengths.
- The society provides institutions and associated discourses and social practices for cultivating those strengths and virtues.

Think about it...

Have a go at completing the VIA Questionnaire for yourself at: www.authentic-happiness.org.

You will receive a read out of your top 5 signature strengths and information on what to do with the results.

The alternative or rival to the VIA is the *Clifton Strengths Finder*, which is organized into 34 themes of talent (Lopez and Ackerman, 2009). They propose that talents are the basis of strengths, which are thereby produced when talents are refined with knowledge and skills. This tool was created by Donald Clifton who interviewed thousands of top performers from several organizational contexts (mainly business and academia) and analysed the data accordingly to determine success. This data was then used to develop a semi-structured interview schedule, which was delivered to millions of participants across skill, job and culture contexts. Statistical analysis reduced the data to 34 themes. The tool is said to have high validity and internal reliability, although most of the data collected on the Strengths Finder is internally conducted, with outside, unbiased researchers rarely given the opportunity to full access of the properties. At present, millions of people from across the world have taken this tool, and research suggests that organizations that focus on their employees' strengths, rather than weaknesses, can reduce turnover, increase productivity and, in turn, profitability (Delichte and Evers-Cacciapaglia, 2010).

Think about it...

You can access the Clifton Strengths Finder via http://www.strengthsfinder. com and by purchasing one of the several Clifton Strengths Finder books.

Strengths Profile

The strengths profile assessment (previously known as Realise2 or R2) was developed at the Centre for Applied Positive Psychology (CAPP) in Warwickshire, England. The Strengths Profile can be accessed online, and the reader can take the test asking them to assess 60 attributes (ranging from Spotlight to Courage to Relationship deepener) and determine three major factors: whether or not these attributes have the ability to re-energize them; whether they are good at them; and how often they get to use them in their daily life.

According to this model, Strengths Profile divides individuals' attributes into four dimensions:

1 *Realized strengths* are the strengths that we already are aware of and use, which in turn enable us to perform at our best.

2 *Unrealized strengths* are strengths that we may not be able to express on a daily basis due to our environment and work situations. However, when we do display them we derive energy and satisfaction from exhibiting these attributes.

3 *Learned behaviours* encompass the behaviours that we have, over time, learned to do well; however, we do not derive pleasure or energy from completing them. These are not considered strengths in the Strengths Profile, but attributes that we have learned to do well, but which drain us, therefore inhibiting our ability to perform and live at our best.

4 *Weaknesses* encompass the behaviours that we have not managed to do well over time and they drain us. These attributes can create issues and need to be managed so that they do not hinder our success in life.

The first two quadrants can hold up to seven attributes, whereas learned behaviours can hold up to four and weaknesses can hold up to three. In the report, the order in which the attributes are numbered demonstrates the potency of the attribute.

Once you have completed the online assessment tool at www.strengthsprofile.com and reviewed the detailed report, Strengths Profile creates a development and prioritization plan for you to enhance your unrealized strengths, moderate your learned behaviours and minimize your weakness. By doing this, you can tangibly maximize your daily performance. The corresponding website offers additional resources, tools and tips related to this assessment instrument.

The value of strengths

Now that we have taken the tests and know our strengths, what is the value of them and how can they be applied to help us live our life to its fullest?

Research has demonstrated that by simply following our strengths, we can gain insight and perspective into our lives, generate optimism, confidence and even enhanced sense of vitality (Clifton and Anderson, 2001). More importantly, strengths appear to have a preventative mechanism in terms of buffering against certain types of physical dysfunction such as allergies, diabetes, chronic pain and even some mental disorders. Finally, strengths help build psychological resilience with the use of signature strengths in work, love, play and parenting generating positive emotions. Finally, the strengths approach is argued to be at the heart of successful psychological therapies (Peterson and Seligman, 2004).

Distribution and demographics

One of the most popular questions we get asked is whether or not certain strengths are more amenable to certain demographics, countries and even age groups. The answer seems to be 'yes' to all three. Based on the data from 117,676 respondents, within the USA and other Western nations, the most commonly endorsed strengths are: kindness, fairness, honesty, gratitude and judgement, and the lesser strengths included prudence, modesty and self-regulation (Park et al., 2004). Hope, teamwork and zest were more common among adolescents than adults whereas appreciation of beauty, authenticity, leadership and open-mindedness were more common among adults.

Biswas-Diener (2006) conducted an in-depth empirical examination of strengths and virtues from a cross-cultural perspective. Among 123 members of the Kenyan Maasai, 71 seal hunters in Northern Greenland and 519 University of Illinois students there was a high rate of agreement about the existence, desirability and development of virtues. Despite strong similarities, there were differences between cultures based on gender, the perceived importance of specific virtues (such as modesty), and the existence of cultural institutions that promote each strength. In the UK, bother genders tend to score similarly among their top five strengths (open-mindedness, fairness, curiosity and love of learning). In addition, as British citizens get older, they tend to have higher strengths relating to curiosity and love of learning, fairness and forgiveness and self-regulation (Linley et al., 2007).

In relation to well-being, it appears that it is better to have some strengths rather than others. Research suggests that the strengths of curiosity, gratitude, hope, love and zest are the strengths most robustly associated with life satisfaction (Park et al., 2004). So, should we be worried that we are doomed to never be happy if we do not have these correlated strengths? We would argue, on the basis of other well–documented research, that there is a lot we can do, regardless of what strengths we have, to enhance our well-being.

For example, simply taking the VIA online and identifying our top 5 signature strengths can significantly enhance our well-being levels. This, in itself, is considered to be a positive psychosocial interventions (PPI) (Seligman et al., 2005). From there, we can do many things with this information to create a strength-based approach to life. When deciding on which career to follow or what job to take as we decide on the future, trying to match your top 5 strengths with a job is very important, as the most valued job, relationship and hobbies are the ones congruent with people's strengths. Thus, if a top strength is kindness, then we should try to source a job with some form of mentoring element. Or if we score high on curiosity, we should try to inject some adventure into our romantic relationships.

Finally, we can try using our signature strengths in a new way every day, for at least one week. Infusing daily life with variety in how we express our strength has a lasting effect on increased happiness and decreased depressive symptoms for up to six months (Seligman et al., 2005).

Can my strengths change over time?

Strengths have the ability to morph over time and circumstances. Although the test is considered reliable, it is subject to changes in environment. One of the biggest influences is tragedy. For example, after 9/11, researchers compared pre- and post- 9/11 VIA surveys and found a significant increase in faith, hope and love (Peterson and Seligman, 2003). Furthermore, Peterson and his colleagues have started to look into the connections between illness (both physical and mental) and strengths. More specifically, they have found, from a large sample of US citizens, that individuals who recover from a serious physical illness (e.g. cancer, heart disease) score higher on greater appreciation of beauty, bravery, curiosity, fairness, forgiveness, gratitude, humour, kindness, love of learning and spirituality. Those who have recovered from a psychological disorder score higher on appreciation of beauty, creativity, curiosity, gratitude and love of learning (Peterson et al., 2006).

Think about it...

If you do not like online tests, we would suggest reviewing the strengths lists (either the VIA, Strengths Finder or Strengths Profile) and pick the top five you feel are most authentic to you. When you are doing this, think about the following:

- Does the strength identify who you really are?
- When you are demonstrating this strength, do you truly enjoy yourself?
- Are you energized during and after its use?

Positive therapy

When we hear the word 'therapy', many of us automatically equate it to something negative, defunct, broken. *Positive psychology therapy* is, at present, a non-governed field (Joseph and Linley, 2006; 2009). Many psychologists who affiliate themselves with the positive psychology movement offer ideas and approaches on how to conduct 'positive psychology therapy'. The underlying principles are that therapy shouldn't focus just on diagnosing and treating disorder, maladjustment, suffering and so on (Rashid, 2009b; Joseph and Linley, 2009). In addition, therapy should recognize, utilize and build on the client's existing strengths and resources rather than view the client as flawed and disordered.

time out

Types of therapy
What is therapy and what type of therapies are currently in practice? In modern-day psychology, you can choose a variety of schools of thought when considering therapy, such as:

1 *Behavioural:* this is aimed at changing behaviour (thereby changing thought processes).

2 *Cognitive–behavioural:* aimed at changing thought processes and changing your action.

3 *Psychoanalytic:* aims to uncover and deal with unconscious emotional issues developed from the past.

4 *Psychodynamic:* similar to the above methods, however less intense and shorter in duration.

5 *Gestalt:* part of the existential branch, this therapy aims to uncover personal responsibility.

6 *Client-centred:* this aims to be non-directive and assumes that the client is better equipped to figure out their own answers to their own problems.

7 *Transactional analysis:* a mixture of several therapies, this assumes that all people are ok, we can all think for ourselves, and that we have the power to change our situation.

8 *Integrative therapy:* aims to adopt a pragmatic approach to therapy, thereby using the positive elements of several types of therapy and combining them into one new cohesive framework.

(Adapted from Boniwell, 2008: 110–111).

Positive therapy is also not just concerned with enhancing strengths and qualities within the individual but the prevention of mental illness and ill-being (Seligman, 2002b). There are issues with trying to decipher the effects of psychotherapy. As Seligman points out, field studies versus controlled lab settings consistently show better results; furthermore, when researchers try to isolate the specific elements that appear to be working, there appears to be no large difference between techniques. Finally, as in all psychology, we have to negotiate the placebo effect (Goldacre, 2009), with on average 50 per cent of clients demonstrating positive effects when being administered placebo drugs/therapies (Seligman, 2002b).

THERAPIES

Do all therapies work the same? And if not, which ones have shown better results than others? In 2002, Lambert and Barley wrote and published a controversial chapter on the effects of the therapeutic relationship and positive outcomes of psychotherapy. After reviewing the psychotherapy literature, they concluded that only 15 per cent of therapy success could be attributed to the therapeutic technique (method used). The remainder was attributed to expectancy (15 per cent), common factors (such as empathy, warmth confidentiality) (30 per cent) and extratherapeutic change 40 per cent). Wampold (2005) conducted a similar review of laboratory-controlled psychotherapy interventions, and found evidence supporting Lambert and Barley's findings. His results showed that it was the therapists themselves that were the largest predictor of therapy success whereas the treatment technique had only a minute effect on the final outcome.

See Lambert and Barley (2001, 2002) and Wampold (2005) for the original articles.

Seligman argues that generic therapy works because it can be broken down into tactics and deep strategies, and that the utilization of these can account for the beneficial outcomes of psychotherapy. Tactics that all good therapy must include are: attention, authority figure, rapport, paying for services, trust, opening up, naming the problem and utilizing tricks of the trade (e.g. 'Let's pause here', rather than 'Let's stop here') (Seligman 2002b: 6). Deep strategies are arguably theoretical and scientifically based techniques within positive psychology. These strategies include: instilling hope and building strengths (such as courage, rationality capacity for pleasure, etc.). By using these strategies, therapists will engage with enhancing and nurturing what is already strong, rather than trying to fix or remedy what's wrong.

Indeed, even in the late 1960s, therapists were aware that therapy existed in two formats: helping with psychological disorders and enabling psychological growth (Mahrer, as cited in Bernard et al., 2010). A positive therapy stands in sharp contrast to attempts that seek to classify every problem of living as a psychological disorder. The next section will review some of the existing and new therapies that may be considered under the 'positive' umbrella, including rational emotional behavioural therapy (REBT), motivational interviewing (MI), acceptance and commitment therapy (ACT), quality of life therapy (QOLT), well-being therapy (WBT) and positive psychotherapy (PPT). Of course, this is not an exhaustive review of all the types of 'positive' therapies available; however they are the ones with the most evidence behind them to date.

Distinct approaches within positive clinical psychology and therapy[2]

Rational emotional behavioural therapy (REBT)

Contrary to popular belief (even within positive psychology), Ellis's REBT was aimed at both helping individuals, with and without emotional problems, to deal with emotional distress as well as lead a fulfilling and happy life (Bernard et al., 2010). Based on the concept of rationality this scientific model aimed at restructuring cognition, which enables individuals to harness their own inner strengths and abilities to live rational lives, 'rationality is characterised by positive emotions, (pleasure, joy excitement), an absence of dysfunctional negative emotions, a determination to solve life's problems and goal directed behaviour' (Bernard et al., 2010: 303). By doing so, the individuals can experience short-term positive affect as well as long-term goal attainments and psychological well-being.

Ellis proposes that there are 11 rational principles of living as follows:

- Self-interest: individuals need to pursue their own interests before others; not give over themselves to others (be kind to yourself).
- Social interest: while you are pursing your happiness make sure it is not at the expense of others, and be kind to others.
- Self-direction: do not wait for others to 'serve' you happiness or remove dissatisfaction; you need to do this yourself.
- Self-acceptance: remove the belief in a 'rating scale', when comparing yourself to others. There is no 'global standard'.
- Tolerance of others: people who understand that all humans are fallible will be better equipped to deal with flaws and diversity.

■ Short-term/long-term hedonism: it's about the short-term and the long-term happiness of individuals. Don't take the easy route.

■ Commitment to creative, absorbing activities and pursuits: similar to the concept of flow, try to engage in activities of 'vital absorption'.

■ Risk taking and experimenting: continue to explore and take on new projects; this will expand your mind and helps development of the self. Also take risks; failure is a part of life so take a chance!

a) High frustration tolerance and willpower: don't expect that life provides you with what you want comfortably and easily. In order to achieve something pleasant in the long term, you often have to do something unpleasant in the short term.

b) Problem solving: recognize that there are almost always alternative solutions to any problem.

c) Scientific thinking: think in a more objective, rational, but also more flexible manner.

Even Ellis was a balanced scientist, highlighting the importance of negative emotions. He argued that people who exhibit sadness are rational and therefore able to deal with their situation. The next section will move away from REBT and focus on Rogers' concept of unconditional positive regard.

Organismic valuing process

Therapists are also directed to encourage clients to use the *organismic valuing process* (Rogers) and provide unconditional positive regard to strip away external and internal conditions of worth. Therapists should form an authentic relationship with clients (Rogers) as this satisfies the need for relatedness and has been shown to be the strongest predictor of therapy outcome (Orlinsky et al., 1994). Thus, it is not so important what therapists do (i.e. what techniques they use); what matters instead is the extent to which they use 'deep strategies', such as instilling hope, building strengths and facilitating coherence in mental functioning (Joseph and Linley, 2006).

Positive psychologists also acknowledge that some psychopathologies (e.g. schizophrenia, bipolar disorder, temporal lobe epilepsy and organic brain diseases) are best considered as disorders and treated within the medical field by psychiatrists and clinical psychologists.

Motivational interviewing (MI)

MI is a short-term intervention methodology that works by facilitating and engaging intrinsic motivation within the client in order to change behaviour (Miller and Rollnick, 2002). It is a practical and empathetic process that takes into consideration how difficult it is to make life changes. In a supportive manner, a motivational interviewer encourages clients to talk about their need for change and their own reasons for wanting to change. The role of the interviewer is mainly to evoke a conversation about change and commitment. The interviewer listens and reflects back the client's thoughts so that they can hear their reasons and motivations expressed back to them. Research has shown that this intervention works well with individuals who start off unmotivated or unprepared for change.

As initially formulated, MI was based on client-centred therapy (Rogers, 1951) and assumed an actualizing tendency and organismic process as central aspects of its meta-theory. However, in recent formulations, more substantial emphasis has been put on change talk – that is, on clients expressing cognitions that are concerned with changing key behaviours – and less emphasis on the autonomy and actualizing that were more central in the earlier formulation (Miller and Rose, 2009).

Acceptance and commitment therapy (ACT)

Acceptance and commitment therapy is one of a family of behaviour therapies, dialectical behaviour therapy and functional-analytic psychotherapy. It draws on a functional contextualist worldview, in which suffering or unhappiness can be seen either as normal or problematic, depending on the context in which they occur. A model for behaviour change, ACT has six core processes that contribute to the development of psychological flexibility, and moving away from inflexibility:

1 Acceptance versus avoidance.
2 Cognitive defusion versus cognitive fusion.
3 Present moment versus thinking the past or the future.
4 Self-as-context versus self-as-content.
5 Valued living versus lack of values.
6 Committed action versus inaction/impulsivity/avoidance.

The strengths of ACT are its sound evidence base (e.g. Öst, 2014; 2017) and the fact that it can be used in both clinical and non-clinical settings (Hayes et al., 1999). Its interventions entail a mix of acceptance and mindfulness approaches, and are identified in major positive psychology meta-analyses (e.g. Weiss et al., 2016).

Quality of Life (QOL) Therapy

Quality of Life Therapy/Coaching (QOLTC) is an approach to positive psychology intervention, offering a comprehensive package (Frisch, 2006). Clients are taught tools for boosting their satisfaction and fulfilment in any one of 16 specific areas of life in order to enhance overall contentment or quality of life. These areas include life goals and values, spiritual life, self-esteem, health, relationships, work, play, helping, learning, creativity, money, surroundings – home, neighbourhood, community – and relapse prevention. While QOL Coaching is aimed at non-clinical populations who wish to be happier and more successful, QOLT allows clinicians to integrate the latest in positive psychology into their clinical practice.

In QOLTC the therapist or a coach works with the client to select two to five areas of life that are seen by the client as highly essential for their well-being, but which have high levels of dissatisfaction. In subsequent sessions, cognitive-behavioural strategies are used to facilitate changes in the attitudes or perceptions of this area. These strategies include but are not limited to the following: expressive writing, relaxation, meditation, daily stress diary, problem solving, volunteering, creating a *Playlist* (identification of a wide range of mood-enhancing activities that the reader can try out at the end of this chapter), worry management techniques, goal-setting tools and so on. In essence, clients are taught to put their time where their values are. The package also includes regular homework between sessions.

QOLTC has been evaluated as successful and superior to the standard treatment in randomized controlled trials (see e.g. Rodrigue et al., 2006). In one of the trials, using QOLTC with wait-listed lung transplant patients led to significant improvement in quality of life, mood disturbance and social intimacy. Improvements in quality of life and mood appear to be maintained for as long as three months after treatment (Rodrigue et al., 2005).

Well-being Therapy (WBT)

WBT is a short-term psychotherapy created by Giovanni Fava that aims to develop well-being and resilience. This type of therapy is conceptually based on Ryff's psychological well-being model, targeting environmental mastery, personal growth, purpose in life, autonomy, self-acceptance and positive relations with others. It consists of eight sessions, 30–50 minutes in length with an emphasis on self-observation with a structured diary. Essentially, clients simply monitor whether or not episodes of PWB occur. Episodes (or the lack thereof) are then discussed in therapy, and obstacles are targeted with traditional CBT techniques (e.g. refuting negative automatic thoughts). Evidence suggests the potential of this therapy for relapse prevention in mood and anxiety disorders, as well as in the treatment of post-traumatic stress disorder (Ruini and Fava, 2004; Fava and Ruini, 2009; Ruini and Fava, 2012).

Positive psychotherapy (PPT)

PPT is a therapeutic endeavour within positive psychology to broaden the scope of traditional psychotherapy. Its central working mechanism is to activate clients' positive resources such as positive emotions, character strengths and meaning while treating psychopathology. PPT is based on three assumptions (Rashid and Seligman, 2013; in press). First, clients inherently desire growth, fulfilment and happiness instead of just seeking to avoid misery, worry and anxiety. Psychopathology happens when a person is no longer growing. Second, positive resources such as strengths are authentic and as real as symptoms and disorders. These are not defences, illusions or clinical by-products of symptom relief. The final assumption is that effective therapeutic relationships can be formed through the discussion and manifestation of positive resources, not only thorough lengthy analysis of weaknesses and problems. PPT is primarily based on Seligman's PERMA conceptualization of well-being (2002b; 2011) that includes positive emotion, engagement, relationships, meaning and accomplishment. Importantly, pain and trauma are not ignored in the therapeutic process, but more emphasis is placed on the positive aspects of human experience and the growth potential of each client. A brief overview of PPT is presented in Table 10.2. A number of validation studies of PPT have been completed, establishing its effectiveness (Seligman et al., 2006; Rashid and Anjum, 2007; Meyer et al., 2012).

To conclude, critiques of positive approaches to clinical psychology and therapy stem from the perception that many conventional therapies already use positive psychology principles to reduce suffering and increase happiness and well-being (but usually without making this explicit). For example, some therapies facilitate positive emotions; meaning and purpose (self-determination/ autonomy); self-efficacy, perceived competence/mastery; relatedness and interpersonal functioning (Weinberger, 1995). We accept the above, yet would argue that the approaches reviewed above are more explicit in putting the positive forward.

Applying positive psychology to coaching

Over the last decade, the integration of positive psychology (theory and practice) into the coaching world has increased exponentially (Boniwell et al., 2014). Although an obvious pairing, it is only recently that the publication of accessible, and scientifically supported, positive psychology manuals and tools (e.g. *The HOW of Happiness*; *Positivity*; *Practising Positive Psychology Coaching*; *Positive Psychology and Coaching*; *Positive ACTIONS*, etc.), has enabled coaches access to the existing validated PPIs, which offer innovative and invigorating exercises for coaches to use in their client sessions.

The process of coaching typically involves identification and development of strengths and competences, goal setting, and a focus on achieving results within a specified time-scale. Coaching psychology is for enhancing performance in work and personal life domains with normal, non-clinical populations,

Phase One

Theme	Skill	Practice
1. Orientation to PPT Positive Emotions	• Discussing ground rules, client-clinician role & responsibilities • Importance of practicing skills in and between sessions • Developing a coherent self-narrative	Positive Introduction: Client recalls, reflects and writes a one-page Positive Introduction sharing a story with a ginning, middle and a positive end, in concrete terms which called for the best in the client
Gratitude (ongoing exercise) Positive Emotions	• Honing gratitude skills by developing awareness, acknowledging and appreciating everyday good events and experiences	Gratitude Journal: Client starts an on-going journal to record three good things every night (big or small) and also writes what made these happen
2. Character strengths Engagement	• Understanding that character strengths are intrinsically valued attributes which can be used, refined and developed towards self-development • Understanding that exploring character strengths are as real and authentic as symptoms and weaknesses	Character Strengths: Client compiles his client signature strengths profile by collecting information from multiple resources including self-report, an online measure, a family member and a friend
3. Signature strengths action plan (A Better Version of Me) Accomplishment	• Integrating character strengths from various perspectives to determine signature strengths	A Better Version of Me: Client writes a self-development plan 'A Better Version of Me' which uses her strengths adaptively through specific, measurable and achievable goals
4. Practical Wisdom	• Learning and practicing skills of practical wisdom to use one's signature strengths in a balanced and adaptive way, especially in the context of one's presenting concerns.	Under & Over Use of Strengths: Client applies five practical wisdom strategies (specificity, relevance, conflict, reflection and calibration) to resolve three specific scenarios

TABLE 10.2 Brief overview of positive psychotherapy (PPT) session-by-session description

Phase Two

Theme	Skill	Practice
5. Open vs. Closed Memories Meaning	• Reflecting and exploring consequences of holding on to open (bitter) memories including those that perpetuate his psychological distress.	Positive Appraisal: After practicing relaxation, client writes bitter memories and explores a variety of ways to deal with them adaptively.
6. Forgiveness Relationships	• Discerning forgiveness as a process of decreasing negative resentment-based emotions, motivation and thoughts. • Learning how forgiveness can help to heal and empower. • Learning what forgiveness is and isn't	Forgiveness: Client learns about REACH – a process of forgiveness and/or writes a letter of forgiveness but not necessarily deliver it.
7. Gratitude Positive Emotions & Relationships	• Attuning awareness towards good Exploring gratitude as a process of enduring thankfulness. Broadening the perspective and building other positive emotions	Gratitude Letter & Visit: Client writes a letter of gratitude to someone whom Client never properly thanked; Client polish the draft and make arrangements to deliver it in person
8. Therapeutic Progress Accomplishment	• Discussing motivation and therapeutic progress; elicit and offer feedback • Discussing potential barriers and generate strength-based solutions	Client completes the Forgiveness and Gratitude exercises Client discusses his experience regarding A better Version of Me
9. Satisficing vs. maximizing Positive Emotions & Meaning	• Learning about maximizing which entails getting the best possible option, or making the best decision while satisficing entails settling for the good enough in most domains of life • Understanding the cost of maximizing	Satisficing: Client explores in which domains of life he maximizes or satificizes Client drafts a plan to increase satificizing

TABLE 10.2 (Continued)

(Continued)

Phase Three

Theme	Skill	Practice
10. Hope and optimism	• Developing ability to see the best possible, yet realistic side of most things • Believing that challenges faced are temporary and one is capable of overcoming them	One Door Closed, One Door Opened: Client reflects and writes about three doors that closed and three door that opened.
Positive Emotions	• Hoping that most goals are attainable	
11. Post-traumatic Growth (PTG)	• Exploring that Post-Traumatic Growth (PTG) can potentially occur even after the trauma • Learning that PTG is often accompanied by a renewed philosophy of life, resolve to prevail, commitment to improve relationships and prioritizing what really matters	Reflection & Writing about PTG: Client can complete an optional exercise of transporting troubling and traumatic experiences on a piece of paper with assurance that writing is only for her own eyes, kept in a secure place The exercise is completed after client develops healthy coping skills and is not overwhelmed by current stressors
Meaning		
12. Slowness and Savouring	• Learning about the psychological hazards of being fast and about specific applied ways to slow down • Developing awareness about savouring as an ability which represents the completeness of human experience • Learning to attend mindfully the positive features of an event, experience or situation.	Slow & Savor: Client selects one slowness and one savouring technique that fit client's personality and life circumstances
Positive Emotions & Engagement		
13. Positive relationships	• Learning that connecting with others not only meets biological needs but motivates us to achieve and maintain well-being.	Active-Constructive Responding (ACR): Client explores strengths of his significant other and also practices active-constructive responding.
Relationships	• Learning about Capitalization—a process of being seen, felt and valued–the sum that is greater than its part	

TABLE 10.2 (Continued)

Phase Three

Theme	Skill	Practice
14. Altruism Meaning	• Learning about belonging to and serving something larger than oneself can be a potent antidote to psychological distress	Gift of Time: Client plans to give the gift of time doing something that also uses client signature strengths
15. Positive Legacy Meaning & Accomplishment	• Integrating elements of well-being together and reflecting on group exercises • Maintaining client therapeutic progress	Positive Legacy: Client writes how she would like to be remembered, especially in terms of her positive footprints

Source: Reproduced with permission from Rashid and Seligman (in press).

underpinned by models of coaching grounded in established therapeutic approaches (Grant and Palmer, 2002).

Executive coaching takes place in business contexts and is commonly aimed at 'key' employees at times of change and transition. Furthermore, when coaching is undertaken by professional versus peer coaches, research shows a greater commitment and progression, as well as higher levels of well-being (environmental mastery) (Spence and Grant, 2007).

Positive psychology and coaching psychology both claim that attention should be redirected away from 'fixing' the client, from looking for signs of pathology or viewing the client as 'broken', flawed, disordered, and so on. Both coaching and positive psychology are natural allies in sharing an explicit concern with the enhancement of optimal functioning and well-being, arguing for performance improvement, finding what is right with the person and working on enhancing it. Good coaching helps clients discover their skills and resources and fits with the premise of positive psychology: helping clients identify their strengths and find ways to use them more often in all aspects of their lives. Positive psychology provides an excellent theoretical framework for coaching and likewise, coaching can serve as a good soundboard to their scholarly ideas (e.g. positive emotions; resilience; strengths, etc.)

Positive psychology coaching (PPC) can be defined as a scientifically rooted approach to helping clients increase well-being, enhance and apply strengths, improve performance and achieve valued goals. At the core of PPC is a belief in the power of science to elucidate the best approaches for positively transforming clients' lives. The PPC orientation suggests that the coach views the client as 'whole' and that the coach focuses on strengths, positive behaviours and purpose. These, in turn, are used as building blocks and leverage points for coachee development and performance improvement.

Positive psychology coaching (PPC) uses positive psychology theories and tools to offer practical help to its clients. This help may centre around positive psychology assessment (Biswas-Diener, 2010), coaching for strengths deployment (Francis and Zarecky, 2017), increasing positive emotions and well-being by using validated PPIs (Boniwell, 2017; Tunariu et al., 2017a), increasing motivation by applying the SDT framework (Boniwell et al., 2014), resilience coaching (Lawton-Smith, 2017) or using PPC to accompany leaders (Boniwell and Smith, 2018).

Given the executives' multiple time management issues, and the distinct lack of evidence-based time management interventions (Claessens et al., 2007), another distinct and much asked for line of work is time perspective coaching (Boniwell et al., 2014). Time perspective theory, which distinguishes between five different time perspectives – past negative, past positive, present fatalistic, present hedonistic and future (see Chapter 7) – offers a framework for coaches working on temporal-related problems: from performing initial diagnostics, to distinguishing problems associated with excessive reliance on particular time frames and providing practical tools that can help individuals to overcome the negative consequences associated with them. This is an alternative, theory-based approach to working with time management-related issues and to developing a healthier relationship with time in general.

Research found that the combination of several PPC interventions (360-degree feedback, one-half day leadership workshop and four one-to-one coaching sessions[3]) over 12 weeks significantly increased employees' goal attainment, resilience and workplace well-being and reduced depression and stress when compared to controls (Grant et al., 2009).

time out

Towards an integrative future: the emergence of positive psychology coaching

Encouraged by the dynamic ongoing development within positive psychology, we see rich and necessary opportunities for a closer integration with a related field which pivots on conceptual and professional endeavours that are too concerned with scaffolding flourishing and well-being: namely, the field of coaching psychology. Both these fields aim to support people, groups and organizations to reach subjectively meaningful goals in personal, professional domains of life through scientifically embedded lenses, principles and techniques. Specifically, coaching psychology focuses on enhancing the 'well-being and performance in personal life and work domains, underpinned by models of coaching grounded in established adult and child learning or psychological approaches' (Palmer and Whybrow, 2007: 2). Academics and practitioners have noted the natural complementarity of the two fields for a while (e.g. Biswas-Diener, 2010; van Nieuwerburgh and Green, 2014).

The primary drivers of integration are that both disciplines are interested in the improvement of performance and well-being; both are dedicated to understanding the workings of the human condition – its resources, vicissitudes and discontents – and argue for the existence of optimal conditions for human growth and flourishing; and both promote the use of human strengths as part of an overall asset vs. deficit based approach. The benefits of such integration are being considered as part of pioneering pedagogical dialogues (e.g. Van Nieuwerburgh and Tunariu, 2013) and are embedded in the development of psychological interventions alongside insights from other areas of psychology such as existential and social psychology, and the psychology of relating (e.g. Tunariu et al., 2017a).

The term 'positive psychology coaching' (Biswas-Diener, 2010) per se is gaining momentum as useful nomenclature and delivers a common starting point for thinking, planning and application where in positive psychology, coaching psychology and their associated practices intersect to offer equally significant contributions. Positive psychology coaching tends to represent an integrated framework which, overall, seeks to improve 'short term (i.e. hedonic well-being) and sustainable ▶

▶ well-being (i.e. eudaimonic well-being) using evidence-based approaches from positive psychology and the science of well-being and enable the person to do this in an ongoing manner after coaching has been completed' (Passmore and Oades, 2014: 68).

This new integrated discipline would be research-informed and highly applied, with 'a shared focus on unlocking potential, building on people's strengths, enhancing subjective well-being and supporting sustainable optimal functioning' (van Nieuwerburgh and Oades, 2017: 2). Recent developments show that practitioners are already applying integrative approaches (e.g. Tunariu, 2015; Leach and Green, 2016; Pritchard and van Nieuwerburgh, 2016) and that it can be explicitly taught at postgraduate level. For instance, the Masters in Applied Positive Psychology and Coaching Psychology (MAPP-CP) programme at the University of East London, UK is committed to teaching the conceptual fertilization of the two fields and, as a collective of academics in conversations with their students, are immersed in pioneering and evaluating best ways to achieve their optimal union. International Masters in Applied Positive Psychology (iMAPP) at Anglia Ruskin University has had a dedicated positive psychology coaching track for experienced coaches.

At the July 2017 International Positive Psychology Association Conference, the emerging observations formed part of a timely round-table discussion and the following areas were introduced for elaboration and debate:

1 thoughts towards a conceptual definition of Positive Psychology Coaching (PPC), in terms of existing knowledge and its potentiality for expansion;

2 thoughts towards the prospect for PPC to generate distinct knowledge;

3 PPC's potentiality for framing direction in relation to research and theory of change;

4 PPC's scope for informing applied and professional practice;

5 PPC's scope for enhancing curriculum as well as pedagogical approach at all levels of education

We are enthusiastic about these possibilities and continue to recognize the need for further debate, deliberations and research to refine integrative endeavours, their translation at conceptual and applied levels, and appropriate efforts to establish their robustness and fit.

(Tunariu et al., forthcoming)

Applying positive psychology to education

One of the fastest growing directions in applied positive psychology is within the domain of positive educational curricula. There are multiple curriculums worldwide, incorporating the principles of positive psychology to varying degrees.

Positive education aims to develop the skills of well-being, flourishing and optimal functioning in children, teenagers and students, as well as parents and educational institutions. In doing that it adopts both the preventative and enabling developmental functions. Importantly, positive education is underpinned by the principles and methods of empirical validation, which is what differentiates positive psychology from self-help initiatives (Boniwell and Ryan, 2012).

Schools in the USA, UK, Australia and across the world have for some time included work on social and emotional issues in the curriculum (e.g. personal, social and health education, service learning, citizenship) and helped pupils reflect on the importance of good social and emotional skills. Much has been done to promote such learning through stand-alone programmes and/or the whole-school environment, with more and more programmes being evaluated empirically through RCTs and controlled studies.

Positive education programmes in primary and secondary schools

Empirically tested programmes such as the Penn Resiliency Programme from the USA (Gillham et al., 2007), the Bounce Back! programme from Australia (McGrath and Noble, 2003), SPARK Resilience programme and Personal Well-Being Lessons from the UK have provided clear evidence that the teaching of social competence, resilience and optimism can offer clear benefits to children through reducing psychological disorders.

The Penn Resiliency Programme (PRP) has been developed and researched for several years and consequently has acquired a solid base of evidence showing that it helps prevent depression and anxiety and has long-lasting effects (see e.g. Reivich et al., 2007; Gillham et al., 2007).

PRP is a schools-based intervention curriculum designed to increase resilience and promote optimism, adaptive coping skills and effective problem solving through the applications of the principles of CBT to normal populations. Based on the seven 'learnable' skills of resilience, the programme teaches children: how to identify their feelings; tolerance of ambiguity; the optimistic explanatory style; how to analyse causes of problems; empathy; self-efficacy; and how to reach out or try new things. The PRP, therefore, educates adolescents to challenge a habitual pessimistic explanatory style by looking at the evidence and considering what is realistic, while avoiding unrealistic optimism.

A further applied classroom resiliency programme is *Bounce Back!* Devised by two Australian psychologists, Helen McGrath and Toni Noble (2003), it is a highly practical, teacher-friendly programme. It is based on the conclusions, reached by a meta-review of school-based programmes, that benefits of the vast majority of short-term programmes are, in fact, not sustainable. Bounce Back! is delivered in both primary and secondary schools, revisiting fundamental concepts in developmentally appropriate ways over time. Research evidence indicates beneficial effects of the programme on depression (McGrath and Noble, 2003).

The *SPARK Resilience Programme* is a universal school-based positive education intervention (Boniwell and Ryan, 2009; 2010) that builds on CBT and positive psychology concepts with the explicit goal of fostering emotional resilience and associated skills, as well as preventing depression (Pluess and Boniwell, 2015; Pluess et al., 2017). Organized around the SPARK acronym, the programme teaches children to break down their responses to stressful situations into five components: Situation, Perception, Autopilot, Reaction and Knowledge. Through the use of hypothetical scenarios, children are taught how everyday Situations, as a function of their individual Perceptions, tend to trigger their Autopilot (i.e. automatic emotional responses). Children are instructed to identify their subsequent behavioural Reactions and observe what Knowledge they gained from the experience. To help students understand these concepts, they are introduced to the 'parrots of perception' – imaginary creatures representing common maladaptive cognitive distortions. The programme teaches students how to challenge their interpretation of adverse situations and consider other alternatives by putting their parrots 'on trial', understanding and modifying their automatic emotional responses, and learning to control negative behavioural reactions. Alongside this, students are introduced to the skills of assertiveness and problem solving, and are helped to build their 'resilience muscles' through identifying their strengths, social support networks, sources of positive emotions and reflection on previous experiences of resilience and self-efficacy. SPARK Resilience has been extensively implemented in the UK, France, Netherlands, Japan and Singapore, with the large international charity Partnership for Children choosing the updated version of the programme as one of their flagship projects.

Well-being is not a mere absence of depression, just as the person who is not ill is not necessarily in good physical shape. Development of well-being needs to include skills over and above successful coping, including the enhancement of positive emotions, flow, positive relations and meaningfulness.

With the expansion of the positive psychology field, the last decade has seen a surprising wealth of curricula being developed around the world to address different aspects of positive functioning. For example, the *Wisdom Curriculum* encourages the intellectual and moral development of children through the medium of mainstream subjects (Reznitskaya and Sternberg, 2004). Students can formulate their own ideas about wise thinking, thus it's not what to think, but how to think. This education programme incorporates 16 pedagogical principles and six procedures such as reflective thinking, dialogical thinking and dialectical thinking, and so on.

Positive Self	Positive Body	Positive Emotions	Positive Mindset	Positive Direction	Positive Relationships
Happy Talk!	Image Matters	Understanding Emotions	Fixed or Flexible?	Egg Yourself On	Tonic or Toxic
Me, Inc.	Supersize Me!	The Negativity Bias	Hope	Nail, Nag, Nudge	Forgiveness
My Strengths Portfolio	Nutrition Quiz	Boost your Positive Emotions	Creative Problem Solving	Flow and Engagement	Listening and Empathy
Confident You	Mindfulness for Life	Just for Fun	Money, Money, Money!	Big Hairy Goals	Sweet Trading
My Best Possible Self	Go to bed, Sleepyhead!	Surprising, Sponta-neous Savouring!	The Tyranny of Choice	Five Little Pigs	Kindness and Gratitude
Strengths Songbook	The Power of Exercise	Mental Time Travelling	Thinking Your Way to Happiness	The Balancing Act	Happiness across Cultures

Source: Adapted with permission from Boniwell and Ryan (2012)

TABLE 10.3 Personal well-being lessons organized into six modules

Emotional intelligence has been widely used as an umbrella concept for various programmes around social and emotional learning, the most successful of which are *Self Science* and *The South Africa Emotional Intelligence Curriculum* (Salovey et al., 2004).

Another example is the *Personal Well-Being Lessons* curriculum. Originally a joint project of a partnership between the Haberdashers' Aske's Academies Federation and the University of East London, it has evolved into a free-standing programme. The curriculum targets every known major predictor and correlate of well-being using individually tested interventions to enhance learning. It has been successfully implemented and evaluated in secondary schools in London (Boniwell et al., 2016) for many years, with the best 36 lessons published in a dedicated book by McGraw-Hill (see Table 10.3). Some of the best-known Australian schools (e.g. St Peter's School in Adelaide) have been running the curriculum for the past five years.

Whole-school approach to well-being

Looking beyond programmes targeting the development of specific skills, evidence suggests that school-wide programmes (involving all staff and pupils) to promote psychological well-being are more likely to be effective than class-based interventions (Wells et al., 2003), probably owing to the impact of all staff modelling positive behaviours outside of class time. A positive climate in the school as a whole is associated with teacher and student satisfaction, lower stress levels and better academic results (Sangsue and Vorpe, 2004).

Although it is difficult to define what makes a good school, researchers agree that it is a type of school that encourages students to be engaged with and enthusiastic about learning. Common features of such schools include a safe environment, an articulated and shared vision of the school's purpose, explicit goals for students, emphasis on the individual student and rewarding their efforts or improvements (Peterson, 2006). Student satisfaction with the school, feelings of security and belonging play a crucial role in their engagement in learning and achievement (Brand et al., 2003).

There are several institution-wide initiatives, such as Wellington College in the UK and Geelong Grammar School in Australia, that have received worldwide acclaim (Morris, 2013; White, 2013). In September 2006, Wellington College – a private, co-educational school in the UK – embarked on a two-year Skills of Well-Being programme for its pupils. The course was originally designed by Ian Morris and Dr Nick Baylis and was delivered fortnightly to Years 10 and 11 (ages 14–16) with the specific aim of 'redressing the imbalance in modern education caused by an emphasis on exam results and measured outcomes' (Baylis and Morris, 2006: 3). The ultimate outcome of the course was to give Wellington College pupils practical skills for living well that are useful, easily understood and can be applied on a daily basis. The course has attracted unprecedented media coverage, placing the well-being debate firmly in the heart of the British political agenda, and culminating in a popular book (Morris, 2015).

A project aiming to create a 'positive school' has been implemented in Geelong Grammar, a fee-charging Australian boarding school. Under the leadership of Professor Martin Seligman, a team of 35 positive psychologists from the University of Pennsylvania spent several months re-designing the school on the basis of positive psychology principles. All staff were trained in positive psychology and resilience using the Penn Resilience Programme and elements of the Positive Psychology Programme for High School Students. In addition to introducing the above programmes as stand-alone elements, the positive psychology team collaborated with subject teachers to discover and highlight elements of optimal functioning in mainstream subjects, such as English, history and maths (White, 2013; White and Murray, 2015).

Noble and McGrath proposed the *Positive Educational Practices (PEPs) Framework* (2008) to facilitate better understanding, clarification and utilization of positive educational practices. The PEPs Framework specifies five foundations of well-being, which were derived from research in positive psychology and other related psychological and educational areas. The five foundations are as follows: 1) social and emotional competence, 2) positive emotions, 3) positive relationships, 4) engagement through strengths, and 5) a sense of meaning and purpose. The first foundation further includes three components: resilience skills, emotional literacy skills and personal achievement skills. The second foundation contains five subcategories of positive emotions: feelings of belonging, feelings of safety, feelings of satisfaction and pride, feelings of excitement and enjoyment, and feelings of optimism. The authors suggested the PEPs Framework should be used to supplement traditional educational psychologists' work, aiming to 'shift the direction and mindset of both educational systems and school personnel from deficit model of pupil learning and behavioural difficulties to a preventative well-being model'. Ultimately, the PEPs Framework is intended to assist students in finding a sense of meaning and purpose at school and in life (Noble and McGrath, 2008).

Applying positive psychology to business settings

Organizational use of positive psychology is probably the fastest growing branch of positive psychology applications, with many terms to define related sub-fields. Let us introduce some of these. *Positive organizing* is the term used to describe the links between positive psychology and organizational theory, 'in general terms, it refers to the generative dynamics in and of the organizations that enable individuals, groups and organizations as a whole to flourish' (Frederickson and Dutton, 2008: 1). *Positive organization scholarship* regards organizations as macro contexts that shape positive states and positive outcomes for individuals, groups and whole organizations. It investigates positive deviance, or the ways in which organizations and their members flourish and prosper in especially favourable ways. Positive refers to an affirmative bias focused on the elevating processes and dynamics in organizations. Organizational refers to the processes and conditions that occur in and through organizations, especially taking into account the context in which positive phenomena occur. Scholarship refers to the scientific, theoretically based and rigorous investigation of positive phenomena (Fredrickson and Dutton, 2008). *Positive organizational behaviour* is a vein of this work that focuses more narrowly on developed positive psychological states and psychological capacities that can be measured, developed and effectively managed for performance improvement in today's workplace. *Positive leadership* is a study of what elevates individuals and organizations (in addition to what challenges them), what goes right in organizations (in addition to what goes wrong), what is life-giving (in addition to what is problematic or life-depleting), what is experienced as good (in addition to what is objectionable), what is extraordinary (in addition to what is merely effective), and what is inspiring (in addition to what is difficult or arduous). Finally, the *Great Place to Work*® Institute, Inc. is a management consultancy based in the USA with international affiliate offices throughout the world that also carry out research into positive organizational functioning. The Institute works to select 'Lists of Best Workplaces' that appear in 44 different countries. The Fortune's '100 Best Companies to Work For List' is also based on their results. The surveys utilized in assessment priorities the measures of trust, pride and enjoyment.

The benefits of focusing on the positive in the workplace

Why apply positive psychology to the workplace? Between a half and two thirds of our life is spent working. Let's assume the reader is an average person working from the age of about 20 to retirement at, say 65; and assume they take about five weeks holidays a year. Now, let's imagine they work about a 40-hour week. This means that over a lifetime they will probably spend 80,000 hours at work. This figure does not take into account emails and phone calls answered during evenings, weekends or holidays, thinking of work or working well over time. For many executives, on the other hand, even 90,000 hours is a conservative underestimation. Nevertheless, whether the figure is 80,000 or 150,000, it represents a huge chunk of life. We need to ask ourselves: Do we feel we are spending it well? Do we feel happy during all these hours?

Even though feeling happy is appealing in itself, it has many more tangible benefits (which we examined earlier), some of which are potentially interesting for the employer, and not just the employee. In a nutshell, happier employees set their challenges higher and achieve their goals faster; generate better and more creative ideas; interact better with colleagues and bosses; get promoted faster;

earn more; give more help and support; receive superior reviews; learn more; achieve greater success; and are healthier.

Let us consider some of these in more detail. Looking at health benefits first, happy workers help keep costs down because they are *healthier*. They take fewer sick days and thus the organization requires fewer employees for the same volume of work. Because of better health, happy workers can help keep down the healthcare costs of their organizations. Healthcare is becoming a major expense for organizations and for any nation, the better health of happy workers is a significant asset. Putting some numbers onto these findings, Gallup research has shown that the average annual new disease burden cost for people with high well-being is $723, compared with $1,488 for those with low well-being – a per-person difference of $765.

Happy individuals are more likely to *focus on external challenges* rather than on themselves. They more often pursue what psychologists call 'promotion goals' (attaining new things), rather than prevention goals (avoiding possible bad things). Research clearly shows that happy workers are more cooperative and collaborative in negotiations than unhappy ones. They are also more willing to make more concessions during negotiation. Through cooperation, they usually reach a better joint solution to negotiation. There is also a clear link between happiness and being a better work colleague. Good citizenship in the workplace includes activities such as helping each other on the job, even when it is not part of one's job description. Even more, being happy at work predicts lower workplace deviance (such as stealing, taking excessive breaks, intentionally working slowly and spreading rumours about colleagues), whereas unhappiness at work predicts the exact opposite.

In an ever-increasing competitive business environment where innovation is a key driver of success, it is noteworthy that happiness has been shown to enhance curiosity and *creativity*. Happy people are more likely to feel energetic and interested in doing things, as well as scoring higher on curiosity scales. Further, there is a large experimental research literature showing that people put in a good mood tend to be more original and creative, and show greater cognitive flexibility. So forget the myth of an unhappy genius; two recent meta-analyses of research studies showed that although the strength of effects depend on the context and motivational focus, happiness is directly related to and generates creativity (De Neve et al., 2013).

So if the company wants to reap all these benefits, focusing on happiness becomes an obvious thing to do at any stage of a company's development (or at least when a new company starts stabilizing). Of course, from the company's perspective the profit is the most important, and it is the profit that enables them to pay the wages, thus satisfying the employees' basic needs. Yet, if it wants healthier, more collaborative, reliable and innovative staff, their well-being needs should be taken into account to achieve the win-win outcomes.

As we can see, happiness/well-being can impact performance, albeit indirectly, with studies showing engagement playing an even more important role (Harter et al., 2002; Schaufeli, 2013). And the great news is that the drivers (objective and subjective factors that we can impact) of both happiness and engagement are actually quite similar.

Drivers of well-being and engagement in the workplace

There exist several models that investigated drivers or predictors of well-being, engagement, and subsequently, performance at work. Among these is the *Self-Determination Theory* of Deci and Ryan (2000), the *Vitamin Model of Employment* of Warr (2007), the *Quality of Work Life* of Martel and Dupuis (2006) and *ASSET 6* essentials model of well-being at work (Robertson and Cooper, 2011). Here we summarize common factors/drivers that are highlighted by these models (Boniwell, in preparation).

First, there is a cluster of *personal resources* that an individual brings with them to work. These are the energy (or health) capital, cognitive flexibility, emotional intelligence, time use and self-confidence. Although companies have a lesser role to play here, because these are more personal characteristics, they can provide environmental context that supports the development of these skills. Access to gym, yoga or meditation classes during the breaks would build energy capital and emotional agility. The culture that accepts and celebrates errors as a learning opportunity provides conditions for developing confidence. There is solid evidence that resilience can be developed through structured training and workshops (the best example of that is the US army in which all personnel were resilience trained). Time use can also be promoted through training, but also through organizational interventions, such as establishing email rules, taking active steps to reduce the need for email communication or ensuring that employees fully disconnect (and thus recover) during holidays.

Where organizations have far more control is in the provision of *organizational resources,* shown to impact happiness and engagement at work. The common-sense wisdom of 'buying' engagement through higher salary and bonuses does not match up with a wealth of existing evidence. While pay and benefits need to be sufficient to satisfy employees' needs and must be perceived as fair, bigger annual bonuses would not translate to better performance the next year. Evidence suggests that delivering smaller, quarterly bonuses may be a better strategy, as it is the frequency of positive boosts that has the longest effect. Furthermore, given the limits to the impact of financial bonuses, on-the-job benefits and rewards appear to offer a far better motivational value. Establishing a *climate of trust,* in which every employee knows that things can be brought out into the open and discussed, and fairness considerations are vital, is another important driver, as are *managerial support* (we will discuss this further below), *environmental conditions* (work space, natural light, presence of greenery) and *social importance* (clear mission and vision, communicating company's history and narrative to ensure pride, and corporate social responsibility actions beyond compliance and statutory requirements). All of these five factors are more objective in nature.

Finally, there is another cluster of factors that are both objective and subjective and are concerned with employee *job experience*. These are autonomy, mastery, variety, structure and relationships. Most of these appeared in the chapter on motivation. Autonomy is facilitated by flexible work environment, defining the outcome rather than the process (thus giving people the ownership of the process) or letting employees explore the solutions and showing them that the organization values such explorations. Mastery comes from ensuring a great strengths-job fit and growth opportunities, such as training on the job and cultivating learning culture. Talent mobility, sabbaticals, passion clubs and accelerator experiences are great ways to ensure variety that in itself is a direct predictor of productivity. Role clarity/structure is one of the strongest predictors of engagement at work. The lack of it is also one of the biggest predictors of burnout. Finally, quality relationships are a number one predictor of work well-being and also motivation, and can be facilitated in diverse ways from informal socializing opportunities to establishing reciprocity and appreciation rituals.

The role of a manager

Although the tide is turning, many organizations still adopt a weakness, troubleshooting approach, which has been found to be inefficient in enhancing productivity and flourishing within the organization and the employee themselves. Furthermore, the manager role holds one of the keys for engagement and flourishing within business organizations. For example, employees who feel ignored by their manager have a 40 per cent likelihood of disengaging from their job. Conversely, managers who listen to their employees, and encourage them to utilize their strengths, reduced the likelihood of disengaging to only a 1 per cent.

A great manager is capable of motivating and engaging employees not by applying the 'command and control' method (even though at times it may be necessary), but rather through enabling and respecting autonomy, helping employees to find meaning in their activities, matching employees' strengths to their job tasks and creating a positive working climate. There are multiple actions and practices that can be adopted to achieve the above, such as frequent recognition and encouragement. Recognition consists of a comment or small act that signals to the employee that they are valued. Managers who provide frequent recognition and encouragement have significantly higher project performance from their team. Specifically, scoring in the top quarter on giving recognition equates to a 42 per cent increase in productivity compared with managers who score in the bottom quartile. By providing recognition, these managers satisfy two needs – for competence (signalling that someone is doing well) and relatedness (there is a human being taking an interest in us). Anyone who uses Facebook will have experienced a surge of satisfaction on seeing the 'likes' accumulating around a piece of news shared with others. On the other side of the coin, feeling unrecognized has effects that aren't merely neutral, but negative because we are likely actively to withdraw our labour.

Think about it...

To what extent do you think your boss has an influence on your overall well-being? Interestingly, new research shows that when asked to rank the people we **DON'T** like to be around, both genders ranked their boss as number one!

(Krueger et al., 2008)

Positive psychology interventions within business organizations

Flow interventions are argued to be very important for a 'good business' (Csikszentmihalyi, 2003). The main reasons why flow doesn't happen on the job stem from the idea of not bringing out the *best* in people but getting the *most* out of them. Few jobs have clear goals and feedback is seldom provided. Furthermore, when the skills and the opportunities for action are not well matched, the employee will experience a sense of lack of control.

At present, a strengths approach as a framework for career development, performance appraisal and team building has been adopted by several companies. A strengths-based approach includes incorporating a strengths language into the environment in which to communicate or discuss issues with colleagues. Recent research has found that people who are thriving in career well-being are able to use their strengths on a regular basis within their work environment. By using their strengths, workers have been found to be up to six times more engaged then those who do not. Furthermore, people who use their strengths report enjoying up to 40-hour work weeks where as those that do not report experiencing burnout at the 20-hour mark (Rath and Harter, 2010).

Some companies use strengths assessment tools such as the Strengths Profile for recruitment and selection purposes; however this should not be the sole determinant in the final decision. In terms of appropriateness of job allocation, businesses have started to match people with their strengths with promising results. Furthermore, constructing teams on the basis of complementary strengths profiles and managing weaknesses through complementary partnering or strengths-matched teams has also delivered successful outcomes. Ultimately, businesses that create further opportunities for the use of strengths have reported enhanced productivity and well-being among employees (Buckingham and Clifton, 2005).

In business, the application of a *reflected best selves exercise (RBSE)* intervention has gained increasing popularity. New research has shown that when RBSE uses both professional and personal sources, individuals experience more enhanced positive emotions, agency and relation resources than when just delivered by the professional source. Furthermore, the exercise can be strengthened by adding improvement suggestions as well as strengths-based RBSE (Spreitzer et al. 2009).

Positive psychology and public policy

Countries around the world have traditionally measured the wealth of their nation by Gross Domestic Product (GDP). Robert Kennedy famously criticized this method of analysis, claiming that governments measure everything but what makes life worth living. Positive psychologists have made progress within the area of public policy, recommending the implementation of subjective well-being measures into a government's assessment of individuals and societal quality of life and subjective well-being (Diener et al., 2009b). Not only can these tools give governments an idea of how 'happy' their people are, it can help distinguish between what projects and schemes actually increase/ decrease their citizens' well-being. Governments around the world have heeded this information (e.g. Britain) and are currently employing well-being measurements in their general citizen polls (Stiglitz et al., 2009).

A notable public policy initiative was undertaken by the Royal Government of Bhutan that in 2012 united 800 delegates at United Nations headquarters in New York to launch a new development paradigm. This paradigm was designed to nurture human happiness and the well-being of all life on earth, based on a healthy balance among thriving natural, human, social, cultural and built assets, and recognizing ecological sustainability and the fair distribution and efficient use of resources as key conditions for the new model. As a result of this meeting, the Kingdom of Bhutan was also requested to elaborate the details of the new development paradigm. Coordinated by Ilona Boniwell, 60 members of the United Nation's International Well-being Expert Group – a group of leading international experts from distinct disciplines – worked with the Royal Government of Bhutan and United Nations to create a New Development Paradigm based on well-being, which went into effect in 2015 when the UN's Millennium Development Goals (MDGs) expired and became the Sustainable Development Goals (SDGs).

Evidence shows that above a certain level, economic growth does not produce an increase in human happiness; on the contrary, it appears that economic growth strategies in the world market economies have damaging effects on human and planetary well-being (Eckersley, 2005, 2006; Marks et al., 2006; Pickett et al., 2006). The report published by the Centre for Bhutan Studies and GNH (2017) argues that in the developed world, we have reached the limits of the benefits of affluence, demonstrates how consumerism promotes individual anxiety and undermines social solidarity, reveals the short- and long-terms costs of inaction and offers and elaborates on concrete action steps for happiness-based public policy.

Overall, the application of positive psychology into therapy, coaching, education, organizational settings and public policy is rapidly growing. The increase in funding for evaluating larger scale and longitudinal programmes will give positive psychology further validation within the psychological sciences.

Chapter Summary

Reflecting on the learning objectives the reader will now understand the concept of strengths and several applications of positive psychology, more specifically:

- There are three main models of strengths, including the VIA, strengths finder and strengths profile.
- The most research in positive psychology is on the VIA and its 24 strengths, classified into six virtues (wisdom, courage, humanity, justice, temperance and transcendence).
- Coaching is an excellent medium for testing out theories within positive psychology, helping to bridge the gap between the ivory tower and the real world.
- Positive therapy uses 'deep strategies' approaches.
- Rational emotional behavioural therapy, well-being therapy and quality of life therapy attempt to work on building strengths.
- Organizations that adopt a positive psychology approach can increase productivity, reduce turnover and enhance the well-being of their staff.
- The use of positive psychology within schools is growing, ranging from one-off workshops to three-month interventions, to even the re-organization of entire curriculums to embed the theoretical concepts of positive psychology.
- The use of positive psychology measurement tools is currently being adopted by governments to assess their citizens' subjective well-being scores.

Suggested Resources

www.ipen-network.com/
Browse through this website to access information regarding positive education developments around the world, as well as multiple free resources.

www.contextualpsychology.org
Log on to this website to find extensive research and treatment materials for ACT.

www.bhutanstudies.org.bt/happiness-transforming-the-development-landscape/
Glance through the report if the question of happiness-based public policy inspires you.

Further questions for the reader

1 What would the good university be like?

2 How would you create a truly positive psychology department?

3 What do you think children should be learning in school? Are academic skills enough?

4 What three things could your workplace do to create a flourishing environment?

Personal Development Interventions

Playlist

Adults aren't really good 'players'. We tend to leave imagination and the fun stuff to children. However, recreational activities are essential ways to relax, have fun, forget worries, be creative and learn something new. These activities can renew and refresh us so that we perform better in our work and relationships. We spend too little time 'playing' when we are adults. Therefore, this exercise asks you to list the activities that you think you might enjoy as a recreational outlet. Do not think about what is best, most practical or easiest to do. If possible, try to choose active rather than passive leisure activities as these are proved to enhance rather than hinder well-being (Holder et al., 2009). Ideas on the Playlist

▶

▶

can include visiting your favourite (or new) sections of a book, video or music store; playing cards or board games, singing, dancing, going to the museum or the botanical garden, visiting a neighbour, sightseeing in the city, going to an antique sale, doing woodwork, hiking, bird watching, people watching, bowling, reading do-it-yourself materials, baking, scrap booking, looking at pictures, cuddling and many others! Try to follow a leisure plan in which you regularly – preferably daily even for just five minutes – engage in some of these activities.

Notes

1 Whereby building these strengths, a person can achieve the associated virtue.
2 For more information, please see Seligman and Peterson's (2003) chapter on positive clinical psychology.
3 Using cognitive behavioural solution focused approach, with trained, external coaches.

CHAPTER 11

Summing Up
Positive Psychology

❖ **LEARNING OBJECTIVES**

Does positive psychology overemphasize the positive, neglecting the useful functions of negative psychological processes, such as pessimism, complaining and doubt? Likewise, does positive psychology underestimate the intricate role of negative emotions in relation to well-being and growth? Does it overemphasize psychological factors, such as positive affect and cognition, at the expense of cultural, social and environmental predictors of adjustment? This chapter discusses some of the limitations and criticisms aimed at positive psychology.

Topics include:

- Top 10 critiques of positive psychology.
- The many futures of positive psychology.
- A summary of the textbook.

MOCK ESSAY QUESTIONS

1 Can positive psychology evolve and establish itself as a distinct field of scientific study with useful applications to real-world issues?

2 Discuss the criticism of imbalance.

3 Is positive psychology all about the 'positive'? Critically argue for or against.

Top 10 critiques of positive psychology

There are a number of critics who would vehemently oppose the very notion of positive psychology as an area of psychology. Is positive psychology just another temporary by-product of capitalist America's self-absorbed, individualistic fixation with the pursuit of happiness? In what ways can positive psychology's distinctive focus and emphasis on scientifically knowing and systematically promoting conditions for human flourishing be achieved? We have collated the top ten criticisms of positive psychology that encompass critics from all areas of science and the humanities.

1 Why study positive when negative is more important and immediate?

A notable critique comes from the renowned emotion/coping researcher Richard Lazarus who proposed that positive psychology is indeed just another fad that promises too much and will not deliver. Lazarus suggested that positive psychology is looking to 'accentuate the positive, eliminate the negative, and don't mess with Mr. In-between' (Lazarus, 2003: 93). While the point about overemphasizing 'positivity' is valid and well made, it is important to take time and examine what is meant by 'positive' in the positive psychology literature. This examination would indicate 'positive' as part of an appreciation of what-works-well-in-spite-of; and as part of an appreciation of 'asset' vs. 'deficits or limitations' when delineating features of the human mind, action and experience and so forth.

2 Methodology used

As with any area of study in psychology, methods and methodologies have and need to continue to be scrutinized. For a while, there has been a great deal of emphasis on cross-sectional correlation research design in positive psychology. These types of methods are able to show relationships; however, not causal directions. Most positive psychologists agree and as the field grows, the issue of limited range of methodological techniques is becoming a less prominent critique, with longitudinal research and world studies also becoming more commonplace. Likewise, there is a growing recognition of a balanced inclusion of inductively rigorous qualitative and mixed methods studies to support and corroborate holistic theory development processes (see e.g. Hefferon et al., 2017).

3 The concept of positive and negative

Another oft-used criticism of positive psychology is its simplistic viewpoint on the dimensionality of emotions; emotions are regarded as either positive or negative, but in reality they are often mixed (Larsen et al., 2001; 2004). For example, hope (positive), which is a wish for a desired outcome, can cause incredible amounts of uncertainty and anxiety (negative). Joy may be pleasant but is usually short-lived. Pride is one of seven deadly sins; love is pleasant, but only when reciprocated; anger can be positive when a person needs to assert themselves. Thus, positive psychology would do well to heed this critique and continually identify the complexity of emotions and the blends that can occur within human life.

Held (2002) supports this argument, claiming that positive psychologists convey polarizing messages without nuances (positive is good, negativity is bad). Some positive psychologists (i.e. Seligman) seem to suggest that 'we must think positive thoughts, we must cultivate positive emotions and attitudes, and we must play to our strengths to be happy, healthy, and wise' (Held, 2004: 12). An examination of the current state of play would make apparent positive psychology's growing appreciation of the dialectical relationship between 'positive' and 'negative' while retaining the overall ethos of a 'positive' mindset and its inherent beneficial domino effect.

4 Unbalanced perspective on topics and research findings

Lazarus (2003) also criticizes positive psychology's advocacy of optimism, which is incredibly one-sided and unbalanced. In reality, pessimists ('realists') mobilize valuable outrage against cruelty, murder, slavery, genocide, prejudice and discrimination. Held (2004) proposes that Seligman's message was sometimes too one-sided and messianic: 'Pessimists are losers on many fronts' (authentic happiness). There is an implicit message that 'accentuating the positive' (and ignoring the negative) is maximally beneficial (Held, 2004). However, research suggests that co-activation of negative emotions and memories is also necessary for integration and growth (Larsen et al., 2003). The task for positive psychology is to remain mindful of and accountable for negotiating the essence of this criticism in its scholarly or applied work.

5 Negative as necessary

Van Deurzen's (2009) critique of positive psychology focuses on the notion of positive psychology filling a void/hole in this century's lost people, who find their lives devoid of meaning. Most notably, Van Deurzen states that struggle and hardship are necessary in human existence, and that positive psychology fixates on a happy ending. In response to the latter criticism, the areas of resilience and post-traumatic growth (PTG) focus specifically on these concepts and that how, through suffering, we can learn something and change something valuable about ourselves. The concepts of 'happiness' and 'subjective well-being', as the reader will know by now, are not the sole focus of positive psychology.

6 Positive psychology as a cult

Is positive psychology little more than an ideological movement? A dogma for the increasingly secular societies in which we live? Some researchers argue that positive psychology gives people a bandwagon on which to hop; however, this comparison clearly oversimplifies the issue. Yes, positive psychology might have overemphasized novelty, but this was understandable to identify, from the start, its perspective shift. The researchers and students within the area of positive psychology work hard to put scientific evidence behind important topics and phenomena, and not to advocate self-help techniques that have not been properly validated through psychological experimentation.

7 Ethics of positive psychologists

Van Deurzen argues that positive psychologists offer quick fixes, taking complex issues and turning them into easy to access sellable commodities. But aren't we always trying to bridge the gap between research and the ivory tower and practice- application? What good are ideas if not put into practice? Thinking about as well as 'doing' psychology will unavoidably involve transparency and accountability for the processes of 'knowledge–production', the 'truth' that it communicates and the implications this can/may have in shaping the collective knowledge and practices 'out there'.

Van Deurzen argues that positive psychology's aim is to alter unhelpful and negative thoughts/emotions to more productive/positive entities, likening it to a sort of mind control. It is relevant to recall that traditional clinical psychology has for decades 'interfered' with patient's negative thinking and attempted to tackle what it considered detrimental patterns. Positive psychology too challenges unhelpful habits of thinking and looks to usher changes via adaptive thought processes. Positive psychology is not asking for exclusivity of positive thoughts; rather it studies, values and highlights the propagating force inherent to the positive mindset – across its possible configurations and complexity.

8 Tyranny of positive thinking

Held (2002) argues that there is a major 'dark downside' to the positive psychology movement, with a side effect being that victims of unfortunate circumstances, and other sufferers, are blamed for their own misery. When victims fail to exhibit the necessary optimism, strength, virtue and willpower, it is their own fault. The tyranny of the positive attitude may paradoxically reduce subjective well-being, the very condition it is designed to enhance. The implicit cultural mandate that unhappiness is intolerable and should be abolished may be harmful (Held, 2002):

> 66 The single most remarkable fact of human existence is how hard it is for human beings to be happy. If we add up all those humans who are or have been depressed, addicted, anxious, angry, self-destructive, alienated, worried, compulsive, workaholic, insecure, painfully shy, divorced, avoidant of intimacy, stressed, and so on, we are compelled to reach this startling conclusion: Suffering is a basic characteristic of human life.
>
> *– (Hayes et al., 1999: 1; see also ACT website).* 99

9 The separatist stance of (some) positive psychologists

Seligman dismisses humanistic psychology as unscientific (Taylor, 2001; Held, 2004) and simultaneously defines quantitative, empirical research as the only legitimate scientific basis for positive psychology. This dismissal can be understood in the context of positive psychology's dominant, separatist message: if one claims that one's movement constitutes a discrete approach within the social sciences, then one must eliminate competing approaches that can challenge that distinction (Held, 2004).

As positive psychology matures and reaches out to incorporate insights from across psychology and beyond, the relevance and magnitude of this critique diminishes.

9½ Lack of cohesive guiding theory

Critics argue neither logical nor empirical relationships between variables are clearly established within the area of positive psychology. We put this as 9½ because we feel that there is a guiding theory that binds the areas of research, namely, asking a different question: what is going *right* rather than what's going *wrong*. Yes, there are several areas that seem not to link well; however, each one is trying to understand how humans flourish. Furthermore, if we were to look within cognitive psychology, many of the topic areas bear little resemblance or connection to the others, with the main thread being to look at the brain and how it influences human behaviour.

10 Positive psychology meglects positive aspects of 'negative thinking'

Critics would argue that there is a definite case for the positive effects of negative thinking and positive psychology should not neglect the positive features of negative interpersonal behaviours (Kowalski, 2002: 1027). For example defensive pessimism, as discussed earlier, can be a good thing, depending on the individual. Likewise, there may be benefits to initiation of complaints. For example, complaining in novel, unpleasant situations can be an effective form of social bonding (e.g. when in a waiting room, at a new college or in any other unfamiliar situation, expression of complaints about unpleasant circumstances can be effective in breaking the ice).

The future of positive psychology: what would it be?

Interestingly, the major figures (e.g. Diener, Linley, Joseph) within the discipline believe that the integration of positive psychology (and therefore the disappearance of it as an actual field) is the ideal future of positive psychology. Ultimately the purpose of Seligman's American Psychological Association (APA) terms as president was to readdress this imbalance within 'psychology as usual'. Now that this has been addressed, then perhaps there is no 'need' for a separate discipline. The timeline in which this could potentially take place is debatable however, integration and a shift in perspective may continue depending on funding, researchers and a need for developed theories and applications (Linley et al., 2006).

As researchers, consultants and lecturers within the field of positive psychology we have a unique insight into the field and have made an educated prediction for the future of positive psychology. We feel that if positive psychology continues in what Joseph and Linley once described as marginalization (the segregation of positive psychology from the other fields within psychology), it would damage the integrity and growth of the subject. The more a discipline isolates itself, the more it loses in terms of depth, richness and understanding of its outer counterparts. Indeed, we feel that as positive psychology progresses and grows, its strength will double with the integration into other areas of the science, with continued specialization. This proposed future has elements of pragmatics in it in terms of funding and structural issues guaranteed to exist within psychological bureaucracy. Positive psychology must recognize, however, that while studying the positive there needs to be an acknowledgement of the negative, since imbalance was what originally drove us to the field in the first place.

In 2000 Seligman and Csikszentmihalyi posited that the future will witness positive psychology as 'a science and profession' with a good grasp of how to best 'understand and build the factors that allow individuals, communities, and societies to flourish' (2000: 5). To this end, Seligman and Csikszentmihalyi encouraged psychologists to seek to ascertain knowledge about 'what makes life worth living' (2000: 5) through the development of positivity – including personal and collective well-being reflected at home, in the workplace and in governing policies (resulting in enhanced civic engagement). Notwithstanding the criticisms presented above – such as scrutinizing its selective attention on positivity; the risk of sliding into becoming a temporary movement; its methodology and unbalanced emphasis between *who* (e.g. psychometric measures of individuals differences) and *how* (e.g. psycho-social-cultural and subjectively underpinned processes and mechanisms); its traditionally poor engagement with the 'negative' features integral to the human condition – the field is evolving and the core tenets of its mission statement (as above) retain their strengths.

The second wave of positive psychology is committed to remedying its engagement with the 'dark side of life'; scholars are outlining proposals for addressing ethics and professional governing for positive psychology practitioners (see Lomas and Ivtzan, 2016a) and also continue beneficial interdisciplinary work with other areas of psychology (e.g. the emergence of positive psychology coaching – see Chapter 10).

Chapter Summary

Reflecting on the learning objectives the reader now understands the current critiques of positive psychology. In summary:

- We have identified 10 major critiques of the positive psychology movement, most of which are the result of a misunderstanding of the discipline.
- The second wave of positive psychology is committed to remedying its engagement with the 'dark side of life' – as discussed and illustrated with reference to the study of emotions in Chapter 2.
- There are still several questions left to answer, such as to try to understand why interventions work for some people and not others.
- There are several perceived futures for the area of positive psychology: separation, integration and complete dissolution.

Suggested resources

www.uel.ac.uk/postgraduate/courses/msc-applied-positive-psychology-and-coaching-psychology
> The link to the new MAPP programme at the University of East London, England (via distance learning or on-campus delivery) which is now integrating positive psychology and coaching psychology.

www.sas.upenn.edu/lps/graduate/mapp
> If the reader is curious about a US perspective, they should check out the MAPP USA website for information on their programme.

Textbook Summary

So as the textbook, and the course, comes to the end of the journey, let's review what we set out to achieve from this textbook, as well as from the course in general. We set out to provide an up-to-date, critical textbook to enhance the reader's journey through positive psychology. We hope the reader has engaged with the textbook, taking the time to stop and reflect on the *'think about it'* sections. Furthermore, we hope they have enjoyed reading the interesting and sometimes obscure experiments that we feel each positive psychology student should know.

Finally, we hope that the reader has taken the time, each week, to attempt the personal development interventions that we have chosen according to the topics within the relevant chapters. These interventions are based on scientific evidence and, if initiated with intrinsic engagement, can have a significant impact on well-being. Overall, we hope we have engendered a balanced perspective of positive psychology through critical thinking and we wholeheartedly encourage the reader to undertake further independent study.

Further questions for the reader

1 What do you intend to do with your knowledge of positive psychology?

2 Do you think the discipline is biased and exclusive?

3 How would you describe the discipline in one sentence?

4 What would your ideal future be for positive psychology?

Personal Development Interventions

1 Creating your own mind map

We would like you to now set aside some time, review the mind map you created within the first chapter, and create a new, more intricate version. How does it compare to the mind map you created when you started reading the book? What do your main branches look like? What now stems off of them? If you need reminding of how to do the mind map, use the example in the first chapter to guide you.

2 Creating an 'emotion' scrapbook

This last intervention is aimed to giving you a personal development intervention that you can keep doing long after you have finished reading this book. It's similar in concept to the portfolio from the personal development intervention in Chapter 8. We would like you to create a portfolio based on one of the 10 positive emotions (e.g. a gratitude or serenity portfolio) (Fredrickson, 2009). For this intervention, you need to collect photographs, memorabilia, and so on that help you feel the emotion you are trying to encapsulate. You can be as creative as you like, just make sure you are choosing meaningful and relevant entries. Once you've completed one, try and create, in your own time, a portfolio for all 10 emotions (Fredrickson, 2009). Remember, this is an ongoing task that you can return to many weeks or months from now and reflect upon or add to.

References

Abramson, L.Y., Seligman, M.E.P. and Teasdale, J.D. (1978) Learned helplessness in humans: critique and reformualtion, *Journal of Abnormal Psychology*, 87(1): 49–74.

Ackerman, C. (2009) Dopamine, in S. Lopez (ed.) *The Encyclopedia of Positive Psychology*. Chichester: Blackwell Publishing Ltd.

Ai, A.L., Tice, T.N., Whitsett, D.D. et al. (2007) Posttraumatic symptoms and growth of Kosovar war refugees: the influence of hope and cognitive coping, *Journal of Positive Psychology*, 2(1): 55–65.

Ajzen, I. (1988) *Attitudes, Personality, and Behavior*. Milton Keynes: Open University Press.

Ajzen, I. (1991) The theory of planned behaviour, *Organisational behaviour and Human Decision Processes*, 50: 179–211.

Ajzen, I. and Fishbein, M. (1980) *Understanding Attitudes and Predicting Social Behaviour*. Englewood Cliffs, NJ: Prentice- Hall.

Aked, J., Marks, N., Cordon, C. and Thompson, C. (2008) *Five Ways to Wellbeing*. London: New Economics Foundation.

Algoe, S.B., Haidt, J. and Gable, S.L. (2008) Beyond reciprocity: gratitude and relationships in everyday life, *Emotion*, 8(3): 425.

Allred, L. (2015) 6 Traits for Growing Old with Grace. 9 September. Available at: https://blogs.sas.com/content/efs/2015/09/09/6-traits-for-growing-old-with-grace (accessed 19 November 2018).

Antoni, M.H., Lehman, J.M., Kilbourn, K.M. et al. (2001) Cognitive-behavioral stress management intervention decreases the prevalence of depression and enhances benefit finding among women under treatment for early-stage breast cancer, *Health Psychology*, 20(1): 20–32.

Antonovsky, A. (1979) *Health, Stress and Coping*. San Francisco, CA: Jossey-Bass.

Antonovsky, A. (1987) *Unraveling the Mystery of Health: How People Manage Stress and Stay Well*. San Francisco, CA: Jossey-Bass.

Antonovsky, A. (1993) The structure and properties of the Sense of Coherence Scale, *Social Science and Medicine*, 36: 725–73.

Antonovsky, H. and Sagy, S. (2001) The development of a sense of coherence and its impact on response to stress situations, *Journal of Social Psychology*, 126(2): 213–25.

Aquilina, D. (2013) A study of the relationship between elite athletes' educational development and sporting performance, *The International Journal of the History of Sport*, 30(4): 374–92.

Ardelt, M., Gerlach, K.R. and Vaillant, G.E. (2018) Early and midlife predictors of wisdom and subjective well-being in old age, *The Journals of Gerontology*, 73(8): 1514–25.

Armon-Jones, C. (1986) The social functions of emotion, in R. Harré (ed.) *The Social Construction of Emotions*. Oxford: Basil Blackwell.

Ashfield, A., Harrison, J. and Giles, S. (in press) Performance lifestyle in Olympic and Paralympic sport: where positive psychology informs practice, in A. Brady and B. Grenville-Cleave (eds) *Positive Psychology in Sport and Physical Activity: An Introduction*. Abingdon: Routledge.

Bab, M. and Boniwell, I. (2016) *HEX: The HEX Guide*. Paris/Aarhus: Positran/Gnist.

Baltes, P., Staudinger, U., Maercker, A. and Smith, J. (1995) People nominated as wise: a comparative study of wisdom-related knowledge, *Psychology & Aging*, 10: 155–66.

Bandura, A. (1977) *Social Learning Theory*. Englewood Cliffs, NJ: Prentice Hall.

Bandura, A. (1986) *Social Foundations of Thought and Action: A Social Cognitive Theory*. Englewood Cliffs, NJ: Prentice-Hall.

Bandura, A. (1997) *Self-Efficacy: The Exercise of Control*. New York: Freeman Press.

Bandura, A., Ross, D. and Ross, S.A. (1961) Transmission of aggression through imitation of aggressive models, *Journal of Abnormal and Social Psychology*, 63: 575–82.

Barrett, L.F. (2017a) *How Emotions Are Made: The Secret Life of the Brain*. (Air Iri OME edition). London: Macmillan.

Barrett, L.F. (2017b) Many fairy tales about the brain still propagate through our field, *The Psychologist*, 30: 54–7.

Baumeister, R.F. (2003) Ego depletion and self-regulation failure: a resource model of self-control, *Alcoholism: Clinical and Experimental Research*, 27(2): 281–84.

Baumeister, R.F., Muraven, M. and Tice, D.M. (2000) Ego depletion: a resource model of volition, self-regulation, and controlled processing, *Social Cognition*, 18(2): 130–50.

Baumeister, R.F., Gailliot, M., DeWall, C.N. and Oaten, M. (2006) Self-regulation and personality: how interventions increase regulatory success, and how depletion moderates the effects of traits on behavior, *Journal of Personality*, 74(6): 1773–801.

Baylis, N. and Morris, I. (2006) *The Skills of Well-being: Course Overview*. Tunbridge Wells: Wellington College.

Beck, A.T. (1976) *Cognitive Therapy and the Emotional Disorders*. New York: International Universities Press.

Berger, B.G., Pargman, D. and Weinberg, R.S. (2015) *Foundations of Exercise Psychology*, 3rd edn. Morgantown, WV: Fitness Information Technology.

Bernard, M.E., Froh, J.J., DiGiuseppe, R. et al. (2010) Albert Ellis: unsung hero of positive psychology, *Journal of Positive Psychology*, 5: 302–10.

Biddle, S.J.H. and Mutrie, N. (2008) *Psychology of Physical Activity: Determinants, Well-being and Interventions*, 2nd edn. London: Routledge.

Biddle, S.J., Wang, C.K.J., Chatzisarantis, N.L.D. and Spray, C.M. (2003) Motivation for physical activity in young people: entity and incremental beliefs about athletic ability, *Journal of Sport Sciences*, 21: 973–89.

Biswas-Diener, R. (2006) From the equator to the North Pole: a study of character strengths, *Journal of Happiness Studies*, 7(3): 293–310.

Biswas-Diener, R. (2010) *Practicing Positive Psychology Coaching: Assessment, Activities and Strategies for Success*. Hoboken, NJ: John Wiley and Sons.

Biswas-Diener, R. (ed.) (2011) *Positive Psychology as Social Change*. Oregon: Springer.

Black, A.E. and Deci, E.L. (2000) The effects of instructors' autonomy support and students' autonomous motivation on learning organic chemistry: a self-determination theory perspective, *Science Education*, 84, 740–56.

Blanchflower, D.G. (2001) Unemployment, well-being, and wage curves in eastern and central Europe, *Journal of the Japanese and International Economies*, 15(4): 364–402.

Blanchflower, D.G., Oswald, A.J. and Stutzer, A. (2001) Latent entrepreneurship across nations, *European Economic Review*, 45(4–6): 680–91.

Boecker, H., Sprenger, T., Spilker, M. et al. (2008) The runner's high: opioidergic mechanisms in the human brain, *Cerebral Cortex*, 18 (11): 2523–531.

Boehm, J.K. and Lyubomirsky, S. (2009) The promise of sustainable happiness, in S.J. Lopez (ed.) *Handbook of Positive Psychology* (2nd edn). Oxford: Oxford University Press.

Bohart, A. (1993) Emphasizing the future in empathy responses, *Journal of Humanistic Psychology*, 33(2): 12–29.

Bolier, L. and Martin Abello, K. (2014) Online positive psychological interventions: state of the art and future directions, in A.C. Parks and S.M. Schueller (eds) *The Wiley Blackwell Handbook of Positive Psychological Interventions*. Chichester: John Wiley & Sons.

Bolier, L., Haverman, M., Westerhof, G.J. et al. (2013) Positive psychology interventions: a meta-analysis of randomized controlled studies, *BMC Public Health*, 13(1): 1.

Bonanno, G.A. (2004) Loss, trauma, and human resilience: have we underestimated the human capacity to thrive after extremely aversive events? *American Psychologist*, 59: 20–8.

Boniwell, I. (2008) *Positive Psychology in a Nutshell*. London: Personal Well-being Centre.

Boniwell, I. (2009) European network for positive psychology, in S. Lopez (ed.) *The Encyclopedia of Positive Psychology*. Chichester: Blackwell Publishing Ltd.

Boniwell, I. (2013) *Strengths cards*. Paris: Positran.

Boniwell. I. (2016) *The integrated happiness dashboard*. Paris: Positran.

Boniwell, I. (2017) Positive actions: *evidence-based positive psychology intervention cards*. Paris: Positran.

Boniwell, I. and Henry, J. (2007) Developing conceptions of well-being: advancing subjective, hedonic and eudaimonic theories, *Social Psychology Review*, 9(1): 3–18.

Boniwell, I. and Reynaud, L. (2015) *The happiness box*. Paris: ScholaVie/Positran.

Boniwell, I. and Ryan, L. (2009; 2010) *SPARK Resilience Curriculum (Teacher and Student Materials)*. University of East London.

Boniwell, I. and Ryan, L. (2012) *Personal Well-being Lessons for Secondary Schools: Positive Psychology in Action for 11 to 14 Year-olds*. Maidenhead: McGraw-Hill.

Boniwell, I. and Smith, W.A. (2018) Positive psychology coaching for positive leadership, in S. Green and S. Palmer (eds) *Positive Psychology Coaching in Practice*. Abingdon: Routledge.

Boniwell, I., Kauffman, C. and Silberman, J. (2014) The positive psychology approach to coaching, in T. Bachkirova, E. Duncan and D. Clutterbuck (eds) *The SAGE Handbook of Coaching*, 2nd edn. London: Sage Publications.

Boniwell, I., Osin, E.N. and Martinez, C. (2016) Teaching happiness at school: non-randomized controlled mixed-methods feasibility study on the effectiveness of Personal Well-Being Lessons, *The Journal of Positive Psychology*, 11(1): 85–98.

Boniwell, I., Osin, E. and Sircova (2014) Achieving balance in time perspective: coaching methods, *International Journal of Evidence Based Coaching and Mentoring*, 12(2): 14–40.

Boniwell, I., Osin, E., Linley, P.A. and Ivanchenko, G. (2010) A question of balance: examining relationships between time perspective and measures of well-being in the British and Russian student samples, *Journal of Positive Psychology*, 5(1): 24–40.

Brackett, M. and Crum, A. and Salovey, P. (2009) Emotional intelligence, in S. Lopez (ed.) *The Encyclopedia of Positive Psychology*. Chichester: Blackwell Publishing Ltd.

Brady, A. and Grenville-Cleave, B. (in press) Contemporary findings about the value of well-being and positive psychology in sport and physical activity settings, in A. Brady and B. Grenville-Cleave (eds) *Positive Psychology in Sport and Physical Activity: An Introduction*. Abingdon: Routledge.

Brand, S., Felner, R., Shim, M. et al. (2003) Middle school improvement and reform: development and validation of a school-level assessment of climate, cultural pluralism, and school safety, *Journal of Educational Psychology*, 95: 570–88.

Branden, N. (1994a) Our urgent need for self-esteem: our responses to events are shaped by whom and what we think we are, *Executive Excellence*, 11: 14–14.

Branden, N. (1994b) *The Six Pillars of Self-esteem*. New York: Bantham Books.

Brickman, P., Coates, D. and Janoff-Bulman, R. (1978) Lottery winners and accident victims: is happiness relative? *Journal of Personality and Social Psychology*, 36(8): 917–27.

Bridges, S. and Wertz. F. (2009) Abraham Maslow, in S. Lopez (ed.) *The Encyclopedia of Positive Psychology*. Chichester: Blackwell Publishing Ltd.

Brown, K.W. and Ryan, R.M. (2003) The benefits of being present: mindfulness and its role in psychological well-being, *Journal of Personality and Social Psychology*, 84(4): 822–48.

Brown, N.J.L., Sokal, A.D. and Friedman, H.L. (2013) The complex dynamics of wishful thinking: the critical positivity ratio, *American Psychologist*, 68(9): 801–13.

Bryant, F.B. and Veroff, J. (2007) *Savoring: A New Model of Positive Experience*. Mahwah, NJ: Lawrence Erlbaum Associates.

Buckingham, M. and Clifton, D. (2005) *Now Discover Your Strengths: How to Develop Your Talents and Those of the People You Manage*. London: Pocket Books.

Buettner, D. (2010) *Thrive: Finding Happiness the Blue Zones Way*. Washington: National Geographic Society.

Burton, C.M. and King, L.A. (2004) The health benefits of writing about intensely positive experiences, *Journal of Research in Personality*, 38(2): 150–63.

Burton, C.M. and King, L.A. (2008) Effects of (very) brief writing on health: the two-minute miracle, *British Journal of Health Psychology*, 13: 9–14.

Calhoun, L.G. and Tedeschi, R.G. (1999) *Facilitating Posttraumatic Growth: A Clinician's Guide*. Abingdon: Routledge.

Calhoun, L.G. and Tedeschi, R.G. (2004) The foundations of posttraumatic growth: new considerations, *Psychological Inquiry*, 15(1): 93–102.

Calhoun, L.G. and Tedeschi, R.G. (2008) The paradox of struggling with trauma: guidelines for practice and directions for research, in S. Joseph and A. Linley (eds) *Trauma, Recovery, and Growth: Positive Psychological Perspectives on Posttraumatic Stress*. Hoboken, NJ: John Wiley and Sons.

Campbell, D. (1979) 'Degrees of freedom' and the case study, in T. Cook and C. Reinhardt (eds) *Qualitative and Quantitative Methods in Evaluation Research*. Beverly Hills, CA: Sage Publications.

Cantor, N. and Sanderson, C. (1999) Life task participation and well-being: the importance in taking part in daily life, in D. Kahneman, E. Diener and N. Schwarz (eds) *Well-being: The Foundations of Hedonic Psychology*. New York: Russell Sage Foundation.

Cantril, H. (1965) *The Pattern of Human Concerns*. New Brunswick, NJ: Rutgers University Press.

Carr, A. (2004) *Positive Psychology: The Science of Happiness and Human Strengths.* Hove: Routledge.

Carroll, B., Parker, P. and Inkson, K. (2010) Evasion of boredom: an unexpected spur to leadership, *Human Relations*, 63: 1031–49.

Carron, A.V., Hausenblas, H.A. and Estabrooks, P.A. (2003) *The Psychology of Physical Activity.* New York: McGraw-Hill.

Carstensen, L.L. and Charles, S.T. (2002) Human aging: why is even good news taken as bad?, in L. Aspinwall and U. Staudinger (eds) *A Psychology of Human Strengths: Perspectives on an Emerging Field.* Washington, DC: American Psychological Association.

Carver, C.S. and Scheier, M.F. (1990) Origins and functions of positive and negative affect – a control process view, *Psychological Review*, 97(1): 19–35.

Carver, C.S. and Scheier, M. (1998) *On the Self Regulation of Behavior.* New York: Cambridge University Press.

Carver, C.S. and Scheier, M.F. (2009) Optimism, in S. Lopez (ed.) *The Encyclopedia of Positive Psychology*, Chichester: Blackwell Publishing Ltd (pp. 656–63).

Carver, C.S., Scheier, M.F., Miller, C.J. and Fulford, D. (2009) Optimism, in S.J. Lopez and C.R. Snyder (eds) Oxford library of psychology. *Oxford Handbook of Positive Psychology.* New York: Oxford University Press.

Caspersen, C.J., Powell, K.E. and Christenson, G.M. (1985) Physical activity, exercise, and physical fitness: definitions and distinctions for health-related research, *Public Health Reports*, 100(2): 126.

Cassel, L. and Suedfeld, P. (2006) Salutogenesis and autobiographical disclosure among Holocaust survivors, *Journal of Positive Psychology*, 1(4): 212–25.

Centre for Bhutan Studies and GNH (2017) *Happiness: Transforming the Development Landscape.* Thimphu, Bhutan: The Centre for Bhutan Studies and GNH.

Charney, D. (2004) Psychobiological mechanisms of resilience and vulnerability: implications for successful adaptation to extreme stress, *American Journal of Psychiatry*, 161: 195–216.

Cheavens, J. and Dreer, L. (2009) Coping, in S. Lopez (ed.) *The Encyclopedia of Positive Psychology.* Chichester: Blackwell Publishing Ltd (pp. 232–39).

Chen, L.H. and Wu, C.H. (2014) Gratitude enhances change in athletes' self-esteem: the moderating role of trust in coach, *Journal of Applied Sport Psychology*, 26(3): 349–62.

Chen, L.H., Wu, C. and Chen, S. (2015) Gratitude and athletes' life satisfaction: an intra-individual analysis on the moderation of ambivalence over emotional expression, *Social Indicators Research*, 123(1): 227–39.

Chichekian, C.T. and Vallerand, R.J. (2018) Positive psychology meets education in the context of passion for sports: implications for sports–study programmes, in A. Brady and B. Grenville-Cleave (eds) *Positive Psychology in Sport and Physical Activity.* London: Routledge.

Christakis, N. and Fowler, J. (2009) *Connected: The Surprising Power of Our Social Networks and How They Shape Our Lives.* New York: Little, Brown and Company.

Ciarrocchi, J.W., Dy-Liacco, G.S. and Deneke, E. (2008) Gods or rituals? Relational faith, spiritual discontent, and religious practices as predictors of hope and optimism, *Journal of Positive Psychology*, 3(2): 120–36.

Claessens, B., van Eerde, W., Rutte, C. and Roe, R. (2007) A review of the time management literature, *Personnel Review*, 36: 255–76.

Clark, A.E., Diener, E., Heorgellis, Y. and Lucas, R. (2008) Lags and leads in life satisfaction: a test of the baseline hypothesis, *The Economic Journal*, 118: 222–43.

Clifton, D.O. and Anderson, E.C. (2001) *StrengthsQuest*. Washington: The Gallup Organization.

Cohen, S., Doyle, W.J., Turner, R.B. et al. (2003) Emotional style and susceptibility to the common cold, *Psychosomatic Medicine*, 65(4): 652–57.

Cohen, S. and Janicki-Deverts, D. (2009) Can we improve our physical health by altering our social networks?, *Perspectives on Psychological Science*, 4(4): 375–78.

Cohn, M. and Fredrickson, B. (2009) Broaden-and-build theory of positive emotions, in S. Lopez (ed.) *The Encyclopedia of Positive Psychology*. Chichester: Blackwell Publishing Ltd.

Colahan, M., Tunariu, A.D. and Dell, P. (2012) Understanding lived experience and the structure of its discursive context, *Qualitative Methods in Psychology Bulletin*, 13(1): 48–57.

Compton, W.C., Smith, M.L., Cornish, K.A. and Qualls, D.L. (1996) Factor structure of mental health measures, *Journal of Personality and Social Psychology*, 71(2): 406–13.

Cordova, M. (2008) Facilitating posttraumatic growth following cancer, in S. Joseph and A. Linley (eds) *Trauma, Recovery and Growth: Positive Psychological Perspectives on Posttraumatic Stress*. New Jersey: John Wiley & Sons.

Costa, P.T. and McCrae, R.R. (1980) Influence of extraversion and neuroticism on subjective well-being: happy and unhappy people, *Journal of Personality and Social Psychology*, 38(4): 668–78.

Costa, P.T. and McCrae, R.R. (1992) *Revised NEO Personality Inventory (NEO-PI-R) and NEO Five-Factor Inventory (NEO-FFI) Manual*. Odessa, FL: Psychological Assessment Resources.

Côté, J., Horton, S., MacDonald, D. and Wilkes, S. (2007) The benefits of sampling sports during childhood, *Physical and Health Education Journal*, 74 (4): 6–11.

Craig, C. (2007) *Creating Confidence: A Handbook for Professionals Working with Young People*. Glasgow: Centre for Confidence and Well-Being.

Crawford, S., Diener, E., Wirtz, D. et al. (2002) Wanting, having and satisfaction: examining the role of desire discrepancies in satisfaction with income, *Journal of Personality and Social Psychology*, 83: 725–34.

Crocker, J. and Wolfe, C.T. (2001) Contingencies of self-worth, *Psychological Review*, 108: 593–623.

Csikszentmihalyi, M. (1975) *Beyond Boredom and Anxiety*. San Franscisco, CA: Jossey-Bass.

Csikszentmihalyi, M. (1990) Flow: *The Psychology of Optimal Experience*. New York: Harper and Row.

Csikszentmihalyi, M. (1992) Flow: *The Psychology of Happiness*. London: Ryder.

Csikszentmihalyi, M. (2002) *Flow: The Classic Work on How to Achieve Happiness*. New York: Harper and Row.

Csikszentmihalyi, M (2003) Materialism and the evolution of consciousness, in T. Kasser and A.D Kanner (eds) *Psychology and Consumer Culture: The Struggle for a Good Life in a Materialistic World*. Washington: APA

Csikszentmihalyi, M. (2009) Flow, in S. Lopez (ed.) *The Encyclopedia of Positive Psychology*. Chichester: Blackwell Publishing Ltd.

Csikszentmihalyi, M. and Larson, R. (1984) *Being Adolescent: Conflict and Growth in the Teenage Years.* New York: Basic Books.

Csikszentmihalyi, M. and Csikszentmihalyi, I. (1988) *Optimal Experience: Psychological Studies of Flow in Consciousness.* New York: Cambridge University Press.

Csikszentmihalyi, M. and Lebuda, I. (2017) A window into the bright side of psychology: interview with Mihaly Csikszentmihalyi, *Europe's Journal of Psychology,* 13(4): 810–21, doi:10.5964/ejop.v13i4.1482

Curley, J. and Keverne, E. (2009) Epigenetics, in S. Lopez (ed.) *The Encyclopedia of Positive Psychology.* Chichester: Blackwell Publishing Ltd.

Damasio, A.R. (1999) *The Feeling of What Happens: Body and Emotion in the Making of Consciousness.* New York: Harcourt Brace.

Danner, D.D., Snowdon, D.A. and Friesen, W.V. (2001) Positive emotions in early life and longevity: findings from the nun study, *Journal of Personality and Social Psychology,* 80: 804–13.

Davidson, R.J. (2001) Toward a biology of personality and emotion, in A.R. Damasio, A. Harrington, J. Kagan et al. (eds) *Annals of the New York Academy of Sciences: Vol. 935. Unity of Knowledge: the Convergence of Natural and Human Science.* New York: New York Academy of Sciences.

Davidson, R.J. (2003) Affective neuroscience and psychophysiology: toward a synthesis, *Psychophysiology,* 40(5): 655–65.

Davidson, R.J. and Irwin, W. (1999) The functional neuroanatomy of emotion and affective style, *Trends in Cognitive Sciences,* 3(1): 11–21.

Davidson, R.J. and Schuyler, B.S. (2015) The Neuroscience of Happiness. *World Happiness Report 2015.* United Nations Sustainable Development Solutions Network.

Davidson, R.J., Jackson, D.C. and Kalin, N.H. (2000a) Emotion, plasticity, context, and regulation: perspectives from affective neuroscience, *Psychological Bulletin,* 126(6): 890–909.

Davidson, R.J., Marshall, J.R., Tomarken, A.J. and Henriques, J.B. (2000b) While a phobic waits: regional brain electrical and autonomic activity in social phobics during anticipation of public speaking, *Biological Psychiatry,* 47(2): 85–95.

Davidson, R.J., Kabat-Zinn, J., Schumacher, J. et al. (2003) Alterations in brain and immune function produced by mindfulness meditation, *Psychosomatic Medicine,* 65(4): 564–70.

Davies, M., Stankov, L. and Roberts, R.D. (1998) Emotional intelligence: in search of an elusive construct, *Journal of Personality and Social Psychology,* 75, 989–1015.

Day, A. and Carroll, S. (2008) Faking emotional intelligence (EI): comparing response distortion on ability and trait-based EI measures, *Journal of Organizational Behavior,* 29: 761–84.

De Nazelle, A., Nieuwenhuijsen, M.J., Antó, J.M. et al. (2011) Improving health through policies that promote active travel: a review of evidence to support integrated health impact assessment, *Environment international,* 37(4): 766–77.

De Neve, J.-E., Diener, E., Tay, L. and Xuereb, C. (2013) The objective benefits of subjective well-being, in J. Helliwell, R. Layard and J. Sachs (eds) *World Happiness Report 2013.* New York: UN Sustainable Development Solutions Network.

De Volder, M. (1979) Time orientation: a review, *Psychologica Belgica,* 19: 61–79.

Deci, E.L. and Ryan, R.M. (1995) Human agency: the basis for true self-esteem, in M.H. Kernis (ed.) *Efficacy, Agency, and Self-esteem.* New York: Plenum.

Deci, E.L. and Ryan, R.M. (2000) The 'what' and 'why' of goal pursuits: human needs and the self-determination of behavior, *Psychological Inquiry*, 11(4): 227–68.

Deci, E., Connell, J. and Ryan, R. (1989) Self-determination in a work organisation, *Journal of Applied Psychology*, 74: 580–90.

Deci, E.L., Olafsen, A.H. and Ryan, R.M. (2017) Self-determination theory in work organizations: the state of a science, *Annual Review of Organizational Psychology and Organizational Behavior*, 4:19–43.

Delichte, J. and Evers-Cacciapaglia, R. (2010) The science and application of strengths, Lecture presented 16 April, UEL MAPP.

Delle Fave, A. and Massimini, F. (2004) Bringing subjectivity into focus: optimal experiences, life themes, and person centred rehabilitation, in P.A. Linley and S. Joseph (eds) *Positive Psychology in Practice*. Hoboken, NJ: John Wiley and Sons.

Delle Fave, A., Brdar, I., Freire, T. et al. (2011b) The eudaimonic and hedonic components of happiness: qualitative and quantitative findings, *Social Indicators Research*, 100: 185–207.

Delle Fave, A., Massimini, F. and Bassi, M. (2011a) Hedonism and eudaimonism in positive psychology, in *Psychological Selection and Optimal Experience Across Cultures*. Dordrecht: Springer.

DHSC (Department of Health and Social Care) (2011) UK physical activity guidelines. Guidance from the Chief Medical Office (CMO) on how much physical activity people should be doing, along with supporting documents. Available at: www.gov.uk/government/publications/uk-physical-activity-guidelines (accessed 12 December 2018).

Diab, D.L., Gillespie, M.A. and Highhouse, S. (2008) Are maximizers really unhappy? The measurement of maximizing tendency, *Judgment and Decision Making*, 3: 364–70.

Diener, E. (1984) Subjective well-being, *Psychological Bulletin*, 95: 542–75.

Diener, E. (2000) Subjective well-being: the science of happiness and a proposal for a national index, *American Psychologist*, 55(1): 34–43.

Diener, E. and Biswas-Diener, R. (2008) *Happiness: Unlocking the Mysteries of Psychological Wealth*. Boston, MA: Blackwell Publishing.

Diener, E., Horowitz, J. and Emmons, R.A. (1985a) Happiness of the very wealthy, *Social Indicators Research*, 16: 263–74.

Diener, E., Emmons, R.A., Larsen, R.J. and Griffin, S. (1985b) The satisfaction with life scale, *Journal of Personality Assessment*, 49(1): 71–5.

Diener, D., Lucas, R., Schimmack, U. and Helliwell, J. (2009a) *Well-Being for Public Policy*. Oxford: Oxford University Press.

Diener, E., Kahneman, D., Arora, R. et al. (2009b) Income's differential influence on judgements of life versus affective well-being, in A.C. Michalos (ed.) Social indicators research series: vol. 39. *Assessing Well-Being: The Collected Works of Ed Diener*. London: Springer.

Diener, E., Wirtz, D., Tov, W. et al. (2009c) New measures of well-being: flourishing and positive and negative feelings, *Social Indicators Research*, 39: 247–66.

Diener, E., Sandvik, E., Pavot, W. and Gallagher, D. (1991) Response arifacts in the measurement of subjective well-being, *Social Indicators Research*, 24(1): 35–56.

Diener, E., Suh, E.M., Lucas, R.E. and Smith, H.L. (1999) Subjective wellbeing: three decades of progress, *Psychological Bulletin*, 125: 276–302.

Dietrich, A. and McDaniel, W.F. (2004) Endocannabinoids and exercise, *British Journal of Sports Medicine*, 38(5): 536–41.

Drake, L., Duncan, E., Sutherland, F. et al. (2008) Time perspective and correlates of wellbeing, *Time and Society*, 17(1): 47–61.

Duckworth, A.L. and Seligman, M.E.P. (2005) Self-discipline outdoes IQ in predicting academic performance of adolescents, *Psychological Science*, 16(12): 939–44.

Duckworth, A.L. and Seligman, M.E.P. (2006) Self-discipline gives girls the edge: gender in self-discipline, grades, and achievement test scores, *Journal of Educational Psychology*, 98(1): 198–208.

Duckworth, A.L. and Steinberg, L. (2015) Unpacking self-control, *Child Development Perspectives*, 9(1): 32–7.

Dunn, E.W., Aknin, L.B. and Norton, M.I. (2008) Spending money on others promotes happiness, *Science*, 319: 1687–8.

Dweck, C.S. (2006) *Mindset: The New Psychology of Success*. New York: Random House

Dweck, C. (2017) *Mindset: The New Psychology of Success*. Updated edition. New York: Random House.

Dweck, C.S. and Bempechat, J. (1983) Children's theories of intelligence: implications for learning, in S. Paris, G. Olson and H. Stevenson (eds) *Learning and Motivation in Children*. Hillsdale, NJ: Erlbaum.

Dweck, C.S., Chiu, C. and Hong, Y. (1995) Implicit theories: elaboration and extension of the model, *Psychological Inquiry*, 6: 322–33.

Eckersley, R. (2005) *Well and Good: Morality, Meaning and Happiness*, 2nd edn. Melbourne: Text Publishing.

Eckersley R. (2006) Is modern Western culture a health hazard? *International Journal of Epidemiology*, 35: 252–58.

Ekman, P. (2003) *Emotions Revealed: Recognizing Faces and Feelings to Improve Communication and Emotional Life*. New York: Henry Holt and Company, LLC.

Emmons, R.A. and McCullough, M.E. (2003) Counting blessings versus burdens: an experimental investigation of gratitude and subjective well-being in daily life, *Journal of Personality and Social Psychology*, 84(2): 377–89.

Emmons, R.A. and Shelton, C.M. (2002) Gratitude and the science of positive psychology, *Handbook of Positive Psychology*, 18: 459–71.

Epel, E., Bandura, A. and Zimbardo, P.G. (1999) Escaping homelessness: the influences of self-efficacy and time perspective on coping with homelessness, *Journal of Applied Social Psychology*, 29: 575–96.

Eurobarometer (2010) Sport and Physical Activity. Special Eurobarometer 334. Wave 72.3. Available at: http://ec.europa.eu/commmfrontoffice/publicopinion/archives/ebs/ebs_334_en.pdf (accessed 12 December 2018).

Faulkner, G.E.J. and Taylor, A.H. (2005) Exercise and mental health promotion, in G.E.J. Faulkner and A.H. Taylor (eds) *Exercise, Health and Mental Health*. Abingdon: Routledge.

Fava, G. and Ruini, C. (2009) Well-being therapy, in S. Lopez (ed.) *The Encyclopedia of Positive Psychology*. Chichester: Blackwell Publishing Ltd.

Feder, A., Nestler, E.J., Westphal, M. and Charney, D.S. (2010) Psychobiological mechanisms of resilience to stress, in J.W. Reich, A.J. Zautra and J.S. Hall (eds) *Handbook of Adult Resilience*. New York and London: Guilford Press.

Fenouillet, F. (2016) *Les théories de la motivation*. 2nd edn. Dunod.

Festinger, L., Riecken, H. and Schachter, S. (1956/2008) *When Prophecy Fails*, 2nd edn. London: Pinter and Martin.

Ford, J. D., Tennen, H. and Albert, D. (2008) A contrarian view of growth following adversity, in S. Joseph and P.A. Linley (eds) *Trauma, Recovery and Growth: Positive Psychological Perspectives on Posttraumatic Stress*. Hoboken, NJ: Wiley.

Fordyce, M. (1981) *The Psychology of Happiness: A Brief Version of the 14 Fundamentals*. Fort Myers, FL: Cypress Lake Media.

Fordyce, M.W. (1977) Development of a program to increase personal happiness, *Journal of Counseling Psychology*, 24(6): 511–21.

Fordyce, M.W. (1983) A program to increase happiness: further studies, *Journal of Counseling Psychology*, 30(4): 483–98.

Foret, M.M., Steger, M.F. and Frazier, P. (2004) Time perspective and well-being. Poster presented at the 3rd International Positive Psychology Summit, Washington, DC.

Fowler, J. and Christakis, N. (2008) Dynamic spread of happiness in a large social network: longitudinal analysis over 20 years in the Framingham Heart Study, *British Medical Journal*, 337: 1–9.

Francis, S. and Zarecky, A. (2017) Working with strengths in coaching, in E. Cox, T. Bachkirova and D. Clutterbuck (eds) *The Complete Handbook of Coaching*. London: Sage.

Frankl, V. (1963) *Man's Search for Meaning*. New York: Pocket Books.

Fredrickson, B.L. (2001) The role of positive emotions in positive psychology: the broaden-and-build theory of positive emotions, *American Psychologist*, 56(3): 218–26.

Fredrickson, B.L. (2009) *Positivity: Groundbreaking Research to Release Your Inner Optimist and Thrive*. New York: Crown.

Fredrickson, B.L. (2013) Positive emotions broaden and build, *Advances in Experimental Social Psychology*, 47(1):1–53. http://dx.doi.org/10.1016/B978-0-12-407236-7.00001-2

Fredrickson, B.L. and Dutton, J.E. (2008) Unpacking positive organizing: organizations as sites of individual and group flourishing, *Journal of Positive Psychology*, 3: 1–3.

Fredrickson, B.L. and Losada, M.F. (2005) Positive affect and the complex dynamics of human flourishing, *American Psychologist*, 60(7): 678–86.

Fredrickson, B.L., Cohn, M.A., Coffey, K.A. et al. (2008) Open hearts build lives: positive emotions, induced through loving-kindness meditation, build consequential personal resources, *Journal of Personality and Social Psychology*, 95, 1045–62.

Frijda, N.H., Kuipers, P. and ter Schure, E. (1989) Relations among emotion, appraisal, and emotional action readiness, *Journal of Personality and Social Psychology*, 57: 212–28.

Frisch, M. (2006) *Quality of Life Therapy: A Life Satisfaction Approach to Positive Psychology and Cognitive Therapy*. Hoboken, NJ: John Wiley and Sons.

Froh, J.J., Fives, C.J., Fuller, J.R. et al. (2007) Interpersonal relationships and irrationality as predictors of life satisfaction, *Journal of Positive Psychology*, 2(1): 29–39.

Froh, J.J., Kashdan, T.B., Ozimkowski, K.M. and Miller, N. (2009) Who benefits the most from a gratitude intervention in children and adolescents? Examining positive affect as a moderator, *Journal of Positive Psychology*, 4(5): 408–22.

Fromm, E. (1976) *To Have or to Be*. London: Abacus.

Fullagar, C. and Delle Fave, A. (2017) *Flow at Work: Measurement and Implications* (Current Issues in Work and Organizational Psychology), London and New York: Routledge.

Gable, S.L., Reis, H.T., Impett, E.A. and Asher, E.R. (2004) What do you do when things go right? The intrapersonal and interpersonal benefits of sharing positive events, *Journal of Personality and Social Psychology*, 87(2): 228–45.

Gagné, M. (2003) The role of autonomy support and autonomy orientation in prosocial behavior engagement, *Motivation and Emotion*, 27: 199–223.

Gailliot, M.T., Baumeister, R.F., DeWall, C.N. et al. (2007) Self-control relies on glucose as a limited energy source: willpower is more than a metaphor, *Journal of Personality and Social Psychology*, 92(2): 325–36.

Gainotti, G. (1972) Emotional behavior and hemispheric side of the lesion, *Cortex*, 8(1): 41–55.

Galati, D., Manzano, M. and Sotgiu, I. (2006) The subjective components of happiness and their attainment: a cross-cultural comparison between Italy and Cuba, *Social Science Information Sur Les Sciences Sociales*, 45(4): 601–30.

Gallup (2017) *Gallup 2017 Global Emotions Report*. Available at: http://news.gallup.com/reports/212648/gallup-global-emotions-report-2017.aspx (accessed 31 December 2018).

Garber, C.E., Blissmer, B., Deschenes, M.R. et al. (2011) Quantity and quality of exercise for developing and maintaining cardiorespiratory, musculoskeletal, and neuromotor fitness in apparently healthy adults: guidance for prescribing exercise. ACSM Position Stand, *Medicine & Science in Sports & Exercise*, 43 (7): 1334–59.

Gardner, H. (1993) *Frames of Mind: The Theory of Multiple Intelligences*, 2nd edn. New York: Basic Books.

Gardner, J. and Oswald, A.J. (2006) Money and mental wellbeing: a longitudinal study of medium-sized lottery wins. Discussion paper 2233, Watson Wyatt Worldwide, University of Warwick and IZA Bonn.

Gilbert, D. (2007) *Stumbling on Happiness*. London: Harper Perennial.

Gilbert, D.T., Pinel, E.C., Wilson, T.D. et al. (1998) Immune neglect: a source of durability bias in affective forecasting, *Journal of Personality and Social Psychology*, 75: 617–38.

Gilbert, P., McEwan, K., Mitra, R. et al. (2008) Feeling safe and content: a specific affect regulation system? Relationship to depression, anxiety, stress, and self-criticism, *Journal of Positive Psychology*, 3(3): 182–91.

Gillham, J.E., Reivich, K.J., Freres, D.R. et al. (2007) School-based prevention of depressive symptoms: a randomized controlled study of the effectiveness and specificity of the Penn Resiliency Program, *Journal of Consulting and Clinical Psychology*, 75(1): 9–19.

Gillham, J.E., Reivich, K.J., Jaycox, L.H. and Seligman, M.E.P. (1995) Prevention of depressive symptoms in schoolchildren: two-year follow-up, *Psychological Science*, 6(6): 343–51.

Goldacre, B. (2009) *Bad Science*. London: Harper Collins Publishers.

Goldenberg, J. and Shackelford, T. (2005) Is it me or is it mine? Body self integration as a function of self esteem, body esteem and mortality salience, *Self and Identity*, 4: 227–41.

Goleman, D. (1996) *Emotional Intelligence: Why It Can Matter More Than IQ*. New York: Bantam Books.

Gomez, M. (2009) Albert Bandura, in S. Lopez (ed.) *The Encyclopedia of Positive Psychology*. Chichester: Blackwell Publishing Ltd.

Grant, A.M. and Palmer, S. (2002) Coaching psychology. Meeting held at the annual conference of the Division of Counselling Psychology, British Psychological Society, Torquay, 18 May.

Grant, A.M., Curtayne, L. and Burton, G. (2009) Executive coaching enhances goal attainment, resilience and workplace well-being: a randomised controlled study, *Journal of Positive Psychology*, 4(5): 396–407.

Grenville-Cleave, B., Brady, A. and Kavanagh, E. (in press) Positive psychology of relationships in sport and physical activity, in A. Brady and B. Grenville-Cleave (eds) *Positive Psychology in Sport and Physical Activity: An Introduction*. Abingdon: Routledge.

Grossman, P., Niemann, L., Schmidt, S. and Walach, H. (2004) Mindfulness-based stress reduction and health benefits: a meta-analysis, *Journal of Psychosomatic Research*, 57: 35–43.

Grubb, W. and McDaniel, M. (2007) The fakability of Bar-On's emotional quotient inventory short form: catch me if you can, *Human Performance*, 20: 43–59.

Haidt, J. (2006) *The Happiness Hypothesis: Finding Modern Truth in Ancient Wisdom*. New York: Basic Books.

Hallal, P.C., Andersen, L.B., Bull, F.C., Guthold, R. et al. (2012) Global physical activity levels: surveillance progress, pitfalls, and prospects. *The Lancet*, 380(9838): 247–57.

Hanrahan, S.J. (2018) LifeMatters: using physical activities and games to enhance the self-concept and well-being of disadvantaged youth, in A. Brady and B. Grenville-Cleave (eds) *Positive Psychology in Sport and Physical Activity*. London: Routledge.

Hanson, S. and Jones, A. (2015) Is there evidence that walking groups have health benefits? A systematic review and meta-analysis, *British Journal of Sports Medicine*, 49(11): 710–15.

Hanssen, M.M., Peters, M.L., Vlaeyen, J.W. et al. (2013) Optimism lowers pain: evidence of the causal status and underlying mechanisms, *Pain*, 154(1): 53–8. doi: 10.1016/j.pain.2012.08.006

Harker, L.A. and Keltner, D. (2001) Expressions of positive emotion in women's college yearbook pictures and their relationship to personality and life outcomes across adulthood, *Journal of Personality and Social Psychology*, 80(1): 112–24.

Harmon-Jones, E., Simon, L., Greenberg, J. et al. (1997) Terror management theory and self esteem: evidence that increased self esteem reduces mortality salience effects, *Journal of Personality and Social Psychology*, 72: 24–36.

Harré, R. (1986) An outline of the social constructionist viewpoint, in R. Harré (ed.) *The Social Construction of Emotions*. Oxford: Basil Blackwell.

Harter, J. (2009) Employee engagement, in S. Lopez (ed.) *The Encyclopedia of Positive Psychology*. Chichester: Blackwell Publishing Ltd.

Harter, J.K. and Gurley, V.F. (2008) Measuring well-being in the United States, *APS Observer*, 21(8): 23–6.

Harter, J.K., Schmidt, F.L. and Hayes, T.L. (2002) Business-unit-level relationship between employee satisfaction, employee engagement, and business outcomes: a meta-analysis, *Journal of Applied Psychology*, 87(2): 268–79.

Hayes, S.C., Strosahl, K. and Wilson, K.G. (1999) *Acceptance and Commitment Therapy: An Experiential Approach to Behavior Change*. New York: Guilford Press.

Headey, B. (2008) Life goals matter to happiness: a revision of set-point theory, *Social Indicators Research*, 86: 213–31.

Headey, B., Schupp, J., Tucci, I. and Wagner, G.G. (2008) Authentic happiness theory supported by impact of happiness on life satisfaction: a longitudinal analysis with data for Germany, *Journal of Positive Psychology*, 5(1): 73–82. DOI10.2139/ssrn.1323686

Headey, B. and Muffels, R. (2017) Towards a theory of life satisfaction: accounting for stability, change and volatility in 25-year life trajectories in Germany, *Social Indicators Research*. DOI10.1007/s11205-017-1785-z

Hefferon, K. (2013) *Positive Psychology and the Body: The Somatopsychic Side to Flourishing*. Maidenhead: Open University Press.

Hefferon, K., Ashfield, A., Waters, L. and Synard, J. (2017) Understanding optimal human functioning: the 'call for qual' in exploring human flourishing and well-being, *Journal of Positive Psychology*, 12(3): 211–19.

Held, B.S. (2002) The tyranny of the positive attitude in America: observation and speculation, *Journal of Clinical Psychology*, 58(9): 965–91.

Held, B.S. (2004) The negative side of positive psychology, *Journal of Humanistic Psychology*, 44(1): 9–46.

Helliwell, J., Layard, R. and Sachs, J. (2017) *World Happiness Report 2017*. New York: Sustainable Development Solutions Network.

Hodgins, D. and Engel, A. (2002) Future time perspective in pathological gambling, *Journal of Nervous and Mental Disease*, 190(11): 775–80.

Hoffman, L., Cleare-Hoffman, H.P. and Vallejos, L. (2013) Existential issues in trauma: implications for assessment and treatment. Paper presented as part of the *Developing Resiliency: Compassion Fatigue and Regeneration symposium* (I. Serlin, Chair), at the 121 Annual Convention of the American Psychological Association, August, 2013, Honolulu, HI.

Hogan, C.L., Catalino, L.I., Mata, J. and Fredrickson, B.L. (2015) Beyond emotional benefits: physical activity and sedentary behaviour affect psychosocial resources through emotions, *Psychology & Health*, 30(3): 354–69.

Holder, M. and Klassen, A. (2009) Personality, in S. Lopez (ed.) *The Encyclopedia of Positive Psychology*. Chichester: Blackwell Publishing Ltd.

Holder, M.D., Coleman, B. and Sehn, Z.L. (2009) The contribution of active and passive leisure to children's well-being, *Journal of Health Psychology*, 14(3): 378–86.

Howitt, D. and Cramer, D. (2008) *Introduction to Research Methods in Psychology*, 2nd edn. Harlow: Pearson Education Limited.

Humberstone, B. and Cutler-Riddick, C. (2015) Older women, embodiment and yoga practice, *Ageing & Society*, 35: 1221–41.

Huta, V. and Ryan, R.M. (2010) Pursuing pleasure or virtue: the differential and overlapping well-being benefits of hedonic and eudaimonic motives, *Journal of Happiness Studies*, 11(6): 735–62.

Huta, V. and Waterman, A.S. (2014) Eudaimonia and its distinction from hedonia: developing a classification and terminology for understanding conceptual and operational definitions, *Journal of Happiness Studies*, 15(6): 1425–56. DOI10.1007/s10902-013-9485-0

Huta, V., Park, N., Peterson, C. and Seligman, M.E.P. (2003) Pursuing pleasure versus eudaimonia: which leads to greater satisfaction? Poster presented at the International Positive Psychology Summit, Washington, DC., October, 2003.

Ivtzan, I., Lomas, T., Hefferon, K. and Worth, P. (2016). *Second Wave Positive Psychology: Embracing the Dark Side of Life*. London: Routledge.

Iyengar, S.S. and Lepper, M.R. (2000) When choice is demotivating: can one desire too much of a good thing? *Journal of Personality and Social Psychology*, 79(6): 995–1006.

Izard, C.E. (2009) Emotion theory and research: highlights, unanswered questions, and emerging issues, *Annual Review of Psychology*, 60: 1–25.

Jackson, S.A. and Roberts, G.C. (1992) Positive performance states of athletes: toward a conceptual understanding of peak performance, *The Sport Psychologist*, 6(2): 156–71.

Janoff-Bulman, R. (1992) *Shattered Assumptions: Towards a New Psychology of Trauma.* New York: Free Press.

Janoff-Bulman, R. (2004) Posttraumatic growth: three explanatory models, *Psychological Inquiry*, 15(1): 30–4.

Jimenez, S. (2009) Suffering, in S. Lopez (ed.) *The Encyclopedia of Positive Psychology.* Chichester: Blackwell Publishing Ltd.

Johnson, K.J., Waugh, C.E. and Fredrickson, B.L. (2010) Smile to see the forest: facially expressed positive emotions broaden cognition, *Cognition and d Emotion*, 24(2): 299–321.

Jolley, D., McCready, C., Grenville-Cleave, B. and Brady, A. (in press) My future today: identity development in young professional footballers, in A. Brady and B. Grenville-Cleave (eds) *Positive Psychology in Sport and Physical Activity: An Introduction.* Abingdon: Routledge.

Josefsson, T., Lindwall, M. and Archer, T. (2014) Physical exercise intervention in depressive disorders: meta analysis and systematic review, *Scandinavian Journal of Medicine and Science in Sports*, 24(2): 259–72.

Joseph, S. and Linley, P.A. (2005) Positive adjustment to threatening events: an organismic valuing theory of growth through adversity, *Review of General Psychology*, 9(3): 262–80.

Joseph, S. and Linley, A. (2009) Positive therapy, in S. Lopez (ed.) *The Encyclopedia of Positive Psychology.* Chichester: Blackwell Publishing Ltd.

Joseph, S. and Linley, A. (2006) *Positive Therapy: A Meta-Theory for Positive Psychological Practice.* Hove: Routledge.

Joseph, S. and Linley, A. (ed.) (2008) *Trauma, Recovery, and Growth: Positive Psychological Perspectives on Posttraumatic Stress.* Hoboken, NJ: Wiley.

Joseph, S., Linley, P.A., and Harris, G.J. (2005) Understanding positive change following trauma and adversity: structural clarification, *Journal of Loss and Trauma*, 10(1): 83–96.

Joseph, S., Williams, R. and Yule, W. (1993) Changes in outlook following disaster: the preliminary development of a measure to assess positive and negative responses, *Journal of Traumatic Stress*, 6: 271–9.

Jowett, N. and Spray, C.M. (2013) British Olympic hopefuls: the antecedents and consequences of implicit ability beliefs in elite track and field athletes, *Psychology of Sport and Exercise*, 14: 145–53.

Judge, T., Erez, A., Bono, J. and Thorensen, C. (2002) Are measures of self-esteem, neuroticism, locus of control, and generalized self-efficacy indicators of a common core construct? *Journal of Personality and Social Psychology*, 23: 693–710.

Kahneman, D., Krueger, A., Schkade, D. et al. (2004) A survey method for characterizing daily life experience: the day reconstruction method, *Science*, 306: 1776–80.

Kangas, M., Henry, J.L. and Bryant, R.A. (2002) Posttraumatic stress disorder following cancer: a conceptual and empirical review, *Clinical Psychology Review*, 22(4): 499–524.

Karpinski, A. and Steinberg, R. (2006) The single category implicit association test as a measure of implicit social cognition, *Journal of Personality and Social Psychology*, 91: 16–31.

Kashdan, T. and Biswas-Diener, R. (2014) *The Upside of Your Dark Side: Why Being Your Whole Self – Not Just Your 'Good' Self – Drives Success and Fulfillment*. New York: Hudson Street Press.

Kashdan, T.B., Biswas-Diener, R. and King, L.A. (2008) Reconsidering happiness: the costs of distinguishing between hedonics and eudaimonia, *Journal of Positive Psychology*, 3: 219–33.

Kasser, T., Ryan, R.M., Zax, M. and Sameroff, A.J. (1995) The relations of maternal and social environments to late adolescents' materialistic and prosocial aspirations, *Developmental Psychology*, 31: 907–14.

Keltner, D., Oatley, K. and Jenkins, J.M (2013) *Understanding Emotions*, 3rd edn. Hoboken, NJ: Wiley.

Kendzierski, D. and DeCarlo, K. (1991) Physical activity enjoyment scale: two validation studies, *Journal of Sport and Exercise Psychology*, 13: 50–64.

Keough, K.A., Zimbardo, P.G. and Boyd, J.N. (1999) Who's smoking, drinking and using drugs? Time perspective as a predictor of substance use, *Basic and Applied Social Psychology*, 21: 149–64.

Kesebir, P. and Diener, E.D. (2008) In pursuit of happiness empirical answers to philosophical questions, *Perspectives on Psychological Science*, 3(2): 117–25.

Keyes, C. and Michalec, B. (2009) Mental health, in S. Lopez (ed.) *The Encyclopedia of Positive Psychology*. Chichester: Blackwell Publishing Ltd.

Keyes, C.L. and Lopez, S.J. (2002) Toward a science of mental health, in C.R Snyder and S.J. Lopez (eds) *Handbook of Positive Psychology*, 45–59.

Keyes, C.L., Shmotkin, D. and Ryff, C.D. (2002) Optimizing well-being: the empirical encounter of two traditions, *Journal of Personality and Social Psychology*, 82(6): 1007–22.

Kim, H.W. (2001) Phenomenology of the body and its implications for humanistic ethics and politics, *Human Studies*, 24: 69–85.

Kimiecik, J., Vealey, R., Wright, E. and Morrison, D. (in press) As positive as it gets: flow and enjoyment in sport and physical activity, in A. Brady and B. Grenville-Cleave (eds) *Positive Psychology in Sport and Physical Activity: An Introduction*. Abingdon: Routledge.

King, L.A. (2001) The health benefits of writing about life goals, *Personality and Social Psychology Bulletin*, 27(7): 798–807.

King, L.A. and Napa, C.K. (1998) What makes a life good? *Journal of Personality and Social Psychology*, 75(1): 156–65.

Knobben, S. (2013) A meta-analysis of the effectiveness of yoga on mental health: taking on a dual perspective reflecting the medical and positive perspective of mental health. MS thesis, University of Twente, The Netherlands.

Koch, S., Kunz, T., Lykou, S. and Cruz, R. (2014) Effects of dance movement therapy and dance on health-related psychological outcomes: a meta-analysis, *The Arts in Psychotherapy*, 41(1): 46–64.

Koole, S.L. (2009) The psychology of emotion regulation: an integrative review, *Cognition and Emotion*, 23(1): 4–41.

Kowalski, R. (2002) Whining, griping, and complaining: positivity in the negativity, *Journal of Clinical Psychology*, 58: 1023–35.

Krueger, A., Kahneman, D., Schkades, D. et al. (2008) *National Time Accounting: The Currency of Life.* Princeton, NJ: Princeton University, Department of Economics, Industrial Relations Section.

La Forge, R. (1995) Exercise-associated mood alterations: a review of interactive neurobiological mechanisms, *Medicine, Exercise, Nutrition and Health*, 4: 17–32.

Lambert, M.J. and Barley, D.E. (2001) Research Summary on the therapeutic relationship and psychotherapy outcome, *Psychotherapy*, 38, 4: 357–61.

Lambert, M.J. and Barley, D.E. (2002) Research summary on the therapeutic relationship and psychotherapy outcome, in John C. Norcross (ed.) *Psychotherapy Relationships that Work: Therapist Contributions and Responsiveness to Patients.* New York: Oxford University Press.

Lambert, N.M. and Fincham, F.D. (2011) Expressing gratitude to a partner leads to more relationship maintenance behavior, *Emotion*, 11(1): 52.

Langer, E. (2009) Mindfulness, in S. Lopez (ed.) *The Encyclopedia of Positive Psychology.* Chichester: Blackwell Publishing Ltd.

Langer, E. and Rodin, J. (1976) The effects of choice and enhanced personal responsibility for the aged: a field experiment in an institutional setting, *Journal of Personality and Social Psychology*, 134: 191–8.

Larsen, R. and Diener, E. (1992) Promises and problems with the circumplex model of emotion, in M.S. Clark (ed.) *Review of Personality and Social Psychology*, Vol. 13. Newbury Park, CA: Sage.

Larsen, J.T., McGraw, A.P. and Cacioppo, J.T. (2001) Can people feel happy and sad at the same time? *Journal of Personality and Social Psychology*, 81: 684–96.

Larsen, J.T., Hemenover, S.H., Norris, C.J. and Cacioppo, J.T. (2003) Turning adversity to advantage: on the virtues of the coactivation of positive and negative emotions, in L.G. Aspinwall and U.M. Staudinger (eds) *A Psychology of Human Strengths: Perspectives on an Emerging Field.* Washington, DC: American Psychological Association.

Larsen, J.T., McGraw, A.P., Mellers, B.A. and Cacioppo, J.T. (2004) The agony of victory and thrill of defeat: mixed emotional reactions to disappointing wins and relieving losses, *Psychological Science*, 15: 325–30.

Lawton-Smith, C. (2017) Coaching for resilience and well-being, in E. Cox, T. Bachkirova and D. Clutterbuck (eds) *The Complete Handbook of Coaching.* London: Sage.

Lazarus, R.S. (2003) Does the positive psychology movement have legs? *Psychological Inquiry*, 14(2): 93–109.

Lazarus, R.S. and Folkman, S. (1984) *Stress, Approach and Coping.* New York: Springer.

Leach, C. and Green, S. (2016) Integrating coaching and positive psychology in education, in C. van Nieuwerburgh (ed.) *Coaching in Professional Contexts.* London: Sage.

Leary, M.R., Tambor, E.S., Terdal, S.K. and Downs, D.L. (1995) Self-esteem as an interpersonal monitor: the sociometer hypothesis, *Journal of Personality and Social Psychology*, 68: 518–30.

Lechner, S. (2009) Benefit finding, in S. Lopez (ed.) *The Encyclopedia of Positive Psychology.* Chichester: Blackwell Publishing Ltd.

Lechner, S., Stoelb, B. and Antoni, M. (2008) Group-based therapies for benefit finding in cancer, in S. Joseph and A. Linley (eds) *Trauma, Recovery, and Growth: Positive Psychological Perspectives on Posttraumatic Stress.* Hoboken, NJ: Wiley.

Lent, R. and Hackett, G. (2009) Social cognitive theory, in S. Lopez (ed.) *The Encyclopedia of Positive Psychology*. Chichester: Blackwell Publishing Ltd.

Lepore, S. and Revenson, T. (2006) Resilience and posttraumatic growth: recovery, resistance and reconfiguration, in R.G. Tedeschi and L.G. Calhoun (eds) *Handbook of Posttraumatic Growth*. Mahwah, NJ: Lawrence Erlbaum Associates.

Lerner, R.M., Dowling, E.M. and Anderson, P.M. (2003) Positive youth development: thriving as the basis of personhood and civil society, *Applied Developmental Science*, 7(3): 172–80.

Lev-Wiesel, R. and Amir, M. (2003) Posttraumatic growth among holocaust child survivors, *Journal of Loss & Trauma*, 8(4): 229–37.

Levy, B. (1996) Improving memory in old age by implicit self-stereotyping, *Journal of Personality and Social Psychology*, 71: 1092–107.

Levy, B. (2009) Stereotype embodiment: a psychological approach to aging, *Current Directions in Psychological Science*, 18: 332–3.

Levy, B., Slade M.D. and Kasl, S.V. (2002) Increased longevity by positive self-perceptions of aging, *Journal of Personality and Social Psychology*, 83: 261–70.

Liebenberg, L., Ungar, M. and LeBlanc, J.C. (2013) The CYRM-12 [Child and Youth Resilience Measure]: a brief measure of Resilience, *Canadian Journal of Public Health*, 104(2): e131–e135.

Limonero, J.T., Fernández-Castro, J., Soler-Oritja, J. and Álvarez-Moleiro, M. (2015) Emotional intelligence and recovering from induced negative emotional state, *Frontiers in Psychology*, 6(816). doi.org/10.3389/fpsyg.2015.00816

Linley, A. (2009) Positive psychology (history), in S. Lopez (ed.) *The Encyclopedia of Positive Psychology*. Chichester: Blackwell Publishing Ltd.

Linley, A. and Joseph, S. (2004) Positive change following trauma and adversity: a review, *Journal of Traumatic Stress*, 17(1): 11–21.

Linley, P.A. and Joseph, S. (eds) (2009) Review of trauma, recovery and growth: positive psychological perspectives on posttraumatic stress, *psychiatric rehabilitation journal*, 32(3): 241–2.

Linley, A., Joseph, S., Harrington, S. and Wood, A. (2006) Positive psychology: past, present, and (possible) future, *Journal of Positive Psychology*, 1(1): 3–16.

Linley, P.A. (2003) Positive adaptation to trauma: wisdom as both process and outcome, *Journal of Traumatic Stress*, 16(6): 601–10. Available at https://psychnet.2009-00580-016

Linley, P.A., Maltby, J., Wood, A.M. et al. (2007) Character strengths in the United Kingdom: the VIA Inventory of Strengths, *Personality and Individual Differences*, 43(2): 341–51.

Litovsky, V.G. and Dusek, J.B. (1985) Perceptions of child rearing and self-concept development during the early adolescent years, *Journal of Youth and Adolescence*, 14: 373–88.

Lomas, T. (2016) *The Positive Power of Negative Emotions: How to Harness Your Darker Feelings to Help You See a Brighter Dawn*. London: Piatkus.

Lomas, T. and Ivtzan, I. (2016a) Professionalising positive psychology: developing guidelines for training and regulation, *International Journal of Wellbeing*, 6(3): 96–112.

Lomas, T. and Ivtzan, I. (2016b) Second wave positive psychology: exploring the positive–negative dialectics of wellbeing, *Journal of Happiness Studies*, 17(4): 1753–68.

Lopes, M.P. and Cunha, M.P.e. (2008) Who is more proactive, the optimist or the pessimist? Exploring the role of hope as a moderator, *Journal of Positive Psychology*, 3(2): 100–9.

Lopez, S. and Ackerman, C. (2009) Clifton StrengthFinder, in S. Lopez (ed.) *The Encyclopedia of Positive Psychology*. Chichester: Blackwell Publishing Ltd.

Lucas, R.E. (2007) Long-term disability has lasting effects on subjective well-being: evidence from two nationally representative longitudinal studies, *Journal of Personality and Social Psychology*, 92: 717–30.

Lucas, R.E., Diener, E. and Suh, E. (1996) Discriminant validity of well-being measures, *Journal of Personality and Social Psychology*, 71(3): 616–28.

Lucas, R.E., Clark, A.E., Georgellis, Y. and Diener, E. (2003) Re-examining adaptation and the set point model of happiness: reactions to changes in marital status, *Journal of Personality and Social Psychology*, 84: 527–39.

Lupien, S.J and Wan, N. (2004) Successful ageing: from cell to self, *Philosophical Transactions of the Royal Society B: Biological Sciences*, 359: 1413–26.

Lykken, D. and Tellegen, A. (1996) Happiness is a stochastic phenomenon, *Psychological Science*, 7(3): 186–9.

Lyubomirsky, S. (2006) Happiness: lessons from a new science, *British Journal of Sociology*, 57(3): 535–6.

Lyubomirsky, S. (2007) *The How of Happiness: A Scientific Approach to Getting the Life you Want*. New York: Penguin Press.

Lyubomirsky, S. (2008) *The How of Happiness: A Practical Guide to Getting the Life You Want*. London: Sphere.

Lyubomirsky, S. and Layous, K. (2013) How do simple positive activities increase well-being? *Current Directions in Psychological Science*, 22: 57–62.

Lyubomirsky, S. and Lepper, H.S. (1999) A measure of subjective happiness: preliminary reliability and construct validation, *Social Indicators Research*, 46(2): 137–55.

Lyubomirsky, S., King, L.A. and Diener, E. (2005a) The benefits of frequent positive affect: does happiness lead to success? *Psychological Bulletin*, 131: 803–55.

Lyubomirsky, S., Sheldon, K.M. and Schkade, D. (2005b) Pursuing happiness: the architecture of sustainable change, *Review of General Psychology*, 9: 111–31.

Lyubomirsky, S., Sousa, L. and Dickerhoof, R. (2006) The costs and benefits of writing, talking, and thinking about life's triumphs and defeats, *Journal of Personality and Social Psychology*, 90(4): 692–708.

Lyubomirsky, S., Dickerhoof, R., Boehm, J.K. and Sheldon, K.M. (2009) Becoming happier takes both a will and a proper way: two experimental longitudinal interventions to boost well-being. Manuscript submitted for publication.

Macquarrie, J. (1974) *Existentialism: An Introduction, Guide and Assessment*. Pelican Books.

Maddux, J.E. (2002) Self-efficacy: the power of believing you can, in C.R. Snyder and S.J. Lopez (eds) *Handbook of Positive Psychology*. New York: Oxford University Press.

Maddux, J. (2009) Self efficacy, in S. Lopez (ed.) *The Encyclopedia of Positive Psychology*. Chichester: Blackwell Publishing Ltd.

Magnus, K., Diener, E., Fujita, F. and Pavot, W. (1993) Extroversion and neuroticism as predictors of objective life events: a longitudinal analysis, *Journal of Personality and Social Psychology*, 65(5): 1046–53.

Mallen, G. and Grenville-Cleave, B. (in press) Positive psychology and physical education in schools, in A. Brady and B Grenville-Cleave (eds) *Positive Psychology in Sport and Physical Activity: An Introduction*. Abingdon: Routledge

Mancini, A.D. and Bonanno, G.A. (2010) Resilience to potential trauma: towards a lifespan approach, in J.W. Reich, A.J. Zautra and J.S. Hall (eds) *Handbook of Adult Resilience.* New York and London: Guilford Press.

Marks, N., Thompson, S., Eckersley, R. et al. (2006) Sustainable development and well-being: relationships, challenges, and policy implications. A report by the centre for well-being, nef (New Economics Foundation) for DEFRA (Department of Environment, Food, and Rural Affairs.

Martel, J.P. and Dupuis, G. (2006) Quality of work life: theoretical and methodological problems, and presentation of a new model and measuring instrument, *Social Indicators Research*, 77(2): 333–68.

Martins, A., Ramalho, N. and Morin, E. (2010) A comprehensive meta-analysis of the relationship between emotional intelligence and health, *Personality and Individual Differences*, 49: 554–64.

Maslow, A.H. (1954) *Motivation and Personality.* New York: Harper.

Mason, M. and Tiberius, V. (2009) Aristotle, in S. Lopez (ed.) *The Encyclopedia of Positive Psychology.* Chichester: Blackwell Publishing Ltd.

Masten, A.S. and Wright, M.O. (2010) Resilience over the lifespan: developmental perspectives on resistance, recovery, and transformation, in J.W. Reich, A.J. Zautra and J.S. Hall (eds) *Handbook of Adult Resilience.* New York and London: Guilford Press.

Matsunaga, M., Yamauchi, T., Nogimori, T. et al. (2008) Psychological and physiological responses accompanying positive emotions elicited on seeing favorite persons, *Journal of Positive Psychology*, 3(3): 192–201.

Mayer, J.D., Salovey, P. and Caruso, D.R. (2004) Emotional intelligence: theory, findings, and implications, *Psychological Inquiry*, 15(3): 197–215.

Mayer, J., Roberts R. and Barsade, S.G. (2008) Human abilities: emotional intelligence, *Annual Review of Psychology*, 59: 507–36.

Mayer, J.D., Salovey, P., Caruso, D.R. and Sitarenios, G. (2003) Measuring emotional intelligence with the MSCEIT V2.0, *Emotion*, 3(1): 97–105.

McCarthy, P.J. (2011) Positive emotion in sport performance: current status and future directions, *International Review of Sport and Exercise Psychology*, 4(1): 50–69.

McCullough, M.E., Emmons, R.A. and Tsang, J.A. (2002) The grateful disposition: a conceptual and empirical topography, *Journal of Personality and Social Psychology*, 82(1): 112–27.

McDonald, M. and O'Callaghan, J. (2008) Positive psychology: a Foucauldian critique, *The Humanistic Psychologist*, 36(2): 127–42.

McGrath, H. and Noble, T. (2003) *Bounce Back! Teacher's Handbook.* Port Melbourne, VIC: Pearson Education.

McGregor, I. and Little, B.R. (1998) Personal projects, happiness, and meaning: on doing well and being yourself, *Journal of Personality and Social Psychology*, 74(2): 494–512.

McMakin, D.L., Santiago, C.D. and Shirk, S.R. (2009) The time course of positive and negative emotion in dysphoria, *Journal of Positive Psychology*, 4(2): 182–92.

Meehl, P.E. (1975) Hedonic capacity: some conjectures, *Bulletin of the Menninger Clinic*, 39(4): 295–307.

Meevissen, Y.M., Peters, M.L. and Alberts, H.J. (2011) Become more optimistic by imagining a best possible self: effects of a two week intervention, *Journal of Behavior Therapy and Experimental Psychiatry*, 42(3): 371–8.

Mei-Chuan, W., Lightsey, O.R., Pietruszka, T. et al. (2007) Purpose in life and reasons for living as mediators of the relationship between stress, coping, and suicidal behavior, *Journal of Positive Psychology*, 2(3): 195–204.

Meyer, P.S., Johnson, D.P., Parks, A.C. et al. (2012) Positive living: a pilot study of group positive psychotherapy for people with schizophrenia, *Journal of Positive Psychology*, 7, 239–48.

Michalec, B., Keyes, C. and Nalkur, S. (2009) Flourishing, in S. Lopez (ed.) *The Encyclopedia of Positive Psychology*. Chichester: Blackwell Publishing Ltd.

Miller, W.R. and Rollnick, S. (2002) *Preparing People for Change. Motivational Interviewing*, 2nd edn. New York: Guilford Press.

Miller, W.R. and Rose, G.S. (2009) Toward a theory of motivational interviewing, *American Psychologist*, 64(6): 527–37.

Mischel, W., Shoda, Y. and Rodriguez, M.L. (1989) Delay of gratification in children, *Science*, 244(4907): 933–8.

Morris, I. (2013) Going beyond the accidental: happiness, education, and the Wellington College experience, in S.A. David, I. Boniwell and A.C. Ayers (eds) *The Oxford Handbook of Happiness*. Oxford: Oxford University Press.

Morris, I. (2015) *Teaching Happiness and Well-Being in Schools: Learning to Ride Elephants*. London: Bloomsbury Publishing.

Mueller, C.M. and Dweck, C.S. (1998) Praise for intelligence can undermine children's motivation and performance, *Journal of Personality and Social Psychology*, 75(1): 33–52.

Mutrie, N. and Faulkner, G. (2004) Physical activity: positive psychology in motion, in P.A. Linley and S. Joseph (eds) *Positive Psychology in Practice*. Hoboken, NY: Wiley.

Myers, D.G. (2000) The funds, friends, and faith of happy people, *American Psychologist*, 55(1): 56–67.

Nakamura, J. and Csikszentmihalyi, M. (2005) Engagement in a profession: the case of undergraduate teaching. *Daedalus: Journal of the American Academy of Arts and Sciences*, 134: 60–7.

Nelson, D.W. (2009) Feeling good and open-minded: the impact of positive affect on cross cultural empathic responding, *Journal of Positive Psychology*, 4(1): 53–63.

Nelson, S.K., Kushlev, K. and Lyubomirsky, S. (2014) The pains and pleasures of parenting: when, why, and how is parenthood associated with more or less well-being? *Psychological Bulletin*, 140: 846–95.

Nes, R.B., Czajkowski, N., Røysamb, E. et al. (2008) Well-being and ill-being: shared environments, shared genes? *Journal of Positive Psychology*, 3(4): 253–65.

Noble, T. and McGrath, H. (2005) Helping children and families 'bounce back', *Australian Family Physician*, 9: 34.

Noble, T. and McGrath, H. (2008) The positive educational practices framework: a tool for facilitating the work of educational psychologists in promoting pupil wellbeing, *Educational & Child Psychology*, 25(2): 119–34.

Norem, J.K. and Cantor, N. (1986) Defensive pessimism: harnessing anxiety as motivation, *Journal of Personality and Social Psychology*, 51: 1208–17.

Norem, J.K. and Chang, E.C. (2002) The positive psychology of negative thinking, *Journal of Clinical Psychology*, 58(9): 993–1001.

Nozick, R. (1974) *Anarchy, State, and Utopia*. New York: Basic Books.

Oatley, K., Keltner, D. and Jenkins, J.M. (2006) *Understanding Emotions*, 2nd edn. Malden, MA: Blackwell Publishers.

O'Connell, B.H., O'Shea, D. and Gallagher, S. (2016) Enhancing social relationships through positive psychology activities: a randomised controlled trial, *Journal of Positive Psychology*, 11(2): 149–62.

Oishi, S. and Diener, E. (2001) Goals, culture, and subjective well-being, *Personality and Social Psychology Bulletin*, 27(12): 1674–82.

Oishi, S., Diener, E., Suh, E. and Lucas, R.E. (1999) Value as a moderator in subjective well-being, *Journal of Personality*, 67(1): 157–84.

Olds, J. and Milner, P. (1954) Positive reinforcement produced by electrical stimulation of the septal area and other regions of rat brain, *Journal of Comparative and Physiological Psychology*, 47: 419–27.

Orlinsky, D.E., Grawe, K. and Parks, B.K. (1994) Process and outcome in psychotherapy, in A.E. Bergin and S.L. Garfield (eds) *Handbook of Psychotherapy and Behavior Change*. Hoboken, NY: Wiley.

Öst, L.-G. (2014) The efficacy of acceptance and commitment therapy: an updated systematic review and meta-analysis, *Behaviour Research and Therapy*, 61, 105–21.

Öst, L.-G. (2017) Rebuttal of Atkins et al. (2017) critique of the Ost (2014) meta-analysis of ACT, *Behaviour Research and Therapy*, 97: 273–81.

Otake, K., Shimai, S., Tanaka-Matsumi, J. et al. (2006) Happy people become happier through kindness: a counting kindnesses intervention, *Journal of Happiness Studies*, 7: 361–75.

Padesky, C.A. and Mooney, K.A. (2012) Strengths-based cognitive–behavioural therapy: a four-step model to build resilience, *Clinical Psychology and Psychotherapy*, 19: 283–90.

Palmer, S. and Whybrow, A. (2007) *Handbook of Coaching Psychology: A Guide for Practitioners*. London: Routledge.

Papageorgiou, C. and Wells, A. (2003) Nature, functions, and beliefs about depressive rumination, in C. Papageorgiou and A. Wells (eds) *Depressive Rumination: Nature, Theory, and Treatment*. Chichester: John Wiley & Sons.

Park, C., Cohen, L. and Murch, R. (1996) Assessment and prediction of stress-related growth, *Journal of Personality*, 64: 71–105.

Park, N., Peterson, C. and Seligman, M. (2004) Stengths of character and well-being: a closer look at hope and modesty, *Journal of Social and Clinical Psychology*, 23(5): 628–34.

Park, S., Lavallee, D. and Tod, D. (2013) Athletes' career transition out of sport: a systematic review, *International Review of Sport and Exercise Psychology*, 6(1): 22–53.

Parks, A.C. and Schueller, S. (2014) *The Wiley-Blackwell Handbook of Positive Psychological Interventions*. Hoboken, NY: Wiley.

Passer, M. and Smith, R. (2006) *Psychology: The Science of Mind and Behaviour*. Maidenhead: McGraw-Hill.

Passmore, J. and Oades, L.G. (2014) Positive psychology coaching, *The Coaching Psychologist*, 10(2): 68–70.

Pate, R.R., Pratt, M. Blaire, S.N. et al. (1995) Physical activity and public health: a recommendation from the Centers for Disease Control and Prevention and the American College of Sports Medicine, *Journal of the American Medical Association*, 273: 402–407.

Pavot, W. and Diener, E. (2008) The Satisfaction With Life Scale and the emerging construct of life satisfaction, *Journal of Positive Psychology*, 3(2): 137–52.

Pawelski, J. (2009) William James, in S. Lopez (ed.) *The Encyclopedia of Positive Psychology*. Chichester: Blackwell Publishing Ltd.

Pawelski, J. and Gupta, M. (2009) Utilitarianism, in S. Lopez (ed.) *The Encyclopedia of Positive Psychology*. Chichester: Blackwell Publishing Ltd.

Pedrotti, J.T. (2014) Taking culture into account with positive psychological interventions, in A.C. Parks and S.M. Schueller (eds) *The Wiley Blackwell Handbook of Positive Psychological Interventions*. Chichester: John Wiley & Sons.

Peña-Sarrionandia, A., Mikolajczak, M. and Gross, J.J. (2015) Integrating emotion regulation and emotional intelligence traditions: a meta-analysis, *Frontiers in Psychology*, 6(160). doi.org/10.3389/fpsyg.2015.00160

Pennebaker, J.W. (1997) Writing about emotional experiences as a therapeutic process, *Psychological Science*, 8(3): 162–6.

Pennebaker, J.W. (2004) Expressive writing and the regulation of emotion over time, *Psychophysiology*, 41: S23–S28.

Peterson, C. (2000) The future of optimism, *American Psychologist*, 55: 45–55.

Peterson, C. (2006) *A Primer in Positive Psychology*. New York: Oxford University Press.

Peterson, C. and Seligman, M. (2003) Character strengths before and after September 11, *Psychological Science*, 14(4): 381–4.

Peterson, C. and Seligman, M. (2004) *Character Strengths and Virtues: A Handbook and Classification*. New York: Oxford University Press.

Peterson, C. and Vaidya, R.S. (2001) Explanatory style, expectations, and depressive symptoms, *Personality and Individual Differences*, 31(7): 1217–23.

Peterson, C., Park, N. and Seligman, M.E. (2005) Orientations to happiness and life satisfaction: the full life versus the empty life, *Journal of Happiness Studies*, 6(1): 25–41.

Peterson, C., Park, N. and Seligman, M.E.P. (2006) Greater strengths of character and recovery from illness, *Journal of Positive Psychology*, 1(1): 17–26.

Pickett, K. E., James, O.W. and Wilkinson, R.G. (2006) Income inequality and the prevalence of mental illness: a preliminary international analysis, *Journal of Epidemiology & Community Health*, 60(7): 646–7.

Pink, M., Saunders, J. and Stynes, J. (2015) Reconciling the maintenance of on-field success with off-field player development: a case study of a club culture within the Australian Football League, *Psychology of Sport and Exercise*, 21: 98–108.

Pluess, M. and Boniwell, I. (2015) Sensory-processing sensitivity predicts treatment response to a school-based depression prevention program: evidence of vantage sensitivity, *Personality and Individual Differences*, 82: 40–5.

Pluess, M., Boniwell, I., Hefferon, K. and Tunariu, A.D. (2017) Preliminary evaluation of a school-based resilience-promoting intervention in a high-risk population: application of an exploratory two-cohort treatment/control design, *PLoS ONE*, 12(5): e0177191

Pöhlmann, K., Gruss, B. and Joraschky, P. (2006) Structural properties of personal meaning systems: a new approach to measuring meaning of life, *Journal of Positive Psychology*, 1(3): 109–17.

Porter, E. (1913) *Pollyanna*, 2nd edn. Rockville, MD: Tark Classic Fiction.

Positive Psychology Center (1998) Positive psychology network concept paper. Available at: www.ppc.sas.upenn.edu (accessed 31 January 2018).

Pressman, S.D. and Cohen, S. (2007) The use of social words in autobiographies and longevity, *Psychosomatic Medicine*, 69: 262–9.

Pritchard, M. and van Nieuwerburgh, C. (2016) The perceptual changes in life experience of at-risk adolescent girls following an integrated coaching and positive psychology intervention group programme: an interpretive phenomenological analysis, *International Coaching Psychology Review*, 11(1): 57–74.

Prochaska, J. and Prochaska, J. (2009) Stages of change, in S. Lopez (ed.) *The Encyclopedia of Positive Psychology*. Chichester: Blackwell Publishing Ltd.

Prochaska, J.O. and Velicer, W.F. (1996) Addiction versus stages of change models in predicting smoking cessation: on models, methods and premature conclusions – comment, *Addiction*, 91(9): 1281–3.

Prochaska, J.O., Velicer, W.F., Rossi, J.S. et al. (1994) Stages of change and decisional balance for 12 problem behaviours, *Health Psychology*, 13(1): 39–46.

Pury, C. (2009) Perseverance, in S. Lopez (ed.) *The Encyclopedia of Positive Psychology*. Chichester: Blackwell Publishing Ltd.

Pyszczynski, T., Greenberg, J. and Goldenberg, J. (2002) Freedom versus fear: on the defence, growth, and expansion of the self, in M. Leary and J. Tangney (eds) *Handbook of Self and Identity*. New York: Guilford Press.

Pyszczynski, T., Greenberg, J., Solomon, S. et al. (2004) Why do people need self-esteem? A theoretical and empirical review, *Psychological Bulletin*, 130(3): 435.

Public Health England (2016) Health matters: getting every adult active every day. Available at: www.gov.uk/government/publications/health-matters-getting-every-adult-active-every-day/health-matters-getting-every-adult-active-every-day (accessed 12 December 2018).

Rashid, T. (2009a) Authentic happiness, in S. Lopez (ed.) *The Encyclopedia of Positive Psychology*. Chichester: Blackwell Publishing Ltd.

Rashid, T. (2009b) Positive psychotherapy, in S. Lopez (ed.) *The Encyclopedia of Positive Psychology*. Chichester: Blackwell Publishing Ltd.

Rashid, T. (2015) Positive psychotherapy: a strength-based approach, *Journal of Positive Psychology*, 10(1): 25–40.

Rashid, T. and Anjum, A. (2007) Positive psychotherapy for children and adolescents, in J.R.Z. Abela and B.L. Hankin (eds) *Depression in Children and Adolescents: Causes, Treatment and Prevention*. New York: Guilford Press.

Rashid, T. and Seligman, M.E. (2013) Positive psychotherapy, in D. Wedding and R.J. Corsini (eds) *Current Psychotherapies*. Belmont, CA: Cengage.

Rashid, T. and Seligman, M.E.P. (in press) *Positive Psychotherapy: A Manual*. Oxford: New York.

Rasmussen, M. and Laumann, K. (2014) The role of exercise during adolescence on adult happiness and mood, *Leisure Studies*, 33(4): 341–56.

Ratey, J. (2001) *A User's Guide to the Brain*. New York: Abacus.

Rath, T. and Harter, J. (2010) *Well-being: The Five Essential Elements*. New York: Gallup Press.

Rathunde, K. and Csikszentmihalyi, M. (2005) Middle school students' motivation and quality of experience: a comparison of Montessori and traditional school environments, *American Journal of Education*, 111: 341–71.

Ray, J., Esipova, N., Pugliese, A. and Maybud, S. (2017) *Towards a Better Future for Women and Work: Voices of Women and Men*. Geneva: International Labour Organization and Gallup.

Read, J., Fosse, R., Moskowitz, A. and Perry, B. (2014) The traumagenic neurodevelopmental model of psychosis revisited, *Neuropsychiatry*, 4(1): 65–79.

Redelmeier, D.A., Katz, J. and Kahneman, D. (2003) Memories of colonoscopy: a randomized trial, *Pain*, 104(1–2): 187–94.

Reed, J. and Buck, S. (2009) The effect of regular aerobic exercise on positive-activated affect: a meta-analysis. *Psychology of Sport and Exercise*, 10(6): 581–94.

Reed, G.M., Kennedy, M.E., Taylor, S.E. et al. (1994) Realistic acceptance: as a predictor of decreased survival time in gay men with Aids, *Health Psychology*, 13: 299–307.

Reed, J. and Ones, D.S. (2006) The effect of acute aerobic exercise on positive activated affect: a meta-analysis, *Psychology of Sport and Exercise*, 7(5): 477–514.

Reivich, K. and Shatte, A. (2002) *The Resilience Factor: 7 Keys to Finding Your Inner Strength and Overcoming Life's Hurdles*. New York: Broadway Books.

Reivich, J., Gillham, K., Shatté, A. and Seligman, M.E.P. (2007) *Penn Resiliency Project: A Resilience Initiative and Depression Prevention Programme for Youth and Their Parents. Executive Summary*. Philadelphia, PA: University of Philadelphia.

Reznitskaya, A. and Sternberg, R.J. (2004) Teaching students to make wise judgments: the 'Teaching for Wisdom' program, in P.A. Linley and S. Joseph (eds) *Positive Psychology in Practice*. New York: John Wiley & Sons, Inc.

Roberts, R.D., Zeidner, M. and Matthews, G. (2001) Does emotional intelligence meet traditional standards for an intelligence? Some new data and conclusions, *Emotion*, 1: 196–231.

Robertson, I. and Cooper, C. (2011) *Well-Being: Productivity and Happiness at Work*. Basingstoke: Palgrave Macmillan.

Robson, C. (2004) *Small-Scale Evaluation*. London: Sage Publications.

Rodrigue, J.R., Baz, M.A., Widows, M.R. and Ehlers, S.L. (2005) A randomized evaluation of Quality of Life Therapy with patients awaiting lung transplantation, *American Journal of Transplantation*, 5(10): 2425–32.

Rodrigue, J.R., Widows, M.R. and Baz, M.A. (2006) Caregivers of patients awaiting lung transplantation: do they benefit when the patient is receiving psychological services? *Progress in Transplantation*, 16: 336–42.

Rogers, C. (1951) *Client-centered Therapy: Its Current Practice, Implications and Theory*. London: Constable.

Rosenberg, M. (1965) *Society and the Adolescent Self-Image*. Princeton, NJ: Princeton University Press.

Rosenberg, M., Schooler, C., Schoenberg, C. and Rosenberg, F. (1995) Global self-esteem and specific self esteem: different concepts, different outcomes, *American Sociological Review*, 60: 141–56.

Rothschild, B. (2000) *The Body Remembers: The Psychophysiology of Trauma and Trauma Treatment*. New York: W.W Norton & Company.

Rotter, J. (1966) Generalized expectancies for internal versus external control of reinforcements, *Psychological Monographs*, 80 (609).

Rousseau, F.L. and Vallerand, R.J. (2008) An examination of the relationship between passion and subjective well-being in older adults, *The International Journal of Aging and Human Development*, 66(3): 195–211.

Ruini, C. and Fava, G.A. (2004) Clinical applications of well-being therapy, in P.A. Linley and S. Joseph (eds) *Positive Psychology in Practice*. Hoboken, NJ: Wiley.

Ruini, C. and Fava, G.A. (2012) Role of well-being therapy in achieving a balanced and individualized path to optimal functioning, *Clinical Psychology & Psychotherapy*, 19(4): 291–304.

Russell, J.A. (1980) The circumplex model of affect, *Journal of Personality and Social Psychology*, 39: 1161–78.

Ryan, R. and Deci, E. (2000) Self determination theory and the facilitation of intrinsic motivation, social development and well-being, *American Psychologist*, 55: 68–78.

Ryan, R.M. and Deci, E.L. (2017) *Self-determination Theory: Basic Psychological Needs in Motivation, Development, and Wellness*. New York: Guilford Publishing.

Ryan, R.M., Deci, E.L. and Grolnick, W.S. (1995) Autonomy, relatedness, and the self: their relation to development and psychopathology, in D. Cicchetti and D.J. Cohen (eds) *Developmental Psychopathology: Theory and Methods*. New York: John Wiley & Sons.

Ryff, C.D. (1989) Happiness is everything, or is it? Explorations on the meaning of psychological well-being, *Journal of Personality and Social Psychology*, 57(6): 1069–81.

Ryff, C.D. and Singer, B.H. (2006) Best news yet on the six-factor model of well-being, *Social Science Research*, 35(4): 1103–19.

Ryff, C.D. and Singer, B. (2008) The integrative science of human resilience, *Interdisciplinary Research: Case Studies from Health and Social Science*, 198.

Sabiston, C.M., McDonough, M.H. and Crocker, P.R.E. (2007) Psychosocial experiences of breast cancer survivors involved in a dragon boat program: exploring links to positive psychological growth, *Journal of Sport & Exercise Psychology*, 29(4): 419–38.

Sackeim, H.A., Greenberg, M.S., Weiman, A.L. et al. (1982) Hemispheric-asymmetry in the expression of positive and negative emotions: neurologic evidence, *Archives of Neurology*, 39(4): 210–18.

Salmela-Aro, K., Nurmi, J.-E., Saisto, T. and Halmesmäki, E. (2001) Goal construction and depressive symptoms during transition to motherhood: evidence from two longitudinal studies, *Journal of Personality and Social Psychology*, 81: 1144–59.

Salovey, P. and Mayer, J. (1990) Emotional intelligence, *Imagination, Cognition and Personality*, 9: 185–211.

Salovey, P., Caruso, D. and Mayer, J.D. (2004) Emotional intelligence in practice, in P.A. Linley and S. Joseph (eds) *Positive Psychology in Practice*. Hoboken, NJ: John Wiley & Sons.

Salovey, P., Mayer, J. and Caruso, D. (2002) The positive psychology of emotional intelligence, in C.R. Snyder and S.J. Lopez (edss) *Handbook of Positive Psychology*. New York: Oxford University Press.

Sangsue, J. and Vorpe, G. (2004) Professional and personal influences on school climate in teachers and pupils, *Psychologie du Travail et des Organisations*, 10(4): 341–54.

Schacter, D.L. and Addis, D.R. (2007) The optimistic brain, *Nature Neuroscience*, 10(11): 1345–7.

Schaufeli, W. (2013) What is engagement, *Employee Engagement in Theory and Practice*, 15, 321.

Scheier, M. and Carver, C.S. (1987) Dispositional optimism and physical well-being: the influence of generalised outcome expectancies on health, *Journal of Personality and Social Psychology*, 55: 169–210.

Scheier, M. and Carver, C.S. (2009) Optimism, in S. Lopez (ed.) *The Encyclopedia of Positive Psychology*. Chichester: Blackwell Publishing Ltd.

Scheier, M.F., Carver, C.S. and Bridges, M.W. (1994) Distinguishing optimism from neuroticism (and trait anxiety, self-mastery, and self-esteem): a re-evaluation of the Life Orientation Test, *Journal of Personality and Social Psychology*, 67: 1063–78.

Scheier, M., Mathews, K., Owens, J. et al. (1989) Dispositional optimism and recovery from coronary artery bypass surgery: the beneficial effects on physical and psychological well-being, *Journal of Personality and Social Psychology*, 57: 1024–40.

Schmuck, P. (2001) Intrinsic and extrinsic life goal preferences as measured via inventories and via priming methodologies: mean differences and relations with well-being, in P. Schmuck and K.M. Sheldon (eds) *Life Goals and Well-Being: Towards a Positive Psychology of Human Striving*. Goettingen: Hogrefe & Huber Publishers.

Schmuck, P., Kasser, T. and Ryan, R.M. (2000) Intrinsic and extrinsic goals: their structure and relationship to well-being in German and US college students, *Social Indicators Research*, 50(2): 225–41.

Schneider, K. (2017) The resurgence of awe in psychology: promise, hope, and perils, *The Humanistic Psychologist*, 45(2): 103–8.

Schotanus-Dijkstra, M., Pietersea, M.E., Drossaerta, C.H.C. et al. (2017) Possible mechanisms in a multicomponent email guided positive psychology intervention to improve mental well-being, anxiety and depression: a multiple mediation model, *The Journal of Positive Psychology*. https://doi.org/10.1080/17439760.2017.1388430

Schroder, K.E.E. and Ollis, C.L. (2013) The Coping Competence Questionnaire: a measure of resilience to helplessness and depression, *Motivation and Emotion*, 37(2): 286–302.

Schueller, S.M. (2014) Person-activity fit in positive psychological interventions, in A.C. Parks and S.M. Schueller (eds) *The Wiley Blackwell Handbook of Positive Psychological Interventions*. Chichester: John Wiley & Sons.

Schulz, U. and Mohamed, N.E. (2004) Turning the tide: benefit finding after cancer surgery, *Social Science & Medicine*, 59(3): 653–62.

Schutte, N.S., Malouff, J.M., Simunek, M. et al. (2002) Characteristic emotional intelligence and emotional well-being, *Cognition and Emotion*, 16: 769–86.

Schwartz, B. and Ward, A. (2004) Doing better but feeling worse: the paradox of choice, in P.A. Linley and S. Joseph (edss) *Positive Psychology in Practice* . Hoboken, NJ: John Wiley & Sons.

Schwartz, B., Ward, A., Monterosso, J. et al. (2002) Maximizing versus satisficing: happiness is a matter of choice, *Journal of Personality and Social Psychology*, 83(5): 1178–97.

Schwartz, S.H. (1994) Are there universal aspects in the structure and contents of human values? *Journal of Social Issues*, 50: 19–45.

Schwartz, S.H., Cieciuch, J., Vecchione, M. et al. (2012) Refining the theory of basic individual values, *Journal of Personality and Social Psychology*, 103(4): 663.

Schwarzer, R. and Jerusalem, M. (1995) Generalized Self-Efficacy scale, in J. Weinman, S. Wright and M. Johnston (eds) *Measures in Health Psychology: A User's Portfolio. Causal and Control Beliefs*. Windsor: NFER-Nelson.

Scollon, C.N. and King, L.A. (2011) What people really want in life and why it matters: contributions from research on Folk Theories and the Good Life, in R. Biswas-Diener (ed.) *Positive Psychology as Social Change*. Portland, OR: Springer.

Seifert, T. and Hedderson, C. (2010) Intrinsic motivation and flow in skateboarding: an ethnographic study, *Journal of Happiness Studies*, 1(3): 277–92.

Seligman, M. (1998) *Learned Optimism: How to Change Your Mind and Your Life.* New York: Free Press.

Seligman, M. (2002a) *Authentic Happiness: Using the New Positive Psychology to Realize Your Potential for Lasting Fulfilment.* New York: Free Press.

Seligman, M. (2002b) Positive psychology, positive prevention, and positive therapy, in C.R. Snyder and S.J. Lopez (eds) *Handbook of Positive Psychology.* New York: Oxford University Press.

Seligman, M. (2011) *Flourish.* London: Nicholas Brealey Publishing.

Seligman, M. and Csikszentmihalyi, M. (2000) Positive psychology: an introduction, *American Psychologist*, 55(1): 5–14.

Seligman, M. and Peterson, C. (2003) Positive clinical psychology, in L.G. Aspinwall and U.M. Staudinger (eds) *A Psychology of Human Strengths.* Washington, DC: American Psychological Association.

Seligman, M.E.P. and Schulman, P. (1986) Explanatory style as a predictor of productivity and quitting among life insurance agents, *Journal of Personality and Social Psychology*, 50: 832–8.

Seligman, M.E.P., Rashid, T. and Parks, A.C. (2006) Positive psychotherapy, *American Psychologist*, 61: 774–88.

Seligman, M., Steen, T.A., Park, N. and Peterson, C. (2005) Positive psychology progress: empirical validation of interventions, *American Psychologist*, 60(5): 410–21.

Shapiro, L.S. (2009) Meditation and positive psychology, in S.J. Lopez (ed.) *Handbook of Positive Psychology*, 2nd edn. Oxford: Oxford University Press.

Sharot, T., Riccardi, A.M., Raio, C.M. and Phelps, E.A. (2007) Neural mechanisms mediating optimism bias, *Nature*, 450(1): 102–5.

Sheldon, K. (2009) Authenticity, in S. Lopez (ed.) *The Encyclopedia of Positive Psychology.* Chichester: Blackwell Publishing Ltd.

Sheldon, K.M. and Deci, E.L. (1995) The Self-Determination Scale. Unpublished manuscript, University of Rochester, New York.

Sheldon, K.M. and Kasser, T. (1995) Coherence and congruence: two aspects of personality integration, *Journal of Personality and Social Psychology*, 68: 531–43.

Sheldon, K.M. and Lucas, R.E. (eds) (2014) *Stability of Happiness. Theories and Evidence on Whether Happiness Can Change.* London: Academic Press Elsevier.

Sheldon, K.M. and Lyubomirsky, S. (2004) Achieving sustainable new happiness: prospects, practices, and prescriptions, in A. Linley and S. Joseph (eds) *Positive Psychology in Practice.* Hoboken, NJ: John Wiley & Sons.

Sheldon, K.M. and Lyubomirsky, S. (2006a) Achieving sustainable gains in happiness: change your actions, not your circumstances, *Journal of Happiness Studies*, 7: 55–86.

Sheldon, K.M. and Lyubomirsky, S. (2006b) How to increase and sustain positive emotion: the effects of expressing gratitude and visualizing best possible selves, *Journal of Positive Psychology*, 1(2): 73–82.

Sheldon, K.M. and Lyubomirsky, S. (2007) Is it possible to become happier? (And if so, how?), *Social and Personality Psychology Compass*, 1: 129–45.

Sheldon, K.M. and Lyubomirsky, S. (2009) Change your actions, not your circumstances: an experimental test of the Sustainable Happiness Model, in A.K. Dutt and B. Radcliff (eds) *Happiness, Economics, and Politics: Toward a Multi-Disciplinary Approach.* Cheltenham: Edward Elgar.

Sheldon, K.M., Abad, N., Ferguson, Y. et al. (2010) Persistent pursuit of need-satisfying goals leads to increased happiness: a 6-month experimental longitudinal study, *Motivation & Emotion*, 34(1): 39–48.

Sheldon, K.M., Frederickson, B., Rathunde, K. et al. (1999) Positive psychology Manifesto. Akumal, Mexico, January 1999.

Shiota, M.N., Keltner, D. and John, O.P. (2006) Positive emotion dispositions differentially associated with Big Five personality and attachment style, *Journal of Positive Psychology*, 1(2): 61–71.

Shoda, Y., Mischel, W. and Peake, P.K. (1990) Predicting adolescent cognitive and self-regulatory competences from preschool delay of gratification: identifying diagnostic conditions, *Developmental Psychology*, 26(6): 978–86.

Sin, N.L. and Lyubomirsky, S. (2009) Enhancing well-being and alleviating depressive symptoms with positive psychology interventions: a practice-friendly meta-analysis, *Journal of Clinical Psychology*, 65(5): 467–87.

Smith, C. (2008) Mind map of positive psychology. Available at: http://positiveintegration. com/positivepsychology.htm

Snyder, C.R. (2002) Hope theory: rainbows of the mind, *Psychological Inquiry*, 13: 249–75.

Solnick, S. and Hemenway, D. (1998) Is more always better? A survey on positional concerns, *Journal of Economic Behaviour & Organisation*, 37: 373–83.

Sorabji, R. (2000) *Emotions and Peace of Mind: From Stoic Agitation to Christian Temptation.* Oxford: Oxford University Press.

Spence, G.B. and Grant, A.M. (2007) Professional and peer life coaching and the enhancement of goal striving and well-being: an exploratory study, *Journal of Positive Psychology*, 2(3): 185–94.

Spreitzer, G., Stephens, J.P. and Sweetman, D. (2009) The Reflected Best Self field experiment with adolescent leaders: exploring the psychological resources associated with feedback source and valence, *Journal of Positive Psychology*, 4(5): 331–48.

Springer, C., Misurell, J., Kranzler, A. et al. (2014) Resilience interventions for youth, in A.C. Parks and S.M. Schueller (eds) *The Wiley Blackwell Handbook of Positive Psychological Interventions.* Chichester: John Wiley & Sons.

Steger, M. (2009) Meaning, in S. Lopez (ed.) *The Encyclopedia of Positive Psychology.* Chichester: Blackwell Publishing Ltd.

Steger, M.F. (2012) Making meaning in life, *Psychological Inquiry*, 23: 381–5.

Steger, M.F., Fitch-Martin, A.R., Donnelly, J. and Rickard, K.M. (2015) Meaning in life and health: proactive health orientation links meaning in life to health variables among American undergraduates, *Journal of Happiness Studies*, 16(3): 583.

Steger, M.F., Frazier, P., Oishi, S. and Kaler, M. (2006) The Meaning in Life Questionnaire: assessing the presence of and search for meaning in life, *Journal of Counseling Psychology*, 53: 80–93.

Steger, M.F., Shin, J.Y., Shim, Y. and Fitch-Martin, A. (2013) Is meaning in life a flagship indicator of well-being?, in A.S. Waterman (ed.) *The Best Within Us: Positive Psychology Perspectives on Eudaimonia.* Washington, DC: American Psychological Association.

Stenseng, F., Forest, J. and Curran, T. (2015) Positive emotions in recreational sport activities: the role of passion and belongingness, *Journal of Happiness Studies*, 16(5): 1117–29.

Sternberg, R. (2009) Wisdom, in S. Lopez (ed.) *The Encyclopedia of Positive Psychology*. Chichester: Blackwell Publishing Ltd.

Stiglitz, J.E., Sen, A. and Fitoussi, J. (2009) Report by the commission on the measurement of economic performance and social progress. Available at: www.stiglitz-sen-fitoussi.fr/documents/rapport_anglais.pdf (accessed).

Stolarski, M., Bitner, J. and Zimbardo, P.G. (2011) Time perspective, emotional intelligence and discounting of delayed awards, *Time & Society*, 20(3): 346–63.

Strauss, G.P. and Allen, D.N. (2006) The experience of positive emotion is associated with the automatic processing of positive emotional words, *Journal of Positive Psychology*, 1(3): 150–9.

Sweeney, A., Clement, S., Filson, B. and Kennedy, A. (2016) Trauma-informed mental healthcare in the UK: what is it and how can we further its development? *Mental Health Review Journal*, 21(3): 174–92.

Takkinen, S., Suutama, T. and Ruoppila, I. (2001) More meaning by exercising? Physical activity as a predictor of a sense of meaning in life and of self-rated health and functioning in old age, *Journal of Aging and Physical Activity*, 9(2): 128–41.

Taylor, S. (1989) *Positive Illusions: Creative Self-Deception and the Healthy Mind*. New York: Basic Books.

Taylor, S. (2001) Positive psychology and humanistic psychology: a reply to Seligman, *Journal of Humanistic Psychology*, 41: 13–29.

Taylor, S. (2009) Positive illusions, in S. Lopez (ed.) *The Encyclopedia of Positive Psychology*. Chichester: Blackwell Publishing Ltd.

Taylor, S. and Brown, J. (1994) Positive illusions and well-being revisited: separating fact from fiction, *Psychological Bulletin*, 116: 21–7.

Taylor, S.E., Kemeny, M.E., Reed, G.M. et al. (2000) Psychological resources, positive illusions, and health, *American Psychologist*, 55: 99–109.

Teasdale, J.D., Segal, Z.V., Williams, J.M.G. et al. (2000) Reducing risk of recurrence of major depression using Mindfulness-based Cognitive Therapy, *Journal of Consulting and Clinical Psychology*, 68: 615–23.

Tedeschi, R.G. (1999) Violence transformed: posttraumatic growth in survivors and their societies, *Aggression and Violent Behavior*, 4(3): 319–41.

Tedeschi, R.G. and Calhoun, L.G. (1995) *Trauma and Transformation: Growing in the Aftermath of Suffering*. Thousand Oaks, CA: Sage Publications.

Tedeschi, R.G. and Calhoun, L.G. (1996) The posttraumatic growth inventory: measuring the positive legacy of trauma, *Journal of Traumatic Stress*, 9: 455–71.

Tedeschi, R.G. and Calhoun, L.G. (2003) Routes to posttraumatic growth through cognitive processing, in D. Paton, J.M. Violanti and L.M. Smith (eds) *Promoting Capabilities to Manage Posttraumatic Stress: Perspectives on Resilience*. Springfield, IL: Charles C Thomas Publisher.

Tedeschi, R.G. and Calhoun, L.G. (2006) Foundations of posttraumatic growth, in R.G. Tedeschi and L.G. Calhoun (eds) *Handbook of Posttraumatic Growth*. Mahwah, NJ: Lawrence Erlbaum Associates Inc.

Tedeschi, R.G. and Calhoun, L.G. (2008) Beyond the concept of recovery: growth and the experience of loss, *Death Studies*, 32: 27–39.

Tellegen, A., Lykken, D.T., Bouchard, T.J. et al. (1988) Personality similarity in twins reared apart and together, *Journal of Personality and Social Psychology*, 54: 1031–9.

Tennen, H. and Affleck, G. (2004) Benefit-finding and benefit-reminding, in C.R. Snyder and S. Lopez (eds) *Handbook of Positive Psychology*. Oxford: Oxford University Press.

Thompson, S.C. (2002) The role of personal control in adaptive functioning, in C.R. Snyder and S.J. Lopez (eds) *Handbook of Positive Psychology*. Oxford: Oxford University Press.

Thornton, A.A. (2002) Perceiving benefits in the cancer experience, *Journal of Clinical Psychology in Medical Settings*, 9: 153–65.

Thornton, A.A., and Perez, M.A. (2006) Posttraumatic growth in prostate cancer survivors and their partners, *Psycho-Oncology*, 15(4): 285–96.

Tkach, C. and Lyubomirsky, S. (2006) How do people pursue happiness?: relating personality, happiness-increasing strategies, and well-being, *Journal of Happiness Studies*, 7: 183–225.

Tribe, R. and Tunariu, A.D. (2017) Psychological interventions in the context of cultural psychiatry, in D. Bhugra and K. Bhui (eds) *Textbook of Cultural Psychiatry*. Cambridge: Cambridge University Press.

Tugade, M.M., Fredrickson, B. and Barrett, L.F. (2004) Psychological resilience and positive emotional granularity: examining the benefits of positive emotions on coping and health, *Journal of Personality*, 72(6): 1161–90.

Tunariu, A.D. (2015) *The iNEAR Psychological Intervention: A Resilience Curriculum Programme for Children and Young People*. Teacher and Student Guides. London: University of East London.

Tunariu, A.D. (2017) Coaching for resilience within an Islamic context: a case study, in C. van Nieuwerburgh and R. Al-Laho (eds) *Coaching in Islamic Culture: The Principles and Practice of Ershad*. London: Karnac.

Tunariu, A.D. and Reavey, P. (2007) Common patterns of sense making: interpreting numeric and textual data on sexual boredom qualitatively, *British Journal of Social Psychology*, 46: 815–37.

Tunariu, A.D., van Nieuwerburgh, C. and Boniwell, I. (forthcoming) Integrative psychological interventions: issues for development and implementation within a context of multidisciplinary collaborative action. *Journal of Applied Psychology*.

Tunariu, A.D., Boniwell, I., Ruffion, A. and Clamy-Sebag, V. (2017a) *Towards Sustainable Prevention of Youth Radicalization. The Philosophical Dialogues Program – An existential positive psychology intervention for resilience, wellbeing and affirmative mindset*. Manual, materials and training (English and French). Nice: UNISMED and London: UEL.

Tunariu, A.D., Tribe, R., Frings, D. and Albery, I.P. (2017b) The iNEAR programme: an existential positive psychology intervention for resilience and emotional wellbeing, *International Review of Psychiatry*. 29(4): 362–72.

Ungar, M. (2008) Resilience across cultures, *The British Journal of Social Work*, 38(2): 218–35.

Ungar, M. (2011) The social ecology of resilience: addressing contextual and cultural ambiguity of a nascent construct, *American Journal of Orthopsychiatry*, 81(1): 1–7.

Updegraff, J.A. and Suh, E.M. (2007) Happiness is a warm abstract thought: self-construal abstractness and subjective well-being, *Journal of Positive Psychology*, 2(1): 18–28.

Urcuyo, K.R., Boyers, A.E., Carver, C.S. and Antoni, M.H. (2005) Finding benefit in breast cancer: relations with personality, coping, and concurrent well-being, *Psychology & Health*, 20(2): 175–92.

Vaillant, G. (2004) Positive aging, in P.A. Linley and S. Joseph (eds) *Positive Psychology in Practice*. Hoboken, NJ: John Wiley & Sons.

Vaillant, G.E., DiRago, A.C. and Mukamal, K. (2006) Natural history of male psychological health, XV: retirement satisfaction, *American Journal of Psychiatry*, 163(4): 682–8.

Vallerand, R.J. (2015) *The Psychology of Passion*. New York: Oxford University Press.

Vallerand, R.J., Ntoumanis, N., Philippe, F.L. et al. (2008) On passion and sports fans: a look at football, *Journal of Sport Sciences*, 26: 1279–93.

Van Deurzen, E. (2009) *Psychotherapy and the Quest for Happiness*. London: Sage.

van Nieuwerburgh, C. and Green, S. (2014) Developing mental toughness in young people: coaching as an applied positive psychology, in D. Strycharczyk and P. Clough (eds) *Developing Mental Toughness in Young People: Approaches to Achievement, Well-Being and Positive Behaviour*. London: Karnac Books.

van Nieuwerburgh, C. and Oades, L. (2017) Editorial, *Coaching: An International Journal of Theory, Research and Practice*, 10(2): 99–101.

van Nieuwerburgh, C. and Tunariu, A. (2013) Responding to a new landscape: towards integrative practice, *Coaching Today*, 8: 6–10.

Vealey, R. and Chase, M. (2016) *Best Practice for Youth Sport: Science and Strategies for Positive Athlete Experiences*. Champaign, IL: Human Kinetics.

Vella, S.A., Oades, L.G. and Crowe, T.P. (2011) The role of the coach in facilitating positive youth development: moving from theory to practice, *Journal of Applied Sport Psychology*, 23(1): 33–48.

Vella, S.A., Oades, L.G. and Crowe, T.P. (2013) The relationship between coach leadership, the coach-athlete relationship, team success, and the positive developmental experiences of adolescent soccer players, *Physical Education and Sport Pedagogy*, 18(5): 549–61.

Vittersø, J. (2004) Subjective well-being versus self-actualization: using the flow-simplex to promote a conceptual clarification of subjective quality of life, *Social Indicators Research*, 65(3): 299–331.

Vittersø, J., Oelmann, H.I. and Wang, A.L. (2009a) Life satisfaction is not a balanced estimator of the good life: evidence from reaction time measures and self-reported emotions, *Journal of Happiness Studies*, 10(1): 1–17.

Vittersø, J., Overwien, P. and Martinsen, E. (2009b) Pleasure and interest are differentially affected by replaying versus analyzing a happy life moment, *Journal of Positive Psychology*, 4(1): 14–20.

Vittersø, J., Vorkinn, M. and Vistad, O.I. (2001) Congruence between recreational mode and actual behavior: a prerequisite for optimal experiences?, *Journal of Leisure Research*, 33(2): 137.

Vodanovich, S.J. and Watt, J.D. (2016) Self-report measures of boredom: an updated review of the literature, *The Journal of Psychology*, 150(2): 196–228.

Vohs, K.D., Schmeichel, B.J., Nelson, N.M. et al. (2008) Making choices impairs subsequent self-control: a limited-resource account of decision making, self-regulation, and active initiative, *Journal of Personality and Social Psychology*, 94(5): 883–98.

von Haarena, B., Haertel, S., Stumpp, J. et al. (2015) Reduced emotional stress reactivity to a real-life academic examination stressor in students participating in a 20-week aerobic exercise training: a randomised controlled trial using Ambulatory Assessment, *Psychology of Sport and Exercise*, 1(20): 67–75.

Wampold, B.E. (2005) Do therapies designated as ESTs for specific disorders produce outcomes superior to non-EST therapies? Not a scintilla of evidence to support ESTs as more effective than other treatments, in J.C. Norcross, L.E. Beutler and R.F. Levant (eds) *Evidence-based Practices in Mental Health: Debate and Dialogue on the Fundamental Questions.* Washington, DC: American Psychological Association.

Wang, C., Bannuru, R., Ramel, J. et al. (2010) Tai Chi on psychological well-being: systematic review and meta-analysis, *BMC Complementary and Alternative Medicine,* 10(1): 1.

Warr, P.B. (2007) *Work, Happiness, and Unhappiness.* Mahwah, NJ: Erlbaum.

Wasko, L. and Pury, C. (2009) Affective forecasting, in S. Lopez (ed.) *The Encyclopedia of Positive Psychology.* Chichester: Blackwell Publishing Ltd.

Waterman, A.S. (1993) Two conceptions of happiness: contrasts of personal expressiveness (eudaimonia) and hedonic enjoyment, *Journal of Personality and Social Psychology,* 64: 678–91.

Waterman, A.S., Schwartz, S. and Conti, R. (2008) The implications of two conceptions of happiness (hedonic enjoyment and eudaimonia) for the understanding of intrinsic motivation, *Journal of Happiness Studies,* 9: 41–79.

Waterman, A.S., Schwartz, S.J., Zamboanga, B.L. et al. (2010) The Questionnaire for Eudaimonic Well-Being: Psychometric properties, demographic comparisons, and evidence of validity, *The Journal of Positive Psychology,* 5(1), 41–61.

Watson, D., Clark, L.A. and Tellegen, A. (1988) Development and validation of brief measures of positive and negative affect: the PANAS scales, *Journal of Personality and Social Psychology,* 54(6): 1063–70.

Waugh, C.E. and Fredrickson, B.L. (2006) Nice to know you: positive emotions, self–other overlap, and complex understanding in the formation of a new relationship, *Journal of Positive Psychology,* 1(2): 93-106.

Waugh, C.E., Wager, T.D., Fredrickson, B.L. et al. (2008) The neural correlates of trait resilience when anticipating and recovering from threat, *Social Cognitive and Affective Neuroscience,* 3(4): 322–32.

Wehmeyer, M. and Little, T. (2009) Self-determination, in S. Lopez (ed.) *The Encyclopedia of Positive Psychology.* Chichester: Blackwell Publishing Ltd.

Weinberger, J. (1995) Common factors aren't so common: the common factors dilemma, *Clinical Psychology: Science and Practice,* 2: 45–69.

Weis, R. and Speridakos, E.C. (2011) A meta-analysis of hope enhancement strategies in clinical and community settings, *Psychology of Well-being: Theory, Research and Practice,* 1(1): 1.

Weiss, L.A., Westerhof, G.J, Bohlmeijer, E.T. (2016) Can we increase psychological well-being? The effects of interventions on psychological well-being: a meta-analysis of randomized controlled trials, *PloS One,* 11(6).

Wells, J., Barlow, J. and Stewart-Brown, S. (2003) A systematic review of universal approaches to mental health promotion in schools, *Health Education,* 103: 197–220.

White, M.A. (2013) Positive education at Geelong Grammar School, in S.A. David, I. Boniwell and A.C. Ayers (eds) *The Oxford Handbook of Happiness.* Oxford: Oxford University Press.

White, M.A. and Murray, A.S. (eds) (2015) *Evidence-based Approaches in Positive Education: Implementing a Strategic Framework for Well-being in Schools.* New York: Springer.

WHO (1948) The World Health Organization 1948 Constitution. Available at: https://www.encyclopedia.com/science/encyclopedias-almanacs-transcripts-and-maps/constitution-world-health-organization.

WHO (World Health Organization) (2010) Global Recommendations on Physical Activity for Health. Available at: www.ncbi.nlm.nih.gov/books/NBK305057/ (accessed 12 December 2018).

Wiberg, M., Sircova, A., Wiberg, B. and Carelli, M.G. (2012) Operationalizing balanced time perspective in a Swedish sample, *The International Journal of Educational and Psychological Assessment*, 12(1): 95–107.

Williams, G.C., Grow, V.M., Freedman, Z. et al. (1996) Motivational predictors of weight loss and weight-loss maintenance, *Journal of Personality and Social Psychology*, 70: 115–26.

Willig, C. (2013) *Introducing Qualitative Research in Psychology*, 3rd edn. Maidenhead: Open University Press.

Wilson, T.D. and Gilbert, D.T. (2003) Affective forecasting, *Advances in Experimental Social Psychology*, 35: 345–411.

Winkelmann, L. and Winkelmann, R. (2008) Personality, work, and satisfaction: evidence from the German Socio-Economic Panel, *Journal of Positive Psychology*, 3(4): 266–75.

Wirtz, D., Stalls, J., Napa Scollon, C. and Wuensch, K.L. (2016) Is the good life characterized by self-control? Perceived regulatory success and judgments of life quality, *The Journal of Positive Psychology*, 11(6): 572–83.

Wong, P. (2009) Existential psychology, in S. Lopez (ed.) *The Encyclopedia of Positive Psychology*. Chichester: Blackwell Publishing Ltd.

Wong, P.T.P. (2010) What is existential positive psychology? *International Journal of Existential Psychology and Psychotherapy*, 3: 1–10.

Wong, P.T.P. (2011) Positive psychology 2.0: towards a balanced interactive model of the good life, *Canadian Psychology*, 52(2): 69–81.

Wood, A.M. and Tarrier, N. (2010) Positive Clinical Psychology: a new vision and strategy for integrated research and practice, *Clinical Psychology Review*, 30(7): 819-29.

Zaleski, Z., Cycon, A. and Kurc, A. (2001) Future time perspective and subjective well-being in adolescent samples, in P. Schmuck and K.M. Sheldon (edss) *Life Goals and Well-being: Towards a Positive Psychology of Human Striving*. Goettingen: Hogrefe & Huber Publishers.

Zhang, J.W., Howell, R.T. and Stolarski, M. (2013) Comparing three methods to measure a balanced time perspective: the relationship between a balanced time perspective and subjective well-being, *Journal of Happiness Studies*, 14(1): 169–84.

Zimbardo, P.G. (2002) Just think about it: time to take our time, *Psychology Today*, 35: 62.

Zimbardo, P.G. and Boyd, J.N. (1999) Putting time is perspective: a valid, reliable individual-differences metric, *Journal of Personality and Social Psychology*, 77: 1271–88.

Zimbardo, P.G. and Boyd, J.N. (2008) *The Time Paradox: The New Psychology of Time That Can Change Your Life*. London: Rider Books.

Zimbardo, P.G., Keough, K.A. and Boyd, J.N. (1997) Present time perspective as a predictor of risky driving, *Personality and Individual Differences*, 23: 1007–23.

Zullow, H.M., Oettingen, G., Peterson, C. and Seligman, M.E.P. (1988) Pessimistic explanatory style in the historical record: CAVing LBJ, presidential candidates and East versus West Berlin, *American Psychologist*, 43(9): 673–82.

Index

Note: Page numbers in *italics* denote boxes, figures and tables.

POSITIVE PSYCHOLOGY IN A NUTSHELL
The Science of Happiness

Third Edition

Ilona Boniwell

9780335247202 (Paperback)
October 2012

eBook also available

'What makes us fulfilled?' and 'Is happiness necessary for a good life?' Discover the latest thinking on the topics of happiness, flow, optimism, motivation, character strengths and love, and learn how to apply it to your life. Ilona Boniwell presents an engaging overview of the science of optimal functioning and well-being, which combines real readability with a broad academic base applied to day-to-day life.

Now fully updated and enhanced with new material on how to:

- Change your mindset
- Practice mindfulness
- Develop better resilience
- Enhance your well-being at work
- Adopt positive leadership

Introducing positive psychology in a friendly, straightforward way, this international bestseller is peppered with many simple tools and tips for daily living that will help you love your life.

www.mheducation.com